STARVING THE BEAST

Starving the Beast

RONALD REAGAN AND THE TAX CUT REVOLUTION

Monica Prasad

Russell Sage Foundation   NEW YORK

The Russell Sage Foundation, one of the oldest of America's general purpose foundations, was established in 1907 by Mrs. Margaret Olivia Sage for "the improvement of social and living conditions in the United States." The foundation seeks to fulfill this mandate by fostering the development and dissemination of knowledge about the country's political, social, and economic problems. While the foundation endeavors to assure the accuracy and objectivity of each book it publishes, the conclusions and interpretations in Russell Sage Foundation publications are those of the authors and not of the foundation, its trustees, or its staff. Publication by Russell Sage, therefore, does not imply foundation endorsement.

LIBRARY OF CONGRESS CATALOGING-IN-PUBLICATION DATA

Names: Prasad, Monica, author.
Title: Starving the beast : Ronald Reagan and the tax cut revolution / Monica Prasad.
Description: New York : Russell Sage Foundation, 2018. | Includes bibliographical references and index.
Identifiers: LCCN 2018028875 (print) | LCCN 2018047839 (ebook) | ISBN 9781610448765 (ebook) | ISBN 9780871546920 (paperback)
Subjects: LCSH: Finance, Public—United States—History. | Taxation—United States—History. | Income tax—United States—History. | Corporations—Taxation—United States—History. | Political parties—United States—History. | Reagan, Ronald. | BISAC: SOCIAL SCIENCE / Sociology / General. | POLITICAL SCIENCE / History & Theory. | POLITICAL SCIENCE / Public Policy / Economic Policy. | SOCIAL SCIENCE / Research. | POLITICAL SCIENCE / Political Process / Political Parties.
Classification: LCC HJ9801 (ebook) | LCC HJ9801 .P73 2018 (print) | DDC 336.2/060973—dc23
LC record available at https://lccn.loc.gov/2018028875

The paper used in this publication meets the minimum requirements of American National Standard for Information Sciences—Permanence of Paper for Printed Library Materials. ANSI Z39.48-1992.

Text design by Linda Secondari.

RUSSELL SAGE FOUNDATION
112 East 64th Street, New York, New York 10065
10 9 8 7 6 5 4 3 2 1

CONTENTS

ILLUSTRATIONS

Figures

Tables

ABOUT THE AUTHOR

MONICA PRASAD is professor of sociology and faculty fellow in the Institute for Policy Research at Northwestern University.

Introduction

ONCE YOU START to think about it, everything seems to come down to taxes. I began this project wondering why the United States has so much more poverty than other similarly wealthy countries.[1] Why is there such a concern to cut taxes in America—even though total taxes here are already lower than in almost any other developed country—instead of using government revenue to bring poverty down?[2]

But taxes and tax cuts affect more than poverty. Climate change? Experts agree that a carbon tax would be the best, least economically disruptive method to address climate change, but it's impossible to say the t-word in American politics today. Economic growth? Long-term growth requires spending on education, research and development, and infrastructure. But all of that depends on tax money. Inequality? Thomas Piketty, the economist who has done so much to put inequality back on the public agenda, comes back again and again to tax reductions as the reason for rising inequality in the United States and tax increases as a possible solution.[3] Automation? The difference between a utopian future in which machines do all the work and a dystopian future in which machines do all the work is a well-functioning tax system. The lead poisoning of Flint, Michigan? Partly about the economic collapse of Detroit, but also partly about the state's refusal to raise taxes.[4] Black Lives Matter? Two of the central cases that inspired that movement, the deaths of Sandra Bland and Michael Brown, are tax stories.

Because the states of Texas and Missouri lowered their taxes, their police departments began raising revenue by aggressively pursuing minor infractions, like changing lanes without signaling (in Bland's case) and walking in the middle of the street (in Brown's). Doing so multiplies the number of altercations that police get into with citizens, and some of these are bound to go wrong. Underlying the direct racism of the police is a form of structural racism and classism that often goes unnoticed: working-class members of society, including working-class police officers, have borne the brunt of our unwillingness to support a sufficient tax base.[5] Responding to the opioid epidemic, implementing policies that would address the root causes of populism, maintaining public education, subsidizing child and elder care, upgrading infrastructure—all of it comes back to taxes.

Some of these problems would have occurred even without the constraints imposed by tax cuts. For example, an ideologically inclined Congress might not agree to an infrastructure program even if we had the money to spend on it. But no one *wants* children to suffer from lead poisoning, or innocent prisoners to languish in jails for lack of legal representation.[6] Even most libertarians agree that the state should fund courts and police—indeed, libertarians were horrified when a wealthy white man was killed by police who concocted a story about marijuana possession so that they could claim his property.[7] The tax cut program has gone off the rails and is causing real damage to the capacity of the American state to provide the framework, the rules, the roads and the water pipes that allow an economy to function. Every few years we have another round of budget brinkmanship in Washington, and many observers wonder how much longer this can go on without damaging the country's reputation as a safe place to invest. Why are tax cuts always on the agenda, whether the economy is doing well or doing poorly, whether the budget is in surplus or deficit, whatever the actual needs of the moment, and despite the findings of economists that tax cuts are not a reliable recipe for economic growth?

This book is the story of how it all began. It traces the history of the tax cut that started the tax cut fervor in 1981—the "Laffer curve" tax cut, the "supply-side" tax cut, the "trickle-down economics" tax cut that has gone down in so much fame and infamy.

It was at the time the largest tax cut in American history.[8] More properly called the Economic Recovery Tax Act (ERTA) of 1981, this tax cut turned out to be only the beginning of a decades-long push for tax cuts by Republican politicians that continues to today. This first tax cut taught Republicans that tax cuts could be popular—something that was not clear at the time, because for decades before then opinion polls had shown strong and consistent opposition to deficits.[9] In demonstrating the electoral appeal of tax cuts even at the cost of deficits, and in eventually showing that deficits could be financed by foreign capital, the ERTA transformed the Republican Party from a party of fiscal rectitude into a party whose main domestic policy goal is cuts in taxes. This first tax cut remains a touchstone of both left and right, and many scholars see in it the rise of the era of the market in which we currently live.

Reagan's administration reoriented the economy toward the market in other ways, including through deregulation, free trade policy, tight monetary policy, and an aggressive stance against labor. But the ERTA can make a claim to being the most important of Reagan's free market policies, one of the most durable, the most controversial, and the most surprising given prior historical trends. The major financial deregulations came before and after Reagan, under Jimmy Carter and Bill Clinton. In environmental deregulation, Reagan's achievements were overturned by later presidents and subverted at state level. Reagan broke a strike of the Professional Air Traffic Controllers (PATCO), but in doing so he only accelerated a trend of labor decline that had begun long before his arrival. Reagan signed a free trade agreement with Canada in 1988 and proposed a free trade zone between Canada, the United States, and Mexico, a vision that would later be realized in the North American Free Trade Agreement (NAFTA), but his main efforts were not oriented to trade, and his administration ended up increasing trade barriers. Reagan was also president during a time of tight monetary policy under Federal Reserve Chairman Paul Volcker. But it was the Democrat Jimmy Carter who had originally appointed Volcker, also a Democrat, and the "Volcker shock" began in 1979 under Carter; in the context of the 1970s, when inflation had reached double digits, there was broad bipartisan support for fighting inflation. And both free trade and tight monetary policy, unlike the ERTA, rest on a large body of supporting academic evidence.[10] Reagan's other main achievement in taxes, the Tax Reform Act of 1986, has received a great deal of attention for its even-handed and revenue-neutral framework of lowering tax rates and eliminating exemptions, but over time exemptions have proliferated in the tax code, and it is the lower rates—the element introduced in 1981—that remain.[11]

Reagan and his successors never succeeded in controlling spending, or in limiting the growth of government regulation. The successful effort to transform Aid to Families with Dependent Children (AFDC) into Temporary Aid for Needy Families (TANF) was symbolically potent, but these policies are a small part of the budget, and the decreases have been matched by increased spending through the Earned Income Tax Credit (EITC) and the Affordable Care Act (ACA) of 2010. For several decades, the two largest non-defense items of government spending have been Social Security and Medicare. Any serious attempt to control or cut back government spending must cut back one or both of these programs. But as Reagan discovered, core welfare state programs are enormously popular. Although members of the administration did attempt substantial cuts, they could not find support even among Republican members of Congress.[12]

The ERTA, on the other hand, has only become more popular as time passes, and similar tax cuts have been implemented again and again.[13] And unlike policies like welfare reform, lower tariffs, or even financial deregulation, tax cuts affect everything the state can do—by threatening state capacity itself. Even though the ERTA's many tax breaks for special interests made it an imperfectly market-conforming tax policy, as the largest tax cut in American history and the fountainhead of the era of tax cuts that followed it dealt a significant and lasting blow to state capacity. More striking is that although there is vigorous opposition to most free market policies, on the issue of tax cuts for the middle classes there is no opposition. No significant force currently argues that taxes need to rise on the middle classes. On this question the Reagan victory has been so successful that the enemy has ceased to exist. The ERTA is thus a central episode, perhaps the central episode in the rise of economic conservatism in America since the 1970s.

Over the years the worst possible effects of the decades-long program of tax cuts, such as drastic cuts in popular programs, have been avoided through a sustained and decades-long policy of borrowing. But survey the country today, and stories abound of police departments stopping drivers for no reason and seizing their property to enhance departmental budgets, or cities making up for lost tax revenue by slapping exorbitant fees on citizens for "wearing pants below the waist in public [or] having a hedge above three feet in the front yard."[14] It turns out that if you try to starve the beast of government of tax revenue, it eats whatever else it can find.

Across-the-board cuts in tax rates for individuals at the expense of higher deficits represent more of a break with midcentury conservatism than other policies do. Although elements of the right have always criticized the income tax, after the 1940s antitax sentiment was largely relegated to the fringes of mainstream politics.[15] The colorful history of the antitax resisters on this fringe has recently been chronicled by several scholars, but in the 1950s and 1960s the mainstream of the Republican Party was committed to balanced budgets, even at the price of tax increases.[16] As the Kennedy administration considered tax cuts, Republican senator Barry Goldwater thundered: "Deficit spending is not now and never has been the answer to unemployment."[17] After Kennedy went ahead and cut taxes, it was the Democrats rather than the Republicans who were the tax-cutting party, especially because Republicans decided after Goldwater's defeat in the 1964 presidential race that the antitax fringe was a liability for their party. There was rhetorical obeisance from Republicans to the goal of cutting taxes (including by Goldwater himself), but in practice, Republicans increased taxes as much as they lowered them.[18] Richard Nixon and Gerald Ford both faithfully increased taxes in the mid-1970s. Nixon did propose tax cuts during the campaign of 1960, and his presidency did produce some tax cut legislation. But it also produced tax increases, and Nixon's tax cuts were for businesses, not for individuals.[19] Ford had no overarching philosophy favoring tax cuts, staggering from a tax increase in 1974 meant to address inflation to a tax cut in 1975 meant to address recession.[20]

Indeed, unlike other aspects of the rise of conservative economic politics, our contemporary fear of high taxes, particularly on the wealthy, is unprecedented in American history. From the late nineteenth century to the 1970s, America pioneered a politics of progressive taxation that was extreme in comparative perspective. Thomas Piketty writes: "Over the period 1932–1980, nearly half a century, the top federal income tax rate in the United States averaged 81 percent. It is important to emphasize that no continental European country has ever imposed such high rates (except in exceptional circumstances, for a few years at most, and never for as long as half a century). . . . In the United States, the top estate tax remained between 70 and 80 percent from the 1930s to the 1980s, while in France and Germany the top rate never exceeded 30–40 percent except for the years 1946–1949 in Germany."[21] Piketty is talking about nominal rates, but effective tax rates— the rates actually paid after deductions and exemptions and all the loopholes are accounted for—were also higher on capital in the United States than in other countries at this time.[22]

But those high tax rates did not necessarily bring in more tax revenue than less dramatic but more effective forms of tax collection in other countries, such as national sales taxes; moreover, the high American rates were undone by an increasingly bold attack on taxes that gathered force at century's end. The consequence is that if we examine tax revenue as a percentage of GDP from 1965 to 2016, no other rich OECD country shows both stable and relatively low tax revenues. The United States has kept total tax revenue for all levels of government at around 25 percent of GDP throughout this period. Only Ireland had lower tax revenue as a percentage of GDP in 2016, and then only because its revenues had declined recently because of economic crisis. A few other rich OECD countries have managed to keep revenues stable at higher levels—the United Kingdom at around 33 percent, and Germany at around 35 percent. But the United States is unique in having low levels as well as the smallest standard deviation during this period.[23]

Maintaining a steady rate of low tax revenue as an economy grows is unusual in historical perspective, because demands on the government grow as an economy becomes wealthier. This phenomenon is so pervasive that social scientists even have a name for it: "Wagner's Law."[24] For example, as GDP rises and the economy changes, demands on education rise, so that a population that had been educated to primary school levels now needs to be educated to high school or college level; as GDP rises medical care and medical technology improve, enabling people to live longer in conditions of health that do not allow them to work and therefore require care from the community; as GDP rises society's expectations change, so that electrification and telephone wires are no longer enough and communities start wanting to provide Wi-Fi access to all citizens; as productivity increases in the private sector, to compete for workers, government jobs have to raise salaries;[25] and as GDP rises, citizens may simply become able to collectively demand more from their governments.

For all of these reasons, the United States is unusual in having hovered around the same relatively low level of tax revenue as a percentage of GDP despite a stunning rise in GDP over the last several decades. Whether one thinks this is a positive or a negative accomplishment, it is an accomplishment, not something that happens naturally, and the question is why the United States was able to do this when other nations have not wanted to, or been able to.

This focus on tax cuts gives American conservatism a unique profile: in other countries, populists support the welfare state instead of threatening it. And the focus on tax cuts gives a material edge to the partisan polarization of the country. In wider perspective, as can be gleaned from the considerable scholarly work on "state building" compared to the much smaller literature on tax cut movements, it is unusual that a state "unbuilds" itself in this manner.[26] As a member of the Reagan administration noted in the run-up to the 1981 tax cut, "We're going to make history . . . no government has before voluntarily reduced itself in size."[27] Even more unusual is that this project of unbuilding the American state has lasted for several decades now. A generation-long project of attempting to decrease tax revenue is a curiosity in world history.

So why did the Republican Party suddenly abandon its historical commitment to the balanced budget and its acceptance of progressive taxation? And why did it do so in such wholesale fashion that tax cuts remain the main domestic policy that Republicans offer even today, nearly forty years later?

In the late 1990s, when I was working on my PhD, I decided this would be my research question. I was sure that free market policies in general, and the ERTA tax cut in particular, had arisen because of pressure from business groups. I knew that every other advanced capitalist country in the world had a comprehensive set of policies, including national health care, that kept poverty and inequality rates much lower than in the United States. I also knew that the United States allows money to influence politics to a greater extent than any other developed country does, and it was easy to surmise that the one thing led to the other—that business group pressure had led to Reagan's successes. I thought my role in life would be to document this outrage with such clear and convincing evidence that no one could ever doubt it again, and to show that other countries resist and contain business pressure and are therefore able to implement policies in the general interest.

There was only one problem. There was no such evidence. As I show in this book, the main part of the tax cut, the part that blew up the deficit, had not arisen from business group pressure at all. Instead, Reagan had to convince business to support it. Business groups did eventually come on board with this part of Reagan's plan, but they were not the initiators of it and were always reluctant supporters of it. This became clear within just a few months of investigating the topic.

But if it had not been business group pressure at the origins of this change, then what was it? This was much harder to figure out. I had to get inside the world of Reagan's decision-making to do so. In 2005, in the process of turning my research into a book, I traveled to the Reagan Presidential Library in Simi Valley, California. Many documents from the early Reagan administration were now available to researchers, and in the library's catalogs I found page after page of descriptions of relevant material. But although all of this material was legally accessible, before it could be seen by researchers it had to be hand-vetted by an archivist to make sure it did not contain any information about national security, or personnel, or the location of oil wells, or one of the other categories that Congress had deemed too sensitive to be seen by the public.[28] The Reagan Library archivists were so overwhelmed and understaffed that the only way to get them to vet the specific documents needed, they said, was to submit Freedom of Information Act (FOIA) requests. And those requests would take six or seven years to be processed because there were already so many requests in the queue.

I submitted FOIA requests for thousands of pages. But by then, I had an academic job and tenure to earn and could not wait six or seven years for the documents, and so I turned to other projects, including a brief version of the ERTA story drawn from newspaper accounts and secondary sources.[29]

Eventually the years did pass, the requests were processed, and out of the depths of the library's massive holdings emerged gems of history. And while I was waiting for all of the material I had requested, another interesting thing happened: Nancy Reagan decided, of her own accord, to let researchers access Reagan's pre-presidential records. There is a sharp legal dividing line between presidential records—documents created by the executive branch in the exercise of government—and pre-presidential and post-presidential records—documents created by an eventual president and his or her staff before inauguration as president and after relinquishing the presidency. Only presidential records are subject to FOIA requests. As for pre- and post-presidential records, if a family or estate wishes, it can keep them inaccessible forever, or even destroy them. During one of my early visits to the Reagan Library, a staff member had told me about the pre-presidential records and explained that there was nothing that could be done to access them, so in my mind I had written them off. But miraculously, when I visited in 2009 to check up on the progress of my FOIA requests, all the pre-presidential records were open.

As it happens, these pre-presidential records turned out to be as useful to me, or even more so, as all of the records I had pried open with FOIA.[30] Much of the story told in these pages comes from the pre-presidential records, because the policies that Reagan implemented in his first year were the most important ones, and these had been endlessly discussed and debated by his team long before the election. Reagan arrived in office with a fully worked-out policy agenda in place, and the papers from after he became president showcase mainly the administration's sales effort to get the plan through. I don't think I ever imagined that I would one day have a concrete personal reason to say: Thank you, Nancy Reagan.

Given its historical importance, the ERTA has not lacked for commentary, and as with a literary classic or a religious text, several rival schools of interpretation have arisen seeking to explain it. The dominant interpretations see the tax cut as the product of business interests, small government ideology, or racial backlash. Most of this commentary has been based on media accounts of the events, which are themselves based on interviews with the key actors. The Reagan Library materials, which include minutes and transcripts from meetings at which the key policies were discussed, memos and briefings, notes and letters between the key actors, and ephemera such as newsletters, reports, and campaign items, allow a fresh evaluation of these rival interpretations. These documents allow us to see the 1981 tax cut as it was being debated and decided.

What emerges from these records is a story that is new in the voluminous literature on Reagan and the free market revolution. I knew that Reagan had fixated on individual income tax cuts after he saw evidence of their popularity among the public. But what made these policies so popular in the United States at that time, when there was no such groundswell of support in other countries? Could it be what some analysts have suggested, that Americans are in general a market-loving people? But if so, why did opinion polls not show support for such policies before the 1970s? What happened then to increase this support?

The story I eventually pieced together is that the United States witnessed the rise of free market policies in the 1980s because, quite contrary to our general picture of American capitalism, the United States had adopted a stance toward its businesses that was unusually hostile in comparative perspective. At the time, no other developed country ringed its businesses with environmental and health and safety regulations as voluminous as those of the United States, few other developed countries raised so much revenue from the taxation of corporations, only one other developed country had banking regulations that were so stringent, and in general no other government in the developed world adopted as adversarial an attitude toward capital as the United States did. As we will see in the chapters to follow, even Social Democratic Sweden was in some ways more accommodating to business than the United States.

These policies had always made American businesses grumble, and in the 1970s, combined with a worsening economy, they ignited an organized counterattack by business groups. That counterattack had mixed success, however. In fact, the real success of free market policies came not from the complaints of business, but from the way adversarial policies also divided the public and may have hurt economic growth. In particular, adversarial policies combined with the inflation of the 1970s to produce increasingly heavy rates of taxation and therefore increasing support for cutting taxes among the general public, a sequence not seen in most other countries.

But how could it be that a country so suspicious of governmental intervention that it refused to take responsibility for the basic health of its citizens until well into the twenty-first century—over one hundred years after the first European health care programs—had policies that were so adversarial to business? And why were the European countries, champions of the public welfare state, also revealing themselves to be coddlers of capital? Although it seemed mystifying at the time, in the end the question answered itself. European policymakers, worried about what the growing welfare state would do to the economy, had embedded it in measures that were favorable to capital. It is not clear whether an extensive welfare state actually harms the economy—we discuss this in chapter 11—but it is clear that European policymakers thought it might; therefore, they tried to design welfare programs so as not to damage work incentives and embedded them in a broader political economy that was supportive of businesses in many ways. This broader political economy featured reliance on regressive forms of taxation and lighter regulation and even allowed the self-regulation of business. In a few cases, the bargain of extensive welfare benefits embedded in a political economy that encouraged business in several ways was struck explicitly by actors who were aware of what they were doing, at identifiable points in time.[31] In other cases, the bargain developed only haphazardly over years and decades as national sales tax emerged as the historical anchor that allowed the growth of an extensive state.[32] Only the United States, with its small and residual welfare state, had the luxury of burdening businesses with regulations and taxation, or the need to do so—until it ran into the economic crisis of the 1970s, at which point the limits to this strategy became clear.

For the purposes of our examination of the ERTA, the key feature that explains the rise of tax cuts in America is disproportionate reliance on income, profit, and capital gains taxes as compared to sales taxes and other kinds of taxes. This tax structure, when combined with inflation, led to tax dissatisfaction, which the Republican Party—newly desperate to find winning issues in the wake of Watergate—picked up and mobilized as its route into power. This was the origin of the tax cut movement.

I emphasize, however, that this explanation does not accord final primacy to the preferences of the public, nor is it a story of a grassroots movement in favor of the free market. It's true that polls in the 1970s captured rising tax dissatisfaction, and that this dissatisfaction was rooted in objective factors having to do with a political economic structure that is unusual in comparative perspective. On the other hand, public preference was essentially contradictory: polls also showed respondents wanting to preserve spending and avoid deficits. It was not that public preference moved politicians in a particular direction; rather, Republican politicians *sought out and nurtured* potential dissatisfaction within the public, playing to the tax dissatisfaction and doing their best to downplay the concerns about spending and balanced budgets, because spending was an issue that did not offer a contrast with the Democrats, and balancing the budget was an issue without electoral potential. Cutting taxes was certainly not an issue with perfect electoral potential either. But it was better than any of the alternatives.

Rather than a median voter model, then, I elaborate here a theory of politics based on the efforts of the entrepreneurial politician, who forges a coalition in favor of a policy out of occasional polls, media stories, willing economists, periodic meetings and conferences, and a gut sense of where the votes are. Analysts of the rise of free market policies often jump to the conclusion that those who benefited from the tax cut—businesses and the wealthy—must have been the ones who brought it about, or try to root the origins of tax cuts in social conflicts around race or in the social and intellectual currents of the time. But in the case of the tax cut, the movement to wind back the state originates in the state. Changes including the rise of polling and the weakening of committees in Congress led to a democratization of the state that strengthened the role of such entrepreneurial politicians in mid- to late-twentieth-century America.[33]

Most of this book is devoted to tracing the course of the innovation of the policy: from its origins, to getting on the agenda, to winning in the decision-making arena over many obstacles—and then to being scaled partway back and resurrected. I then turn to explaining the context to ask why tax cuts were the mobilizable issue. I examine American political economy in historical and comparative perspective to explore how the consumer economy of the postwar period led to the free market policies of the post-1973 period, both as a backlash to the consumer orientation on the part of business and as an outgrowth of the consumer orientation on the part of voters and politicians.

These theoretical points lead to a practical implication: the key lever for change is not campaign finance reform, or developing intellectual counter-narratives. Rather, the tax cut agenda will be abandoned only if and when the Republican Party can find an issue to mobilize around with greater electoral potential. This is not easy, because as we will see, the Democratic Party owns most of the popular issues.

Part I of the book, "Tax Cut Clientelism," tells the story of the tax cut as seen through the Reagan Presidential Library documents and other archives. Part 2, "American Conservatism and American Hegemony," draws three lessons from the story:

1. Don't overestimate business power. Much of American progressive politics revolves around complaints about business power. In fact business power, or the power of wealthy individuals more generally, was not responsible for the 1981 tax cut or for many of the free market policies we have seen over the last several decades. In some cases where businesses were victorious (such as the repeal of Glass-Steagall), the victory took a great deal of effort and brought American businesses only to a position that European businesses took for granted, without having had to struggle.

The focus on business power in America is good and necessary: without that vigilance from journalists and scholars and the public, business probably *would* be politically powerful. And if we shouldn't overestimate business power, we should not underestimate it either. As we will see, business groups were often quite capable of defining their interests, organizing around them, and winning political concessions. An examination of American business power in comparative perspective gives a better appreciation of both its extent and its limits.

But business power is not the end of the story, and understanding what is really going on requires moving past the question of business power.

2. *Lack of democracy is not the problem.* If the literature on the rise of free market policies begins with the assumption of business power, it generally ends with a ringing call for more democracy. In fact, the dominance of tax cuts is the result of democracy at work—although saying that, as we will see, is a compliment neither to democracy nor to the tax cuts. The democracy demonstrated in the story of tax cuts is not democracy understood as the median voter's views reflected in policy, but actually existing democracy, in which the views of voters are conflicted, and politicians gain power by creating as much as following voter preference.

In our hyperpartisan and polarized moment it may be hard to believe that in 1950 a distinguished group of political scientists concluded that the problem of American democracy was that the parties were not partisan and polarized *enough*. At that moment there was so little partisanship that the problem, according to these observers, was voters couldn't tell what each party stood for, and there was no reason to believe a candidate would or could do what had been promised in the campaign—partly because it was not clear what had actually been decided by an election.

A "responsible" party system, the political scientists wrote in a famous report, was one in which the voter had a clear choice, in which each party promised some specific policy or program and strove to implement it if elected.[34] This might be called the "mandate model" of democracy: a political party works hard to unify so it can promise something clear to voters and, if victorious, strives genuinely to implement it. Only such a model of democracy presents the voters with an actual choice and allows them to hold parties accountable to voters.

It is possible to see the story chronicled here as the rise of a mandate model of democracy under the Republicans, who strove to unify on the issue of tax cuts and then to deliver those tax cuts when they gained power. They did this not because of any philosophical commitment to responsible party systems, but because it seemed to them to offer a route to electoral victory. From this point of view, the Republicans' efforts are exactly the definition of democracy at work.

What the authors of that midcentury report did not foresee is that a politics that gives voice to fundamental debates and divisions would be a more democratic politics, but also a more divisive one. Moreover, the mandate model, in which a politician adheres to the platform she promised in the campaign, can lead to situations where the politician is voting against public opinion but still upholding the vision of the responsible party. The mandate model asks only that the politician make a clear promise during the election and strive to implement that promise in office—even if the opinions of voters change in the interim. Whether voters actually chose the party for the stated reason is not always clear. And there is generally enough scope in public preference to allow politicians latitude in what they choose to focus on, making the mandate a weak constraint. Most importantly, the mandate model can lead parties to emphasize certain issues—those on which they can visibly demonstrate accountability—over others on which accountability is harder to demonstrate. Thus, the mandate model can remove from politics issues whose solutions politicians are unable to deliver during short terms of office, thereby making it difficult to address problems whose benefits will become visible only in the long term.[35]

Nevertheless, these are all problems of a different nature than what is generally envisioned by scholars who argue that free market policies reflect an absence of democracy: the real problems are problems *within* democracy and the incentives that politicians in particular democratic contexts face to mobilize particular issues.

The Republicans' development of a mandate around the politics of tax cuts and the perceived electoral consequences of this provide the best explanation for the rise of the tax cut movement and for its persistence even after the high levels of support for tax cuts withered. But the parameters within which politicians are able to make mandates are very narrow, and because of this, Republicans are trapped in the politics of tax cuts as much as the rest of us are. It's not that they don't believe in tax cuts. Indeed, at the height of the battle over the ERTA, one legislator wrote, "I am prepared to work for, fight for, bleed for, die for the tax package."[36] Another of the central actors would say later, "This is a mission I have. There is a power moving me that I don't quite understand. I truly believe that I can save people and that the supply-side revolution can save the world from decline, poverty, disease and war."[37]

But there are other Republicans who believe equally deeply in the need to bring back manufacturing jobs, or balance the budget, or lessen the country's polarization. What the tax cut story shows is how much effort went into making tax cuts the centerpiece of Republican strategy. The tax cut movement depends on Republicans walking a very fine line to convince voters, and themselves, that tax cuts will not lead to spending cuts or higher deficits, and on being able to keep a quarrelsome coalition together. We will see in the following chapters that the tax cut magic may be weakening. Nevertheless, the effort and difficulty chronicled here are also, in another way, a source of strength for the tax cut movement: this story makes clear how much effort would need to go into finding any new issue to displace tax cuts, and therefore how daunting is the task to move the party away from tax cuts. Over the last few years we have seen only one other issue—xenophobia—that is able to appeal to the Republican coalition with anything like the power of tax cuts. The policy of tax cuts is resilient because, for Republicans who don't want to travel the xenophobia route and are unwilling to accept that Americans like their welfare state, tax cuts are all they have to offer.

In short, the tax cut movement is the realization of what some prescient thinkers noticed early in the twentieth century: when a democracy is not forced to choose between higher taxes and lower spending, it chooses neither.[38] These are democracy's deficits.

3. Welfare states work best when they are embedded in pro-market policies. The most surprising discovery I made from this decades-long investigation is the degree to which Ronald Reagan—the recent president who is perhaps most successfully identified with American patriotism—was promoting a program that, in at least some respects, imitated European countries. This element of the conservative resurgence, some aspects of which I have explored in prior work, helps to explain both the similarities and differences between American and European capitalism, but it has been almost entirely overlooked in all of the scholarship on conservatism.[39]

This observation allows us to take the scholarship on the resurgence of the American right, which is by now well developed, in a global direction. Two specific elements of the country's economic role in the world are central. First, as the world's consumer of last resort, characterized by a large market as well as an orientation toward consumption rather than savings, the United States was fundamentally different from other countries in its postwar politics, and Reagan's free market policies developed out of these midcentury trends. Second, with the internationalization of capital, the United States has lost a constraint that kept tax cuts on the periphery of politics until Reagan's tax cut eventually showed that deficits could, at least in the short term, be financed with foreign borrowing.

Examining the events in an international context also leads to a way forward in rethinking how states can and should oversee the welfare of their citizens. European welfare states at midcentury managed to lower poverty and inequality while striving to give businesses what they needed for economic growth; indeed, in some ways Europe was more solicitous of capitalist growth than the United States. This is the good news: there is actually a path forward that identifies an area of cooperation that could improve citizens' welfare while also helping the economy. The European model cannot be imitated blindly because the United States played and to some extent continues to play a role in the global economy that pulls it down different paths, and both its economic and political circumstances are too different. But the observation that progressive policies have been most successful where progressive policymakers have been careful to avoid damaging economic growth is the central lesson to take away from the history of the European welfare states. The absence of this bargain in twentieth-century American history is the best explanation for the unique nature of American economic conservatism.

Part I

TAX CUT CLIENTELISM

CHAPTER 1

The Tax Cut Santa Claus

NO ONE WHO knew him ever had anything bad to say about Jack Kemp. Washington, D.C., is not a place that leaves reputations unscathed, and Kemp, the football player turned politician who championed tax cuts before any other politician did, was a central figure in one of the most politically contentious episodes in recent American history. But scrape away the layers of everything that has been written about the origins of the tax cut movement, and at its heart is a man whom even his opponents seemed to like.

He was in his own small way an activist for racial integration. Growing up in Los Angeles, Kemp had wanted nothing more than to play professional football, and although he was a bit too small, he eventually got his wish, playing for the short-lived American Football League in the 1960s. He was shocked to see his black teammates relegated to inferior hotels or even dormitories when the team played games in the South, while the white players stayed in the Hilton. "'This is not acceptable,'" a teammate remembers him saying. "'Either we stay as a team or we don't play.' And Kemp was the guy that actually did it. We all ended up in the crappiest hotel in Grand Prairie, Texas."[1] As president of the AFL Players' Association, Kemp supported a boycott of New Orleans, which had banned African Americans in nightclubs and taxicabs, and got an all-star game moved to Houston instead.[2] Benjamin Hooks, head of the National Association for the Advancement of Colored People, called Kemp a "liberal with a big L" on civil rights issues, and the African American journalist Michel Martin of National Public Radio wrote: "Of all the people I have ever met, let alone public figures I have ever met, he might be one of the few I can think of as colorblind. . . . Not blind in the sense of a convenient indifference to other people's real-life circumstances, but a real lack of interest in race—or class or status, for that matter—as a determining factor in his opinions about people."[3] Later in Kemp's life, this concern for equality would translate into an unrelenting—if unsuccessful—effort to develop a Republican approach to fighting poverty.[4] A *New York Times* reporter who covered Kemp cites all of the ways in which the Reagan tax cut was "a disaster" but nevertheless says that he "became convinced that [Kemp's] concern for the poor was sincere."[5] The socialist writer Michael Harrington once said to Kemp on television, "Your heart is in the right place, amazing for a Republican."[6] The liberal icon Daniel Patrick Moynihan wrote to Kemp, "I have talked about you to a half dozen reporters in the past few months. All in the warmest terms—which *I feel*."[7]

He was perhaps too nice to be a politician. He blew his big chance to move from the House of Representatives to the Senate because the incumbent, Senator Jacob Javits, had just announced that he had been diagnosed with a serious disease, and Kemp allegedly couldn't stomach the thought of attacking a man when he was down.[8] (Compare this to Ronald Reagan's cool professionalism when his daughter from his first marriage complained that his campaign managers wanted her to disappear, to avoid reminding voters of Reagan's divorce. "I couldn't shake the feeling of being kicked in the stomach," she wrote. But her father's response, she said, was: "'If you pay someone to manage a campaign. . .then you've got to give them the authority to do it as they see fit.' And that was that."[9])

And yet Kemp had more influence on the course of policy than most politicians have ever managed in American history. Kemp's political career began just as the Republican Party seemed on the verge of ending. He had used his football celebrity to campaign for and work for Nixon and Reagan in the 1960s before transitioning into politics himself in 1970 as a representative for a suburb of Buffalo.[10] He was one of an increasing number of celebrities who had begun in the 1960s to parlay their fame into political careers.[11] "Pro football gave me a good perspective," Kemp said. "When I entered the political arena, I had already been booed, cheered, cut, sold, traded, and hung in effigy."[12]

Kemp would need that perspective, because it was not easy to be a Republican in the 1970s. In 1974, Richard Nixon had resigned the presidency in disgrace, and Republicans worried that he would drag the party down with him. Nearly a third of survey respondents reported in 1973 that Watergate had made them less likely to vote for Republicans. "Nixon is likely to kill us for the next 40 years the way Hoover has killed us for the past 40 years," concluded one Republican pollster. He was not exaggerating about the previous forty years: from 1933 to 1974, there were only four years when Republicans controlled either house of Congress. The Republican Party was for most of the twentieth century a minority party. Generations grew up believing that the natural order of things was for Democrats to control Congress. One observer concluded in 1952 that the Democrats were the "sun party," dominating the solar system, and the Republicans were the "moon party," a pale reflection. Two Republicans, Eisenhower and Nixon, had won the presidency on national security issues, but even that success turned out to be a mixed blessing as Nixon climbed into the helicopter that swept him away from the White House, leaving his troubled legacy to Republicans in Congress.[13]

One aspect of the conservative resurgence that does not receive the attention it deserves is how desperate the Republican Party was in the wake of Watergate. In 1974, only 23 percent of Gallup poll respondents called themselves Republicans, an all-time low up to that point, compared to 44 percent who called themselves Democrats.[14] Between 1972 and 1974, the party had lost five percentage points in affiliation among the public, the sharpest drop since polling began.[15] The midterm elections of 1974 reflected this lack of trust in the Republicans, as the Democrats picked up several seats in the Senate and forty-six in the House, along with governorships and seats in state legislatures.[16] An editor at the *Los Angeles Times* mused, "After the latest shellacking, who can even imagine a Republican congress being elected in our lifetime or perhaps in our children's lifetime?"[17] In 1975, the party was running an ad called "Republicans Are People, Too," and the Republican National Committee could not pay the mortgage on its Capitol Hill Club, which was about to be foreclosed.[18]

"I am a member of an endangered species," said Kemp. "The Republican Party."[19]

The Republicans' political crisis coincided with an economic crisis that Kemp was particularly well attuned to as a congressman from upstate New York. Buffalo was in the Rust Belt, a part of the country experiencing staggering rates of unemployment in the 1970s. In the mid-1970s, Buffalo's unemployment rate was sometimes as high as 16 percent, almost twice as high as the national rate.[20] The lack of jobs was leading to unprecedented levels of frustration—as, for example, in a letter Kemp received from Thomas A. Klinck, a father of nine who had fought in the Second World War and was now unemployed. "In 1945 World War II veterans were awarded a Victory medal by the president and Congress," Klinck wrote. "I am returning this medal to you with instructions to return it to the president as I no longer care to own it, because the very inscription on its reverse side is a lie. Freedom of fear and want, freedom of speech and religion, it sounds good but isn't it laughable. I fear the loss of my home for which I worked 24 years, 30 year mortgage. I fear also the loss of self respect and the respect of others." Kemp passed on the medal to President Ford, whose office wrote: "I hope the day will soon arrive when Mr. Klinck will feel that circumstances in this nation warrant a request by him for the return of his medal."[21]

Nor was unemployment helping to bring down inflation, as had usually been the case during the Cold War period. Instead, a new word entered the lexicon, "stagflation," to describe the simultaneous appearance of inflation and unemployment. According to the economic theory still dominant at the time, stagflation was not supposed to be possible, because unemployment should have led workers to accept lower wages, bringing prices down.

It was inflation that particularly vexed Americans. In the most systematic attempt to measure public concern about inflation, the University of Michigan's Survey Research Center showed that a substantially higher proportion of respondents believed that inflation was a greater problem than unemployment throughout the late 1970s.[22] In 1978 Gallup's "most important problem" series showed 83 percent of respondents citing inflation as the nation's most important problem. This was the highest score *any* issue had received since the inception of the series in 1939—not even unemployment in any of the peak periods of unemployment received such a high level of disapproval.[23] Carter's Communications Director Gerald Rafshoon told him, "It is impossible to overestimate the importance of the inflation issue to your Presidency . . . It affects every American in a very palpable way. It causes insecurity and anxiety. It threatens the American dream."[24] Inflation, not the hostage crisis, most worried Americans during the Carter presidency.

One reason for the inflation was the oil crisis, which sent Americans into a period of fear that the fuel-intensive way of life they had pioneered in the

1950s and enjoyed in the 1960s was coming to an end. The crisis reached into the daily lives of Americans. During the first oil crisis shock in the winter of 1973–1974, motorists waited as long as seven hours for gas in lines that were several miles long, and fistfights erupted between frustrated customers. In January 1974, truckers, demanding lower prices, blockaded highways, tossed nails across the road to puncture the tires of strikebreakers, and even resorted to arson, gunshots, and throwing rocks from overpasses. There were 228 shootings across the country related to these issues, and eight states declared martial law. Moreover, the goods those trucks would have transported were not reaching supermarkets. Shoppers faced store shelves empty of meat, milk, and eggs, and some shopkeepers were rationing flour. Some companies organized plane lifts of food to ensure supplies. The crisis continued intermittently for years and periodically saw previously unthinkable spectacles such as automakers shutting down for lack of electricity, school being canceled for a month in Ohio, and the New Jersey governor asking residents to refrain from doing their laundry and threatening to arrest those who refused to turn their thermostats down.[25]

And Washington did not seem to know what to do about any of it, careening from wage and price controls to half-hearted efforts at conservation. The Democrats doubled down on traditional anti-recession measures such as big jobs bills (some of which many Republicans, including Jack Kemp, voted for) and suggested new approaches such as developing industrial policy and national economic planning, but in truth the experts were empty-handed.[26] Economists were quite willing to attack what politicians were doing but did not have clear answers themselves: "By and large economists are chastened, more aware of their inability to direct the economy toward the commonly accepted nirvana of full employment without inflation."[27] Economists' proposals were timid, with suggestions such as giving businesses incentives to keep prices low or asking "labor and management to accept some sort of voluntary program for reducing wage and price settlements,"[28] or simply "slow economic growth, which would take some of the pressure off prices and wages by means of an increase in the unemployment of both men and machines."[29] Economists had pieced together a monetarist theory of inflation, particularly in a memorable address by Milton Friedman in 1968, but they had not yet reached a consensus on what to do: in 1975 Friedman himself, today identified with the thesis that tight monetary control is necessary to bring down inflation, was testifying that the Federal Reserve was not creating *enough* money.[30] As Alice Rivlin, an economist who was a key critic of the Reagan program, noted later: "It was just almost impossible to say what good economy policy would have been. Nobody had thought through what you do when we have stagflation . . . It was easy to criticize what they were doing, but it wasn't clear, even in hindsight, what should have been done."[31]

Three presidents hurled themselves against inflation without success. Richard Nixon had implemented wage and price controls, which were popular but did not achieve much. Gerald Ford's program attempted to rely on voluntary efforts at price control and conservation, symbolized by buttons that said WIN for "Whip Inflation Now." It was never popular and went nowhere. Jimmy Carter tried various measures, from credit controls to price decontrol to a heartfelt but ineffectually delivered program involving restrictions on imported oil, a big push on alternative fuels, a windfall tax on domestic oil production, and energy conservation.[32]

If no one knew how to solve the economic crisis, no one knew how to solve the Republicans' political crisis either. Over the decades, the Republicans had lurched from suggested solution to suggested solution for their "minority problem," as the historian Robert Mason calls it. Mason catalogs the range of responses that Republicans gave to their decades-long problem of being in the perpetual minority in Congress: from the argument that the party needed to become more moderate to appeal to voters to the argument that the party needed to offer a clear, conservative alternative; from complaining that Democrats had "bought" votes by extending welfare benefits to more and more constituencies to blaming the Republican Party's weak organizational efforts; from emphasizing anti-Communism and the Constitution to looking for new, conservative solutions to new urban problems or advocating isolationism; from looking longingly at the success of the British Conservatives and hoping to learn their lessons to insisting that success lay in the personal qualities of the candidates. From the 1940s through the 1970s, the party experimented with one approach after another to get control of Congress. Nothing worked.[33]

What puzzled Kemp was how the Democrats did it. When he looked around himself in 1974, he saw a country and an economy in crisis. And although it was true that a Republican had been president during the most recent decline, Nixon had not, Kemp believed, single-handedly created inflation or brought about unemployment in a few short years, though his wage and price controls were not a particularly effective response. Kemp's diagnosis was that four decades of Democrats in Congress must have put the country on a wrong path. And yet, they kept winning. What was going wrong?

Kemp's first instinct in responding to his constituency's problems was to suggest cutting taxes for business. In 1974, he put forth a bill lowering capital gains taxes and corporate taxes and giving businesses faster depreciation. There were only two paths, he said, to growth: "The workers can work harder and longer" or "we can have more and better tools." Tax incentives for capital accumulation represented the path of better tools. Kemp's bill, the Jobs Creation Act, was an ill-fated private-enterprise response to the Humphrey-Hawkins Full Employment Act of 1978.[34] Formulated with the help of Paul Craig Roberts and Norman Ture, the Jobs Creation Act would have reduced overall tax amounts for business and on dividends.[35] The bill went nowhere.[36]

That defeat and the criticism from others—including other Republicans who resented this upstart celebrity who wasn't even on the tax writing committees—did not dampen Kemp's energy. He would try to convert anyone, anywhere—at committee meetings, in the halls of Congress, at fund-raisers. He would not stop talking about tax cuts, to the point that a joke began to circulate: when the Gestapo gets a hold of Jack Kemp they say, "Vee have vays of making you stop talking."[37] One contemporary remembers: "Other Members of Congress seeing him approaching in a hallway would bail into a cross-corridor to avoid being buttonholed by Kemp and given a long lecture."[38]

Although no one knew what to do about the economic crisis and Kemp's bills all failed, others were also struggling with the question. Unbeknownst to Kemp, a little group had formed and was thinking about tax cuts in a different way. It began with Jude Wanniski, Robert Mundell, and Arthur Laffer.

Wanniski would seem to be an unusual candidate for the role of conservative Rasputin: a New York intellectual of Central European descent, he was the grandson of a Communist coal miner who had given him a copy of *Das Kapital*.[39] But many of those who created the conservative movement came from exactly this kind of social background. If Kemp was the all-American football player from California, Wanniski represented another America, the cosmopolitan, ethnically diverse East Coast that had begun to abandon progressivism.[40] One of the stories of the rise of American conservatism is the shift to the right of many of the leaders of this other America, from Irving Kristol to Norman Podhoretz to Milton Friedman. For Murray Weidenbaum, who would become the first chair of Reagan's Council of Economic Advisers—and whose route through the City College of New York was also common for many in this group—what did it was a deep confrontation with a union. He had originally seen labor as the "little guy," but after analyzing the Teamsters, and especially after studying the case of an independent trucker who had gone up against the union, he felt that "the roles were reversed . . . The little employer was dealing with the giant union."[41] For the many others in this demographic whose families had roots in Central or Eastern Europe, the convincing factor was fear of communism.[42]

By the 1970s, Wanniski was working as a journalist for the *Wall Street Journal* and hanging around with two economists who would go on to become prominent—Robert Mundell, who would later win the Nobel Prize, and Arthur Laffer, whose last name became synonymous with Reagan's tax cut. Laffer and Mundell had met in 1967 at the University of Chicago, and Laffer had met Wanniski sometime in the 1970s, but the real meeting of minds happened when Laffer, with funding from the American Enterprise Institute (AEI), organized a conference in 1974 that Wanniski attended and at which Mundell spoke.[43]

We see in the background of these meetings the institutions that are often associated with the rise of free market policies, such as the University of Chicago and the AEI think tank. And yet Laffer and Mundell were mostly outsiders to the main strands of free market thinking at these institutions. Laffer had an economics PhD and a job as a professor, but he was more of a policymaker and gadfly than a serious researcher.[44] Neither he nor Mundell would stay long at the University of Chicago. Mundell was well regarded among economists for his work on optimum currency areas, but when he began thinking about taxes, he did not find a favorable hearing among fellow economists; indeed, years later, the Nobel Prize committee citation pointedly left out any mention of his work on supply-side economics.[45] The tax cut movement in America did not develop out of the traditions, networks, or main actors we generally associate with free market policies, such as Friedrich Hayek, Milton Friedman, and the Mont Pèlerin Society. Although Friedman would later become an adviser to Reagan and would support the tax cut program, in fact his favored tax policy was a flat rate tax with a high personal exemption and eradication of the corporate tax and the tax on inheritances.[46]

Mundell's thinking, perhaps drawing on recent developments in the economics of taxation, was different. It was first introduced to the world in 1974 in an article by Wanniski in the pages of the *Wall Street Journal* titled "It's Time to Cut Taxes," which Mundell would later describe as the best account of his thinking at the time.[47] Pulling the issues of taxes and inflation together into one problem, Mundell argues that if tax rates were lower, the incentives created to work and invest would produce so much supply that the problem of inflation would be solved. "The level of U.S. taxes has become a drag on economic growth in the United States," Mundell says in Wanniski's article. "Taxes have increased even while output has fallen, because of the inflation. The unemployment has created vast segments of excess capacity greater than the size of the entire Belgian economy. If you could put that sub-economy to work, you would not only eliminate the social and economic costs of unemployment, you would increase aggregate supply sufficiently to reduce inflation."[48]

He puts forward what would become one of the main arguments for tax cuts not being inflationary: "To stop inflation you need more goods, not less. . . . The Keynesians only look at [a tax cut's] effect on demand and have always considered it inflationary. . . . They neglect the financing side, aggregate supply and inventory effects." Mundell also argues that a tax cut will not raise interest rates: "The classical economists are only concerned about the 'crowding-out' effect [government borrowing raising interest rates]. . . . Both of these extreme views do not see that there is a middle position. . . . The government budget recycles tax dollars into the spending stream through expenditures, but in so doing it reduces the incentive to produce and lowers total production."[49]

Mundell states in words what Laffer would later construct as a figure: "After all, if total taxes and expenditures become confiscatory, all economic activity would cease and the government tax bite would be 100% of nothing."[50] Wanniski steps in to elaborate that "with announcement of a major tax cut, the capital market would instantly perceive that it is more profitable to do business in the United States than the rest of the world. Capital that is now flowing out would remain; foreign capital going elsewhere would come in."[51] Mundell notes that the issues are intertwined: "[The nation's problems] feed on themselves through the effects of inflation on the progressive income-tax schedules and through the negative multiplier effects thus generated. . . . They feed on themselves through the ever-increasing percentage increases in wages needed to maintain workers' purchasing power. And they feed on themselves through the international escalation of world money supplies that has taken place since the breakdown of the gold-exchange standard." He puts a price tag on the tax cut he wants: "The $30 billion tax cut is needed immediately to arrest the world slump, and if it is delayed by even one month, the figure required will be higher"[52]—in fact the eventual cut would be much higher.

These themes of inflation raising income tax burdens, of taxes affecting the supply side of the economy, and of the need for a gold standard would become the foundation of the argument expounded by the supply-siders over the next few years. The basic supply-side argument was that if inflation is a matter of too much money chasing too few goods, then to bring down inflation one can either restrict the amount of money available (addressing the demand side) or make more goods available (boosting the supply side). If there was a tradeoff between unemployment and inflation, as economists thought at the time—because unemployment meant higher wages to attract workers, which meant higher prices—then the solution to inflation was to raise unemployment, which would induce workers to accept lower wages and stop the wage-price spiral. Supply-siders argued this was unnecessary: tax cuts would give incentives to businesses to produce more and workers to work more, which would lead to both greater employment and lower inflation. The supply-siders focused on cuts in the marginal tax rate, which is the rate that a taxpayer pays on the next increment of income. In progressive tax systems, the marginal rate can be much higher than the average rate, because high-income taxpayers pay lower rates on their first increments of income. The supply-siders argued it was that additional taxation, the marginal rate, that mattered to work incentives.

In this vision, the mechanism through which tax cuts have their effect is different from a Keynesian mechanism, which sees tax cuts increasing consumption and thereby increasing employment. The supply-side mechanism is tax cuts raising employment by increasing incentives to work and produce, as well as raising productivity at a *given* level of employment—not only through more workers in the labor force, but also through those workers' "overtime, moonlighting, [and] working harder and better"—which would then increase economic growth and increase employment. Thus the "supply-side" label; originally coined by a critic of the movement, the economist Herbert Stein, to distinguish the argument from the familiar Keynesian argument that tax cuts boost demand, it was later adopted proudly by Wanniski.[53]

Figure 1.1 The Purported Laffer Curve Napkin

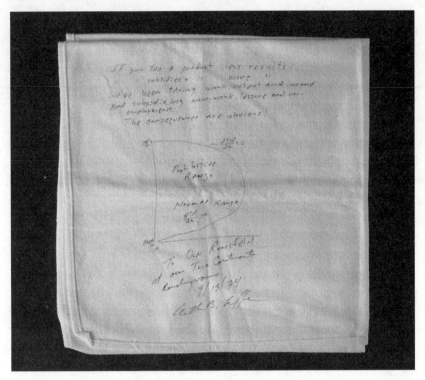

Source: National Museum of American History, gift of Patricia Koyce Wanniski.
Note: Above the figure, Laffer wrote: "If you tax a product, less results. If you subsidize a product, more results. We've been taxing work, output, and income and subsidizing non-work, leisure, and un-employment. The consequences are obvious!" Below the figure, he wrote: "To Don Rumsfeld at our Two Continents rendezvous, 9/13/74, Arthur B. Laffer."

Wanniski was well connected in politics and journalism, and he managed to get the idea in front of many people—including, in September 1974, two staffers from the Ford administration, Donald Rumsfeld and Dick Cheney, who agreed to drop by to see what the group was up to. This particular meeting was at the Two Continents restaurant. Laffer argued to the gathered principals that high taxation reduces work incentives and can therefore reduce tax revenue. Following this logic, reducing taxation should increase work incentives, which should lead to economic growth and bring in more tax revenue. Laffer drew a diagram on a napkin summarizing the point; a version of it is now in the Smithsonian (figure 1.1), but there are some doubts about whether it is the authentic version or a later re-creation.[54]

The diagram shows a parabola on its side. At a 0 percent tax rate and at a 100 percent tax rate, tax revenue will be zero, the endpoints of the legs of the parabola. But we know that, in between, the tax revenue generated is not zero. That means that somewhere on the parabola lies the maximum point—the tax rate that will generate the most revenue. The key point is that, on the declining leg of the parabola, lowering tax rates will actually produce more tax revenue.[55]

The idea, as Laffer always noted, is not new and seems to appear wherever taxation appears. The supply-siders often dug out historical examples of others who had made the point, from the fourteenth-century Tunisian scholar Ibn Khaldun to Andrew Mellon and John F. Kennedy.[56] They loved to quote Kennedy, who had said in 1962:

> It is a paradoxical truth that tax rates are too high today and tax revenues are too low and the soundest way to raise the revenues in the long run is to cut the rates now. The experience of a number of European countries and Japan [has] borne this out. This country's own experience with tax reduction in 1954 has borne this out. And the reason is that only full employment can balance the budget, and tax reduction can pave the way to that employment. The purpose of cutting taxes now is not to incur a budget deficit, but to achieve the more prosperous, expanding economy which can bring a budget surplus.[57]

Keynes himself, the supply-siders pointed out, had said: "Nor should the argument seem strange that taxation may be so high as to defeat its object, and that, given sufficient time to gather the fruits, a reduction of taxation will run a better chance than an increase of balancing the budget." But of course, Keynes was arguing about increasing *demand*.[58]

For all of the political attention it attracted, and despite the terrific tale it makes—who can resist a story that begins with a napkin and ends as the law of the land?—the Laffer curve argument was never taken seriously by economists. Although there have been some arguments that tax cuts affect income shifting at the top of the income distribution, there do not seem to be any professional academic economists who believe that tax cuts necessarily lead to increases in revenue. This is partly because the effect of taxes on economic growth depends on what the money is spent on, although there is debate over which specific expenditures are beneficial and which are not. Many scholars argue that spending tax revenue on education, infrastructure, health, and other productive investments can benefit economic growth.[59] Others point out that increases in taxation could lead to increased work effort if workers try to maintain the same after-tax standard of living, and that although there is in theory a point at which the costs of taxation exceed the benefits—the midpoint of the curve in Laffer's diagram—no one knows whether the United States has passed that point.[60] This last criticism was made repeatedly by many observers at the time, and the curve was criticized as "an awesomely casual way to reach firm conclusions about the desirability of major changes in our tax system."[61]

Perhaps for these reasons, the Ford administration officials were not convinced, so Wanniski and Laffer took their napkin to others—in 1976, they seem to have drawn this diagram for anyone in Washington who would sit still long enough. Wanniski meanwhile had convinced the *Wall Street Journal* editorial board, and the newspaper's opinion pages became a prominent outlet for the supply-side argument. But the ideas did not find much traction in the political world until Wanniski met Kemp. In this meeting, the two Americas retreating from progressivism found a way forward.

Wanniski knocked on Kemp's office door in January 1976, without an appointment. Wanniski had been advised by Robert Bartley, the editor of the *Wall Street Journal,* to go meet Kemp. Kemp was familiar with Wanniski's name and his op-eds in the *Journal* and had been wanting to meet him. The two hit it off immediately and spent the whole day talking about economics. Wanniski canceled all his appointments that day and accompanied Kemp on all of his, and then they traveled to Kemp's home and continued talking over a macaroni and cheese dinner.[62]

Kemp told Wanniski about his efforts with the Jobs Creation Act, and Wanniski responded that the bill kept losing because it was too complex. In his telling of it, he eventually persuaded Kemp to make individual income tax cuts the centerpiece of the bill and to focus on cutting tax rates rather than overall amounts, arguing that marginal tax rates had the greatest effect on production incentives.[63]

There is some dispute regarding who should get credit for inventing the idea. If the supply-side term is taken to mean any claim that tax cuts can pay for themselves, then it is clear that Kemp's congressional office had already pioneered a supply-side approach even before Kemp met Wanniski. For example, Kemp aides Paul Craig Roberts and Norman Ture had already developed econometric models incorporating the principle that business tax cuts could pay for themselves by generating greater economic activity.[64] In March 1975, Kemp wrote to Ford's treasury secretary about his bill for capital formation: "We believe that almost all loss in revenue would be eventually recaptured through increased national productivity and resulting tax revenues in sections of the Code not affected by the bill."[65] Indeed, Roberts claims that Wanniski "had discovered the budding supply-side movement in the Congress and rushed in to take over as its interpreter."[66]

But the proposals took a different direction after Kemp met Wanniski. Before the meeting, Kemp's office had been focusing on *business* tax cuts, or tax cuts on savings and investment. In fact, what Reagan would later come to be known for was cuts in general tax rates for *individuals*. It's worth pausing on this distinction a moment, because the difference between tax cuts for businesses or for savings and investment on the one hand, and general cuts in individual income tax rates on the other, turns out to be crucial to the entire story and is generally overlooked. As discussed in more detail in chapter 7, the bill that eventually became the ERTA had two main parts, a business tax cut and a tax cut for individuals. These two parts had different origins, drew on different sources of support, and resulted in very different outcomes. Business tax cuts were a more traditional Republican solution, approved by economists, but rate cuts on individual taxes were unusual and more provocative.

Kemp's office had been focusing on business tax cuts, and it was only after meeting Wanniski that Kemp began to push for individual tax rate cuts as well. For example, in a letter to Ronald Reagan in October 1975, Kemp outlined his full tax program, which was focused on cutting taxes for capital and did not mention individual rate cuts.[67] In an article in the Washington *Evening Star* that year he explicitly came out *against* the notion that would later become a centerpiece of the argument for the tax cut—that "inflation has hurt the consumer so badly, that he needs tax relief"; instead he stresses that the problem is savings, and the need is for a tax cut to stimulate savings.[68] As late as February 1976—after he had met Wanniski, but presumably before he had been thoroughly converted to the cause—Kemp did not mention rate cuts in individual income taxes at all in a speech to the Republican National Committee. The speech veered from complaints about regulation and the growth of government to arguments that Republican policies were good for minorities and the poor, to the German hyperinflation of the 1930s, to complaints about deficits and spending, and to preserving the "small entrepreneurial spirit." Only toward the end did Kemp mention tax reform, and the only tax reform he mentioned concerned the taxation of savings and investment.[69]

The move toward individual tax rate cuts happened after Kemp met Wanniski, but whether it happened because of Wanniski is less clear. Wanniski and the *Wall Street Journal* had been arguing for across-the-board rate cuts for individuals since 1975. For example, when discussing the tax cuts proposed by the Ford administration, the editorial board was already making comments such as, "The most effective method would be to winnow an effective across-the-board tax cut out of the complex of measures incorporated in the budget," and, "The cut in individual taxes would be more beneficial to the economy if it were applied across the board; a reduction in taxes in the lower incomes implies a higher relative tax on the upper incomes, which can only mean a disincentive to the higher incomes to produce."[70]

These early proposals were vague, however, and nowhere near as detailed as the work that had been done on business tax cuts by Kemp's office. It seems that the Kemp office's econometric work trying to show that business tax cuts could pay for themselves combined with the Wanniski-Laffer-Mundell arguments for the Laffer curve and the simplicity of across-the-board cuts in individual taxes to produce an alchemy that transformed both approaches. Wanniski in the *Journal* often compared Kemp's tax cuts to Kennedy's tax cuts, and at some point the idea came up to simply repeat the permanent across-the-board reductions in individual tax rates of the Kennedy/Johnson tax cut of 1964.[71] This would serve as the guiding thread of the program for the next several years. Kemp's group might have gotten to individual rate cuts on their own—Roberts says that he realized by himself the political benefits of cutting individual taxes, although apparently several months after the meeting of Wanniski and Kemp.[72] And others at the time were also thinking about cuts in individual income tax rates. For example, Martin Anderson, an aide to Reagan, claims in passing that he suggested individual tax rate cuts to Reagan, and in 1975 Walter Heller—Kennedy's chief economic adviser and later a critic of supply-side—had proposed repeating the Kennedy tax cuts.[73]

Nevertheless, the meeting of these various groups yielded something different from what any of them had produced prior to the meeting. The joining of the two groups produced a congressional staff committed to the idea, economists willing to argue for it, and a public relations wing on the opinion page of the *Wall Street Journal*. All of the proponents of supply-side were outsiders in their institutions—Kemp a lonely if verbose voice in Congress, Laffer and Mundell iconoclastic among economists, the *Journal* unusual among major newspapers. Mundell in particular has remained out of the limelight to a surprising extent, such that there is still no biography of him, even though his work laid the foundations for the development of the euro and our understanding of international capital flows. But although they were unusual within the institutions, all the main supply-side actors were located firmly within those institutions.

Wanniski's influence is also clear in how Kemp communicated the goal once he was converted to it. For example, after 1976 Kemp adopted, and began to repeat over and over, the phrases on Laffer's napkin, none of which had appeared in his speeches or writings before the Wanniski meeting: "If you tax something, you get less of it. If you subsidize something, you get more of it. We tax work, growth, investment, savings, and productivity, while subsidizing non-work, consumption, and debt."[74] Indeed, this wording would be used years later in the Reagan administration's official attempt to sell the tax program.[75]

Wanniski also turned the arguments, in his usual flashy way, into what he called his Two Santa Claus Theory:

> For the U.S. economy to be healthy and growing, there must be a division of labor between Democrats and Republicans; each must be a different kind of Santa Claus. The Democrats, the party of income redistribution, are best suited for the role of Spending Santa Claus. The Republicans, traditionally the party of income growth, should be the Santa Claus of Tax Reduction. It has been the failure of the GOP to stick to this traditional role that has caused much of the nation's economic misery. . . . It isn't that Republicans don't enjoy cutting taxes. They love it. But there is something in the Republican chemistry that causes the GOP to become hypnotized by the prospect of an imbalanced budget. Static analysis tells them taxes can't be cut or inflation will result. They either argue for a tax hike to dampen inflation when the economy is in a boom or demand spending cuts to balance the budget when the economy is in recession. . . . Either way, of course, they embrace the role of Scrooge, playing into the hands of the Democrats, who know the first rule of successful politics is Never Shoot Santa Claus. The political tension in the

market place of ideas must be between tax reduction and spending increases, and as long as Republicans have insisted on balanced budgets, their influence as a party has shriveled, and budgets have been imbalanced.[76]

Going beyond the economic effects of tax cuts that Mundell and Laffer had focused on, Wanniski tried to argue that tax cuts could be a winning political issue as well. Other Republicans had suggested this before, of course, as far back as Margaret Chase Smith in 1948, but only now would it begin to underpin a transformation of the Republican Party.[77]

By late 1976, Kemp's policy of permanent cuts in individual tax rates had emerged, with a lot of borrowing from Wanniski about Republicans becoming hypnotized by balanced budgets, Santa Claus, and so on.[78] Kemp would go on to argue that Republicans needed to stop offering a moderate version of the welfare programs that Democrats offered and instead start offering an alternative:

> Think about a wagon. . . . The wagon is loaded here. It's unloaded over there. The folks who are loading it are Republicans. The folks who are unloading it are Democrats. You need both parties. The Republicans are the party of growth. The Democrats are the party of distribution. The system works best when each party does its job. What I'm saying is that the System has been breaking down because the Republican Party has not been doing its job. Instead of loading the wagon, some Republicans have jumped away to complain about the unloading job the Democrats have been doing. Others have argued that the unloaders have more fun, and the trouble with the GOP is that it spends too much time complaining about the unloaders when it should be in the wagon, helping them unload. Surely, it's obvious that you can't unload a wagon faster than you load it. Sooner or later it's empty, and while you're then living from hand to mouth, the unloaders will start to complain. They'll persuade the populace that since the loaders have failed, what you need is a new system of loading, perhaps one that rewards collective effort instead of individual effort, so nationalize the wagons and redistribute all the goods.[79]

Kemp was attempting to avoid either echoing the Democrats, or attacking the basic premises of the welfare state.

Most importantly for Kemp, the idea of a broad tax cut helped solve his and the Republicans' political problem. And this is the point developed by the little group that most appealed to other Republicans—not only that tax cuts would bolster the economy or increase revenue, but that they would win votes. Kemp, Wanniski, and other Republicans began to articulate in the late 1970s a vision of how the Republican Party could reconcile free market principles with the need for popular approval. Kemp, who came from a labor district and was the son of a social worker, was able to translate Republican principles into language that resonated with his labor constituents. Now he would use that ability to transform the issue of tax cuts into a new power structure.

The argument was that the Democrats emerged from World War II with an extremely durable framework of power based on government programs. This had been a familiar refrain in Republican circles ever since the New Deal, and it continues to resonate among Republicans today. Many Republicans, starting in the 1930s, explained Democratic victories as the result of votes that had been "bought" by spending programs. In 1936, the journalist Raymond Clapper wrote, "What Civil War pensions and protective tariff favors have been to the Republican party for many years"—means of patronage with which to secure electoral support—"relief is coming to be for the Democratic party."[80] Complaints about the "bought vote" proliferated. As Robert Mason notes, there was some substance to the argument, since relief recipients were likely to be grateful to the Democratic administration that had helped them in times of trouble. Moreover, there was evidence of favoritism at the local level, with use of Works Progress Administration (WPA) money to influence votes. One observer noted that in Michigan support for Roosevelt declined in 1933 but picked up again when money started to flow in from the Civil Works Administration (CWA). Particularly infuriating to Republicans, government programs often promoted pro-government messages; for example, the National Housing Agency put out a pamphlet called "Home loans under the G.I. Bill of rights: How your Government will help you finance the building or buying of a home." As Republicans saw it, taxpayer funds were being used to promote a message that helped Democrats electorally. Examples like these made Republicans conclude that Roosevelt's welfare state was "calculated virtually to Tammanyize the whole United States—the good old theory that those who get money out of a Government will vote for the Party which sponsored the payments."[81]

Not only did such programs relieve short-run suffering, but, fortuitous economists had elaborated a theory—Keynesianism—that such program would actually be good for the economy. Keynesian principles advocated government spending as an answer to weak economic growth, when the economy needed stimulus. But Democratic politicians adopted a strategy of taking care of their constituents through spending even when the economy was growing robustly and did not need particular stimulation. As Republicans saw it, the Democrats "can always *out*-promise us on economic issues," as Nixon said.[82] The Republicans, meanwhile, in the words of one of the proponents of tax cuts, "were perceived by the recipients of government benefits as the party always threatening to cut back on government programs such as social security, while the taxpaying part of the electorate saw Republicans as the party that was always threatening to raise taxes in order to pay for the benefits that others were receiving."[83]

It was hard for opponents of state expansion to break through this power colossus—as the Republicans saw it—and until the late 1970s most didn't even try. The few who did were not very successful. When in 1973 Ronald Reagan, as governor of California, proposed to limit the amount that the state could collect in taxes, he was lucky in suffering only the defeat of the proposal. Richard Nixon was not so lucky: his clumsy attempt to control the welfare state through impoundment succeeded only in making him enemies in Congress, who seethed and raged and eventually reacted.[84]

Kemp, Wanniski, and others began to see in tax cuts a chance to alter these basic building blocks of American power.[85] In December 1976, just after meeting Wanniski, Kemp wrote a letter to President Ford worrying that "the national platforms available for spokesmen of our Republican Party will shrink significantly" and offering a plan that would "project a positive image with positive programs which will provide the basis for an effective alternative by the Congressional Republican Minority." The Democrats, he wrote, had solved a crucial problem: "Ever larger government spending is the way the Democrats have brought the divergent interests of divergent groups of people together to be satisfied under one political umbrella." In opposing these programs and the deficit spending they required, Republicans had fallen into the trap of having "good economics" but "bad politics."[86]

A few months later, he diagnosed the Democratic path to power as trying "to offer something for nothing for everybody," with consequent large deficits, and noted that "the Republican Party has recognized these adverse effects of spending deficits and has long fought against them. While politically courageous, this has had the effect of giving the party a negative image. In fighting these spending programs, we have been put in the position of opposing what many of the electorate wants and perceives as costless . . . we have been placed in the untenable position of being the tax collector for the Democratic spending programs . . . politically, our good economics has been bad politics, and the Democrats' bad economics has been good politics." When phrased in this way, the strategy was obvious: "Let the Democrats be the party of deficit spending. We are the party of lower taxes. Let the Democrats be the party of quick-fixes and more government jobs. We are the party of private enterprise jobs. Let the Democrats be the party of inflation. We are the party of a sound dollar. . . . This should be the program of the Republican Party. It's positive, consistent with our philosophy, and economically sound."[87]

Over the years, Wanniski and Kemp and their increasingly large coterie of supply-siders would have to convince, in turn, primary voters, the media, general election voters, economists, business groups, Congress, and stock market investors about the virtues of this program. But they could not do any of that without first convincing an equally formidable foe: other Republicans.

CHAPTER 2

Convincing the Republicans

THE REPUBLICAN PARTY was not against tax cuts in the 1970s, but the party's lodestar was a balanced budget. Outright hostility to taxation had turned into resigned acceptance under Eisenhower and Nixon and to the task of ensuring that government spending commitments were properly financed. The party was not against tax cuts, but cautious about them.

This preference for balanced budgets emerged as the American state grew in the 1940s, 1950s, and 1960s, and it formed part of the midcentury compromise around taxation that scholars have labeled "the era of easy finance." This compromise was composed of three parts. First, tax rates were very high, extraordinarily high compared to all other Western democracies. This was a legacy of the prewar period, when agrarian Democrats from the Midwest and the South had ganged up against the industrializing Northeast to place high tax rates on capital and the wealthy and to reject national sales tax because it would burden workers and consumers. These high tax rates reached only the very wealthy, however. In the 1920s Secretary of the Treasury Andrew Mellon managed to reduce those rates somewhat, arguing that lower rates would reduce tax avoidance. The second element of the midcentury compromise was that because of depression and war more and more people became taxpayers. The war turned the income tax from a tax on the wealthy into a tax on the middle classes. Nor did those taxes go down after the war, when a prospering economy and generally increasing paychecks reduced concerns about taxation. But—third—the policy of carving out exemptions and deductions proliferated in the 1950s and 1960s, serving as a profitable source of campaign donations for politicians. While the development of tax systems during and because of the Second World War is common for the advanced industrial countries, the very high tax rates, the rejection of national sales tax, and the practice of deductions and exemptions are unusual. The Republican Party had been an unwilling accomplice throughout all this. After Mellon's reforms in the 1920s, the Party mounted an opposition to Harry Truman's tax policies, but under Eisenhower the party concluded that the New Deal order and the taxes it rested on were here to stay. Reduction of taxes through deductions and exemptions helped to reconcile the party to taxes, and Republicans began to focus on making sure that the government had enough money to pay for its increasing number of programs. For this reason they were not fans of the 1964 Kennedy/Johnson tax cut. Politically these cuts cemented the Republican Party's status as deficit hawks and as the "tax collectors for the welfare state," in Newt Gingrich's phrase. Republicans never left behind the ideal of a smaller state, occasionally trying things such as tax limitation movements; but before the Reagan Revolution they never figured out a successful way to implement it.[1]

A former chair of the Council of Economic Advisers summed up the Republican Party's traditional stance as: "generalized resistance to spending in order to achieve a balanced budget, thereby winning the right to tax reduction."[2] In fact, Republicans only rarely won that right: when Democrats called for Keynesian pump-priming tax cuts in the 1970s, it was the Republicans, and especially the right wing of the party, who pushed for budget balance. In signing the 1975 tax cut, Ford worried that the Republican right would be upset about the resulting deficit, musing that "if I did not do something for conservatives soon, I would risk a party polarization that would damage my attempts to win the GOP nomination in 1976."[3] Indeed, conservatives wanted him to veto the 1975 tax cut because of the deficits it would cause, and because it provided $6 billion *more* in tax cuts than Ford had originally asked for.[4] The Republicans, and especially the Republican right, were still the champions of budget balance, even if it meant higher taxes. And when Republicans thought about their route back to power in the mid-1970s, their analyses settled on other issues: broadening their image and their appeal, for example, or recruiting better candidates.[5] Thus, when Kemp presented his arguments to the Ford administration, he was dismissed as a nuisance. Kemp's proposal "is no doubt well intentioned," an internal memorandum sniffed, but it "overpromises almost as much as the Humphrey-Hawkins bill does at the other extreme."[6]

The first success for Kemp and his team was convincing the Republican National Committee of the electoral appeal of tax cuts. In early 1977, the RNC, struggling to overcome the aftereffects of Watergate and the 1976 presidential loss, developed a series of advisory councils to debate policy issues and develop programs independently from Republicans in Congress, who they believed were too involved with the details of legislating to look at the big picture of policymaking. These were small groups—the thirty-six advisory councils and their subcommittees comprised no more than four hundred members in all—with a total budget of $100,000 and a shoestring staff of three or four. Kemp and company took over the Advisory Council on Economic Affairs with the supply-side idea, their first institutional foothold, small as it was.[7] In May 1977, Charlie Black of the RNC wrote to Jack Kemp: "You have indeed produced 'the issue' on which this party can win some elections. I know that Bill Brock [chairman of the RNC] agrees with me that we must continually hammer home the Republican Party's support for permanent tax reductions. The party unity demonstrated in the Senate on the Javits-Danforth [tax cut] amendment was particularly encouraging to me."[8] Indeed, Brock said, "every day it becomes clearer and clearer that the Democrats are the party of taxes. We need to be the party of tax reduction. We simply cannot support another assault on the middle-income people of America."[9] The RNC was interested in tax cuts.

Republicans in Congress had already started introducing rate-cut bills, to consistent defeat. In February 1977, an across-the-board tax rate cut had been offered as an amendment and defeated. In July, Kemp introduced with William Roth of Delaware the bill that would eventually be immortalized as "Kemp-Roth," legislation for a 30 percent cut in individual income tax rates. It was defeated that year and also in March 1978. By April 1978 the RNC had produced a video emphasizing the need for a repeat of Kennedy-style tax cuts.[10]

But although the RNC was convinced, tax cuts were only one proposal among many. In truth, most of the RNC's efforts were organizational ones—beefing up state-level party structures, focusing on communication efforts, reaching out to minorities.[11] And the intellectual discussions were not just about tax cuts: there was excitement, for example, about an idea developed by Peter Berger and Michael Novak that the Republican Party's focus on individualism should be replaced by a focus on "mediating structures" such as families, churches, neighborhoods, and voluntary associations. Many in the party adopted this focus, including Ronald Reagan.[12]

And then, in the summer of 1978, the property tax revolts ripped across California and across the nation. Just as inflation drove federal income taxes higher because of bracket creep—taxpayers getting pushed into higher tax brackets as their nominal wages rose to keep pace with inflation—so inflation puffed up the nominal values of houses and the local property taxes that homeowners owed. First in California and then eventually in sixteen other states—out of twenty-three that allowed voter initiatives—voters forced referenda on ballot initiatives to limit property taxes. The attention to these developments in the media was profound. Whatever the actual meaning of the tax revolt, the interpretation that voters were rejecting taxes took over the nation.[13] One journalist called it "the Proposition 13 bomb," after the famous referendum in California. It may have been a factor in the passage of a significant capital gains tax cut that was popular even among Democrats that summer.[14]

Although the Carter administration would succeed in fending off major tax cuts for another couple of years, Kemp rocketed to fame with the reputation of having predicted the popularity of tax cuts. Suddenly, Kemp was all over the media. One prominent national magazine opened an article on Kemp this way:

"Look at that physique, look at that athletic grace. . . . Look at that extraordinary vitality, like an old-time revivalist, all that power and drive. I love to watch him debate on the House floor—one shoulder goes down, one knee bends, and you've got the stance of a statue. Look at the way he moves—I bet he's a wonderful dancer." Was [New Jersey congresswoman Millicent] Fenwick turned on by the custom-tailored, forty-three-year-old conservative with the Kennedyesque swath of blown-dry hair across his forehead? "You bet I am," she replied, without hesitation.[15]

A *National Review* reporter wrote:

I have a guilty secret
That fills me full of shame:

Another bumper sticker
Has set my heart aflame.
I'll keep his campaign buttons
Within my bedroom shrine,
But Jack Kemp is replacing
My former valentine.[16]

Everyone was a little bit smitten with Jack Kemp in the autumn of 1978. Kemp had anticipated the issue that now, in hindsight, struck all observers as the defining issue of the time. Jude Wanniski had just published a book elaborating the tax cut ideas, and suddenly Kemp-Roth went from being one proposal among many to being the central proposal.[17] Now that Kemp had showed them the path, the Republicans followed him eagerly, and tax cuts became the key issue on which Republicans fought the midterm elections of 1978. In a massive and well-financed attempt in the fall of 1978, the party chartered a plane and flew a string of speakers around the country to argue in favor of tax reduction and particularly the Kemp-Roth bill. They distributed materials that included information on current tax burdens and on the Kennedy tax cuts and their purported results in raising revenue as well as suggested answers to tough questions that speakers might be asked. The materials also included a background paper on taxes by Michael Boskin and supporting quotes from various luminaries. Milton Friedman was on the record saying: "I support this bill since I believe that any form of tax reduction under any circumstances must eventually bring pressure to bear to cut spending."[18]

The perceived electoral appeal of tax cuts was a central reason for its popularity among Republicans at this stage. "I think we have an issue today that's gluing the party together from California to Maine and from Florida to Washington," said Roth. "You can go to blue collar workers, you can go into businesses, go talk to housewives, colleges—they're all enthusiastic about it. I've had candidates—I think this is the real proof of it—call me and say, 'Not only are we for it, but when we talk about the Roth/Kemp bill, they stand up and applaud.'" Kemp added that "it touches a responsive chord in the hearts and minds of the young, the minorities, blue collar workers—people who heretofore have not been in the Republican Party. It can truly broaden the base by again restoring hope and opportunity to this country. . . . This is the national theme that can put the Republican party in control of the Congress in 1979. We could actually capture the Congress in 1979 on this issue."[19] Kemp had been working this routine for years at this point, and he was getting so good at it that he could even bring a labor audience to its feet, as he did at an international American Federation of Labor and Congress of Industrial Organizations (AFL-CIO) labor union convention in Miami.[20]

Beyond capturing Congress, many of the actors had convinced themselves that they were in it to save civilization. Consider this internal, unsigned memo to Kemp from an aide: written not for public consumption, it deals mostly with internal matters—how Kemp should communicate, what he should prioritize—but nevertheless ends this way:

> I made the decision at the beginning of this Session that the only emotion—
> one arising from reason—which would keep me here over the long run would
> be one arising from being honestly and fairly thoroughly convinced that *you*
> have a chance of reversing the trend in this country. . . . It does no good to
> be President of the United States on this issue and then not do anything
> about it once one got there. We are seeing the collapse of an entire civiliza-
> tion. . . . If you think you can change the course of Western Civilization—
> and no less—then here's where we start.[21]

Joining the cross-country effort in 1978 to save Western civilization was Ronald Reagan, the defeated 1976 candidate for president and current Republican front-runner and darling of the conservative right. Former governor of California, former spokesman for General Electric, former TV actor and Hollywood heartthrob and union leader battling Communists, Ronald Reagan had already lived several lives. Born near poverty but unaware of it, Reagan was a fascinating character who confounded many, including his authorized biographer. His great gift—and fatal weakness—was his ability to see the world as he wanted to see it. He often told the story of two brothers, an optimist and a pessimist, whose parents try to cure them. They give the pessimist a roomful of toys, but he cries because they will all soon be broken. They give the optimist a mound of manure. He grabs a shovel and cheerfully dives in, because with that much manure, there has to be a pony under there somewhere.[22] Many years later, in the midst of a scandal in which he had falsely denied trading arms for hostages, Reagan said: "My heart and my best intentions still tell me that's true, but the facts and the evidence tell me it is not" —an astounding quote that epitomizes his enduring sense of living in a world better than the one that "the facts and the evidence" told him he was in.[23]

Reagan had come into contact with the Laffer-Mundell ideas as early as 1975, when an adviser brought up the Laffer argument at a policy meeting during Reagan's ill-fated 1976 presidential campaign.[24] Ronald Reagan was certainly open to cutting taxes. Biographers have identified a personal reason for Reagan's opposition to taxes: although he never broke through to the highest levels of the acting profession, Reagan did arrive at the highest levels of wealth within it, earning almost as much as Errol Flynn did in the 1940s. At precisely this time, his personal life was coming apart as his first marriage ended, and "he had a sense that his career was slipping and that his financial future was shaky. Reagan took out some of his negative feelings on the tax system" at a time when marginal tax rates could go as high as 91 percent. In politics Reagan had been pushing for restraining the size of the state for years and had attempted tax cuts and tax limitation as governor of California.[25] In 1977, he had written that "the Democrats are handing us Republicans the best issue we've had in a long time, and it's one on which a majority of working Americans will agree with us. The issue is taxes." In 1978, he wrote that at the recent meeting of his political action committee, people "talked of little else but Proposition 13. . . . No wonder Republicans are beginning to feel good about their party. We have an issue that unites us as a party and links us to the self-interest of the hard-pressed American taxpayer. . . . That sounds like a winning platform for any Republican candidate, come November."[26]

And yet, come November, the 1978 midterm effort proved to be only moderately successful in electing Republicans to Congress. The Republicans did gain seats, but fewer than had been predicted, and fewer than the average for the opposition party in midterm elections.[27] They did not take control of either house.[28] A Democratic National Committee (DNC) head gloated, "The Republicans put all their eggs in the Kemp-Roth basket and they broke one by one."[29] Many pundits considered the whole tax cut chase a bust. "There is now almost universal agreement that the evangelistic crusade Republicans launched this fall on behalf of a one-third cut in federal taxes, unaccompanied by spending cuts, was a political blunder of the first magnitude," one sage intoned, noting that most candidates who campaigned on it "were quickly thrown on the defensive by born-again conservative Democrats arguing that Republicans were fiscally irresponsible and promoting inflation."[30] The pollster Louis Harris found that only 34 percent of respondents in polls supported Kemp-Roth, with 47 percent opposing it, and concluded that voters thought tax cuts would lead either to deficits that could worsen inflation or to cuts in government services.[31] Another poll found only 45 percent of Republicans supporting Kemp-Roth.[32]

One important hinge in the history of the ERTA is the question of how the Republican Party would interpret the role of its tax cut efforts in the midterm election. Was all that work—the chartered plane, the carefully prepared materials—wasted on an issue that did not resonate with the electorate? Or would the gains have been even stronger if the party had put even more resources into the tax cut effort? There was poll evidence supporting both positions. Polls showed, for example, that the public believed that Democrats were more likely to cut taxes than Republicans, presumably because of the hard efforts of the Republican balanced budget wing. If this was the problem, then perhaps Republicans needed to double down and make their efforts on tax cuts more visible. But as President Carter noted, the tax revolts that had taken place across the nation were directed at iniquitous local taxes, suggesting that there may not have been a general aversion to high taxes. Of the 50,000 letters the White House received every week, "never in the 20 months that I have been in office has reducing income taxes shown up" in the top ten subjects, Carter said.[33] Perhaps chasing the tax cut idea in the 1980 election would be throwing good time and effort after bad.

There were several presidential candidates, so there were many different answers to this question, just as there were in the news media and in the scholarly literature.[34] The GOP started talking about moving tax cuts to the back burner and focusing on a constitutional amendment to balance the budget instead, as polls were showing more enthusiasm for this than for tax cuts.[35] Bill Brock, who had been so enthusiastic about the tax cuts two years earlier, now only mentioned them in passing, and Howard Baker, Phil Crane, Bob Dole, and George H. W. Bush were all talking about amendments to limit spending or balance the budget.[36]

Ronald Reagan's support for tax cuts could not be taken for granted either, because he was pragmatic when he needed to be—to such an extent that as governor of California, in order to balance the budget, he had actually presided over the largest tax *increase* that any state had ever seen in the history of America. Under Reagan's governorship, taxes on corporations almost doubled in California, state taxes increased, personal income taxes increased, taxes on cigarettes and alcohol increased, and the tax structure became more progressive.[37] The future of the tax cut movement lay with a politician who had presided over large tax increases.

In mid-January 1979, the Reagan team met to hash out the issues and plot strategy for the general election. The purpose of the meeting as explained to the press was to decide whether Reagan should run,[38] but the actual discussion at the meeting focused on the question of how to run and the meaning of the 1978 results.

Particularly notable at this point in the history of the tax cut is the role of pollster Richard Wirthlin and the entire apparatus of polling that had developed over the prior decades. Despite the outpouring of writings on Reagan, Wirthlin is a key figure who has never gotten his due. He helped Reagan at crucial moments—as in 1976 when his polls had discovered the appeal of the issue of American sovereignty over the Panama Canal and Reagan used it to revive his presidential campaign. Although Reagan eventually fell short that year, it was a much narrower loss than it would have been otherwise, keeping his prospects alive for 1980.[39] While much of the research on polling focuses on whether politicians use polls to decide which policies to champion, or whether they use polls to analyze how best to persuade the public of policies they independently favor—that is, whether the politician is leader or follower—the growth and the increasing ease of public opinion polling was now allowing politicians to do both, and pollsters were beginning to be able to coordinate both activities in a reciprocal dynamic. Public opinion was a constraint, but a loose one, and a greater constraint at earlier stages, before the politician committed to a specific course of action.[40] Wirthlin's method of tracking polls was new and notable in the polling community, and he polled both to identify what people were thinking, and to determine how best to market Reagan's policies.[41]

In the spring of 1978, when Reagan was still an unannounced candidate for the 1980 election and ostensibly was still only thinking about it, Wirthlin had taken some soundings. Wirthlin was a creative pollster, not limiting himself to simple polling of issues. He would sometimes try different scenarios to try to uncover how the voters were thinking and what they were feeling. In one set of polls, he made a particularly intriguing discovery. He asked respondents what they thought of hypothetical candidates who combined particular qualities: wants to attack inflation plus chooses a female vice president, say, or favors military spending plus tax limits. One of the qualities Wirthlin used in his combinations was the candidate's age—Reagan's Achilles' heel as a candidate. If Reagan were to win the presidency, he would be the oldest person to enter the office up to that point, just shy of seventy on inauguration day. It was the one constant in all of the articles about him: conservative leader, confident and charismatic, with a devoted national following—and yet. In his poll, Wirthlin found that "limiting taxes is much more effective than either strong defense or a woman Vice President; at the same time, being 70 years old is the weakest attribute of all (indeed, only when coupled with limiting taxes does the 70-year-old with 'Republican' economic beliefs achieve victory)."[42]

At the January 1979 meeting, when the team met to discuss the message of the 1978 election, Wirthlin pulled together data from various surveys and opinion polls to make a forceful electoral argument for tax reduction. He argued that inflation was going to continue for at least the next two years and that it would push respondents into favoring tax reduction. He noted that even some Democrats, such as Jerry Brown, were jumping on the issue of tax cuts. Wirthlin argued that in the midterm election Republican candidates who had vigorously promoted the tax issue and the issue of spending restraint, as some had done in Minnesota and Colorado, had done very well. "When Republicans clearly get on those issues and express some social concern, invariably, they can use that as a vehicle for election," he said. Ultimately the team saw the 1978 results as extremely successful given the still-lingering shadow of Watergate. Charlie Black of the RNC concluded: "I think the party's image in the public mind has been improved, has been cleaned up substantially since the depths of Watergate in 1974. Just the baggage that any candidate carries around by virtue of being a Republican, I think, has been reduced substantially."[43]

Nothing was decided at this particular meeting, but the argument that tax cuts still had electoral potential received strong backing at this time from a key figure, Reagan's pollster. The Reagan team interpreted the 1978 election as a success given the shadow of Watergate, and they concluded that tax reduction was still an issue worth pursuing. That Reagan's campaign was aware of, and influenced by, the movement around Kemp-Roth is evident by the transformation of the issue as they discussed it: Wirthlin's polls were often about tax limitation, the kind of strategy Reagan had tried as governor of California—setting a limit on the amount of taxes government could collect. But the eventual policy that Reagan would adopt was much simpler, just large cuts in tax rates, of the kind Kemp had been pushing since his meeting with Wanniski, Laffer, and Mundell. By August 1979, Reagan's team had hammered out a comprehensive economic policy, with pride of place given to three years of across-the-board cuts in individual income tax rates, and by January 1980 they had let Jack Kemp know that they were embracing Kemp-Roth.[44] The tax cut torch passed from Kemp, Wanniski, Laffer, Mundell, and all the other supply-siders, who would henceforth be relegated to the margins of the effort, to Ronald Reagan.

Reagan had decided on tax cuts. Now he needed to face all the other Republicans who were skeptical. Reagan entered the campaign season as the Republican front-runner, but as the primary process began in early 1980, his team made a big mistake, allowing a potential rival to emerge.

Because Reagan was so far ahead in the polls, his campaign manager, John Sears, decided on a strategy of not engaging in the debates and the rallies. The idea was to prevent Reagan from losing his lead by making some gaffe or providing material for others to criticize. Richard Nixon had coasted to victory in 1968 on just such a strategy, and Sears had been a high-level adviser in that campaign.[45] As the other Republican candidates raced from one speech or press conference or straw poll to another, Reagan sat tight. "It wouldn't do any good to have him going to coffees and shaking hands like the others," Sears said. "People will get the idea he's an ordinary man, like the rest of us."[46]

So Reagan skipped the first Republican debate, to be held before the Iowa caucus. Primary debates were not yet an established political phenomenon. The Iowa debate of 1980 would be only the second in history, and the first primary debate to be televised. Reagan justified his refusal with the argument that Republicans should not debate each other: "I have worked so hard and so long for party unity that, from the very first, I laid down the law that I would not engage in debates with other Republicans. I felt that it emphasized our differences rather than what we had in common."[47]

The debate, the first of its kind in most viewers' lives, was widely watched. The beneficiary was George Herbert Walker Bush, who had been campaigning hard for over a year, touring forty-two states even before he announced his candidacy. Bush was well qualified, with a background in the oil business, time as a legislator and RNC chair, and stints as ambassador to China, ambassador to the United Nations, and head of the CIA—not to mention that he was a true war hero, the youngest combat pilot in the Navy in the Second World War, while Reagan had spent the war making patriotic films. And if Bush won the presidency in 1980, he would be only fifty-six on taking office.[48] He put in fourteen-hour days and brought up his own age often.[49]

Bush performed only moderately well in the debate, but that was enough when combined with the highly effective ground organization he had put together in all ninety-nine of Iowa's counties to pull off a stunning upset. Bush won the caucuses in January in a record turnout and was transformed, in his own words, from "a little star and an asterisk" into potentially the new front-runner.[50] Suddenly the press and the crowds couldn't get enough of him.[51] His fund-raising rose from $40,000 to $150,000 a day.[52]

Bush was a competent executor of tasks, not an ideologue or a visionary. His diverse resume had given him considerable managerial expertise, confidence in his own administrative talents, and an appreciation for knowledgeable staff, but he never seemed to stay in any one post long enough to develop visions for more substantial change. He entered national politics with no burning desire to alter the course of the nation. He was on both sides of many issues, wanting environmental protection as well as easier coal mining, favoring both nuclear energy and solar energy, supporting a draft for women but not "equality in the foxhole." He opposed the 1964 Civil Rights Act, then voted for the 1968 Civil Rights Act after having voted against it in a preliminary vote.[53] He favored a tax cut, but not a big one. At the Iowa forum, he distanced himself from Reagan's across-the-board tax cuts, favoring tax cuts for investment instead.[54] As an oilman he favored deregulation but otherwise seemed to have had no fixed political goals, wanting only to win the game in order to be in a position to solve the problems. "I just think I know how to go about it better," he said.[55] Perhaps a competent pragmatist with Washington experience was exactly what the voters would want after four years of an ineffective outsider president.

After the Iowa caucuses, the next big test—the decisive one, if Reagan lost again to Bush—was the New Hampshire primary. A few weeks before the contest, polls showed 37 percent for Bush and 33 percent for Reagan. Reporters interviewing voters in New Hampshire repeatedly found concerns about Reagan's age. Said one who had voted for Reagan in 1976: "I think he's a little too old. I'm going on 78 and I know I'm not as smart as I used to be." An undecided voter noted, "If I think Reagan can last another five years, I'll have him."[56]

Reagan tried to be jocular about the Iowa loss, commenting to the press that there would be no changes in campaign strategy before New Hampshire and that a loss there would be only a "bruise, but not fatal."[57] Behind the scenes the attitude was very different. When Wirthlin conducted an extremely detailed poll of New Hampshire in late January, he found Bush leading Reagan among "somewhat conservative voters." He concluded:

> It would seem well advised to open up the ideological gap between ourselves and Bush in two ways. First, efforts should be made to secure the organizational backing of the pro-lifers and gun owners against Bush. Second, the Governor should once again re-emphasize the tax cuts and the economic issues. The data reflects our comparative issue strength over Bush in this area. . . . This would involve, in part, having the Governor speak more frequently about the economic issues of tax cuts, federal budgets and inflation . . . the economic issues rank high in saliency and hit very close to the political soul of many New Hampshire voters.

Wirthlin told Sears that the team should be "emphasizing the themes of taxes, the economy, and what can be done to control inflation. These cut well with all ideological groups." He noted with a hint of desperation that "a maximum-maximorum effort must be mounted to win New Hampshire."[58] Everyone in the campaign knew that if Reagan lost New Hampshire, the game was over. He was too old to try again.

As it happened, Reagan won New Hampshire for entirely different reasons, in one of those curious and unscripted campaign moments that reveal more than months of interviews and press conferences can. Given the Iowa fiasco, Reagan gave up the putative focus on "party unity": "Apparently we are more united and can afford to do these things because I have to admit I did not find the debate [in Iowa] divisive in any way. I, therefore, have agreed to debate in New Hampshire."[59]

But the preparations became confused for the second New Hampshire debate. Bush and Reagan agreed to a one-on-one debate in Nashua, but the Federal Election Commission's rules prevented the newspaper that had agreed to sponsor the debate from doing so, because paying for a debate that excluded the rest of the field would be considered an illegal corporate contribution to a political campaign. Reagan's team agreed to step in and pay, thinking that a burst of attention before the vote would benefit them.[60] When the day came, however, Reagan grew uneasy at the idea of sponsoring a debate that the FEC thought was unfair to the other candidates. He wanted to work out an agreement to let them all participate. Moreover, his campaign manager John Sears sensed that something good would come from the tableau of Reagan as the magnanimous one favoring inclusivity and Bush as the stingy candidate wanting to exclude the others.[61]

Reagan's team invited the other candidates to the debate venue, and Reagan argued for their inclusion. But Bush, having expected a boost from going one-on-one with Reagan, feeling tricked into accepting the larger field, and wanting to abide by the newspaper's rules, insisted on the one-on-one debate—thereby earning the excluded candidates' vocal wrath. The moderator, Jon Breen, refused to let the other candidates participate, wanting to honor the terms of the original agreement.

The confusion continued for over an hour, with the crowd cheering on Reagan's instinct for inclusion. Finally Reagan and Bush were introduced. The four excluded candidates trooped in and stood awkwardly on stage, having nowhere to sit. Reagan began trying to explain to the crowd what had happened. Breen, exasperated, ordered the technician to cut off Reagan's microphone. "I am paying for this microphone, Mr. Green," Reagan exploded, seemingly getting Breen's name wrong in his anger. The crowd cheered wildly, and the newspapers the next day put the dramatic story on the front pages, with the excluded candidates lambasting Bush endlessly.[62] Although Bush had been even with Reagan in the polls or slightly ahead, Reagan won the state in a landslide. Observers would later comment that that was the moment Reagan won the nomination.[63]

Although the content of the debate took backstage to the preliminary drama, at the debate George Bush had clearly come out against Reagan's three-year, 30 percent tax cut, arguing that it would contribute to inflation. It's tempting to suggest that that unscripted moment changed the course of history, because had Bush won the primary and then the election that year, he certainly would not have implemented such a big tax cut. But Reagan was already rising in the polls before the debate, and even without the microphone moment, Bush's performance in the debate was panned.[64] Here are Reagan's and Bush's answers, for example, to how they would deal with the Iran hostage crisis. Reagan: "The time has long passed when we should have set a date certain for their release." Bush: "I have been supporting the President [Carter] because I have not been able to come up with a quick fix for the situation."[65] The microphone moment revealed a certainty in Reagan and a caution in Bush that resonated differently with voters at that particular time of American crisis. That moment was a distillation of the campaign rather than an aberration. As a member of Bush's team told him: "The bad news is that the media is playing up the confrontation. The good news is that they're ignoring the debate, and you lost that too."[66]

In policy terms, the lasting effect of Reagan's Iowa loss and the campaign's determined and all-out effort to win New Hampshire was to open up "the ideological gap between ourselves and Bush" and boost the profile of the tax proposals.[67] A second effect of these events was the forced departure of campaign manager John Sears, who had made the poor call on Iowa. Sears was more moderate in policy terms, and his replacement, William Casey, was more ideologically conservative.[68]

Having saved the campaign from disaster in a way that thrilled all of Reagan's longtime supporters and vindicated their hopes in him, Reagan turned to the task of continuing the momentum the microphone moment had generated. Bush eked out a victory in Massachusetts as well as in his home state of Connecticut in March, keeping the contest alive. He tried to portray Reagan as too ideological to get elected. Before the Pennsylvania primary in April Bush called the tax cut "voodoo economics" and overcame a thirty-point deficit to beat Reagan.[69] Wirthlin, meanwhile, was discovering tax-cutting to be a popular issue in many states, and not just among conservative Republicans. A poll in Vermont found that Republicans there "overwhelmingly agree that an absolute tax ceiling should be placed on the federal government's revenue-raising powers."[70] Tax limitation was also popular in Illinois, where "strong agreement with this statement corresponds to strong support for Reagan."[71] While the campaign was divided over how much to emphasize tax cuts, there was no suggestion that Reagan was going to drop Kemp-Roth.[72]

Thus, the tax cut battle moved to the center of the primary fight as Bush tried to draw attention to the policy and Reagan would not back away from it. Each candidate played to his base. There were factions within the Republican electorate as much as within the general electorate, and Reagan would not have wanted to alienate his base of conservative Republicans by moving away from the tax cut policy, just as Bush would not have wanted to disappoint his base of Republican moderates by embracing the untested idea. That Wirthlin was even polling tax limitation so regularly is a reflection of Reagan's stance as the most conservative of the candidates, the one who had made an attempt at tax limitation in California.

By the close of the primary battle Reagan was so thoroughly on board with tax cuts that there was even talk in the Reagan camp of Jack Kemp as a possible vice presidential pick. Kemp's prescience in anticipating "the issue" had made him a favorite with conservatives, such that he was now being talked about as the successor to Reagan—or perhaps even the youthful alternative to Reagan. The Reagan campaign had been worried enough about this to ask pollster Wirthlin to keep an eye on Kemp's name-recognition numbers. They briefly considered Kemp as a running mate, but eventually settled on giving him a role in policy development and putting the Kemp-Roth tax cut at the heart of Reagan's platform, in return for Kemp's vow not to run himself and thereby split Reagan's conservative support. Ever after, Kemp would be the "good soldier" in Reagan's cause.[73] As observers noted, talk of tax cuts and of Jack Kemp had "replaced the notorious 'welfare queen' of 1976 as a stock character in Reagan's stump oratory . . . pushing tax relief for blue-collar workers has replaced flogging welfare recipients."[74]

The primaries were not exactly run on the issue of tax cuts, but especially after Pennsylvania, tax cuts emerged as a central theme, with the main question being whether the large across-the-board tax cuts that Reagan championed were excessive. Bush and many other Republicans at the time wanted to continue the Republican Party's cautious approach to tax cuts. But for Reagan, tax cuts proved to be a way to reconcile the conservatism favored by primary voters with the optimism that would eventually become his hallmark.

As for George Bush, in what would prove to be a leitmotif in his political career, overzealous speechwriting on taxes came back to haunt him. Years later, he denied having spoken the "voodoo economics" phrase and was forced to back down when video of the statement immediately emerged.[75]

CHAPTER 3

Convincing the Voters

AS REAGAN MOVED into the general election phase of the campaign, the question for the team was how much to emphasize the tax cut issue, and how much to subordinate discussion of specifics. In the press, a narrative took shape that there was a battle within the campaign on whether to cut taxes at all.[1] Over the course of the summer, Reagan talked less and less about the tax cut. Observers wondered if the embrace of tax cuts had just been to appease the primary electorate. Would Reagan actually be committed to tax cuts when it came down to it? Had he just swung right for the primaries, and was he now swinging to the center to try to appeal to more moderate voters? And if so, what did that suggest for his actual commitment to tax cuts?

Reagan was in fact trying to move toward the middle, where possible, on other issues, such as providing aid to New York City or to Chrysler.[2] So it was reasonable to wonder if he would give up the ideological red meat on taxes too. Various advisers were also saying confusing things. In March 1980 an unnamed Reagan adviser told the *Wall Street Journal*, "Many Republicans ran on the big Kemp-Roth tax-cut bill in the 1978 elections and managed to let the Democrats paint them as economically irresponsible . . . .We can't let that happen this time." Wanniski also fed the perception that there was irresolution over tax cuts.[3]

In fact by this point the team was committed to tax cuts. The only battle was over how much to emphasize the issue in the general election campaign.

One of the hardest questions for a campaign team is whether, and when, to focus on specifics, particularly if the opponent is not doing well. There were many within the campaign who wanted Reagan to come out with a bold and detailed program, to commit to it publicly, and essentially to run the campaign based on it—including Wanniski, who wanted a big summertime debate on the issue of tax cuts. He wrote that without such a big, bold proposal, "we are preparing to play into Jimmy Carter's hands with a backward-looking, negative, non-issue campaign . . . if the contest is going to be decided at that level, Jimmy will win easily. . . . How mindless to spend $12 million to $15 million to focus on President Carter's 'failure of leadership,' which is the commercial equivalent of spending that amount to inform the American people that Hershey bars are made out of chocolate. . . . People want to know about the future; they already know about the past."[4] A marketing team wrote: "WE MUST GIVE PEOPLE A REASON TO VOTE FOR GOVERNOR REAGAN, NOT JUST AGAINST PRESIDENT CARTER."[5] After all, trying to stay above the fray had been the big mistake in Iowa.

Meanwhile, the media and Reagan's opponents also insisted on a certain level of explicit discussion of the program. As he moved into the general election, Reagan's plan was getting a great deal of scrutiny because of the seemingly implausible nature of the promise to increase defense spending, cut taxes, and balance the budget. Bush's "voodoo economics" phrase hung around the entire effort, and independent presidential candidate John Anderson had repeatedly hammered Reagan by saying "The only way Reagan is going to cut taxes, increase defense spending, and balance the budget at the same time is to use blue smoke and mirrors." The press hounded Reagan at every stop, and articles were coming out with titles like "Reagan Plan Figures Called Way Off Base."[6] The campaign had to produce some details soon.

But there were big problems with getting into the specifics of the program. Reagan's late-season primary loss in Pennsylvania was at least partly caused by media focus on his tendency to get facts both small and large wrong in service of his beliefs. For example, he claimed that giving $1 in poverty benefits cost $3 in overhead, when the actual cost of overhead was 12 cents. He claimed that Kennedy cut taxes by 30 percent when the actual figure was 19 percent. He said that the federal workforce had grown by 131,000 employees in 3 years when in fact it was fewer than 60,000. What was particularly dangerous about these mistakes was how they fed into the picture of "an old man who's beginning to lose his grip."[7] Wirthlin found that media attention to Reagan's alleged misquoting of facts was "the fundamental explanation for the dramatic shift in the Reagan support in Pennsylvania": fully 16 percent of the sample had indicated a preference for Reagan before the primary, heard about his misuse of facts, and changed their vote.[8] And launching a bold discussion of an untested economic program with many tricky details would be an invitation for Reagan to get tripped up in more questions and more dangerous off-the-cuff technical discussions.

These, then, were the tight parameters within which the campaign operated: they had to get across to voters that they *had* a plan and that the plan added up, but somehow avoid getting into too many of the specifics of the plan. The strategy that emerged was best described by the *Wall Street Journal:* to make a technical case for a policy, "you find a Friendly Expert—in government, a university, a think tank—and have him give you the numbers. When reporters ask where the numbers came from, you should be able to lay some Recognized Authority on them. As it turns out, once reporters sense the aura of such authority around a campaign they give up asking the questions."[9] It was necessary only to find numbers that would get the journalists to shut up. But although it's possible to find a wide variety of numbers from universities and think tanks, the malleability of experts is not infinite.

These constraints explain much of the shape of the program that emerged. In fact, these requirements completely blew apart the Mundell program. The original idea that had united Mundell, Laffer, Wanniski, and Kemp was tax cuts *plus returning the country to a gold standard.* But unlike the story of tax cuts, an idea that rewrote history, the story of the gold standard is the opposite—the story of an idea that is now considered quackery, to the extent that even comparing the two proposals seems suspect.

Comparing the proposals is justified because of how much is similar about them. The original push from Mundell, Laffer, and Wanniski, the conversion of Jack Kemp to the cause, Ronald Reagan's adoption of the idea—all of it is the same in the two stories. But the two issues played out in very different ways, and examining why gives important insight into the politics of tax cuts.

Mundell argued that the regime of floating exchange rates had been responsible for inflation because it allowed governments to finance budget deficits by selling bonds with impunity and thereby increasing their money supply. Under fixed exchange rates, selling too many government bonds would lead to outflows of foreign reserves because the increased money supply would make that government's money less valuable compared to the fixed exchange rate. This would act as a constraint on the money supply and thus on inflation. Gold, Mundell argued, was the best asset to underpin the whole system, and if politics did not get in the way, he thought gold would be "the natural solution." Laffer picked up the idea and tried to operationalize it by figuring out exactly how to price gold. Wanniski pushed it in an early article in *Public Interest* and relentlessly in the editorial pages of the *Wall Street Journal;* Kemp advocated for the gold standard in a book published in November 1979.[10] Most economists, on the other hand, had concluded that the gold standard had failed miserably over the course of the twentieth century, artificially constraining productive economies.[11]

It's true that the tax cut idea and the gold standard idea did not play completely equivalent roles in the program. The memorandum that outlined the campaign's agenda in August 1979 did not include the gold standard, for example—but then, that memo also did not include increases in defense spending. Support from economists was probably somewhat weaker for the gold standard than for tax cuts—but then, the role of economists was to provide cover rather than to give direction, and economists such as Mundell could always be found to fulfill that purpose.

The idea of the gold standard also had some distinct political advantages over the idea of tax cuts. Selling the notion of a dollar as good as gold would arguably have been easier than trying to explain how tax cuts and increased spending would create a balanced budget. Only in 1971 had convertibility of the dollar into gold been abandoned, and re-establishing it would not have seemed as far-fetched in the 1980s as it does to us today. Indeed, the argument would have been that restoring convertibility would mean returning to a period of lower inflation, arguably an easier argument to make than the tortured argument of how tax cuts would ease inflation. As the *New York Times* put it, "The idea is no less realistic politically than . . . wholesale firings of striking air controllers."[12]

Most importantly, the gold standard was a live possibility because Ronald Reagan himself was a big fan of the gold standard. "No nation can survive under 'fiat money,'" he lectured his advisers. Economist Alan Greenspan, an adviser to the campaign, tried to argue him out of it. It wasn't that abandonment of the gold standard had caused inflation, Greenspan suggested, but rather that the United States could no longer adhere to the gold standard because of inflation. Greenspan argued that if inflation can be resolved, then there is no need to return to the gold standard, and if inflation cannot be resolved, then it is not possible to.[13] In Reagan's camp were many monetarists who argued that control of the money supply rather than a gold standard should be the key mechanism for control of inflation, and that with control of the money supply in place, even with a regime of floating exchange rates, fears of exchange rate depreciation would keep inflation in check.[14]

But Reagan was still thinking about the gold standard as late as January 1980, bringing it up during a wide-ranging meeting with Milton Freedman to discuss economic policy. The conversation began with a discussion of taxes and how best to reduce them. But the real fireworks occurred on the issue of monetary policy, with Reagan again probing the idea of the gold standard and Friedman set against it. Friedman argued that gold was an unstable basis for an economy, and that there was no way a gold standard could work with government spending 40 percent of national income. The real discipline for monetary policy, Friedman argued, was "limitation on increase of [the] money supply"; gold was a "speculative commodity" and did not form a "good basis for monetary discipline." The key to fighting inflation was to "hold down monetary growth" and "control [the] budget." The recipe to fight inflation was therefore to "slow monetary growth" reasonably, reduce "spending gradually over [a] period of time," and "reduce taxes," including by indexing tax rates to inflation. As to Kemp-Roth, Friedman pronounced the bill "OK." "Combined [with] sensible monetary policy, it will be worthwhile to increase productivity."[15]

But Friedman could not argue Reagan and the team out of the gold standard. In March 1980, Martin Anderson, in a draft of "An Economic Program for the 1980s," wrote: "A return to some form of a gold standard will not automatically solve the overwhelming economic problems that face us today. But the reestablishment of the dollar's link to gold should be one of our first economic priorities once we have made substantial progress toward setting our economic house in order . . . it will help mightily, once we have repaired our economy, to ensure that the economy stays sound."[16] As of that point in the campaign, the gold standard was still part of the platform, although it is clear the team was seeing the gold standard as a less immediate goal.[17]

Campaign manager William Casey—thought of as more ideologically conservative than the pragmatic John Sears—made the pragmatic decision to move the team even further away from the gold standard, with an assist from Wirthlin. Because of the issue of misuse of facts, a strategy memo from Wirthlin in May noted that Reagan needed to "stay away from specific and arguable statements . . . stay away from unnecessary predictions. . . . Economists can argue but no-one knows how fast tax cuts will generate enough new revenue to make up for the revenue lost by lower rates. . . . Stay away from statements or positions that are too technical for public understanding, i.e. the gold standard."[18] Casey eventually turned this argument into campaign policy. In drawing up new policy documents, he eliminated the gold standard completely and backed away from making tax cuts the centerpiece in order to

> get us out of a looming "numbers game" on whether tax cuts will generate revenues fast enough to avoid inflationary deficits. At this point, we should point a direction rather than commit ourselves to specific reductions. We should pursue that direction by tax cuts in combination with other steps to increase production and reduce overhead. . . . Don't let it all hang on tax cuts. I've eliminated reference to gold because it's too technical, the public is not interested now and we're not ready to take a position. I've deferred expenditure limitations and the economic bill of rights because they slow down the articulation of how the immediate concern with inflation can be met.

By October, the gold standard issue had been firmly pushed "until several years down the road." It was eventually referred to a commission, and then it disappeared altogether.[19] Postponing the gold standard discussion had the effect of abandoning the gold standard, because a few years later inflation was no longer the main problem and the Reagan economic program had fallen apart. The gold standard would ever after remain several years down the road, and Mundell's program would lose one of its key pieces.

Because of the same requirement to be careful with discussions over technical issues, Reagan and the campaign began talking less about the tax cut as well. There were also several other reasons for subordinating discussion of the tax cut. First was the problem that the 1978 peak of tax hatred had subsided by the summer of 1980. In a July focus group "there seemed to be some recognition that Reagan plans to cut taxes, but there was relatively little emphasis on this area and it did not provoke an intense response . . . in the few instances when Reagan's California record was raised, it was discussed in a negative light (raising taxes and cutting services) rather than as proof of his ability to get things done." A meeting on July 9 reinforced those worries, noting declining support among older voters that might have resulted from fear of loss of services as a consequence of the tax cut. Also noted was that four out of ten voters weren't clear about Reagan's stances. Although in September 5 percent of respondents named reduction of taxes as a "good thing" that would happen if Reagan was elected, 3 percent thought that he would *increase* taxes—perhaps because of his record of having done so in California. Moreover, the team had become aware that, whatever the polls said about taxes, primary votes for Reagan did not necessarily reflect agreement with his ideological positions. In March, as it was becoming clear that Reagan had locked up the nomination, Casey wrote for a major strategy session: "Survey research conducted in the primary states shows that Ronald Reagan won *not* because his ideological positions were congruent with the electorate, but rather in spite of a rather substantial ideological gap between himself and the average Republican." Wirthlin's experiment of trying to open up a gap between Reagan and Bush had ultimately failed, as it was not because of those issues that Reagan won. This ambivalence on the tax cut issue continued throughout the summer. On October 8, less than a month before the election, a campaign strategy document said "Strong Top-Of-Mind Reaction to Governor's Positions Are *Double Edged*," including on taxes, welfare, defense, and "Russians." Moreover, there was worry that if tax cuts became the central theme of the campaign, Carter could undercut the whole campaign with an October surprise tax cut of his own.[20] A mail report for late October shows that exactly one letter on taxes was sent to the Reagan campaign headquarters, out of a total of several hundred.[21]

Another reason for subordinating supply-side rhetoric emerged as the team prepared for the debates: the economic news was starting to look better, and some thought "that the 'economic issue' may not help the GOP as expected, and that some of Ronald Reagan's more controversial economic positions may come under fire," among them tax cuts.

> By most national poll yardsticks (Harris, NBC News/AP), public support for a tax cut has ebbed in recent months. Press analyses agree that Congressmen came back from their 4th of July recess convinced that the public is suspicious of tax-cutting nostrums. . . . All in all, Democrats are gearing up to attack the Kemp-Roth 30% tax cut as the "Reagan-Kemp-Roth" tax cut. . . . Jimmy Carter has already called it "sugar-coated poison," and Carter, [Edward Kennedy,] and other Democrats are gearing up to attack Reagan-Kemp-Roth as welfare for the wealthy, a tactic that worked against statewide income tax cut referenda in Oklahoma . . . and California . . . Kemp-Roth will also be attacked as wildly inflationary. . . . Kemp-Roth will not be a winner for the GOP in 1980 anymore than it was in the 1978 offyear elections.[22]

The team did not give up the focus of the economy, but they did worry that Carter was planning a negative campaign on Reagan with the argument that he was "naïve, inexperienced, deceptive, and dangerous." The Carter team—the Reagan team thought—planned to show Reagan as "anti-black, anti-labor, anti-elderly," and "captive of [the] Right Wing." Tax cuts played right into this theme. They allowed Carter to portray Reagan as willing to gamble with the deficit, adhering to an extremist ideology that abandoned the balanced budget, and driven by ideologues of the right. Especially given that Reagan's own vice presidential pick had criticized them, the case for tax cuts would be a difficult one to make.[23]

The problem was only reinforced when, in March, Michael Boskin, the economist whose work on the effect of taxation on savings supported the Kemp arguments and the later tax cut legislation, wrote to Ed Meese: "[T]here is little evidence with which to have confidence that the response would be so large, so rapidly as to dispel the fears of large deficit increases (I speak as someone whose own research is usually cited by Kemp et al)." It would thus be important, Boskin continued, that Reagan's program also reduce the rate of growth of spending. Writing in all caps to make his point, Boskin emphasized that "ALL THAT NEEDS TO BE DONE TO MAKE KEMP-ROTH–type TAX CUTS AN EMINENTLY REASONABLE PART OF AN OVERALL FISCAL POLICY IS TO COMBINE IT WITH

SOME MINIMAL MODERATION OF SPENDING GROWTH AND PHASE IT IN GRADUALLY." This proposal might have seemed reasonable to Boskin, but it was a blow to the Kemp-Wanniski politics of joy and would have required argumentation more deft than the kind of revival meeting rhetoric that brought Kemp's audiences to their feet.[24]

Reagan accepted Boskin's position over Kemp's, as he wrote to a Congressman: "I was under the impression that Jack had given up his single-minded approach on the tax bill and that it had been amended to include a reduction in spending. If that isn't so, at least I'm amending it that way because I think both are necessary. Much as people want lower taxes I think it is true that they are hard to sell on the idea that those lower taxes alone would generate additional funds and solve our deficit problems."[25]

And so tax cuts did not become a major issue in the general election. It is also clear, however, that in spite of talking less about the tax cut in order to avoid getting caught in a "numbers game," the team never actually backed away from the commitment to a policy of tax cuts. This commitment was made explicit and official in September 1980, when the team finally bowed to media pressure for details on the program and decided to have Reagan give a big economic speech in which the numbers for the tax cut program, they promised, would add up. Some called it Reagan's "mirrors" speech, after John Anderson's complaint about Reagan's "blue smoke and mirrors" economic proposals.[26]

Just before the speech, a big problem arose: the Congressional Budget Office's numbers had dropped precipitously, so that in fact the projections no longer added up. "There were eighty-six reporters traveling with us," Martin Anderson noted, "representing three major television networks, *Time, Newsweek,* the *Wall Street Journal,* the *New York Times,* the *Washington Post,* and dozens of other media outlets. We also had eight foreign reporters with us from Germany, Australia, Switzerland, Canada, and England. They had been anticipating this speech for weeks and we could expect some very close questioning on the details of Reagan's economic plan."[27] The Reagan Revolution could have died in its cradle if not for what happened next.

The Senate was controlled by Democrats, and the Senate Budget Committee came out with economic numbers that were much more optimistic than the nonpartisan CBO's numbers. They had "used the basic CBO computer model," Anderson told Reagan, "but they modified the assumptions used in that model. Assuming they are right, their projected results show a deficit that is $26 billion *less* for FY1981, and $21 billion *less* for FY1982."[28]

In a remarkable piece of political jujitsu, the Reagan campaign seized on these more optimistic numbers and used them in their own projections. Because these numbers showed that the economy under Carter was doing better than the CBO thought, they also showed that Reagan's plan would not create as high a deficit as the CBO feared. By modifying the Senate Budget Committee estimates only slightly, the Reagan team was able to show a budget coming into balance by 1983. The SBC numbers had the required air of authority. Martin Anderson writes: "I got out my Hewlett-Packard calculator and our current economic forecasts. About ten minutes later I knew we had it. We could go for the full tax cut, the full increase in defense spending, and still balance the budget by 1983, maybe even by 1982. . . . The political problem was gone."[29] A key reason the numbers added up was their assumption that high rates of inflation would continue, thus pulling more tax revenue into the government and thereby keeping the deficit down.[30]

It's not clear whether the SBC numbers were an attempt by the Democratic-controlled Senate to put a more optimistic gloss on Carter's economic performance. If so, the irony would be rich: the Reagan tax cut revolution would have been made possible by partisan Democratic numbers. Even better, by using the Democrats' numbers the Reagan team could not be accused of partisanship.

All of the key players in the administration defended their fiddling with numbers by arguing again and again that econometric modeling was an uncertain art. Donald Regan, in testimony to Congress, complained about the nature of forecasts, saying, "Rather than relying on specious forecasts, our approach will be to develop economic scenarios which embody the president's program for revitalizing the economy."[31] When questioned about the models, Murray Weidenbaum, an economic adviser to the campaign, said: "All models, whether they be the traditional Keynesian or the more recent 'supply-side' variety, are based on the assumption that the complex behavior which determines our economic actions can be summarized in a relatively few mathematical relationships." Elsewhere he wrote: "Economics is too important to be left to statisticians and mathematicians. It requires judgment—and that is the basic source of our forecast." Anderson said: "It cannot be emphasized too strongly that all these economic projections are uncertain and somewhat volatile." They were guided by their belief in the theoretical rationale behind their policies, some academic work on the effect of taxation on savings, and the use of budget numbers to assess whether a given legislation was *plausible*. Different assumptions gave different numbers, but none of the assumptions were completely impossible, and therefore, if the Senate Budget Committee numbers led to the program adding up, Anderson was only too happy to use them.[32]

And this turned out to be just enough to pass media scrutiny. Although the numbers really did not look likely, they were not impossible, and they had the requisite air of authority. That was all it took to get the issue off the front pages. The *New York Times* noted after the September "mirrors" speech, for example, that "the moderation of Mr. Reagan's new program has reduced the numbers debate to arcane disputes."[33] The *Washington Post* wrote:

> The new move by Reagan last week represented a clear shift—a victory for main-line Republicans, who had sought to convince Reagan to adopt a more traditionalist approach. . . . What Reagan did last week was to pare back his tax-cut program. . . . The result was to close off the opportunity for Carter and the Democrats to dismiss his program as outlandish, while retaining the basic tax-cut plan he has backed from the start . . . [although questions remain,] Reagan's rejuggling effort blunted any outside criticism that his economic plan didn't add up.[34]

Although other elements of the tax cut were scaled back, the cut in individual income tax rates was not: the plan was still three years of across-the-board rate cuts. Reagan did not spedify what programs he wanted to cut, and took some of the SBC's numbers and modified others, but to readers this must have seemed more like the kind of argument over numbers that partisans always engage in, rather than the wholesale fabrication that Reagan had been accused of.[35]

One reason Reagan never backed down on tax cuts, despite the fluctuating opinion polls on them, was that opinion polls also showed consistent, unwavering, and strong support for fighting inflation. Without the tax cut, Reagan had nothing to offer that would address that concern. Tax cuts were the Reagan team's attempt to tackle the most popular issue of the time. As a memo from pollster Wirthlin put it a few months before the election, "a

candidate is elected President because he correctly identifies the central issue
of his time and generates the public expectation that he is capable of effec-
tively dealing with that issue." Wirthlin well knew that inflation was the
runaway concern, and had been for years:

> Over half of the electorate now identifies inflation as *the most important prob-*
> *lem* the United States faces today . . . fully 56% of the voters say that Reagan,
> not Carter (14%) "offers the best hope to reduce inflation." Thus the pock-
> etbook issue cluster and, specifically, the inflation module strongly reinforce
> our strengths and Carter's weaknesses. We must, therefore, do all we can to
> keep the electorate's attention focused on this issue as the campaign builds
> and, thereby, keep Carter on this "hook" right through to November.[36]

He and his team would only have abandoned tax cuts if some other bold
new policy that could be sold as a solution to inflation could have been
found. As Richard Nixon, watching from the sidelines, put it shortly after
Reagan's inauguration in a letter to Kemp: "Not pretending to know anything about economics I am not *sure* your tax program will work. However
I *am* sure that what we have been doing *won't* work."[37] Tax cuts were something—anything—at a time when something was desperately called for. As
Sean Wilentz suggests, the public was "looking for any bold move that
promised to remedy the economy," and that is exactly what Reagan gave
them—a bold move that promised to remedy the economy.[38] In many ways,
the actual content of that promise was less important than the promise itself, especially if it was possible to avoid talking about the specifics of the
policy.

Moreover, Reagan, having hammered the issue of tax cuts for over a year,
could hardly back down now. Independent candidate John Anderson had
already been complaining of his opponents' "flip-flops."[39]

Another reason Reagan did not back down was that the polls did not
speak with one voice. Although many polls were suggesting that the tax
issue had peaked, it was possible to find contrary signals if one looked carefully. For example, in September 1980, Gallup found that 54 percent of respondents favored a 10 percent rate reduction and that 55 percent thought
tax cuts would lead to greater work effort.[40] Supporters of tax cuts argued
that the recent lack of enthusiasm for tax cuts stemmed only from the campaign's flagging promotional effort.[41] There was enough murkiness in the

polling tea leaves to make a radical change of course unwise. Unlike the gold standard, which never generated much polling enthusiasm, the idea of tax cuts could be claimed to have led in the last few years to a taxpayer revolt and a season of taxpayer outrage. In a way, just as Reagan was the frontrunner in the Republican Party, after Proposition 13 tax cuts were the frontrunner within the Reagan team. Just as some other politician would have had to mount a strong and credible attack to dismount Reagan, so some other issue would have had to be able to give the Republicans a somewhat plausible, bold new answer to the problem of inflation. George Bush came closest to knocking out Reagan, but no other policy came anywhere close to knocking out tax cuts.

Having gotten the press to stop asking questions about it, the campaign itself now stopped talking very much about tax cuts. Reagan began to talk not specifically about tax cuts, but in more general terms about his program to combat inflation. But this was a rhetorical, not a substantive, change. In March, a strategy memo had put the issue squarely: "Without question, the electorate must view Ronald Reagan in less extreme conservative terms in the Fall if we are to win. This can be done without altering any issue positions. By rounding out the total perception of Ronald Reagan as a more human, warm, approachable individual, and by stressing some issues and leaving others for the opponents to develop, we can 'moderate' the archconservative characterization of the Governor."[42] In May, two advisers tasked with policy development wrote: "We could not agree more that RR must abandon the idea that cutting tax rates will necessarily increase tax revenues. Though he may well be right, at least over the longer term, the public will not buy it. Moreover, it would be irresponsible to base national budgetary policy on such an uncertain phenomenon." All that was needed was a general sense that "the tax burden is already too great and growing; even Kemp-Roth will not fully offset projected tax increases. . . . Tax reduction, carefully employed, can and should be used as a club to force down spending. . . . We must emphasize that: spending restraint accompanies the tax reduction; Kemp-Roth only reduces the increase in taxes; and tax rate reductions are necessary to get the economy moving again." They also note that "it is expected that Carter will cut taxes this summer—perhaps in the neighborhood of $20 billion."[43]

A Wirthlin memo from before the debate with Carter made this observation:

If the Governor succeeds Tuesday in making Jimmy Carter's record the major issue of the debate and the campaign, we will succeed in the debate and win the general election. If, however, Carter makes Ronald Reagan the issue of the debate and the campaign, we will lose both. . . . The major debate task turns on enhancing Ronald Reagan's perceived trustworthiness. . . . This can be accomplished if the debate focuses on Carter's incompetence and weak record in office, and Reagan's compassion. Neither position can be reinforced when the Governor defends past positions. . . . Carter's attack strategy will undoubtedly try to represent Reagan's policies as "naive, unrealistic, anachronistic, and Alice-in-Wonderlandish." In response to this attack, the Governor has an excellent opportunity to show constraint, thoughtfulness and strength. And, when the attack becomes overblown, he should use disarming humor which will build rapport and trust with the electorate.[44]

In fact, the Reagan campaign had heard that the Carter team's analysis of the looming election was very similar to their own. Ed Meese told Richard Wirthlin what he had heard about the Carter strategy: "Their plan is to try to make RR an issue in the campaign. They have stated 'that if Jimmy Carter is the issue, we lose, but if RR becomes the issue, we will win.'"[45]

By subordinating supply-side rhetoric during the general campaign, the Reagan team was able to make Jimmy Carter the issue. Wanniski did not get the summertime debate on economic policy he wanted.[46] The team walked a careful line of promising they had a plan without getting caught up in the specifics of the plan.

The team's calculation that inflation and economic factors were their main political strengths was rewarded. In July, August, and September 1980, "improve economy" and "reduce inflation" were the top positive expectations the electorate had if Reagan were to be elected, with "reduce taxes" a bit further down the list ("possibility of war" was the top negative expectation).[47] And the Reagan camp did not have to worry about Carter stealing the tax cut issue. Over in D.C., Carter's team was concluding that "by jumping on [the tax cut issue] now, Carter is going to be perceived as flip-flopping on yet another issue. It will be a case of 'me-tooism.' . . . He gets no political mileage by coming out for a tax cut to be enacted this year. . . . Those who think that the taxpayers only want tax cuts misjudge the intelligence of the American voter."[48]

Reagan won the election, not necessarily on the issue of tax cuts, but more because of a general sense among the public that Carter had failed—in foreign policy in his handling of the Iranian hostage crisis, but more importantly, in his efforts to revive the economy. Opinion polls showed respondents overwhelmingly giving economic issues as the main reasons for their votes.[49] Reagan and his campaign had successfully navigated the parameters by promising that they had a plan to combat inflation but avoiding getting into too many details about that plan. Thus, voters may not have explicitly voted for tax cuts, but they put into the White House a politician who over the previous two years had become committed to cutting taxes.

CHAPTER 4

Beasts and Dogs

TWO ARGUMENTS THAT are often made for the rise of the tax cut have not yet shown up in our story: that the tax cut movement was driven by "ideas," and that it was driven by racial animus.

Was the Tax Cut Movement Driven by Ideas?

Looking from inside the process that led to the Reagan tax cut, Martin Anderson said, "Ideas come out of the intellectual world and affect political forces and . . . those political forces give rise to candidates."[1] This echoes an argument put forth by some scholars that the right-wing turn in economic policy of recent decades was the result of new intellectual developments at midcentury. If you're inside the winning campaign, it's easy to think that the "ideas" that motivated you are what led to your victory. But ideas also affected the political forces that lost. If you are inside those losing campaigns, the idea that influenced you does not seem particularly powerful at all. For example, Jimmy Carter was in his own way a visionary for the environment, installing solar panels on top of the White House and attempting to rally the nation to the cause of conservation. But those ideas went nowhere. Reagan had the solar panels removed, and instead of conservation, the nation settled on the strategy of using military power to preserve an environmentally expensive way of life.[2] An absence of ideas is not what makes the difference. All campaigns are inspired by ideas, but the context rewarded only some campaigns, inspired by only some of the ideas, over others.

Two arguments highlighting "ideas" have been particularly influential in explanations of the Reagan tax cut. The first is the "Laffer curve" argument—the suggestion that the idea of the Laffer curve kicked off the whole thing. But we saw that the idea that tax cuts raise revenue has been around for a long time—all the way back to Ibn Khaldun in the fourteenth century, by some accounts. There has to be some other reason why the idea was revived at this particular moment. Moreover, we will see that the Reagan administration did not actually make Laffer curve assumptions about tax cuts leading to higher revenue in its budget documents. Those documents drew on more measured arguments about the effects of tax cuts on savings.

The second ideological explanation for the tax cut is the "starve the beast" argument. This explanation—the exact opposite of the Laffer curve explanation—is that the Reagan administration sought to create a deficit in order to force cutbacks in government spending. Where the Laffer curve explanation argues that the administration thought tax cuts would lead to greater revenue, which would be good for the government, this explanation argues that the administration thought tax cuts would lead to less revenue, and this would be good for the country because it would force government to lower spending.[3] The argument seems to have been propounded as early as 1983, when Daniel Patrick Moynihan suggested that by cutting taxes and not cutting spending the administration knew full well that it would generate a deficit.[4] By 1988, observers were noting: "The greatest achievement of President Reagan's Administration may prove to be the roughly $155 billion budget deficit he is leaving to his successor, which is nearly twice the deficit he inherited from President Carter."[5] As one conservative commentator explained, "It has certainly put a lid on the welfare state. . . . The Democrats have sort of trapped themselves because they've said this is all terrible and horrible and that closing the deficit should be the first priority."[6]

There is no doubt that the administration wanted spending cuts, thought tax cuts would be a way to bring about spending cuts, and made this clear throughout the episode. In his very first televised speech as president, Reagan said: "Over the past decades we've talked of curtailing government spending so that we can then lower the tax burden. Sometimes we've even taken a run at doing that. But there were always those who told us that taxes couldn't be cut until spending was reduced. Well, you know, we can lecture our children about extravagance until we run out of voice and breath. Or we can cure their extravagance by simply reducing their allowance."[7] As one key figure put it, "Tax reduction will force spending reduction just as spending reduction will force tax reduction."[8]

This much is uncontroversial: the administration thought that tax cuts would put immediate pressure on government to cut spending. This narrow version of the "starve the beast" argument is correct. However, a broader version of the argument goes further in contending that the administration actually *wanted a deficit* and strategically engineered a deficit in order to put pressure on government to cut spending later. In the late 1980s and early 1990s, many Republicans did indeed adopt a variant of this position.[9] But during the 1981 episode, this more extreme version of the "starve the beast" argument is implausible. First, because polls suggested that deficits were unpopular, politicians feared them. An internal Reagan administration strategy document said that "it is thought likely to be somewhat tougher to put together the necessary tax cut coalition [in Congress] than it was the budget coalition. . . . As you know from your telephone conversations, the question of prospective deficits is one of the most important issues for many key Congressmen."[10]

Second, both internal and external documents show widespread agreement in the Reagan administration that deficits were a factor in inflation and higher interest rates. Although the supply-siders did predict that foreign investors would step in to finance American investment—including Wanniski in that very first article introducing Mundell's arguments—this was not a widespread belief at the time.[11] For example, the Treasury document presenting the tax plan noted matter-of-factly that the deficit was "dissaving which absorbs private sector savings which would otherwise be used for investment," and it forecast a lower deficit raising the savings rate and increasing investment—indeed, the plan depended on the deficit falling.[12] In comments to House Republicans, David Stockman noted that the financial markets "fear continued huge deficits" because congressional inability to cut spending "will mean large deficits and high interest rates—and the high interest rates, in a vicious circle, will make the deficits worse still because of the higher cost of paying the interest on the national debt."[13] A few months before the passage of the plan, Murray Weidenbaum noted, "*The financial markets are also concerned that our program will be inflationary. . . .* They worry about large deficits in '81 and '82, especially reports of overruns from our targets. . . . They worry about 10-10-10 [the Kemp-Roth individual income tax cut plan]."[14]

Another reason it seems unlikely that the administration strategically engineered a deficit is that, as late as August 1980, projections using the Congressional Budget Office's numbers were actually showing that the deficit would come under control under Reagan's plan: "The deficit as a percentage of total federal spending, which will be well over 10 percent under Carter in FY1980, drops steadily . . . from 8.3 percent in FY1981, to 7.1 percent in FY1982, 4.0 percent in FY1983, 2.9 percent in FY1984 and disappears in FY1985."[15] That the CBO tried to be nonpartisan and was not known for supporting Reagan in general made these numbers even more convincing. The economic condition worsened over the next few months, but the more optimistic projections released by the Senate Budget Committee showed Reagan's plan bringing the deficit under control in a few years.[16] This switch to a more optimistic forecast suggests legerdemain, but in investigating the origins of the tax cut it is important to note that this fiddling with projections came long *after* the decision to focus on tax cuts. It is best interpreted, not as a deliberate attempt to create a deficit, but as an attempt to save face at the last minute when confronted with economic numbers that all actors believed were imprecise. Finally, the main reason to doubt the idea that the administration sought to engineer a deficit lies in its actions when the size of the deficit began to become clear—as we will discuss in later chapters, they raised taxes in order to try to cover it.[17] During the ERTA episode, the main actors seem to have assumed that the widespread fear of deficits would act as a constraint forcing immediate reductions in spending; they did not foresee, or want, a deficit, and when a deficit appeared, they acted quickly to try to erase it.

These two ideological explanations for the tax cuts—the Laffer curve explanation and the explanation that the administration wanted to create a deficit—do not hold up to scrutiny. Ideas had little to do with what was happening, except in the sense that if an intellectual peddler's prescriptions happened to coincide with what the party wanted to do, the politicians were more than happy to use them. Free market ideas did abound at around the time that free market policies began to be implemented. But that does not mean that one caused the other. It is more accurate to understand the ideas and policies as both emerging from the dissatisfaction with the economy that began in the 1970s. Of course, in one sense, the "ideas" explanation is trivially true—any policy will always be initiated by someone with some thoughts about the best way forward. But the real question is, do those thoughts arise from the context and the incentives, or are they in some sense autonomous from the context and the incentives? The story of tax cuts seems to be one of many people grappling with the material conditions, not a story of independent ideas as a causal force.

Nevertheless, both ideological explanations of the Reagan tax cut continue to resonate because the participants give confused accounts of their own motivations. In his autobiography Reagan himself gives *both* the Laffer curve argument—that cutting taxes will lead to more revenue for government—*and* the "starve the beast" argument—that cutting taxes will curb the growth of government—in successive sentences:

> I have always thought of government as a kind of organism with an insatiable appetite for money, whose natural state is to grow forever unless you do something to starve it. By cutting taxes, I wanted not only to stimulate the economy but to curb the growth of government and reduce its intrusion into the economic life of the country.
>
> By the way, that philosopher, Khaldoon, and I weren't alone in believing lower tax rates result in higher revenues for government.[18]

In fact, the documentary record lends credence to this contradictory picture: Reagan and his administration wanted tax cuts because they would lead to less revenue (thus forcing government spending down) and because they would lead to more revenue (thus paying for themselves). Psychologists would find nothing unusual here—if anything, holding contradictory beliefs may be the norm. But this does cast doubt on the idea that their potential effects on revenue were the *reason* for the tax cuts, as the administration could not actually simultaneously have preferred lower revenues to higher revenues as well as higher revenues to lower revenues. It does not seem correct to call this state of affairs a "preference" at all. Indeed, the very same people seemed able to argue simultaneously that the tax cuts were not really that big and were just preventing further growth in tax collections, that the tax cuts were in fact so big that they would create a great economic stimulus and no revenue loss, and that the tax cuts would produce revenue loss and thereby constrain spending.[19] The contradictions suggest that Reagan and the administration did not necessarily want either higher or lower revenues—what they wanted was tax cuts.

Was the Tax Cut Movement Driven by Racism?

In 1980, Ronald Reagan gave a campaign speech at the Neshoba County Fair. There was strong disagreement within the campaign as to whether he should do it, given the history of the area: in 1964, three civil rights activists working to register voters had been murdered nearby, giving the town and the fair a chilling claim to fame. Even Nancy Reagan asked him not to do it. But Reagan not only went through with the speech, he also used this line, in a speech that was otherwise mostly about the failings of Jimmy Carter: "I believe that there are programs like that, programs like education and others, that should be turned back to the states and the local communities with the tax sources to fund them, and let the people [applause drowns out end of statement]. I believe in state's [sic] rights; I believe in people doing as much as they can for themselves at the community level and at the private level."[20]

The speech has gone down in Reagan legend as a "dog whistle," an attempt to appeal to white voters' racism that is ambiguous enough to be deniable.[21] The phrase "states' rights," used in the South, at the site of an infamous murder of civil rights workers, invokes an ugly history of Southern resistance to civil rights and integration. But it is not possible to prove Reagan's intent in either making the speech or using the phrase. As Reagan correctly pointed out, the phrase "states' rights" means something different to Californians than it does to Southerners.[22] For some analysts, that deniability is precisely the power of the appeal.

A popular explanation of Reagan and the rise of free market conservatism in America is that the nation's racial fragmentation makes it difficult to sustain the solidarity necessary for the development of a welfare state and may have undermined the willingness of Americans to pay taxes. Because racial and class divisions overlap, white Americans may not want to pay taxes that they believe will benefit black Americans. According to this interpretation, tax cuts and other free market policies represent a culmination of the Republicans' "Southern Strategy," which was inaugurated in the 1960s to appeal to white voters alienated by the Democrats' support of civil rights for

African Americans.[23] Although the South had voted Democratic for nearly a century, in the 1960s many Republican analysts thought that the depth of racial animosity and opposition to civil rights could break the Democrats' lock on the region. In 1961, Republican Barry Goldwater had said: "We're not going to get the Negro vote as a bloc . . . so we ought to go hunting where the ducks are. . . . Why is the South turning? . . . It is because liberalism has stifled the southern conservative voice in the Democratic party."[24] Lyndon Johnson is purported to have said, upon signing the Civil Rights Act of 1964, "I think we just delivered the South to the Republican party for a long time to come."[25]

Kevin Phillips, a child of the Bronx who had grown up observing racial antagonisms and was skeptical of optimistic talk of racial harmony, made the case most systematically in *The Emerging Republican Majority*, published in 1969.[26] Phillips argued that not only the South but also the Midwest and California had already started to move toward the Republicans, primarily for racial reasons. These areas of the country could be welded together into a stable coalition that would marginalize New England. Phillips insisted that his aim was not to provide "a strategy or a blueprint,"[27] but Richard Nixon did seem to turn these principles into a blueprint for victory.[28] It is worth noting that Republicans were not the only ones who made appeals to race. For example, although Phillips's book is often cited, another book, Richard Scammon and Ben Wattenberg's *The Real Majority*, gave similar advice to Democrats.[29] Many Democrats engaged in race-baiting, including Jimmy Carter in his campaign for governor of Georgia in 1966.[30] By Reagan's time, explicit race-baiting could get a politician in trouble, and therefore—according to the dog-whistle hypothesis—politicians began to send coded signals to white voters, appeals whose racial nature was subtle and deniable. In line with this thinking, many scholars have argued that tax cuts were part of the racial backlash that brought Republicans into power.[31]

Richard Wirthlin gives an inside glimpse of the decision-making around the Neshoba speech. Wirthlin had planned for the campaign's opening speech to be in inner-city New York, to dramatize Reagan's commitment to the plight of urban African Americans. But Reagan committed to speaking at Neshoba a few days before the New York event. Wirthlin was well aware of how this would look and thought it could even doom the campaign. He rushed to Reagan's California mansion to try to argue him out of it:

"You simply *cannot* give this speech," I implored.

"Dick, one thing I learned as an actor was that once the billing is set you don't pull out. Now, don't tell me what I can and can't do. *I'm* the one running for president. I'm giving this speech, and I'm giving it at the Neshoba County Fair!" he exclaimed.

"Governor, as your friend, I can tell you that despite your best intentions, and despite what you may think about the importance of keeping your word to your supporters in Neshoba, the media is going to make you out to be an insensitive raci—"

He'd heard enough.

"I'M GIVING THIS SPEECH!" he barked.

At this, he swung back his arm, stared me in the eyes, and hurled all thirty-plus pages of his speech into the air, leaving me sitting on his bed in a blizzard of cascading papers.[32]

Wirthlin gives the explanation that "Ronald Reagan believed that his personal commitment to people and his message were worth fighting for . . . He was willing to endure the political costs our opponents' spin might exact in order to make good on his word."[33] Whatever happened to "If you pay someone to manage a campaign . . . then you've got to give them the authority to do it as they see fit"?[34] Reagan was clearly able to put aside personal commitments for his political interests when he wanted or needed to. In this case, he sided against his advisers and with local Republicans who thought showing up at the fair would help him win Southern states.[35]

Wirthlin gives the even less likely suggestion that Reagan wanted to speak at Neshoba precisely because it was a site sacred to the civil rights movement, because Reagan had grown up committed to the ideals of anti-discrimination.[36] If this were true, the speech would have said something about civil rights or evoked the events of 1964 or at least Martin Luther King, Jr.'s visit to Neshoba. Of course it did nothing of the kind.[37]

It is hard to prove or disprove the dog whistle hypothesis, because it is a hypothesis about things unspoken. There is no reason to think that a strategy of making racial appeals would have been committed to paper or survived archival vetting. But it is possible to test theories of the importance of race using polling data available from the American National Election Study (ANES).[38] In 1980, the ANES conducted eight waves of surveys with a sample of Americans designed to be representative. Two of the eight surveys, conducted from September through November and carried out on 2,383 people, included topical questions on Reagan's proposed tax cut. These questions form the basis for the analysis in this chapter.

When asked their general opinion of whether they paid too much in taxes, 36 percent of respondents replied that they paid "much more" in federal income taxes than they should, and another 32.6 percent said that they paid "somewhat more." When asked if federal income taxes should be cut, only 17.8 percent responded that they should not be cut, the remainder supporting tax cuts of 10 percent (21 percent), 20 percent (20.6 percent), 30 percent (28.6 percent), and over 30 percent (12 percent). Most respondents thought that Jimmy Carter did not want to cut taxes, or that he wanted to cut them by less than 10 percent. Impressively, over half the sample knew that Reagan wanted to cut taxes by 30 percent, reflecting the success of the Reagan team's public relations effort throughout the primaries and the general election campaign.

The survey then asked: "There has been a great deal of talk about the probable effects of a 30% reduction of federal income taxes over the next three years. Have you read or heard anything about this?" Of the sample, 53.7 percent (746 respondents) had, and they were the ones who were asked the more detailed questions about the tax cut. Of this subsample, 39.6 percent thought the tax cut would make inflation worse, while 60.4 percent thought it would not, and 53.7 percent thought it would increase employment. More than two-thirds of the respondents (64.2 percent) thought the benefits would go to business and not to ordinary taxpayers, 83.2 percent thought spending would be cut, and 64.5 percent thought the tax cut would increase the deficit. And when asked a version of the Laffer curve question—whether they agreed with the statement "The government would receive about the same amount of tax money as now because the economy would be stronger"—58.4 percent agreed this would happen.

It should not surprise us by now to note that these responses reveal some contradictions: some respondents seemed to believe both that the tax cut would not decrease revenue (because the economy would be stronger) and that the tax cut would decrease revenue (hence requiring spending cuts or increased deficits). This was in fact the position of the key actors, as we have seen, and it was faithfully represented among the public.

Overall, a strong majority were in favor of some cut in taxes, and a plurality were in favor of Reagan's 30 percent cut. These respondents thought that a tax cut would increase employment without worsening inflation; it might also require some spending cuts or increases in the deficit, but could make the economy stronger, even if they saw it as benefiting business rather than ordinary taxpayers.

The data also allow us to examine more carefully the factors that led respondents to say that their taxes were too high, to favor tax cuts, and to believe that a tax cut would pay for itself. We can thus examine the hypothesis that tax cuts were a "dog whistle." Since the "tax cut as dog whistle" hypothesis is about why tax cuts have been so popular with white voters, I first analyzed white respondents only. Table 4.1 shows the results of racial attitudes on three different variables: the respondent's sense that he or she paid too much tax (models 1 to 3), whether the respondent favored a tax cut (models 4 to 6), and whether the respondent believed that tax cuts could pay for themselves (models 7 to 9).

Models 1, 4, and 7 examine the effect of demographic factors (gender, age, subjective social class, whether the respondent's personal finances were worse compared to a year earlier, and whether the respondent thought the economy in general was worse than a year earlier) and political ideology (party identification as a seven-point scale from "strong Democrat" to "strong Republican" and seven-point scales measuring liberal/conservative ideology, preference for government services, preference for defense spending, and opinion on whether government should "see to it that every person has a job and a good standard of living") as control variables.

The remaining models measure the effects of racism in two different ways. Because there will be disagreements about how to measure racism, I have employed both a minimal and a maximal measure. The minimal measure, used in models 2, 5, and 8, is the "feeling thermometer," a set of questions the ANES asked to gauge how the respondent felt toward political candidates as well as toward certain named groups, from "big business" to "farmers," "Hispanics," "young people," and "evangelical groups active in politics, such as the Moral Majority." The instructions for the feeling thermometer were: "You may use any number from 0 to 100 for rating. Ratings between 50 degrees and 100 degrees mean that you feel favorable and warm toward the person. Ratings between 0 degrees and 50 degrees mean that you don't feel too favorable toward the person. If you don't feel particularly warm or cold toward the person, you would rate the person at the 50 degree

Table 4.1 Racism and White Respondents' Attitudes toward Tax Cuts, 1980

	(1) Whether Respondent Pays Too Much Tax	(2) Whether Respondent Pays Too Much Tax	(3) Whether Respondent Pays Too Much Tax	(4) Whether Respondent Favors Tax Cut
Gender	0.0123	0.00188	0.0130	0.190
	(0.0774)	(0.0777)	(0.0766)	(0.149)
Age	0.00657*	0.00600*	0.00751**	−0.00381
	(0.00275)	(0.00278)	(0.00274)	(0.00534)
Education	0.0220	0.0211	0.0141	−0.00180
	(0.0206)	(0.0206)	(0.0206)	(0.0392)
Household income	−0.000112	−0.000124	0.0000782	0.00382
	(0.00172)	(0.00172)	(0.00170)	(0.00337)
Subjective social class	0.00126	0.00391	−0.00116	−0.0494
	(0.0263)	(0.0263)	(0.0260)	(0.0499)
Personal finances worse	−0.0442*	−0.0405+	−0.0364	0.0764+
compared to a year ago	(0.0222)	(0.0223)	(0.0221)	(0.0416)
Economy worse compared	−0.0937+	−0.0926+	−0.0926+	0.152+
to a year ago	(0.0492)	(0.0491)	(0.0487)	(0.0900)
Party identification	−0.0199	−0.0197	−0.0179	−0.0165
	(0.0232)	(0.0231)	(0.0229)	(0.0446)
Ideology	−0.0417	−0.0434	−0.0278	0.0827
	(0.0335)	(0.0335)	(0.0335)	(0.0655)
Support for spending on	0.0696**	0.0678**	0.0587*	−0.172***
government services	(0.0253)	(0.0253)	(0.0253)	(0.0476)
Support for spending on	−0.0384	−0.0375	−0.0236	−0.0460
defense	(0.0298)	(0.0298)	(0.0300)	(0.0577)
Should government provide	−0.00562	0.000452	0.0157	0.0594
job	(0.0284)	(0.0288)	(0.0291)	(0.0565)
Feeling thermomenter		0.00300		
toward blacks		(0.00233)		
Racial tolerance			0.161**	
			(0.0563)	
_cons	2.201***	2.012***	2.020***	2.495***
	(0.381)	(0.408)	(0.383)	(0.719)
N	389	389	389	330
R^2	0.107	0.111	0.126	0.129

Source: 1980 American National Election Studies (ANES).

Notes: Standard errors are in parentheses. Models 1 to 3—factors influencing respondent's sense of how much tax he/she pays: 1 = "much more," 2 = "somewhat more," 3 = "about right," and 4 = "less than should" (respondents who do not pay tax excluded); OLS estimates (results using ordered logistic regression are similar and are available in the full data and calculations). Models 4 to 6—factors influencing whether respondent favors a tax cut: 1 = "should not be cut," 2 = "should be cut by about 10 percent," 3 = "should be

(5) Whether Respondent Favors Tax Cut	(6) Whether Respondent Favors Tax Cut	(7) Whether Respondent Believes Tax Cuts Will Pay for Themselves	(8) Whether Respondent Believes Tax Cuts Will Pay for Themselves	(9) Whether Respondent Believes Tax Cuts Will Pay for Themselves
0.203	0.187	0.0637	0.0176	0.0589
(0.149)	(0.147)	(0.333)	(0.335)	(0.333)
−0.00311	−0.00530	0.0145	0.0129	0.0130
(0.00540)	(0.00532)	(0.0112)	(0.0113)	(0.0115)
−0.00119	0.00905	−0.214*	−0.218*	−0.212*
(0.0393)	(0.0391)	(0.0903)	(0.0907)	(0.0905)
0.00380	0.00342	0.00794	0.00717	0.00842
(0.00337)	(0.00334)	(0.00793)	(0.00805)	(0.00801)
−0.0529	−0.0417	−0.0201	−0.0118	−0.0161
(0.0501)	(0.0496)	(0.111)	(0.111)	(0.111)
0.0718+	0.0585	−0.0829	−0.0735	−0.0909
(0.0420)	(0.0418)	(0.0936)	(0.0948)	(0.0947)
0.154+	0.158+	0.507*	0.483*	0.512*
(0.0901)	(0.0892)	(0.207)	(0.208)	(0.207)
−0.0181	−0.0194	0.0111	0.0175	0.0106
(0.0446)	(0.0442)	(0.0929)	(0.0936)	(0.0929)
0.0853	0.0556	0.222	0.197	0.209
(0.0656)	(0.0658)	(0.148)	(0.150)	(0.150)
−0.170***	−0.151**	0.00162	−0.0142	0.00929
(0.0477)	(0.0478)	(0.106)	(0.107)	(0.107)
−0.0489	−0.0692	−0.0544	−0.0192	−0.0723
(0.0578)	(0.0579)	(0.128)	(0.131)	(0.133)
0.0516	0.0219	0.0217	0.0584	0.00262
(0.0573)	(0.0578)	(0.128)	(0.131)	(0.132)
−0.00356			0.0148	
(0.00430)			(0.0107)	
	−0.280**			−0.140
	(0.108)			(0.251)
2.728***	2.795***	−1.834	−2.766	−1.607
(0.772)	(0.722)	(1.572)	(1.720)	(1.626)
330	330	197	197	197
0.131	0.147	0.081	0.089	0.083

cut by about 20 percent," 4 = "should be cut by about 30 percent," 5 = "should be cut by more than 30 percent"; OLS estimates (results using ordered logistic regression are similar and are available in the full data and calculations). Models 7 to 9—factors influencing belief that tax cuts can pay for themselves, 1 = believes, 0 = does not believe (logistic regression)'; pseudo R^2 for models 7 to 9.

$^+p < 0.1$; $^*p < 0.05$; $^{**}p < 0.01$; $^{***}p < 0.001$

mark." I used the feeling thermometer toward "blacks." It is not clear exactly what the feeling thermometer is measuring, as respondents may have felt pressured to express less racism than they actually felt. It may simply have measured respondents' awareness of a taboo against expressing racism, but this awareness itself may be a meaningful difference.

The maximal measure of racism, used in models 3, 6, and 9, draws on scholarship that suggests how to measure racism in more subtle forms. Recently, political scientists have used the concept of "racial resentment" to try to show the effect of less explicit racism on politics. The argument is that prejudice today is expressed not in ideas of genetic inferiority or the legitimacy of white supremacy, but rather in terms of unfair advantages given to African Americans. Scholars who discuss this concept draw on the following ANES questions, which were introduced into the survey for this very purpose:

· "Irish, Italians, Jewish, and many other minorities overcame prejudice and worked their way up. Blacks should do the same without any special favors."
· "Over the past few years blacks have gotten less than they deserve."
· "It's really a matter of some people not trying hard enough; if blacks would only try harder they could be just as well off as whites."
· "Generations of slavery and discrimination have created conditions that make it difficult for blacks to work their way out of the lower class."
· "Government officials usually pay less attention to a request or complaint from a black person than from a white person."
· "Most blacks who receive money from welfare programs could get along without it if they tried."[39]

These items were not introduced into the ANES until 1986, so an exact replication of the effects of racial resentment for 1980 is not possible. But it is possible to measure something akin to racial resentment by relying on a battery of similar questions that were included in the survey:

· "Some say that the civil rights people have been trying to push too fast. Others feel they haven't pushed fast enough. How about you: Do you think that civil rights leaders are trying to push too fast, are going too slowly, or are they moving at about the right speed?" (1 = "too fast," 3 = "about right," 5 = "too slowly")

- "There is much discussion about the best way to deal with racial problems. Some people think achieving racial integration of schools is so important that it justifies busing children to schools out of their own neighborhoods. Others think letting children go to their neighborhood schools is so important that they oppose busing. Where would you place yourself on this scale or haven't you thought much about this?" (1 = "bus to achieve integration," 7 = "keep children in neighborhood schools")

- "Some people feel that the government in Washington should make every effort to improve the social and economic position of blacks and other minority groups, even if it means giving them preferential treatment. Suppose these people are at one end of the scale at point number 1. Others feel that the government should not make any special effort to help minorities because they should help themselves. Suppose these people are at the other end at point 7. And, of course, some other people have opinions somewhere in between at points 2, 3, 4, 5, or 6. Where would you place yourself on this scale or haven't you thought much about this?"[40]

In addition, in the maximal measure I also included the respondent's self-placement on the feeling thermometer toward blacks, as well as the feeling thermometer toward civil rights leaders. I created a factor variable, racial tolerance (*ractol*), out of these five measures and used it in models 3, 6, and 9.

Table 4.1 shows the results. The full data and calculations for all quantitative analyses in this book are available through the University of Michigan's Inter-university Consortium for Political and Social Research (ICPSR) data repository, as well as through my website.[41]

In models 1 to 3, the dependent variable is the respondent's sense that he or she paid too much tax. Respondents who did not pay tax are excluded. I first estimated the model using ordered logistic regression because the response variable may not be an interval variable (the possible responses are "1 = much more," "2 = somewhat more," "3 = about right," and "4 = less than should").[42] However, the results using ordered logistic regression are substantially similar to results using ordinary least squares (OLS), so in this chapter I show the OLS results for ease of interpretation. The ordered logistic regression results are available in the full data and calculations.

In models 4 to 6, the dependent variable is whether the respondent favored a tax cut, and again the results shown are OLS, with results using ordered logistic regression available in the full data and calculations. The possible responses are "1 = should not be cut," "2 = should be cut by about 10 percent," "3 = should be cut by about 20 percent," "4 = should be cut by about 30 percent," "5 = should be cut by more than 30 percent."

In models 7 to 9, the dependent variable is a dichotomous variable of belief that tax cuts can pay for themselves. The variable has been recoded so that 1 indicates belief in the argument and 0 indicates disbelief.

The strongest of the control variables is the respondent's sense that the country's economic situation was worse compared to the year before. Some association with age, education, and other variables is also seen. Variance inflation factor (VIF) analysis shows that there is a high VIF on several of the control variables, so there may be more of an association with these variables than can be seen here. However, the main variables of interest for us, the two race variables, do not show a high VIF, suggesting more confidence in those results.

The two race variables do show an association with the dependent variables. In models 2 and 3, both the minimal and the maximal measures of racism show an association with the respondent's sense that he or she paid too much tax: those respondents who felt "warmer" toward blacks were less likely to say that they paid more in tax than they should, and those who showed greater racial tolerance as measured by the five variables were less likely to say that they paid more in tax than they should. In models 4 and 5, there is no significant association with the feeling thermometer measure, but the racial tolerance measure does show an association: those showing greater racial tolerance were less likely to say that taxes should be cut. There is no statistically significant association between the race measures and belief in the Laffer curve, although the minimal measure is near significance.

We can also use the NES data to assess the role of tax cuts in getting Ronald Reagan elected. As table 4.2 shows, tax cuts may have been one factor in leading some voters to choose Reagan over Carter. Overall, the workhorse variables of political science—party identification, political ideology, and perceptions of the economy—are strongly associated with voting for Reagan over Carter, but the tax cut issue also played some part.

Thus, it is not unreasonable to think that race was playing some role in the politics of the tax cut: Reagan's insistence on giving the Neshoba speech, the fact that those who give answers that may be considered to be racist in some way are more supportive of the tax cut, and the fact that tax cuts played a role in increasing votes for Reagan all support an interpretation of the tax cut as a dog whistle that helped Reagan's electoral chances.

However, this argument, while not completely implausible, is not very strong. First of all, the effect of racial attitudes on support for the tax cut, and the effect of support for the tax cut on votes for Reagan, are both very small. In table 4.1 the models that include the race measures provide only a marginally better fit than the models that do not include race. Likewise, in table 4.2 the models that include tax cut attitudes provide only a marginally better fit than the models that do not. Reagan's victory over Carter was so large (51 percent to 41 percent in the popular vote) that it swamps the minor effect of the dog whistle.

Second, as table 4.3 shows, among respondents to the survey who had an opinion on the tax cuts, there was no statistically significant difference in support for tax cuts by race, with blacks actually slightly more likely to support them than whites. (Although only 41.38 percent of African American respondents had an opinion on the tax cut, compared to 65.63 percent of whites.) Presumably a dog whistle would not work to rally African American voters. But African American voters were drawn to the tax cut as much as white voters. Indeed, the supplemental materials show that African American respondents were as likely to support the tax cut as *racist* white voters, that is, white voters with racial tolerance scores below the mean and scores below the mean on the feeling thermometer toward blacks.

Third, the entire attempt to define racism as "racial resentment" has been criticized for conflating individualist ideology with racism.[43] Someone who is thoroughly individualist, but not racist at all, would agree with the phrase "blacks can succeed if they work hard" because such a respondent thinks anyone can succeed if they work hard. If what we are trying to show is that individualism is racism in disguise, we cannot begin by assuming that individualism is racism in disguise.

Fourth, the Neshoba speech does not actually mention individual income tax cuts. Reagan mentions taxes only twice, both times in passing: once in the context of returning "programs like education and others . . . with the tax sources to fund them" back to the states, and again in praise of

Table 4.2 Tax Cuts and the Presidential Vote of 1980

	(1) Vote	(2) Vote	(3) Vote	(4) Vote
Gender	−0.236	−0.238	−0.285	−0.287
	(0.411)	(0.414)	(0.417)	(0.421)
Race	0.414	0.741	0.864	0.845
	(1.247)	(1.263)	(1.278)	(1.274)
Age	0.00265	−0.00241	0.00104	0.00727
	(0.0135)	(0.0141)	(0.0140)	(0.0139)
Education	−0.0433	−0.0553	−0.0373	−0.0522
	(0.106)	(0.108)	(0.110)	(0.110)
Household income	−0.00526	−0.00664	−0.00594	−0.00562
	(0.00896)	(0.00903)	(0.00916)	(0.00911)
Subjective social class	−0.165	−0.160	−0.195	−0.189
	(0.135)	(0.136)	(0.139)	(0.138)
Personal finances worse compared to a year ago	−0.237*	−0.205+	−0.216+	−0.197
	(0.117)	(0.120)	(0.120)	(0.120)
Economy worse compared to a year ago	−0.689**	−0.633*	−0.668**	−0.641**
	(0.242)	(0.247)	(0.245)	(0.244)
Party identification	−0.589***	−0.613***	−0.596***	−0.618***
	(0.104)	(0.108)	(0.107)	(0.109)
Ideology	−0.412*	−0.426*	−0.435*	−0.413*
	(0.171)	(0.176)	(0.178)	(0.176)
Support for spending on government services	0.194	0.120	0.153	0.165
	(0.123)	(0.130)	(0.127)	(0.127)
Support for spending on defense	−0.104	−0.0807	−0.162	−0.114
	(0.165)	(0.168)	(0.172)	(0.169)
Should government provide job	−0.0248	0.0213	0.0387	0.0168
	(0.137)	(0.142)	(0.144)	(0.142)
Whether respondent pays too much tax		0.569*		
		(0.264)		
Whether respondent favors tax cut			−0.457**	
			(0.164)	
Whether respondent believes tax cuts will pay for themselves				−1.076**
				(0.406)
_cons	7.043***	5.985**	8.550***	7.272***
	(2.024)	(2.081)	(2.172)	(2.052)
N	271	271	271	271
Pseudo R^2	0.406	0.421	0.432	0.429

Source: 1980 ANES.

Notes: Standard errors are in parentheses. Models 1 to 4: all voters; models 5 to 8: white voters only. Vote = binary vote choice between Reagan and Carter (respondents voting for other candidates excluded); whether respondent pays too much tax, 1 = "much more," 2 = "somewhat more," 3 = "about right," and 4 = "less than should" (respondents who do not pay tax excluded); tax cut = whether respondent favors tax cut, 1 = "should not be cut," 2 = "should be cut by about 10 percent,"

| (5) | (6) | (7) | (8) |
Vote	Vote	Vote	Vote
−0.228	−0.243	−0.272	−0.280
(0.412)	(0.415)	(0.419)	(0.422)
0.00183	−0.00349	0.000752	0.00690
(0.0136)	(0.0142)	(0.0141)	(0.0140)
−0.0571	−0.0647	−0.0501	−0.0638
(0.107)	(0.109)	(0.110)	(0.110)
−0.00654	−0.00746	−0.00752	−0.00704
(0.00915)	(0.00913)	(0.00943)	(0.00936)
−0.134	−0.133	−0.166	−0.158
(0.136)	(0.136)	(0.139)	(0.139)
−0.235*	−0.203[+]	−0.213[+]	−0.194
(0.117)	(0.121)	(0.121)	(0.120)
−0.639**	−0.588*	−0.608*	−0.592*
(0.242)	(0.248)	(0.245)	(0.244)
−0.593***	−0.617***	−0.600***	−0.621***
(0.104)	(0.108)	(0.107)	(0.109)
−0.392*	−0.398*	−0.422*	−0.400*
(0.174)	(0.178)	(0.182)	(0.179)
0.169	0.102	0.121	0.138
(0.123)	(0.130)	(0.128)	(0.127)
−0.106	−0.0803	−0.167	−0.117
(0.165)	(0.167)	(0.173)	(0.170)
−0.0606	−0.0108	−0.00303	−0.0217
(0.138)	(0.143)	(0.145)	(0.143)
	0.545*		
	(0.268)		
		−0.472**	
		(0.166)	
			−1.067**
			(0.407)
7.086***	5.991**	8.670***	7.332***
(2.035)	(2.093)	(2.192)	(2.064)
262	262	262	262
0.377	0.391	0.405	0.401

3 = "should be cut by about 20 percent," 4 = "should be cut by about 30 percent," 5 = "should be cut by more than 30 percent"; whether respondent believes tax cuts will pay for themselves, 1 = believes, 0 = does not believe (logistic regression).

[+]$p < 0.1$; *$p < 0.05$; **$p < 0.01$; ***$p < 0.001$

Table 4.3 Tax Cuts and Race of Respondents, 1980

"Over the next three years, federal income taxes . . .	White Respondents	Black Respondents	Total
. . . should not be cut."	255	21	276
	(19.78%)	(19.63%)	(19.77%)
. . . should be cut by about 10 percent."	258	18	276
	(20.02%)	(16.82%)	(19.77%)
. . . should be cut by about 20 percent."	257	18	275
	(19.94%)	(16.82%)	(19.7%)
. . . should be cut by about 30 percent."	368	29	397
	(28.55%)	(27.10%)	(28.44%)
. . . should be cut by more than 30 percent."	151	21	172
	(11.71%)	(19.63%)	(12.32%)
Total	1,289	107	1,396
	(100%)	(100%)	(100%)

Source: 1980 ANES.

Note: χ^2 statistic of test of difference between white and black respondents 6.0895; *p*-value 0.19.

lower taxes for savings and investment: "I'm going to try also to change federal regulations in the tax structure that has made this once powerful industrial giant in this land and in the world now with a lower rate of productivity than any of the other industrial nations, with a lower rate of savings and investment on the part of our people and put us back where we belong."[44] If the Neshoba speech was a dog whistle, it was in the more traditional mode of Nixonian dog whistling, not an instance of using tax cuts as a dog whistle.

Indeed, one could wonder whether the Neshoba episode shows not dog whistling, but the exact opposite of dog whistling. The dog whistle hypothesis takes as a premise that white voters know something—some symbol, some fact of history—that allows them to draw the links between a code word used by a politician and a racial appeal. For example, for Neshoba to work as a dog whistle for white voters in the way analysts have hypothesized, white voters have to be aware of the civil rights murders in 1964.

But one aspect of racial privilege is precisely the ability to remain blissfully ignorant of painful racial history and to remain unaware of how events or symbols affect minorities. A recent article about the Neshoba County Fair gives the impression that those who come to the fair don't think at all about its racially exclusionary nature, much less the racial history of the area.[45] Similarly, voters who favored tax cuts may have been thinking about their own pockets rather than how those tax cuts would affect minorities.

Moreover, it is also worth noting that Ronald Reagan became successful at the national level only when he left behind the rhetoric of the welfare queen. That had been a key feature of the 1976 campaign, but had disappeared by the time of the 1980 campaign. The remarkable aspect of the 1980 campaign is how much race was *not* part of Reagan's approach, given his harping about the welfare queen in 1976. As one observer noted in 1979: "The Ronald Reagan who ran for President in past years was angry—angry at student militants, anti-war demonstrators, draft dodgers, urban rioters, welfare cheats, school-busing supporters, Soviet dictators and Washington bureaucrats. His rhetoric was strident and negative: He called for stopping federal programs, rather than for starting new initiatives. In the words of one former Reagan adviser, he supplied 'red meat to rightwing nuts' across the country. The Ronald Reagan who announced [his 1980 campaign for the presidency] last week hardly attacked anyone—except Jimmy Carter. . . . And the underlying theme of his address was positive, not negative."[46] Indeed, the Ronald Reagan who campaigned for Barry Goldwater in 1964 is unrecognizable in tone, angry and dismissive rather than uplifting and avuncular. His migration from the periphery of politics to the mainstream was enabled by a transformation in tone, and perhaps leaving behind angry rhetoric, including angry racially charged rhetoric, was a part of that transformation.

Finally, while the racial backlash thesis clearly provides one important reason why Republicans became increasingly successful electorally over the latter part of the twentieth century, whether it explains the turn of the Republican Party to free market policies is not so clear. An economically moderate, racist Republican Party on the lines of Richard Nixon (who implemented wage and price controls and applied the Southern Strategy) and George H. W. Bush (who called supply-side theory "voodoo economics" while using racist appeals to win the presidency in 1988) is not hard to imagine. Economically moderate Republicans may be forced to turn to racist appeals precisely because without policies such as tax cuts to offer, all they have to campaign on is race. Racism by itself doesn't get us to free market policy.

Other demographic variables are not correlated with support for the tax cut at all. As table 4.4 shows, labor union members were as supportive of

Table 4.4 Tax Cuts and Labor Union Membership of Respondents, 1980

"Over the next three years, federal income taxes . . .	"Does anyone in this household belong to a labor union?"		
	Yes	No	Total
. . . should not be cut."	101	232	333
	(20.53%)	(16.84%)	(17.81%)
. . . should be cut by about 10 percent."	103	289	392
	(20.93%)	(20.97%)	(20.96%)
. . . should be cut by about 20 percent."	90	296	386
	(18.29%)	(21.48%)	(20.64%)
. . . should be cut by about 30 percent."	132	403	535
	(26.83%)	(29.25%)	(28.61%)
. . . should be cut by more than 30 percent."	66	158	224
	(13.41%)	(11.47%)	(11.98%)
Total	492	1,378	1,870
	(100%)	(100%)	(100%)

Source: 1980 ANES.

Note: χ^2 statistic of test of difference between union and non-union respondents 6.45; *p*-value 0.168.

the tax cut as others. One analyst noted: "Those who belong to unions—and the percentage is declining—are preoccupied with what used to be considered middle-class problems: property taxes, interest rates on loans, the price of a second car or recreational vehicle. They no longer identify with the aging New Deal agenda of social activism."[47] An AFL-CIO poll taken in October 1980 found that union workers laid the nation's economic ills at the doorstep of government, not business, by a margin of three to one, and that union members considered government regulation of business excessive, by a margin of two to one.[48]

For these reasons, the tax cut was a cornerstone of Reagan's attempt in 1980 to draw working-class voters away from the Democrats. Reagan emphasized that Carter had "pushed this nation even further into the depths of recession by causing 889,000 more workingmen and -women to be thrown out of work."[49] The Republican National Committee spent $4.3 million on a series of ads appealing to working-class voters, such as an ad of a worker from a closed-down factory asking: "If the Democrats are good for working people, how come so many people aren't working?"[50]

While the AFL-CIO came out in strong opposition to Reagan's tax cut, Republicans could point to other unions, including the Teamsters, who supported Reagan. The head of the steelworkers' union had called the Carter administration's policies "cruel and unjust," both because Carter seemed unable to do anything about the recession that was causing the steel industry to run at only half its capacity and because by prioritizing the fight against inflation Carter was "inflicting unemployment on working people . . . Inflation is a severe problem . . . but the remedy is not to climb to the heights . . . on the backs of working men and women."[51]

Members of Congress reported that their constituent mail did not show the rank and file of workers supporting organized labor's anti–tax cut stance.[52] By October, polls were showing Reagan had won over a quarter of white blue-collar voters who had chosen Carter in 1976.[53] In the end, Reagan narrowly won the blue-collar vote, getting 48 percent of the votes in working-class precincts compared to 45 percent for Carter.[54]

In 1981 Reagan broke a strike by the Professional Air Traffic Controllers Organization (PATCO) by firing all the strikers. This attack was only the most visible of a trend that had been underway since the 1970s, when "mayors across the country, from Edward Koch of New York to Tom Bradley of Los Angeles, reinforced their popularity by taking on municipal unions."[55] Labor had become increasingly unpopular as the shift to services brought many workers out of unionized areas of the economy. The public supported the president—even union members supported the president, as air traffic controllers were among the highest paid of American workers and therefore not a sympathetic population when making wage claims. PATCO was decertified, and the striking controllers lost their jobs and careers. Employers all over the country, even in the private sector where strikes were legal, were emboldened to adopt a more aggressive stance against unions. Labor leaders became cautious and less willing to strike, for fear that a strike could destroy their unions. But without the willingness to strike, labor could not offer much to union members.[56]

One hypothesis is that the decline of labor makes existing union members more relatively privileged, and therefore less likely to support progressive policies,[57] but as shown in the supplemental materials, low-income union members were no less likely to support the tax cut than low-income non-union members. The decline of labor could have been a factor in the inability of unions to rally their members against Reagan and the tax cut.

But it is also possible that the decline of labor and the support for tax cuts were both outcomes of the same phenomenon, the increasing inability of progressives to provide answers to the problems of the day.

As the supplemental materials show, neither gender, nor education, nor subjective class position had anything to do with tax cut attitudes. Reagan's tax cuts appealed across the board—to racists and nonracists, Southerners and non-Southerners, men and women, whites and blacks, the educated and the less educated, and even many Democrats.

CHAPTER 5

"Thank God, and Bring Down Prices"

WHEN REAGAN TOOK office, he was greeted with scores of letters every day from all over the country. The bass note in many of them was concern over inflation. The second oil shock of 1979 had seen a return of gas lines, and with them, once again, rationing and fighting and panicked proposals for solar power and electric cars, truckers refusing to drive, produce and livestock not making it to market, gas locks being installed on car tanks to prevent the siphoning of fuel, and even shootings and two murders.[1]

The worry over inflation had become so widespread that it had entered the imaginations of children. When Sara Rutland of Aiken, South Carolina, asked her fourth-grade class what the most important thing was for the new president to do, she got a few different responses, from quickly getting the hostages back to their families to improving defense. But almost all of the students—eleven out of thirteen—said that the president's first responsibility should be to bring down inflation. Jennifer wrote: "I hope you change the prices on food and gas. They are getting very high and we don't have much money." John wanted to hold the president to his campaign promises: "I think the first thing you should do is cut down inflation. The reason is because you said [you] would if you became President. Now you are President, and I hope you cut down on inflation first." Zera worried that the prices of "clothes are up so high people don't wear clothes." And Gerome summed up: "I suggest you do first is to thank God, and bring down prices."[2] In Edwina Faulkner's fifth-grade class in Huntington, New York, sixteen out of the twenty students worried about inflation. Jordy, who asked for lower airplane fees and taxes and food prices, generously added, "It's O.K. if you can't do it but can you try," and Robert said, "I just want to tell you to try to do your best." Steven was less accommodating, wanting the president "to take off inflation because my allowance is going lower and lower every week. Just try to do what I tell you." (Inflation wasn't the only thing on the class's minds: Holli wanted a law against having more than four children, Mark suggested a higher allowance, Karen asked for women to be made equal to men, and Christine wondered, "Why don't they have girls on bass ball teams"—apparently a heated topic in the school, also mentioned by Stephanie.)[3] Ruth Noble's third-grade class in Germantown, Ohio, drew pictures of what inflation looked like to them (figure 5.1).[4] The class must have been discussing both lowering prices and lowering taxes, as some students were confused by the two issues and how they related. For example, Dori's picture imagines Reagan saying, "I think I should lower the price on taxex down don't you Mrs. Ragon."[5]

Bringing down inflation was the main concern everywhere, and tax cuts were the main method through which Reagan had promised to do so. Paul Volcker, confirmed as chairman of the Federal Reserve in August 1979, had already begun his tight money regime. But although Reagan would go on to reappoint Volcker, and Volcker's policies would eventually be credited with bringing down inflation, at the time it was not clear that they would succeed. Laffer confidently predicted in early 1980 that they would not work. The immediate result of the tight money policy was to create a recession that probably hurt Carter and helped Reagan win, but as Volcker continued the tight money squeeze and the short-term economic pain continued, Volcker was not particularly popular with the Reagan administration either.[6] Thus, in 1981 the Reagan team still considered tackling inflation through tax cuts their first priority, and they now turned to the task of making specific policy proposals out of the campaign platforms.

Reagan presented the program to the public in a speech on February 18. The tax package included Kemp-Roth and incentives for business; Reagan had hoped to enact changes such as indexing tax brackets to inflation, removing the so-called marriage penalty, and making other smaller changes, but he put those off for later. He supported the Fed in its tight money policy and announced deregulatory initiatives.[7]

In the annals of studies of political communication, this February speech has gone down as a blockbuster. Thirty-nine percent of respondents in a Wirthlin poll said that they had watched or heard all of the speech, another 25 percent had watched or heard part of it, and another 18 percent had read or heard about it later.[8] Moreover, Wirthlin told the president that 78 percent of the respondents who saw or heard the speech were favorably impressed. Wirthlin noted that what really worked was when the president stressed that tax cuts would increase productivity—"they buy it."[9]

If the public was broadly in favor however—or at least could be brought to "buy it" if the team sold the program correctly—Reagan was not getting any help from economists. The media could be convinced to stop asking questions by throwing around some numbers before the election, but now it was time to make actual policy, and economists were not so easily convinced.

A folk theory haunting the edges of the tax cut debate is that economists moved in a conservative direction, and therefore politics moved in a conservative direction. In the 1970s, a revolution was under way within economics against the dominance of Keynesian theory. Keynesian scholars argued that unemployment and inflation were inversely related, because periods of high employment would lead to rising wages, which would touch off inflation. Three sets of arguments criticized this orthodoxy. Monetarist scholars criticized it for ignoring the role that the quantity of money played in generating inflation; if inflation was instead a monetary phenomenon— simply a matter of the quantity of money rising in excess of the demand for goods—it would be possible to have high inflation and high unemployment at the same time, a situation that indeed came to pass in the 1970s. Another set of scholars around Robert Lucas explained the coincidence of high inflation and high unemployment with reference to rational expectations, arguing that it is not possible for policymakers to address unemployment through mechanisms that will raise inflation such as a large-scale government stimulus, because doing so encourages actors to incorporate expectations of inflation into their forecasts, negating any possible benefits of the stimulus; in general, government intervention is ineffectual because rational actors anticipate the intervention and change their behavior to take it into account. The third critique was the argument of Martin Feldstein, Lawrence Summers, and Michael Boskin that the American tax system was providing disincentives to savings and investment.[10]

Figure 5.1 Letters of Pupils in Mrs. Noble's Third-Grade Class to President Ronald Reagan, Germantown, Ohio, February 1981

Source: White House Office of Records Management, Subject Files: "Business—Economics," Box 87, Folder BE004-02 (006000–008499), RRPL.

Figure 5.1 (*continued*)

Because this revolution began a few years before the turn in economic policy under the Reagan administration, and because economists did indeed have rising influence over the course of the twentieth century, many observers naturally wonder whether the revolution in economics played some role in the policies of the Reagan administration. Historians of ideas routinely claim that it does.[11]

But most economists were unconvinced by the administration's plans and tried, unsuccessfully, to resist them. Although there were certainly members of the profession, like Boskin or Friedman, who supported the program, economists surveyed by Congress on the wisdom of across-the-board tax cuts opposed it two to one.[12] In particular, while the part of the tax cut that focused on business tax cuts was supported by many economists, the part that focused on individual income tax cuts was supported by very few. An economist at Yale wrote to the head of Reagan's Council of Economic Advisers: "I sympathize with part of the diagnosis, but feel that you have pushed it a bit far in various directions. I think your job, as chairman of the Council of Economic Advisors, is to fight off the wave of ideology that, if you don't fight against it, is likely to sweep over the administration. Keep it sensible, keep it cool. Don't become part of the problem yourself. I know you agree with me in this diagnosis."[13] As for the Laffer curve, George Stigler of the University of Chicago said, "Laffer is no longer a very serious scholar. . . . He is playing the role of a propagandist, and as such he is performing some service. But I would not base a $125 billion tax cut on his work." Even Alan Greenspan, who supported the tax cut, said, "I'm for cutting taxes, but not for Laffer's reasons. I don't know anyone who seriously believes his argument."[14]

A key concern among economists was that the tax cut would be inflationary. The Reagan team tried many arguments to address this. Tax cuts would boost the savings rate, they argued, thus making it easier to invest. These factors would increase the supply of goods, thereby bringing down the cost of goods. Moreover, tax cuts, unlike monetary measures, would not lead to unemployment and would not require slowing down the economy. Reagan called it "another way to balance the budget and another way to end the inflation" and called the principle of a trade-off between inflation and recession "old fashioned economics."[15] The head of the RNC ridiculed those who believed "in the tired old notion that it is necessary to choose between either inflation or unemployment."[16] Kemp argued: "Cutting tax rates on income has a 'supply-side' effect because it rewards additional production relative to additional leisure, and rewards additional saving relative to additional consumption. Since the former increases productivity and the latter lowers prices, it is absurd to say that cutting tax rates is inflationary."[17]

But economists argued that there was no guarantee that the money returned to taxpayers would be saved rather than spent, or that the incentive effects on labor supply would be as large as needed. Eventually the Reagan team settled on the effect of tax cuts on savings as their key argument, and consequently the battle began to center on how much the tax cut would lead to increased saving. The truth was that no one really knew, although economists tended to be skeptical that the effects would be as strong or as immediate as the Kemp-Roth proponents wanted to believe.[18] The questions were asked so often that the team prepared sets of answers that surrogates could give when asked about it. There were many possible answers, such as, "The tax cut reduces the cost of saving compared with consumption," or "With more output inflationary pressures will be reduced, not increased." Another response was to explain: "These tax reductions will result in substantial increases in saving in the private sector, sufficient to finance the additional deficit as well as large gains in capital formation. No inflation will result unless the monetary authorities mistakenly choose to monetize the deficit. Since the additional saving will be more than adequate to finance the deficit, any such monetary action would be completely uncalled for." And giving an example was suggested: "If you spend $1,000 on a stereo, you get music. If you buy a $1,000 bond, you get . . . $50 after tax. . . . If we lower the tax rate, the $50 becomes $63. . . . Anyone just undecided before will prefer the bond."[19]

None of it convinced skeptics. Robert Lucas called Kemp-Roth a "crackpot proposal."[20] A survey of economists in the 1980s found a core of broad consensus against interference with the price mechanism through policies such as wage and price controls, tariffs, rent ceilings, and employment guarantees, but disagreement among economists on "at the present hotly debated issues such as monetarism or supply-side economics." A later survey found that only about 8 percent of members of the American Economic Association were supporters of free market principles, and only 3 percent were strong supporters. Other surveys since then have continued to find disagreement within the field on the effects of tax cuts on the economy.[21]

Given this state of affairs, Reagan and his advisers could choose those economists who supported the policies the administration had already committed itself to. Instead of the force of economic ideas pushing the administration to action, the picture is instead one of the administration being able to pick the views it preferred among the different views within the field of economics.

The recently created nonpartisan Congressional Budget Office, led by Alice Rivlin, was a bastion of opposition from economists to supply-side policy. Under Richard Nixon, Congress had decided that it needed its own staff of economic experts to be able to respond to the president's experts in the Office of Management and Budget. Rivlin, a technocrat with extensive credentials, became the CBO's first head (but not until Al Ullman, who was crucial in choosing the head of the office but opposed to putting a woman in charge, left to take over at the Ways and Means Committee). Under Rivlin, the CBO quickly acquired a reputation for providing nonpartisan analyses. The CBO had called into question Ford's economic projections as well as Carter's. By Reagan's time, the CBO was widely admired for its independence, but this did not stop the Reagan team from attacking Rivlin and trying to get her removed when the CBO argued that the administration's OMB numbers were too optimistic. She survived because some important Republicans who were not fans of supply-side, particularly Senator Pete Domenici of New Mexico, supported her. In the long run, both the CBO numbers and the OMB numbers were wrong, but the CBO numbers were less wrong, earning it plaudits.[22]

Although the episode has gone down as a triumph for the CBO, it is possible that the attack on Rivlin led the CBO to produce numbers that were more optimistic than was warranted. The CBO was institutionally fragile, and Jack Kemp and the powerful columnists Rowland Evans and Robert Novak were campaigning to remove Rivlin.[23] There is some speculation that the CBO intentionally moved closer to the administration's models in order to avoid retribution from the administration.[24] A staffer on the House Budget Committee would remember saying to Rivlin, "'Alice, this looks to me like unbridled optimism,' and she said, 'No it's bridled optimism.' Alice was doing her best to not pick a fight with the Reagan administration." Rivlin herself denied that there was any intentional effort to produce more optimistic numbers in order to avoid retribution from the administration, and after all, even the slightly more optimistic predictions provided opponents of supply-side with ammunition.[25] Perhaps the simple truth is that, just as economic predictions and calculations usually do not converge enough to support an argument in favor of a particular course of action, neither do they converge enough to justify full-throated opposition.

Moreover, it is also true that the administration was by now making the more tempered claim that tax cuts would keep inflation down *when combined with* tight monetary policy: "The monetary policy in the President's program is aimed chiefly at reducing inflation by slowing the growth of the money supply. The tax package, with its emphasis on increasing after-tax rates of return to labor, saving and investment, both lowers costs directly and increases the growth rate of output. Thus, we have less money chasing more goods."[26] The Council of Economic Advisers concurred: "A frequently raised concern is that the tax reductions will be inflationary. . . . In responding to these assertions, the Administration has emphasized the supply-enhancing effects of the reductions in individual tax rates and the important role that monetary policy plays in translating budget deficits into inflation."[27] The official rationale for the program was that tax cuts "are designed to improve the economy by improving incentives. The purpose is to encourage people to earn more by producing more—to ease the tax barriers that discourage people from providing more labor, capital, and real output. At the same time, the demand policies of government—spending restraint and slower money growth—will be used to prevent excess demand. That combination of policies is designed both to expand employment and output and to reduce inflation."[28] The consequence would be that inflation "should come down rapidly."[29]

The administration had by this point left behind the Laffer curve entirely. Unlike Jack Kemp, who was certainly influenced by the Laffer curve argument, the majority of the administration was not convinced that lowering tax rates would raise revenue.[30] Reagan did make this argument on occasion, contrary to what some administration members later claimed.[31] For example, at a press conference before the tax cut passed, he said, "Every major tax cut that has been made in this century in our country has resulted in even the government getting more revenue than it did before, because the base of the economy is so broadened by doing it," and after its passage he referred to the Kennedy tax cuts: "He cut those tax rates, and the government ended up getting more revenues, because of the almost instant stimulus to the economy."[32] He noted that his hero, Calvin Coolidge, had cut taxes, and "every one of those (Coolidge) tax cuts resulted in more revenues to the government because of the increased prosperity to the government as a whole."[33] In his autobiography, Reagan explicitly writes that lower tax rates result in "more prosperity for all—and more revenue for government," and he notes that Coolidge's tax cuts proved that "the principle mentioned by [fourteenth-century North African scholar] Ibn Khaldoon about lower tax rates meaning greater tax revenues still worked in the modern world."[34] A White House briefing book on the program prepared a few months before its passage noted that after Kennedy's tax cuts, "federal revenues actually increased and deficits shrank."[35] David Stockman said to the House Republican Conference that, "with the growth of the economy, the actual dollars of tax revenue collected will be rising, not falling."[36] Quotes like these will keep commentators musing about the Laffer curve for years to come.

However, there are also signs that the administration was aware of the fragile foundations of the Laffer curve. Most important, the official budget documents never made any assumption that tax cuts would lead to greater revenue. It was necessary to make some assumptions to make the numbers add up, but the Laffer curve assumption of tax cuts leading to greater work effort was not one of them. On March 19, a group composed of representatives from the Council of Economic Advisers (CEA), the Office of Management and Budget (OMB), and the Treasury produced a detailed plan based on the following assumptions: that spending restraint would reduce the deficit; that lower taxes on savings would increase the propensity to save; and that accelerated depreciation schedules would lead to higher business savings.[37] The centerpiece of the plan was the assumption that tax cuts would lead to a moderate increase in savings. This was based not on the work of Arthur Laffer but on Stanford economist Michael Boskin's recent research on the influence of taxes on savings. Although some economists contested Boskin's research, it was not outside the mainstream, and, unlike the Laffer curve, it had been published in peer-reviewed scholarly journals.

Boskin argued that the savings rate was more sensitive to the rate of return than had been appreciated and that reducing taxes on interest income would thus lead to a rise in the savings rate and significant economic benefits.[38] On the strength of this argument, as well as on the assumptions of moderate spending reductions and increased business savings—and not any assumptions about greater growth in revenue because of increased incentives to work—the CEA-OMB-Treasury plan hashed out a budget that foresaw deficits coming under control within three years. The document points out that the assumption made about the rate of savings was "well below the 1966–1975 average. It is even further below 1971–1975 average."[39]

But it would be dubious to conclude that Boskin's work *led to* the tax cut, as his work became prominent only very late in the episode. Boskin was being used in the same way that the Senate Budget Committee numbers had been used by Anderson before the election: to make the program add up. After the election, as the policy got closer to being implemented, it was necessary to find stronger numbers than the Senate Budget Committee numbers, which Boskin provided. And it was also necessary to modify the plan to stress the commitment to tight monetary policy. Making these changes was enough for the CBO to ultimately conclude: "Administration scenario is optimistic, but by no means impossible. More conventional analysis would lead one to expect less rapid improvement in inflation and growth. CBO sees less improvement as likely, but note that we too see improvement in both inflation and growth (productivity). Question of how fast." They noted that the differences in the estimations were "not about supply side. Believe tax cuts will have positive supply side effects, but slowly. . . . Don't perceive that we differ much from Administration here." There was agreement on the basic objectives, including "a substantial and sustained shift from consumption to saving, plus channelling of that saving into productive investment." The CBO also agreed that it was "hardly surprising" that U.S. taxpayers felt that the "tax burden is too heavy" given that the "federal share of GNP has been rising . . . [and] effective tax rates [were] rising." There was "agreement on need for personal tax cut."[40]

Some level of bipartisan agreement can also be seen in a memo earlier in the year to Jimmy Carter from Walter Heller, a former chairman of the Council of Economic Advisers who had not been a fan of Kemp-Roth but nevertheless could agree that at least a small tax cut "could be thought of, quite properly, as a return of some of the tax dollars that have been taken away by inflation and a restoration of some of the purchasing power siphoned away by OPEC."[41] Ultimately, Rivlin concluded that the differences between the CBO and Reagan were a matter of degree.[42]

By the time congressional hearings took place in the spring of 1981, although economists' reviews of the tax plan were decidedly mixed, enough of them could be found supporting the plan to make it viable. The economists who testified against the plan included Joseph Pechman of Brookings, who noted that most economists would prefer depreciation allowances; Lester Thurow of MIT, who argued that the tax cuts would not improve the savings rate, as the benefits were going to the top, and would lead to investment in office buildings and shopping centers instead of factories; Robert Gordon of Northwestern, who spoke of the contradictions of trying to balance the budget and cut unemployment and control inflation at the same time; and Dale Jorgenson of Harvard, who testified multiple times against the business tax cut, arguing that it would not work as intended because of the variability of inflation and would end up as a subsidy to business.[43]

On the other hand, John Rutledge of the Claremont Economics Institute testified vigorously in favor of the tax plan, David Bradford of Princeton commented favorably on the accelerated depreciation provisions, Alvin Rabushka of the Hoover Institution and Martin Feldstein of Harvard both argued that the tax cuts were not tax cuts at all but were simply offsetting projected increases in taxes, and David Meiselman of Virginia Polytechnic Institute argued that tax reductions could lessen inflation by increasing supply.[44]

That many of the economists testifying came from think tanks and lower-ranked universities is an indication of how the process worked. Michael Reay interviewed economists and quotes one who shed light on the dynamics. In the early 1980s, this economist said,

> I always got called with, "Do you have something good to say about supply-side economics?" And the fact of the matter was these guys had gone through lists and lists of people who basically told them that there was no solid economic research to support the supply-side stuff; it was a conjecture which was consistent with economic theory but had no empirical foundation, and that's not very interesting. So I got the impression they just kept calling people. And I was *way* down on the list, being a brand new young prof, but they'd been through everybody who was above me on the list and they were *still* going. . . . So it seems like the people you get throwing things out there, the talking heads, are really the people that are accessible to the press that

tell the story the press wants to tell. It's not clear to me that what you see then is an accurate reflection of what the profession is; it's more an accurate reflection of what the press wants to have put out there.[45]

Reagan's Council of Economic Advisers did not push for supply-side tax policies.[46] Moreover, "Council of Economic Advisers Chairman Murray Weidenbaum, when asked directly what weight of influence, on a scale of one to ten, economists had enjoyed in drafting the original tax program of the administration, replied, 'zero.'"[47] The actual work of the CEA seems to have been public relations, as Weidenbaum himself noted: "Following the release of the Reagan administration's proposed economic recovery program in 1981, the CEA chairman became one of the three major 'salesmen' . . . for the president's economic program. . . . There followed an almost endless array of joint and individual congressional testimonies and press conferences; White House briefings to the cabinet, other officials, and numerous visiting interest groups; and speeches to all sorts of organizations—business, consumers, agriculture, ethnic, regional, religious, and so forth."[48]

Reagan's dismissal of economists has come down in the form of the jokes that he loved to tell. "One of the first things I learned about economists was that they have a Phi Beta Kappa key on one end of their watch chain, and no watch on the other end."[49] "You know, I've heard that there is a new version of Trivial Pursuit, that game; it's called the economist's edition. In this one there are 100 questions, 3,000 answers."[50] Brezhnev and an aide are watching a Russian military parade. After the soldiers and weapons go by, the aide is startled to see a ragtag band of civilians. "Those are my economists," Brezhnev says. "You have no idea how much damage they can do."[51]

There was a reason why Reagan wanted to make fun of economists. By and large, economists did not tell him what he wanted to hear. When that happened, he dismissed their expertise: "I hope you'll keep in mind that economic forecasting is far from a perfect science. If recent history's any guide, the experts have some explaining to do about what they told us had to happen but never did."[52]

Economists worry that even on the areas where the field does express consensus, no one listens. One frustrated economist elevated this to a principle he called Murphy's Law of Economic Policy: "Economists have the least influence on policy where they know the most and are most agreed; they have the most influence on policy where they know the least and disagree most vehemently."[53] Moreover, even the latter kind of influence is limited, as it is only economists who agree with the politician who will be allowed to be "influential." As Paul Samuelson put it, responding to the famous Keynes quote about the influence of economic ideas, "He who picks his doctor from an array of competing doctors is in a real sense his own doctor"[54]—a perfect description of how the Reagan team used Boskin. Because the field of economics is divided on what policies will have which effects—honestly divided, because these are not questions that can be answered easily—it's possible to find economists on all sides of any question and refer to only the ones who agree with a predetermined position.

Economists did give some policy suggestions in 1976, but these were of the kind that eventually led, not to Kemp-Roth, but to the accelerated cost recovery system (ACRS): "The United States had a lower savings rate than almost any other industrialized country between 1962 and 1973, according to Martin Feldstein of Harvard University, who noted . . . that the nation needed to generate more capital."[55] Feldstein and other economists had long focused on the issue of capital depreciation. In other areas, such as free trade, economists' influence may have been greater. But economists did not initiate the movement for tax rate cuts that kicked off the Republican Party's transformation.[56] It makes more sense to see both the developments in economics and the supply-side policies as emerging from the same common cause, the slowdown in growth and rise in inflation of the 1970s.

Later observers would wonder how a policy that seemed so clearly not to add up could have been implemented. The answer is that it added up if you used the right numbers and squinted—using SBC numbers rather than CBO numbers, and slightly modified SBC numbers at that, during the campaign; stressing tight monetary policy, promising spending cuts, and using Boskin's work on savings afterwards. Reagan's ultimate answer to the question of how it was possible to cut taxes, increase defense spending, and balance the budget at the same time was not the Laffer curve argument that tax cuts would pay for themselves. The answer that the team eventually settled on was that this could be done because if taxes were not cut, a substantial tax increase would come about automatically, because of inflation. The Reagan plan was to spend some of that tax increase on tax cuts and some of it on defense spending, leaving just enough to bring the budget into balance within a few years. Disagreements between economists gave Reagan essential cover in arguing that the administration's estimates were not impossible, even though the team systematically took the numbers that were most favorable to their cause. And the goal of increasing productivity and even the sense that some form of tax cut was necessary were shared across the political spectrum.

The need to do something—anything—in response to inflation ultimately drove the events. The main actors themselves often mentioned this. As Arthur Laffer himself put it, in a phrase that accurately sums up the whole episode: "There's more than a reasonable probability that I'm wrong, but . . . why not try something new?"[57] Robert Bartley, the *Wall Street Journal* editor who had helped to bring about the revolution, at the eve of the policy victory said, "I think these are very important ideas. But I couldn't give you any guarantee that they'll work. Maybe they won't. I just can't see anything else on the horizon."[58] Paul Craig Roberts wrote in an internal memo, "What is the alternative to a policy designed to stimulate the productive capacity of the nation? . . . Unless we immediately move to alter fundamentally the policy environment, the expectations of the people that a Reagan administration will significantly improve the economic climate will not be met."[59] Reagan himself, when his advisers worried that Kemp-Roth would not work, was said to have responded that nothing else was working either, so one might as well try it.[60] "They demand proof in advance that what we have proposed will work," he complained. "Well, the answer to that is, we're living with the proof that what they want to continue doing won't work. I believe what we have proposed will work because it always has."[61] "How well did your ideas work: They've had a free hand for about 40 years."[62] The supporters of the tax cut said this over and over again in testimony to Congress, and it became a stock response to complaints that the numbers didn't add up, that the country was not on the declining part of the Laffer curve, or that the tax cut would be inflationary.[63]

The question remained of how to cut spending as much as would be needed, and it was at this point that David Stockman came up with the famous magic asterisk, "Future savings to be identified"—a way to make the budget numbers add up without having to immediately specify what would be cut. Some advisers did worry about this, but the worries were put aside by a sense that Congress would diminish the size of the tax cuts.[64] That turned out to be a naive reading of how tax cuts would fare in the rough and tumble of congressional politics.

CHAPTER 6

Tax Cut versus Tax Cut

ON A SWELTERING day in the summer of 1981, during a particularly tricky impasse in negotiations over the tax cut, Congressman Mickey Edwards wrote to the president. Edwards had been an early Reagan supporter, one of a handful of Republican representatives who had worked for Reagan since long before his election. But now he was threatening to vote against Reagan's tax cut program and side with the Democrats instead. The issue was a special exemption for oil: "If the Democrats come up with this kind of package, and we don't, there is no way we can hold the Texas, Oklahoma, and Louisiana Democrats in our coalition. In fact, it would be very difficult to hold Texas, Oklahoma and Louisiana Republicans. To use my own case as an example: I am prepared to work for, fight for, bleed for, die for the tax package—but if the Democrats offer more relief from the windfall profits tax, I could either vote for the Democrat package or begin to groom a successor and wind up my Congressional affairs."[1]

Between the presentation of the tax cut package to the public in February 1981 and its signing in August, Reagan had somehow found himself in the desperate position of trying to hold on to even his most fervent supporters. Having vanquished the Republican fiscal conservatives, the media, and the economists, Reagan had run into the congressional Democrats. The Democrats still controlled the House of Representatives and many of them thought the purpose of government was to collect tax revenue and spend it in ways that might improve the lives of the poor and others who needed it. The exemplar of this philosophy was their leader, House Speaker Thomas P. "Tip" O'Neill. With his abundant white hair and eyebrows and mottled red nose suggesting late nights of backslapping, O'Neill looked exactly the caricature of the big city Democratic politician that he was. He kept in his office a quote from Hubert Humphrey, the former senator from Minnesota and vice president under Lyndon Johnson: "The moral test of government is how it treats those who are in the dawn of life, the children; those who are in the twilight of life, the aged; and those who are in the shadows of life, the sick, the needy, and the handicapped." Reagan noted in his diary that "Tip is truly a New Deal liberal. He honestly believes that we're promoting welfare for the rich." O'Neill, for his part, thought the problem with Reagan was that he had forgotten his working-class roots.[2]

When Reagan was elected, O'Neill decided that he would not obstruct Reagan's program through procedural maneuvers. He did not want the Democrats to be blamed for being obstructionist while the nation was in economic crisis. Many conservative Southern Democrats wanted compromise—and after the Democratic majority was severely reduced by the election, every vote counted. The liberal wing had nowhere to go and could be taken for granted, whereas the conservative wing could credibly threaten to defect to Reagan. Moreover, for some Democrats, supporting social programs did not necessarily mean opposing tax cuts. It was after all the Democratic John F. Kennedy who had initiated the last big tax cut, and Democrats were not burdened by a balanced budget wing. And despite his own sense of the purpose of government, O'Neill thought that the people had shown they wanted Reagan, and so they should get Reagan—that is, the House should allow Reagan to fulfill his entire agenda and offer a bold program to address the nation's crisis. At the same time, O'Neill also thought that Reagan's plan would fail, and that this failure would become evident by the 1982 midterm elections.[3] Key members of the Democratic leadership also wanted compromise: House Ways and Means Committee chair Dan Rostenkowski, the other Democrat leading the tax cut negotiations, said, "We are still debating exactly what it was that the voters expressed at the ballot box last fall. But this much is clear: The public wants government to shed some weight—to dramatically reduce its expenditures and to reduce inflation."[4]

The Democrats did not use all the procedural tools they could have to block the program, but they did put up strong opposition to Reagan. After losses on budget issues in the spring—and facing headlines like "Budget Fight Shows O'Neill's Fragile Grasp"—the Democrats started itching for a political win and thought that they could craft one on the issue of tax cuts.[5] But here the Democrats made a fateful decision: they decided that instead of opposing tax cuts, they would focus on putting together an alternative plan of smaller and, they believed, more responsible tax cuts and spending cuts. This approach seemed to be supported by the economic wisdom, and it would be a reasonable response to the problem of bracket creep; moreover, public opinion polls showed that although the public liked the idea of tax cuts, they preferred budget balance, and there was no appetite for spending cuts other than on the unpopular but budgetarily minuscule program of welfare for indigent mothers. Although Reagan's February 18 speech did lead to a torrent of mail from constituents supporting his plan, the torrent quickly slowed, and Democrats noted that Reagan was not as popular as new presidents generally are: his 59 percent approval rating was in fact quite low for a president just a few months into the job. There seemed to be room to move for the smaller, more responsible bill they had in mind. O'Neill was planning to start his attack the week of March 30 at a labor union conference.[6]

On the afternoon of March 30, Reagan spoke to the same conference, the meeting of the AFL-CIO Building and Construction Trades Council. Reagan remains the only American president to have once been a labor leader, and one of the odd aspects of the tax cut revolution is that not only was it led by two celebrities—Ronald Reagan, the former actor, and Jack Kemp, the former National Football League quarterback—but by two celebrities who had been union activists, Reagan as head of the Screen Actors Guild and Kemp as cofounder and president of the American Football League Players Association, for which he negotiated the first comprehensive collective bargaining agreement for football players in history.[7] Reagan had thought for years "that labor (the rank and file) really is ripe for the picking. I believe they can even be convinced that a reform of the tax structure on business will be beneficial to them in the sense of creating business prosperity and, therefore, jobs and more profit from which to get pay raises."[8]

This particular audience, however, was not the rank and file but the labor leaders who had strongly opposed Reagan during his campaign, and O'Neill thought that this conference would therefore be a good place to start the counterattack. But he would never get his chance.

It was a Monday in the first spring of Reagan's presidency. Still in the first one hundred days of his first term, Reagan was a hive of activity: that morning he had already had breakfast with presidential appointees; addressed a crowd of 125; met with his chief of staff, James Baker, counselor Ed Meese, and the deputy chief of staff, Michael Deaver; had a conference call with Chancellor Helmut Schmidt of Germany; sat for a national security briefing with the vice president and the assistant for national security affairs; and been in meetings with the assistant for legislative affairs, Hispanic leaders, and his speechwriter. After lunch, he traveled to the Washington Hilton to give his speech before the AFL-CIO audience.[9]

As the president stepped out afterwards, waving to the crowd, surrounded by a phalanx of bored men in suits, would-be assassin John Hinckley raised his gun and took several shots at him. One of the bullets ricocheted off the limousine and entered Reagan's body, narrowly missing his lung. A Secret Service agent shoved him into the limo within seconds and sped him to the hospital, with Reagan coughing up blood along the way. Reagan walked to the hospital doors but collapsed immediately inside. He needed four quarts of blood over the course of the day. The head of the trauma team concluded that had Reagan arrived at the hospital fifteen minutes later, he would have been dead. But he survived, and even joked while he was in the hospital. The very next day—March 31—he signed a dairy bill that had to be signed that day to save $250 million. The shaky signature was reproduced in newspapers across the country.[10]

For historians looking for that one moment in the past when things could have gone in distinctly different directions, March 30, 1981, is a good candidate. Reports of Reagan's courage and good humor during the incident spread. "I hope you're all Republicans," he said to the doctors set to operate on him. The head of the trauma team was a Democrat who responded, "We're all Republicans today, Mr. President." At one point when a nurse held Reagan's hand to reassure him he said, "Does Nancy know about us?" When an adviser reassured him that the government was running normally he quipped, "What makes you think I'd be happy about that?" On his first day back at work he told his staff, "I should be applauding you. I'm just so darned proud of all of you and how things were carried on. There were some days when I didn't think I was needed."[11] His approval rating jumped to 73 percent.[12]

As he recovered from the shooting, his staff tried to figure out how best to use the sympathy to generate more votes for the tax cut. Reagan called Congressman Gene Atkinson of Pennsylvania, who had been reluctant to make a firm commitment, from his sickbed. Atkinson happened to be at a radio station in his district. He committed publicly on the radio to supporting the tax cut.[13] Reagan had sent a message to Democratic representative George Mahon to read out during "festivities at [Texas] Tech," despite the assassination attempt, and now aides wondered if "somebody might try to wrangle from Mahon a usable endorsement, no matter how general, of the President's budget proposals? I'd love to spring *that* on the House Demos during the floor debate."[14]

At an April joint session of Congress, the first time the public would see the president since the assassination attempt, Reagan had another opportunity to make his case. He argued that the tax cut was not really a tax cut at all, just returning the revenue the government had received because of bracket creep: "Our choice is not between a balanced budget and a tax cut. Properly asked, the question is, 'Do you want a great big raise in your taxes this coming year or, at the worst, a very little increase with the prospect of tax reduction and a balanced budget down the road a ways?'"[15]

But the important thing that night in April was not the content of the speech so much as the fact that Reagan was making it, looking healthy and fully recovered, in an appearance that transcended politics as all the assembled politicians cheered.[16] Ken Duberstein remembered it as

> an electric moment. I remember the wild applause from the members up there. . . . The hill had all of a sudden found a leader, a president of the United States who understood the hill, who wanted to work with the hill, who respected them but wasn't going to roll over for them, who was pushing his point of view. The president very much captured the Congress that night. . . . Here was our president standing up there and bringing everybody together and yes he was okay. He's looking fine. I just remember the wild applause and the yelling, the happiness the sheer joy of the moment.[17]

The assassination attempt may have helped Reagan, but it's worth noting that the goodwill did not help him implement cuts in Social Security. There was something different about tax cuts. The assassination attempt merely exaggerated the lines and trends that were visible before it.

More importantly, in many ways the tax cut fight was over before it began, because the Democrats, seeing the polls, had already decided not to battle at all over the principle of a tax cut. Instead, they fought only over *how big* of a tax cut to implement. "They made a strategic decision, I'm not sure it was right, a strategic decision that said they were going to be willing to pay just about any price to win this vote."[18] The price they paid was to abandon the debate on whether a tax cut should be implemented in the first place. They started by offering a one-year tax cut, then compromised their way into a two-year tax cut, and eventually proposed a two-year tax cut with a possible third year to be "triggered" if budgetary factors allowed it. The trigger was a clever mechanism that allowed the Democrats to say they were for tax cuts but also fiscally responsible. The trigger would be pulled if Reagan administration projections for the deficit, interest rates, and inflation proved true in the third year. "We call it the 'take them at their word' trigger," one representative said.[19] Reagan said that this version gave more money back to the American worker "if you only plan on living for two years."[20] Overall, it was clear that the Democrats were pulled further in Reagan's direction than vice versa.

When the Republican bill moved to the Senate Finance Committee in late June, Chairman Robert Dole added a measure to index tax brackets to inflation to avoid bracket creep. In the 1970s, workers faced with inflation were sometimes able to get higher wages in compensation. But because tax brackets were not adjusted for inflation, in a progressive tax structure those higher wages moved the taxpayer into a higher tax bracket, so that the same wage in real terms was leading to a higher tax in real terms. It was a phenomenon that had been identified at least as far back as the Ford administration.[21] As the Associated Press explained it in 1978:

> Suppose you earned $15,000 last year. You're married, with two children; only one spouse works. Assume that at the beginning of this year you got a raise equal to the rate of inflation the government is predicting for 1978—7.4 per cent. Your 1978 earnings would be $16,610 . . . In theory, you should be able to keep pace with rising prices. In practice, however, taxes will slow you down. Your federal income tax bill goes up $239, and you pay $97 more in Social Security. In 1977, 15 per cent of your income went for federal income tax and Social Security; in 1978, 16 per cent of your income goes to the government. Because of the extra taxes, your $1,110 raise shrinks to $774. That $774 is not enough to offset inflation. If you measured your income in con-

stant 1977 dollars, you would find yourself with 1.2 per cent less this year than you had last year.[22]

The problem can be avoided if tax brackets rise in step with inflation—"indexing," in the parlance of the time.

Indexing had been a favored idea of Reagan's at least since the campaign, but he had not made it part of his original proposal.[23] Dole had been pushing the idea unsuccessfully for years and favored it because he thought Congress should have to face the pain of enacting tax increases rather than let them happen automatically.[24] The administration had not put indexing in the bill originally because of cost concerns, but by adding it as an amendment, Dole ensured that it wouldn't be counted as part of the costs of the bill in the first three years. Some argued that indexing was addressing a nonexistent problem, as it was easy for Congress to pass tax cuts to offset bracket creep if it wanted to. But because raising taxes is more difficult—forcing Congress to take responsibility for tax increases—indexing moved the debate onto terrain that was more favorable to Republicans. If automatic tax increases were not going to cover spending, then avoiding deficits would require either tax increases or cutting spending. Once indexing was in the spotlight, it proved impossible to make the political case for tax increases that occur without transparency and open debate. And Reagan and those who thought as he did must have hoped that when the choice was put before voters so clearly, they would prefer cutting spending.[25]

It was at this point, in July, that the media discussion of the tax cut became completely derailed by the "bidding war" that erupted between Democrats and Republicans trying to win swing voters over to their version of the plan. And indeed, the competition for votes was where most of the policymakers' efforts were spent on the tax cut issue. Instead of compromising and merging the two bills, each side decided it wanted not only a tax cut, but a big political win. The orthodox explanation for the size of the tax cut came to be that each side held out additional concessions to try to lure wavering legislators to its version of the bill, thus blowing up the size of the bill. Perhaps because of the appeal of the cut and thrust of political negotiation—Was Rostenkowski winning? How would Reagan save face? Which way were the boll-weevil Democrats and gypsy-moth Republicans leaning?—more ink has been poured on the passage of the bill through Congress than on any other aspect of the tax cut.

The "boll weevils" were a group of Southern Democrats who had made it clear to Reagan that they might cross party lines to vote for his tax cut—especially if the bill included concessions that would help Southern districts. To emphasize their persistence they named themselves after the infamous beetle that destroyed Southern cotton crops during the Depression: "People have been trying to eradicate boll weevils for a long, long time."[26] Seeing the boll weevils' success, a group of Northeastern Republicans, especially those from liberal-leaning districts, made it clear that they also might cross party lines to vote *against* Reagan's tax cut, *unless* the bill included concessions that would help Northeastern districts. These "gypsy moths" named themselves for a type of caterpillar that was destroying New England trees.[27]

To the congressional members involved, the stakes were high, and whether or not the president or the Democrats would respond to their particular demands became a test of each member's ability to deliver for his or her district. For a while, the Democrats thought they had won the whole bill because they were able to unite on offering more to oil interests—leading to Mickey Edwards's anguished cry that he might have to vote for the Democratic bill. The Republicans had originally wanted to keep their bill clean—without any extra concessions for specific constituencies—but they gave up the attempt. Eventually both sides gave significant concessions to oil as well as other interests, from small business to the high-tech industry, from savings and loans to real estate, from utilities to cattle ranchers, from mass transit and volunteer fire departments to adoptive parents of disadvantaged children.[28] "It would probably be cheaper if we gave everybody in the country three wishes," one policymaker grumbled.[29] The process fed on itself, because once it became clear the two sides were offering concessions, it would have been irresponsible for members of Congress not to attempt to get concessions for their constituents.

Because both renegade factions could credibly claim to be wavering between party loyalty and constituent interests—for the boll weevils, party loyalty would have them vote against Reagan but constituent interest would have them vote in favor, and vice versa for the gypsy moths—the Democrats and Republicans both courted them assiduously. The administration brought in Cabinet members and even the vice president to contact several dozen representatives, keeping careful tallies of the tone and substance of the discussions. The concerns expressed provided a microcosm of the debate around the tax cut and a glimpse into specific issues around the country.

For Charles Wilson of Texas, "issues affecting his state—oil and gas taxes, windfall profit tax—will be significant factors in making up his mind." On the other hand, Allen Ertel of Pennsylvania was specifically against "breaks for the oil producers." Margaret Heckler of Massachusetts considered the Democrats' proposal for a one-year write-off more helpful for small business. Several members thought that the Democrats' plan for a two-year tax cut with an optional third year made sense. William Goodling of Pennsylvania wanted "additional federal funding for the clean-up of Three Mile Island," the site of a 1979 nuclear accident. James Watt, contacting Carroll Hubbard of Kentucky, noted, "He needs to be stroked." Several members received multiple calls from multiple contacts, even on the same day. The first time Millicent Fenwick of New Jersey was contacted, on June 18, she said that she would support the president. At 11:30 AM on July 8, she "wants to be friendly and helpful but is sincerely concerned about budget deficit. Anxious to be convinced. Believes people in her home district are not really excited about the tax cut." By 7:40 PM that same day, another caller reported that she "will vote with us."[30] Marge Roukema of New Jersey was troubled by the deficit and said that "she has seen no numbers to prove our newest version" would be better for her district. Glenn Anderson of California, on July 13, felt that "the President is moving in the right direction," but requested a comparison of the Democrats' plan with the president's plan, which was duly delivered; a follow-up call found him "still undecided—truly so." Ben Bilman of New York "wants some help for his area. The Poughkeepsie Rail Bridge caught fire in the mid-70's. He wants Conrail to repair it. He is also interested in more mass transport aid for New York State, and more [Section 8] housing for his area." Ronald Mottl believed that the Democrats' bill was better for lower-income taxpayers. Stephen Neal of North Carolina worried that the "tax cuts will cause interest rates to stay excessively high." Many contacted members wanted to wait to compare the final versions from each side before committing. On July 14, John Myers of Indiana was saying flatly "I oppose Kemp-Roth."[31] A "Gypsy Moth Tentative Wish List" from late July noted that several congressional members had expressed "general uneasiness," while others were worried about which income groups the tax cut was skewed toward as well as the concessions for oil.[32]

The individual attention that Reagan paid to congressional members is worth noting, as low-level members of Congress were not used to such solicitousness. The team had already decided to be much more involved with Congress than Carter had been as president. Ken Duberstein remembered that staff members were "going to visit all 535 members of Congress. It was an important gesture, to open the door. . . . With some of the members my staff and I said, look, we realize you probably won't ever vote for Reagan but we want a relationship, we want you to pick up the phone and call us, we want to be helpful, and perhaps some day there is going to come a time where you can be helpful. That really took the place by storm. . . . The comments we were getting—boy isn't that a refreshing change." One Democrat commented to Duberstein, "Here it was just a couple of weeks into the administration and the president wanted to get acquainted with him and he was deeply honored by that. He pointed out to me that in the previous administration it had been almost two years before he had gotten in to have a private chat with the president, even of his own party." Duberstein remembered one congressman who "had served . . . six or seven terms in the house and it was the first time he had been in an oval office where the president of the United States had asked him what he thought. . . . And, if I'm not mistaken, on that upcoming vote . . . [he] in fact voted with the president."[33] Claude Pepper said in his thirty-three years in the House and Senate there had never been anything like it.[34]

In addition to systematically calling wavering congressional members, Reagan even invited several to Camp David, which was considered a great honor.[35] On one day in late July, Reagan met with several representatives individually or in small groups, including Silvio Conte, Sonny Montgomery, Buddy Roemer, Gus Yatron, Bob Young, Clarence Long, Phil Gramm, John Myers, Carl Pursell, Dan Daniel, Ron Dyson, Bill Nichols, Bob Stump, Bill Boner, and Bo Ginn. Some were wavering, and a legislative aide noted that "the Democratic leadership of the House has been wooing these members heavily."[36] Others were upset about the special concessions being given to oil, or about the potential effects of the package on industrialized areas. The administration countered that the Democratic bill had been driven only by the question "What can we put together to beat Ronald Reagan?"[37] Reagan sent handwritten notes, exhorted members with appeals to the general qualities of his legislation as well as to their own specific needs, and met with them personally when possible.[38] Frank Horton, a gypsy moth, noted that, "unlike most presidents," Reagan actually listened to congresspeople in his meetings with them. Newt Gingrich, a very junior congressman at that point, noted his appreciation for Reagan working with the Republican leadership in the House. Billy Evans, a boll weevil, was satisfied that conservative Democrats had helped to decide the contours of the final legislation.[39] One academic analysis found that 67 percent of the seventy-one Democrats in the House of Representatives who were targeted by the president—Reagan called each of them an average of six times—voted for his tax bill.[40]

Many of these legislators were surely responding to the needs of business in their constituencies, but they were also influenced by the general situation of their constituencies. Goodling of Pennsylvania, for example, succeeded in getting the funding for cleaning up Three Mile Island that he had been holding out for, and he also elicited a promise that the administration would not close a base in his district.[41] But even if these legislators were influenced by business interests, the overall role of business influence on the Reagan tax cuts is different from what we might think. It wasn't businesses pushing Reagan to implement a tax cut, but businesses having to be wooed with special favors to support the tax cut. Rather than supporting free market policies on principle, businesses were supporting particularistic interests. And far from adding individual tax cuts because they gave in to special-interest lobbying, the administration used the concessions as a way to convince special interests to support the individual cuts. Business interests were certainly able to unify and win political victories, for example on the concessions given to the oil industry. But they were not at the origins of the sequence that resulted in the individual tax rate cuts. We take up the theme of business influence on the ERTA more fully in the next chapter.

The bidding war promoted indexing from an amendment to inclusion in the full bill during this stage, but otherwise, it had little effect on the overall size of the bill.[42] The administration did make many concessions in order to attract the boll weevils and keep the gypsy moths and other politicians who needed or demanded other individual measures for their constituents. But all the concessions won through that bidding war did not actually increase the estimates of how much the bill would cost, nor did they add up to the most important part of the estimated revenue loss. The original bill had been expected to lead to a $487.7 billion revenue loss, and the bill that passed was expected to lead to a $480.6 billion revenue loss. The elements that were added in the bidding war were offset by a slight delay in the effective dates of the tax cut and slight reductions in both the individual and business tax cuts.[43] Despite the bidding war, the costliest part of the bill remained the Kemp-Roth individual tax rate reductions, the plank that had been there all along. Other exemptions were necessary to buy off legislators with specific interests who otherwise might not have supported the package of individual tax cuts.

In short, the summer-long bidding war had little effect on the overall size of the bill, and it mattered little in substantive terms whether Reagan won or the Democrats won. One congressional member noted that "the President has brought the whole Congress around," and that even if the Democratic bill were to win in the end, "it will be pretty much what [the] President wants."[44] By the end, both sides were promising large tax cuts.

Of course, in political terms, it was all-important whether the Democrats prevailed with their modified tax cut or whether Reagan's proposal prevailed. Had the Democrats won, it could have handed Reagan a major defeat on his signature issue, severely crippling his presidency just as it was getting started. He might not have been remembered for pioneering the politics of tax cuts at all. He could have tried to argue that he had maneuvered Democrats into a corner so that they had to promise larger tax cuts. But at this time the Republican Party was not yet the party of tax cuts, and this would have been a subtle and difficult case to make. Republicans might still have discovered the appeal of tax cuts eventually and used the issue to revive their party, but they would not have been able to burnish it with the potent combination of a popular issue and a successful president.

On July 27, two days before the House would decide between the administration and Democratic versions of the plan, Reagan gave another televised speech, this time explicitly asking viewers to call their representatives and senators. They complied: Capitol Hill received twice as many calls as usual, and Western Union reported a fourfold rise in telegrams. Immediately after Reagan's speech, one congressman heard from "two Marines, a doctor and a rural letter carrier" supporting the president. A Democrat, in explaining his decision to vote with Reagan, said, "The constituents broke our doors down. It wasn't very subtle."[45] "Even Tip O'Neill was saying 50 to 1," says Ken Duberstein. Congressman "Sam Hall of Texas called me and said Ken, I have to get out of the office . . . I'm all alone and my phones are lit up and everybody is calling me from home and this is only five minutes after the speech telling me support the president, support the president. Sam called back a few minutes later and said Ken it is now 20 to 1 or something like that, I've got to go home, I can't answer the phones." Some of this contact seems to have been orchestrated by business groups, which were now fully behind Reagan's plan. O'Neill complained that "Phillip Morris, Paine Webber, Monsanto Chemical, Exxon, McDonnell Douglas . . . were so kind as to allow the use of their staff to the president of the United States in flooding the switchboards of America."[46]

Both during the bidding war and at the final vote, we can see the influence of business interests—particularistic interests who managed to get specific provisions beneficial to business in particular regions, and more unified business interests working to convince congresspeople to vote for the bill. Nevertheless, it is worth noting exactly how *little* was decided in this final stage: the business interests were influential in determining whether a three-year tax cut would win, or whether a two-year tax cut with a third year trigger would win. When we take a step back from the heat of the battle and examine the stakes, it hardly seems much of a fight at all.

In the end, forty-eight Democrats abandoned their party to vote for the administration's bill.[47] The final plan was to forgo $749 billion in tax revenue over the next five years. The original plan to cut taxes ten percent for each of three successive years had been reduced to five percent the first year and ten percent each of the next two years, but otherwise the rate cuts were intact.[48] The tax cut passed in the House of Representatives on July 29, 1981, the same day as the wedding of England's Prince Charles to Lady Diana Spencer. Speaker of the House Tip O'Neill, grasping at the language of class politics for which the tax cut itself was sounding the death knell, said that it was "a big day for the aristocracies of the world."[49]

The polls showed that Americans did want a tax cut, but a smaller one than the Reagan tax cut. This led Democrats into a situation where they began to offer tax cuts of their own, rather than take a stance against tax cuts. And yet, those same polls also showed Americans approving of Reagan's overall economic program three-to-one. That was the fundamental force that pulled the Democrats closer and closer to Reagan's side.[50] Once the Democrats made the decision to offer an alternative tax cut rather than oppose tax cuts completely, it was clear the nation would embark on a big tax cut adventure.

Lou Cannon, one of the closest observers of Ronald Reagan, concluded: "Reagan has demonstrated once again in these first months of his presidency that it is always dangerous to underestimate him. This is not some Hollywood cowboy who has settled into the White House for early retirement, but a dedicated and serious politician who knows how to grasp the levers of power in the age of television. Reagan plays big-league politics. Even Tip O'Neill knows that now."[51] Others noted that Reagan's achievement was even greater than Lyndon Johnson's, because Johnson had been working with large Democratic majorities in Congress: "Republicans and Democrats alike now openly speculate about a party realignment in which the Democrats relinquish their majority status. . . . Republicans think they can increase their Senate majority and—with the help of the redistricting forced by the 1980 census—capture the House [in 1982]."[52]

When the tax cut bill passed, hundreds of well-wishers poured into Jack Kemp's office to shake his hand and thump his back, and buckets of champagne were produced as Kemp took a congratulatory call from Reagan.[53] He had already received a standing ovation in the House of Representatives earlier that day.[54] Kemp, Reagan, and the Republican Party had come a long way from 1974.

CHAPTER 7

How Ronald Reagan Betrayed Business

THE EVENTS OF 1981 have gone down in conservative myth as a triumph. But in the immediate aftermath of the policy, it seemed like a dramatic failure. After the plan passed and the extent of the deficit quickly became clear, financial markets tumbled, interest rates rose, the media communicated growing pessimism, and Reagan's popularity began to slide. GDP dropped 1.9 percent in 1982, and unemployment hit 9.7 percent, numbers that had not been seen since the 1930s and the 1940s.[1] Many observers, including many within the administration, worried that the rising deficit would lead government to compete for funds with private companies that wanted to expand, worsening interest rates and weakening the recovery. One reason the deficit went up more quickly than expected was that inflation was going down more quickly than expected—from 12.5 percent in 1980 to 4 percent in 1982. As a result, automatic tax increases from inflation were not arriving as planned; indexation was not scheduled to begin until 1985, and the Reagan administration had been counting on those early years of inflation-induced tax increases to get the budget back into balance.[2] All those years of systematically relying on the most optimistic projections caught up with them. When told of the situation, Reagan is said to have marveled, "then Tip O'Neill was right all along."[3]

There were still true believers arguing the need to stay the course, such as Martin Feldstein, who came up with ingenious after-the-fact rationalizations to try to claim that the plan was working,[4] and Jude Wanniski, who blamed Federal Reserve chairman Paul Volcker's tight money policy for any problems.[5]

But the administration panicked. Spooked by the deficit, Reagan and his team prepared to undo much of what they had done. As early as January 1982, every member of the Republican leadership except for Jack Kemp had concluded that the tax cuts needed to be scaled back.[6] In February 1982, the presidents of the American Bankers Association, the Mortgage Bankers Association, the National Association of Home Builders, the National Association of Realtors, and the U.S. League of Savings Associations and the chairman of the Mutual Savings Banks wrote to the president: "In order to bring interest rates down, immediate action must be taken to reduce massive federal budget deficits. More than anything else, it is the spectre of an overwhelming volume of deficit financing which haunts housing and financial markets and poses the threat of economic and financial conditions not seen since the 1930s. . . . There is no alternative to: (1) slowing down all spending, not excluding defense and entitlement programs; and, if necessary, (2) deferring previously enacted tax reductions or increasing taxes."[7] In March 1982, Senator Ernest Hollings moaned to the president that "our tragic situation is that the business community is refusing to take advantage of the supply-side business tax cuts of last year until it can be assured that deficits are reduced and the government will not be elbowing it out of the capital market."[8] Elizabeth Dole, who was conducting outreach with interest groups about an acceleration of the tax cuts, wrote that "business feels the tax cut will not provide the needed purchasing stimulus and, by increasing the deficit, will slow the reduction in interest rates. . . . The Business Roundtable, NAM, Realtors, Home Builders and Forest Products Industry are among the leaders in opposition to tax cut acceleration. The Chamber is modestly in favor, while [the National Federation of Independent Business] is a bit more bullish. The American Farm Bureau Federation supports tax cuts in theory, but do not feel this acceleration will help reduce interest rates, which is their current number one priority."[9] Like many observers, businesses feared that the individual tax cuts would increase deficits.

At a March meeting of the president's Economic Policy Advisory Board, the advisers agreed that high interest rates were the biggest problem, and that deficits were the main reason for high interest rates: "The financial markets are convinced that deficits and prospective deficits matter, regardless of the academic debate on the subject."[10] Former treasury secretary William Simon saw "bigger and bigger trouble" ahead if deficits were not brought under control, and former treasury secretary George Shultz "observed that the budget numbers are leaving people feeling hopeless."[11] Martin Anderson thought that other issues "pale by comparison" to the deficit. Herbert Stein argued that "large deficits will frustrate private investment and slow productivity growth" and Alan Greenspan argued that deficit reduction was a "necessary condition" to any economic recovery.[12] Indeed, the clear assumption of all the participants in the lead-up to the 1981 tax cut was that the tax cuts would immediately be followed by spending cuts and that the deficit would come under control in a few years. The administration's assumption seems to have been that the tax cut would put immediate pressure on Congress to pass spending cuts, thus *preventing* a deficit.

When this did not happen, the administration soon entered the battle to increase taxes in order to close the deficit. In 1982, a year after passing the largest tax cut in American history, the administration oversaw the passage of the largest peacetime tax increase in American history, the Tax Equity and Fiscal Responsibility Act (TEFRA) of 1982. How the battle over the TEFRA proceeded is one of the most surprising elements of the story, for it shows Reagan—the free market president we think of as the most committed to the interests of business—fighting against business interests.

Business versus Kemp-Roth

Recently many scholars have argued that free market policies are the result of a concerted effort by organized business to beat back state intervention. David Harvey is perhaps the best known source of this argument.[13] Jacob Hacker and Paul Pierson as well as Lawrence Lessig have also made versions of this claim.[14] Another influential scholar, Kim Phillips-Fein, writes that "the most striking and lasting victories of the right have come in the realm of political economy rather than that of culture"; she also notes that many businesspeople were involved in the coalition that helped Reagan get elected.[15]

Both of these things are true: the major victories of the right have concerned economic policy, and business was involved in Reagan's coalition. The unarticulated implication here is that business wanted and pushed for

Figure 7.1 Revenue Loss from the Economic Recovery Tax Act, 1981–1986, as Projected in 1981

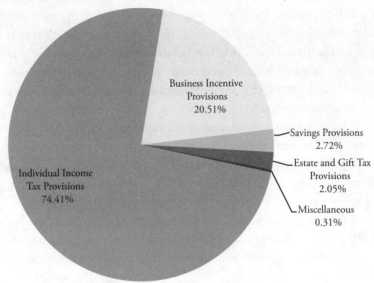

Source: Joint Committee on Taxation 1981.

the economic policies that Reagan implemented. But in the case of individual income tax cuts, this is not true.

To understand this point, it is necessary to rewind the story and retrace the passage of the ERTA from the point of view of business interests. As discussed briefly in chapter 1, the ERTA had two main parts: a tax cut for individuals and a tax cut for business (alongside indexation of taxes and a host of more minor elements). There is no doubt that business wanted the tax cut for business. But cutting tax rates for individuals was the largest part of the plan, projected to lead to the largest revenue loss, as seen in figure 7.1.[16]

The cut for business mainly involved allowing deductions in taxes for business expenses. When a firm purchases new equipment, it is allowed to deduct the amount of that purchase from its tax obligations, since the purchase is seen as a cost of doing business and the assets will wear out in the course of use. This deduction has been allowed since the beginning of the corporate income tax in 1909. But exactly how the deduction should be timed has not been clear. One way to do it is called "straight-line" deduction—simply spreading out the deduction over the life of the machine.

Thus, for a machine that lasts ten years, a deduction of one-tenth of the machine's value would be allowed each year. Straight-line deduction was the standard practice starting in 1934. However, because the value of most machines declines very rapidly in the first few years, the rule before 1981 was that firms could take the bulk of the deduction in the first few years, in what was called "declining balance" depreciation.[17] The system was complex and required that the taxpayer make a complicated decision about the life expectancy of assets and defend that decision if the IRS decided to audit: "This led to a great deal of confusion, needless litigation and conflicting court decisions."[18] Most importantly, inflation was wreaking havoc with the system, because deductions were based on the nominal cost of the old piece of equipment, even though it cost much more now to replace it. In effect, businesses were being taxed for profits that they were not actually making.[19]

"Accelerated depreciation" or the accelerated cost recovery system (ACRS), the rules proposed by business that were eventually adopted as part of the ERTA, allowed companies to take deductions even faster and simplified the deduction rules.

Companies preferred a system of faster deductions because it meant their cash flows were not tied up, they were not paying interest on loans, and— most importantly in the context of the 1970s— their money was not losing value to inflation. The Kennedy administration had liberalized depreciation in its own efforts to stimulate growth. Since the 1970s accelerated depreciation had been the main lobbying issue for business interests, including the Business Roundtable, the Chamber of Commerce, and the National Association of Manufacturers (NAM).[20] The accelerated depreciation provision that ultimately became part of the 1981 tax bill came to be called "10-5-3" because it allowed firms to write off buildings over the course of ten years, machinery over the course of five years, and cars and trucks in just three years.[21] And "under the new system, the guess work of determining the useful life of the asset to be depreciated is eliminated. . . . The taxpayer will have a precise set of rules in determining the annual depreciation deduction for each asset and much less unnecessary litigation."[22] The savings were substantial. Treasury estimated that under ACRS as originally planned the tax savings on a factory worth $100,000 would have been $30,000 over ten years.[23] An administration document noted: "the incentive to invest in new equipment is enormous." It was not obvious that the business community could unify on the issue, as small businesses do not have such large investments and do not benefit as much from depreciation, and other sectors such as finance, housing, and high tech were divided. Eventually a coalition was forged because the simplicity of the formula meant reduction in accounting costs and fewer worries over whether claims would be audited or penalized.[24]

Although not all observers were convinced that accelerated depreciation would have large effects on economic growth, it was a policy that received support from across the political spectrum, including from Keynesian economists such as Walter Heller and Joseph Pechman.[25]

ACRS was the centerpiece of business lobbying, but business groups were not fans of Kemp-Roth. Businesses did not hesitate to make their preferences known, and consequently business opposition to Kemp-Roth has been clear to scholars examining the media record. A former head of the Business Roundtable said, "Kemp-Roth is political rhetoric. Neither Kemp nor Roth are economists or students of the economy. They're politicians. And they arrived at a formula that had a ring to it, and it played politically, and they milked it. But it ought to be discarded now. . . . You can't really commit the country to 30 percent tax cuts for individuals and believe that the Laffer curve is going to save you."[26] The head of the National Association of Manufacturers said Kemp-Roth provided "too much of a stimulus to private consumption" and would be inflationary, and wanted business tax cuts instead.[27] The NAM's chief economist thought the only way to cure inflation was to go through recession: "There's no other way to do it. . . . We'll have to go through a painful period."[28] The president of the International Chamber of Commerce called Kemp-Roth "most dangerous."[29] When George H. W. Bush called supply-side voodoo economics, he was not just engaging in primary season sniping but reflecting the sentiments of the business world.[30]

Kemp complained:

Reagan's appeal is not to the Fortune 500. . . . It never was. He's a populist. . . . We got no support on Kemp-Roth originally from the National Association of Manufacturers and the Business Roundtable because they felt a zero-sum trade-off would occur. Why help the entrepreneur? Why help the investor? Why help the equity market? Why help venture capital? Ultimately—and I'm not accusing them of saying this—but you could make a case that with a healthy venture capital market, in a real spirit of entrepreneurship in America, there would be a heck of a lot more competition for IBM and Du Pont and the other majors. I'm probably going to regret some of the things I've said. I don't like to get into names.[31]

Observers noted that "big business wants to cut spending first (except subsidies to business), business taxes next, and personal taxes last, if at all. Its leaders have frequently warned that Kemp-Roth would be irresponsible or inflationary."[32] At one point during the negotiations, when the business tax cuts were weakened, the chief economist of the Chamber of Commerce complained that "we supported you" on Kemp-Roth, despite business's initial opposition to the policy, and weakening business tax cuts now would be a betrayal. The Reagan administration, in its turn, was testy: at an acrimonious meeting Donald Regan asked business groups if they really needed more when the administration "is voting down food stamps, against the halt, the blind and the poor." Proponents of ACRS opposed Kemp-Roth, and vice versa: supply-siders argued that 10-5-3 privileged capital-intensive firms.[33]

The business view against Kemp-Roth was known within the administration. For example, one internal document rounded up objections from various business voices as well as quotes from well-placed economists calling the plan "an invitation to financial disaster" and conservatives arguing that tax cuts would "touch off an inflationary explosion that would wreck the country and everyone on a fixed income."[34] A letter from the business lobbyist John Davidson gives some of the background of the business push for capital-oriented tax policy and reiterates opposition to Kemp-Roth: "Unfortunately, the original Kemp bill was more of a general tax relief bill than it was a bill to release capital from excessive taxation."[35] A letter notes that Henry Kaufman of Salomon Brothers was testifying to Congress that "in this inflationary setting, across-the-board tax reductions are exceptionally dangerous."[36]

The major business groups had originally supported John Connally of Texas during the primaries. Reagan had said that "he would be the candidate of the entrepreneur, the farmer, the small businessman, the independent," rather than of big business.[37] But after spending $10 million and managing to win only one delegate—Ada Mills of Arkansas, whom newspapers quickly dubbed the "ten-million-dollar delegate"—Connally quietly folded in March 1980 and Reagan picked up his big business backers.[38]

One of these backers was the influential business lobbyist Charls Walker, who had been Connally's chief economic adviser. Walker's mother had given him his unusual first name because she did not want people to call him Charlie and for some reason thought dropping the *e* would prevent that. Inevitably, he was now known to everyone as Charlie.[39] A regular newsletter he sent to clients gives glimpses into Walker's thinking in the late 1970s. In 1977, he imagined the ideal tax reform that Carter should promote, which would include both business and individual tax cuts, but most of his discussion centered on business tax cuts. His brief discussion of individual cuts was limited to changing a particular exemption to a credit and lowering the top tax rate from 70 percent to 50 percent; across-the-board rate cuts were not on the menu anywhere.[40] In fact, later that year Walker specifically came out against a tax cut for "low- and middle-income consumers" because it would be inflationary.[41] In 1978, he, like others in the business community, was obsessed with changing tax laws "to promote the capital formation which increases productivity—the best and only true long-run antidote to inflation"; on individual taxes, his main complaint was against attempts to increase progressivity.[42] In November 1978, Walker was gratified that "there was wide agreement, even from dedicated Congressional liberals, that taxes should be cut to promote productive investment."[43] By 1979, he was intrigued by the developing Kemp-Roth proposal, but thought it could work only if coupled with tight spending controls.[44]

Walker's opinions mirrored those of the business community more broadly. In the meetings of the National Association of Manufacturers, across-the-board cuts for individuals were mentioned in passing, but the focus was on corporate rate reductions, depreciation reform, value-added tax, the double taxation of dividends, and other issues affecting businesses.[45] As late as 1980, NAM had nothing to say about individual tax rate cuts when discussing taxes.[46] Similarly, after Kemp and others had started their push on rate cuts, the Chamber of Commerce came out in support, but from 1977 through 1982 the organization mainly focused on corporate tax cuts.[47] In November 1978, the Chamber's chief economist was pushing for budget balance, not across-the-board rate cuts.[48] In February 1979, the Chamber proposed that Congress "adopt the principle of a budget balanced over the course of the business cycle, running surpluses in periods of strong growth in the private sector of the economy and deficits only in periods of slack growth. To maintain a growing economy, balance should be achieved at the lowest government expenditure level which will provide essential public services and meet the requirements of national security."[49] Only in February 1980—long after the decisions had been made within the Reagan campaign on across-the-board rate cuts in individual taxes—did the Chamber note, after several paragraphs on investment and capital formation, that "general tax relief for individuals in the form of across-the-board reductions in individual income taxes also deserves high priority."[50] The Chamber represented small business, and its greater support of supply-side policy reflects the fact that its members often filed their taxes as individuals and stood to gain from Kemp-Roth. Other business groups not so favorable to supply-side groused about how close the administration had gotten to the Chamber: "To ignore other parts of [the business] coalition, including NAM, the Business Roundtable, the National Federation of Independent Business, and the American Business Conference, is to deny the President a full spectrum of business views," the president of the NAM complained.[51] But even the Chamber offered only cautious acceptance, and not until 1980.

As Reagan locked up the primary nomination, he again tried to bring business on board.[52] His campaign team set up a "Business Advisory Panel." But relations between the Business Advisory Panel and the campaign deteriorated to such a point that the organizer of the panel worried that it would "create more bad publicity for the campaign [and] create ill will among the participants. . . . Even among the acceptances, there has been considerable doubt about the Panel itself. . . . Serious skepticism about whether Governor Reagan is serious about wanting substantive input on issues. They still feel he is not interested in substance. . . . [They fear] that the participants are being used as a public relations gimmick and that the Governor or his staff will not utilize the input."[53]

Reagan met with the group to try to assuage these concerns. After several minutes of venting about the federal government's adversarial approach to business, overregulation, and assorted business complaints, the conversation turned to taxes and the gathered businessmen made their opposition to Kemp-Roth clear. Ed Zschau, a computer industry CEO, contended that a personal income tax cut would "decrease revenues and contribute to inflation," and he argued for a tax cut that would "stimulate investment" instead—a business tax cut. Another participant argued that inflation had been caused by a "consumption bias in this nation since 1966," and that a

personal income tax cut would worsen such a bias; what was needed instead
were policies that would rebuild the "infrastructure and capital base" of the
country.[54] The panel was right to think that the governor was uninterested
in hearing their opinions, and Reagan remained unshakably committed to
Kemp-Roth.

Charlie Walker was the key figure in bringing the ACRS and Kemp-Roth
wings together. First, he got Reagan to commit to ACRS through a per-
sistent campaign in the spring of 1980 over the objections of Kemp and
other advisers.[55] Although these advisers didn't want ACRS, fearing it as
competition to Kemp-Roth, ACRS was popular across the political spectrum at this point; and with ACRS, Walker could try to convince business
to support the plan, whereas without it, business support was a nonstarter.
Then, Walker managed to persuade the business community to support
Reagan's plan,[56] particularly by downplaying the supply-side rationale, and
playing up the argument that tax cuts would simply prevent the government
from generating surplus revenue. Walker actually claims to have invented
this argument, providing "the key memo" that shifted the rationale from
Laffer curve arguments about tax cuts paying for themselves, to the argument that the tax cut was just preventing large surpluses. This would become a common refrain for the whole effort. "I studied the budget messages
and happened to look out at a five-year projection," Walker said. "Lord,
over half a trillion dollars in revenues projected for five years! That's annual
revenues, not accumulated. If we get just a modicum of control of domestic
spending, we can use those revenues to cut taxes. The thrust of my memorandum was not that we would cut taxes and get more revenues to cover a
tax increase. [Instead] we would not cut spending, just reduce its rate of
increase to the size of the economy, relatively speaking, where it was back
during the Kennedy administration. You got revenues coming out your ears,
both to cut taxes and increase defense spending." This argument, and Walker's presence on Reagan's team, reassured business: "The Business Roundtable doesn't know Reagan, and they tend to identify him with right-wing
positions and extremism," Walker noted. "But the publicity that me and
George Shultz and these moderates are in there, and that these wild men
who touted [radical] tax cuts are shunted aside, makes them feel a lot better."[57] The Reagan team was already committed to tax cuts, and Walker's
role was to help persuade business groups, which until then had been skep-

tical about the tax cuts, to support Reagan. The cuts they agreed to were not that different in size from what had been originally proposed; it was only the rationale that had shifted.

When examined carefully, claims that business played a powerful role in bringing about the 1981 tax cuts often boil down to the business community's success in ensuring that ACRS was included in the 1981 tax bill. For example, Hacker and Pierson write that corporate lobbyists "literally wrote many of the key provisions influencing business in the new president's proposals" in the tax cut of 1981; they also call the tax cut "an astonishing acceleration of the . . . formula of big tax cuts for business and the affluent. . . . Ronald Reagan's greatest legislative triumph, a fundamental rewriting of the nation's tax laws in favor of winner-take-all outcomes."[58] Hacker and Pierson do not provide specific citations of provisions written into the bill by business, but they reference Mark Blyth, and the provision Blyth mentions in the cited passage is ACRS.[59] Hacker and Pierson's work is an index of the extent to which the debate on business power and tax policy comes down to business groups' successful implementation of ACRS. For Hacker and Pierson, it is a prime example of how business interests took over Washington. Indeed, it is the only example they give regarding the Reagan tax cut. For Citizens for Tax Justice, ACRS was equivalent to "the virtual elimination of the corporate income tax as a significant source of federal tax revenue."[60]

ACRS was certainly driven by business, but there was wide support for it as a strategy for reviving the economy. The nonpartisan Office of Technology Assessment (OTA) thought that "accelerated depreciation in tax credits could drain government revenues," but also predicted that "in time a healthy industry will result."[61] Indeed, accelerated depreciation was popular enough that one Senate candidate successfully used his opponent's failure to support it as a campaign issue.[62] During the 1980 campaign, even the Carter camp, which had critiques of 10-5-3, nevertheless noted that "there is almost universal agreement that our tax structure is biased against investment. . . . Unlike a business investment oriented business tax cut, a personal income tax cut will be expensive when first implemented. Although a personal income tax will have some 'supply effect,' and may result in somewhat higher personal savings, it will not have as great an impact on productivity, and ultimately, inflation as a business tax cut." Carter said: "The first important step we can take to revitalize America's economy is to provide incentives for greater private investment," and "We need a major increase in depreciation allowances to promote investment in modern plants and equipment." His plan for acceleration was so drastic that the auto and steel industries would actually have received money from the government.[63] Even when public sentiment in favor of a general tax cut fell in the summer of 1980, "the one tax cut voters favor at the federal level is 'to allow business to claim depreciation on investment made in new plant and other expansion more quickly, which would not be as inflationary as certain other tax cuts.'" The ACRS was "favored by a substantial 64–26 percent," an increase from the previous year.[64]

Critics of the measure noted that "depreciation of any kind is basically for the well-off, because one must have money to buy vehicles and equipment before one can depreciate them. For that matter, even the kind of investment tax credit included in the plan presumes profitability, since unless one has earning and is therefore paying a tax, one can hardly take credits against it."[65] To address these issues, the tax bill set up a clever system by which companies could buy and sell depreciation benefits, but this only ended up getting the administration in trouble, because it allowed some firms to end up with zero or negative tax liabilities until the administration walked the provision back.[66]

Investing in Europe

Besides all of the reasons discussed already, businesses also wanted ACRS for another reason: depreciation schedules were much more generous in other countries. The business press was rife with articles pointing out that "in Japan and France, business can write off one-third of the price of a new piece of industrial machinery in the first year for tax purposes. In West Germany, the first year write-off is 17 per cent. Although Congress last year voted adoption of a 7 per cent investment tax credit and accelerated depreciation rules, we are far from reaching the kind of tax write-offs enjoyed by our competitor nations."[67] Observers suggested that this was one reason investment was lower in the United States than in other countries.[68]

In fact, businesses had been aware of European benefits for business investment as far back as the 1960s, when it became clear that European wages were lower (even when the costs of welfare spending were included), while for corporations, "the tax structure is complex but generally lower than in the United States. Depreciation allowances are quick and are attractive to firms who wish to build up their capital."[69]

To meet these problems Kennedy's Treasury secretary, C. Douglas Dillon, had proposed tax credits for business, arguing to Congress that

> the United States for some years had been putting a smaller percentage of its gross national product into machinery and equipment than any major industrial nation—about half as much as devoted to this purpose in West Germany, only three fourths of that of the United Kingdom, and about 60 per cent as much as the combined average of the European members of the Organization for European Economic Development. It is not surprising, therefore . . . that the average annual rate of growth in the United States in the decade of the 1950's was only 3 per cent compared with more than 7 per cent in West Germany and a range of 4 to 6 per cent in other industrial countries of Western Europe.[70]

In 1962, *New York Times* readers were treated to a startling comparison of capital costs. In the United States, machines that had been bought in 1946 for $100 stayed on the books for $100, even though such machinery would cost $200 in 1962. In the Netherlands, on the other hand, plant and equipment and inventories were quoted at replacement value, while in Denmark accelerated depreciation was at the discretion of the company, within some constraints, to such an extent that the Copenhagen Telephone Company had depreciated away all its tax liabilities for "the foreseeable future."[71]

One reason for the significant use of accelerated depreciation in Europe, as we will discuss in chapter 9, is the much different economic situation and world-historical role of European countries compared to the United States for much of the twentieth century. Starting in the 1960s, the Common Market countries used accelerated depreciation in their efforts to attract American capital. For example, in 1966 Belgium put forward a package of policies aimed at luring investors, including low-cost loans, property tax exemptions, and accelerated depreciation, with the goal "to create a psychological impact and provoke a new stream of investments, Belgian and foreign, toward certain regions of the country." The government had the discretion to allow "a double rate of depreciation for three years" under the new law.[72] European countries were outdoing each other with investment credits; accelerated depreciation became a favored policy.[73]

In Sweden, since 1938, corporations had been allowed to "depreciate machinery and equipment according to any schedule they preferred, including a *100 percent first-year write-off.* This was intended as a stimulus to industrial domestic investment and a means by which companies could offset taxes in high profit years against investments made in previous years. . . . This made the system more flexible for companies and further stabilized their investment and employment decisions." As the political scientist Sven Steinmo notes, the depreciation schedules and other pro-capitalist elements of Swedish tax policy were supported by Social Democrats, even though they benefited the wealthy, because Social Democrats "firmly believed that the most important forces which have contributed to income equalization in Sweden have been high growth, full employment, and the generous social welfare programs for which Sweden is so famous. Rather than use corporate taxation as another means of squeezing the rich, corporate tax policy has instead been used as an instrument of government economic policy."[74]

Sweden may be an extreme case, but Great Britain also allowed faster depreciation than the United States did. After the Second World War, a system of capital allowances was implemented to help industry recover from the destruction of war. In 1946, plant and machinery were given a 20 percent deduction the first year and then a 25 percent deduction the following years. Starting in 1954, agricultural and industrial buildings could be written off over ten years, and plant and machinery could be written off in four to seven years. In 1971, this was further reduced to just four years for plant and machinery. Most notably, a 100 percent first-year write-off was available in certain cases and was known to be used even where it did not technically apply. Although these rates and rules were tightened later, when American business groups were writing ACRS into the tax provisions businesses in the United States were at a disadvantage compared to businesses in Great Britain. In the United States, write-offs were thirty years for buildings, ten years for machinery, and three and a half years for vehicles. In Great Britain, by contrast, write-offs were 50 percent for buildings in the first year, followed by a 4 percent per year depreciation, and 100 percent in the first year for machinery. Only vehicle depreciation was similar to the United States, with a four-year write-off period.[75]

In France, depreciation rates in 1975 were 5 percent for buildings, 10 to 20 percent for machinery, and 20 to 25 percent for vehicles, which under the straight-line method then in use translated to a twenty-year write-off for buildings, a five- to ten-year write-off for machinery, and a four- to five-year write-off for vehicles. Additional provisions led to even faster depreciation for some machinery, as well as accelerated depreciation for buildings whose use met certain provisions. Although before ACRS the United States had faster depreciation for vehicles (three and a half years compared to France's four to five years), before ACRS France had faster depreciation for buildings and machinery (thirty years and ten years, respectively, in the United States versus twenty years for buildings and five to ten years for machinery in France).[76]

Germany had depreciation schedules similar to those in the United States before ACRS for machinery and vehicles and much slower depreciation for buildings, but a host of other provisions speeded up depreciation: for example, taxpayers could elect a declining balance method that accelerated depreciation to twice the rate as under the straight-line method, small assets could be written off completely in the first year, and special depreciation was available for purchases that met other goals, such as development in areas near the border with East Germany.[77]

In short, in pushing for faster depreciation—the centerpiece of what scholars have identified as the policies influenced by business in Reagan's tax cut—American capitalists were not out of line with the norm for capital depreciation in other countries, and in fact they were struggling to catch up with the much more generous depreciation schedules in Sweden and Great Britain. In 1981, American capitalists schemed and fought and successfully implemented a policy that was much less generous than what Social Democratic Sweden had offered its capitalists since 1938. American capitalists were governed by depreciation schedules that were nowhere near the flexible schedules—allowing even complete write-off in the first year—offered to Swedish firms. And European depreciation policy, far from being an aberration, was consistent with the larger approach to the taxation of capital in Europe. Reagan argued in a 1978 radio address before he became president, "Our competitors in world trade such as Japan and West Germany—even Sosocialist [sic] England—have no tax on long term capital gains."[78] The result, as he told another radio audience the following year: "In West Germany, Japan and France the increase in per-man hour productivity is twice as great as it is in our own country. It is *almost* twice as great in Italy. . . . We are reinvesting as a percentage of our Gross National Product less than half of what those other countries are investing in research and development. The figures are the same for investment to replace or upgrade aging plants and equipment."[79]

It is worth repeating that capital depreciation is not an obscure issue: it was the central goal of business mobilization in the 1970s. And since the late 1970s and early 1980s are identified by scholars as the peak moment of business mobilization success in contemporary times, this is the key concession that American businesses won through their extensive mobilization efforts.[80]

Winning and Losing on the ACRS

Once they convinced Reagan to adopt ACRS, and were convinced by Walker not to worry about the deficits, business leaders did come to support the entire tax plan. It was always a tenuous arrangement, as again and again the administration seemed to back away from 10-5-3 to make the numbers add up—for example, in the September 1980 "mirrors" speech[81] and again as late as June 1981: "The abrupt and unexpected concession left business's Washington spokesmen sputtering."[82] But in the end tensions were smoothed over, 10-5-3 remained part of the plan, and when Reagan presented his package to the public, business groups as well as executives from individual companies lobbied intensely for it, although their testimony to Congress was significantly more in favor of ACRS than of Kemp-Roth.[83] In 1981, ninety-eight business policy organizations testified in hearings before the House Budget Committee on the tax cut, of which sixty-seven explicitly endorsed ACRS and only twenty-four explicitly endorsed Kemp-Roth. Fifty-nine such organizations were represented before the Senate Finance Committee, of which forty-nine explicitly endorsed ACRS and only eighteen explicitly endorsed Kemp-Roth.[84] Business supported the program, but its particular preferences were clear.

And then, as soon as the ERTA was signed, the deficit skyrocketed. The economic projections had proven worse than predicted. By some accounts, some in the administration had known the deficit would be much worse than expected even before the tax cut bill passed and had chosen to keep silent about it.[85] Ultimately the administration had to pay for having systematically selected the most favorable numbers. They had gotten the plan to add up in the way one tries to stuff a few too many clothes into a suitcase; for a brief while the clasps held, and then they sprang open.

Seeing the situation, the administration decided to raise taxes. But the tax cuts for individuals—the Kemp-Roth plank that business had opposed—were sacrosanct; instead, it was the business tax cuts that were scaled back.[86] Reagan refused to listen to business groups' suggestions for restoring budget balance. He categorically rejected proposals to cut defense spending, so business leaders began to press for cutting back the supply-side tax cuts. In 1982, the chairman of the Business Roundtable led a group of members in trying to convince the administration to scale back the personal individual income tax cuts, arguing that any benefits of lower personal marginal rates were swamped by deficit concerns. Instead, Reagan's team put together a plan that would address the deficit by *raising taxes on corporations:* the administration took back many ERTA provisions for corporations, including about one-third of the ACRS.[87] This decision was the fruit of a thorough quest inside the administration and Congress for ways to raise revenue. The Senate Finance Committee had made twenty-five proposals, which they divided into three categories based on how much they objected to each. The Council of Economic Advisers sounded out each proposal and prepared arguments in favor and arguments against.[88] In the beginning, they stated the condition that "no changes in ACRS schedules or personal income tax rates" would be made. "These are the two basic components of the President's tax program. Revising them would mean a retreat from last year's victory,"[89] they wrote. In the end, however, they did retreat from ACRS.

As the plan wound its way through Congress, business representatives were divided over the question of which was more important, cutting corporate taxes or balancing the budget, and although some business leaders stuck with Reagan, many abandoned him. The administration tried to appeal to business leaders by arguing that Reagan needed to raise these taxes for political reasons, and that it would "be some time before you will encounter a President who so strongly shares your convictions." In other words, business should support these antibusiness measures because they came from a probusiness president. The Roundtable did eventually endorse Reagan's program, but with, as they put it, "serious reservations." At the Chamber of Commerce, the dispute was more bitter. The Chamber's president, Richard Lesher, was unconvinced of the need for deficit reduction at all, and the organization nearly split over the issue when a more proadministration faction, led by W. Paul Thayer, came out in favor of the president's plan. Reagan announced that the administration would work with the Chamber only through Thayer and later rewarded Thayer with a post as deputy defense secretary—an example of the tools available to a president to oppose business interests when necessary. Eventually the administration was able to cobble together a business coalition in support of its plan by appealing to industries for which capital accumulation was a less relevant issue. Benjamin Waterhouse notes that the president personally lobbied the lobbyists, telephoning business leaders to ask them to call Congress on behalf of the bill. The bill narrowly cleared Congress, and Reagan signed the largest peacetime tax increase in the nation's history.[90]

Waterhouse argues that business executives focused on accelerated depreciation over personal income tax cuts, even though personal income tax cuts would have helped them, because the executives involved were all professional managers of firms and thus benefited more from their firm's long-term stability than they would have from individual tax cuts. In later years, as business executives increasingly came to their positions fresh from business school rather than after rising through a firm's ranks, loyalty to specific firms lessened; also, as inflation waned and new regimes of executive compensation rewarded business leaders for short-term increases in stocks, the intense focus on accelerated depreciation faded away.[91]

In sum, far from leading Reagan toward tax cuts, business accepted the Kemp-Roth tax cuts that Reagan wanted in return for corporate tax cuts. When Reagan raised taxes on business afterwards, business felt betrayed. Of course, businesses did get something from the tax cuts. Even after the business tax cuts were scaled back, the tax cut for business stood at around 11 percent—still a huge gain. But even nonpartisan analysts had concluded at the time that incentives for investment would help to revitalize the economy, particularly given that other countries had much more generous depreciation schedules for business. And crucially, business was not behind the ERTA provision that represented the largest revenue loss—the individual tax cuts. Indeed, business opposed that part of the policy, but was powerless to prevent it. Individual tax cuts would remain the unshakable center of politics and policy for several decades. The Tax Equity and Fiscal Responsibility Act of 1982 scaled back much of the ERTA's tax provisions for business, but it did not touch the marginal tax rates that were the centerpiece of the individual income tax cuts.[92]

Some have suggested that across-the-board individual rate cuts were a "Trojan horse" for what the administration really wanted—business tax cuts and cuts in top tax rates. This idea stems from a comment made by OMB director David Stockman to a journalist.[93] It is easily disproved: in fact, the cut in the top tax rate from 70 percent to 50 percent was not part of the official program as presented by Reagan in February 1981, despite the supply-side arguments about marginal tax rates, because Ed Meese had convinced Reagan that such a reduction would be perceived as biased toward the rich. It was Democrats on the House Ways and Means Committee who brought the top tax rate cut back in, having concluded that it would cost very little and that they had bipartisan support for it.[94] And as we have seen, when push came to shove, it was the business tax cuts that gave way, whereas the supposed "Trojan horse," the individual tax cuts, remained.

Moreover, as an internal memo noted, "if the Reagan tax cut were really a 'Trojan horse' to cut taxes for the rich and businessmen. . . . Reagan would have accepted the Democrats' compromise." In the spring of 1981, during the negotiations, the Democrats had suggested giving more of the tax cuts to business and the wealthy, and less to everyone else, than Reagan had wanted.[95] This was an attempt on the part of the Democrats to keep down the size of the revenue loss. It was a perfectly rational alternative proposal, in both substantive and political terms—target the tax cuts where they would have the most effect on savings, investment, and productivity, and keep the overall costs down to keep the budget balanced.

But Republicans responded to this compromise proposal as if it were radioactive: "What an anticlimax," Kemp fulminated. "What an embarrassment for Democrats who are concerned about the state of our economy. . . . Perhaps [Rostenkowski] thinks that only the wealthy respond to incentives. They do; but so do all Americans."[96] Note the distance that Kemp had traveled: his Jobs Creation Act of 1974 had focused largely on business tax cuts and did not contain individual tax rate cuts for the middle classes. In 1975, he was arguing—with the same conviction that he always brought to his arguments—that "the highest priority of our economy should lie in the nurture and stimulation of capital formation for corporations, for small business, for farmers because everything the American people want and need grows out of that capital formation."[97] But now he was mortally offended by the suggestion that taxes be cut for business and the wealthy only. At the beginning of the process, Republicans did want a tax cut that privileged investment, but the route they had traveled had brought them to a point where they were now committed to across-the-board cuts for the middle classes—even when narrow investment tax cuts that would have benefited business alone were politically within reach. They didn't want those cuts as much as they wanted political victory.

Democrats' other strategies to appeal to business were equally unsuccessful. At one point, Democrats offered business a substantially better deal than ACRS, endorsing "expensing"—writing off the entire cost of an investment in the first year—plus lower corporate income taxes. One observer said, "If you'd told me a few years ago that the Democrats would propose expensing, I would have said you were out of your mind." But business lobbyists stuck with the Republican plan, uncertain if they could trust the suddenly business-friendly Democrats.[98] "You dance with him that brung ya," one lobbyist explained.[99] The dynamic here is not of Democrats being pressured by business, but Democrats attempting to woo business in order to get political credit for the tax cut.

Business supported Reagan. This much of the business dominance interpretation is true. But Reagan did not always support business, nor did he always do what business wanted him to do. The story of the tax cut is not a story of business groups persuading Reagan to do what they wanted, but rather, of Reagan persuading business to support what he wanted and then—after he had gotten the policy he wanted—abandoning business interests and scaling back the policy he had given them.

Can Kemp-Roth be seen as an instance of the structural power of business, when policymakers take actions that benefit business without businesses needing to lobby for them, or even over the objections of business interests—"saving capitalism from the capitalists"? Reagan, Kemp, and everyone involved certainly wanted American businesses to prosper. But so did most Americans, and as most Americans also did not want nationalization, it's difficult to distinguish between an argument that business was structurally powerful and an argument that policymakers were simply responding to the preferences of their constituents. Moreover, the disagreements between the administration and the business groups and other politicians on precisely *what* would lead to business prosperity suggest that it is not easy to determine how to help businesses even when one wants to.[100]

Clearly, this story does show business influence: businesses were able to unify around a highly visible policy that was of great benefit to them—contradicting arguments that they are unable to unify,[101] or unable to do so on highly visible issues. They were able to get that policy into the program over the hesitations of some of the key politicians and help rally Congress members to vote for the program. Even after the business tax cuts were scaled back, they represented a clear and substantial victory for business mobilization.

Just as clearly, this story shows the limits of business influence. American business groups were struggling for something that Social Democratic countries offered their businesses as a matter of course. Most importantly, business influence is not enough to explain the origins of Kemp-Roth, the largest part of the tax cut bill. Business actually opposed this part of the bill, but could not prevent it. If we want a full explanation of the tax cut, we have to look beyond business power.

CHAPTER 8

After Reagan

IN 1982, IN the middle of what would retrospectively be called the Reagan Revolution, there was no Reagan Revolution. In fact, Reagan seemed to have fallen into Tip O'Neill's trap. After the tax increases of 1982, the outcome was almost exactly what O'Neill had predicted, and wanted: a smaller tax cut, and voters blaming Reagan for the deficit. The Democrats came roaring back in the House in the midterm elections of 1982, winning enough seats to have a commanding majority. The Republicans' hopes for a permanent realignment were dashed. Particularly sweet for O'Neill was the defeat of one first-term congressman from a wealthy background who had said that O'Neill was exactly like the federal government—"big, fat, and out of control."[1] Both O'Neill and the federal government, it seemed, were back, and wealthy tax cutters were on the run.

So things remained for the rest of Reagan's first term, with another tax increase in 1984. In his second term Reagan presided over a big tax reform in 1986, but this was designed to be a revenue-neutral reform rather than a tax cut; it included increasing business taxes and scaling back accelerated depreciation, despite intense lobbying from business groups and lobbyists like Charls Walker.[2] In fact, Ronald Reagan would never again oversee a big tax cut as he turned increasingly to foreign policy in his second term. His tax-cutting legacy was to have implemented tax cuts and tax increases that netted out to about the size of the tax cuts that the Democrats had wanted in the big battle of the summer of 1981, or even less.

And yet, as the decades passed, tax cut politics moved to the center of the Republican Party and Reagan was retrospectively enthroned as its originator.

Figure 8.1 shows that the remainder of Reagan's time in office after ERTA did not see tax cuts, but starting in 1997, tax cuts have been the rule, under Democratic presidents as well as Republican ones. The most significant progressive legislation of several decades, the Affordable Care Act of 2010, raised tax receipts by an average of just 1 percent in the first four years, a fraction of the total tax revenue lost over this time period.

The tax cuts of George W. Bush represent an inflection point in this chronology, as the first substantial tax cuts after Reagan. In accordance with their historical importance, they have received a great deal of attention from scholars, almost all of it focused on one question: Were the Bush tax cuts popular with voters? If we simply examine the polls, we see that the cuts were remarkably popular, with favorability margins in the double digits—*even though* a majority of respondents understood that the tax cuts would favor the wealthy, and even though a large plurality recognized the increasing inequality in the country and disapproved of it. Analysts have suggested that support for the tax cuts was driven by confusion about what would be in voters' self-interest, that the Bush administration actively misled voters about the nature of the tax cut, specifically, its size and the degree to which it would benefit the wealthy, that the tax cut may have had high favorability ratings but people would have preferred other ways of using that money, or that voters understood their self-interest and the nature of the tax cut but favored it because it gave them absolute benefits that they appreciated, even if it gave the wealthy much more. The debate on the popularity of the tax cuts has overshadowed the perhaps more important debate on why the Bush administration wanted to cut taxes in the first place. On that question, which scholars often answer only in passing, the suggestions are a wish to cater to the partisan base, the power of interest groups who funded the activist elements of that base, and ideological preferences, including a genuine wish to benefit the wealthy, a genuine belief that tax cuts would benefit economic growth, or simply ideological preferences for small government.[3]

Surely each of these factors must have played some role, but each faces

Figure 8.1 Revenue Effects of Major Tax Bills: Percentage Change in Federal Receipts

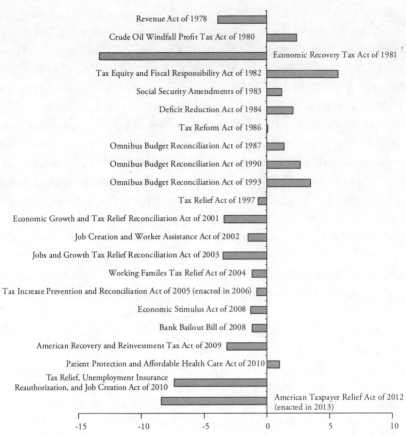

Source: Tempalski 2013.

some problems as a full explanation for why the Bush administration wanted to cut taxes. First, neither the base nor ideological preferences for small government can explain what Bush did after the tax cut, with his large expansion of government in the Medicare Modernization Act of 2003. Ideology and the preferences of the base seem to be a situational constraint, so we still have to determine when ideology and the preferences of the base matter and when they are ignored.

As for the power of interest groups, business groups—in a direct repeat of the Reagan scenario—were not at the origins of the phenomenon, although they did play a role later. For example, the 2001 tax cut did include some provisions that helped business, but it "leaves out most of the business community's wish list, including a cut in the corporate tax rate, accelerated depreciation of equipment, permanent extension of the research and development tax credit, reform of the corporate alternative minimum tax, sweeping changes in U.S. tax haven rules, and an array of smaller items." Many business groups had intended to push for these provisions, and early in the process they seemed to see this as justifiable recompense for the heavy donations by business to Bush's campaign coffers. When business groups saw that the original bill included no tax breaks for business, they signaled their unhappiness and their intention to try to add elements that would help business: "It's too early to be nervous and too early to hyperventilate," said a member of the insurance industry who hoped that later amendments would be more helpful to business. "We're going to get another bite of the apple, and that's when we're going to go after what we really care about," said a representative of the U.S. Chamber of Commerce; a group of high-tech companies and a group of multinationals pushed for their particular tax concerns, and one observer commented: "All the players see the dollars on the table as a way to get into the process. . . . The drop of blood is in the water."[4]

But by March the business community had reversed strategy, apparently under pressure from the administration: "The change of strategy among dozens of trade associations and corporations—which a few weeks ago were eyeing the tax legislation as a golden opportunity—is due in large part to aggressive arm-twisting by Bush and senior administration officials, including Vice President Cheney, Chief of Staff Andrew H. Card Jr. and presidential adviser Karl Rove. 'The message has been "Get with the program,"' said one business lobbyist. 'They're saying if you don't fit into what the president wants, we won't help you and we may even fight you.'" The president of the National Association of Wholesaler-Distributors said: "Lots of folks have come on board where there's no dollar incentive to them of a direct nature. . . . Why are they there? In my judgment they recognize this president is either going to make his bones on this or we find out we have an administration that cannot easily advance its agenda in this city."[5]

Although business groups were not able to enact their preferences in the 2001 tax act, their calculations seem to have paid off in a related domain, regulatory policy.[6] In implied exchange for pro-business action in regulatory realms, business groups disciplined themselves and did not push for the string of corporate tax cuts that they had planned. They were not the originators of the tax cut; indeed, the administration needed to "twist arms" to get business to cooperate. Business did get more in the 2003 tax cut, but the question remains where the 2001 tax cut came from.

As for the suggestion that the administration had a genuine wish to benefit the wealthy, the views of wealthy Americans were not much different than those of others on the issue: only a minority of both groups wanted tax cuts for upper-income groups in 2001 (30.7 percent of the top quintile, 20.4 percent of the bottom quintile) but once those were in place, less than half of both groups wanted to suspend them in 2002 (45 percent of the top quintile compared to 46 percent of the bottom quintile).[7] It is possible that the views of the extremely wealthy—those above the top quintile, not captured in opinion polls of this kind—were different and influential, but if so, those views would have had to contend with business groups' sense that these tax cuts were not the policy that would most benefit business, so we still have to explain why the administration decided to listen to some of its donors over others.

As for the argument that Republicans pushed for tax cuts because they genuinely believed that tax cuts would benefit economic growth, the mystery is why they would believe this, when the Reagan tax cuts seemed to have been such a dramatic failure and the Clinton tax increases of the 1990s had coincided with a period of solid economic growth. Something else was going on.

This chapter will argue that Ronald Reagan's tax cutting agenda succeeded in the long run because it failed in the short run. Reagan inadvertantly created huge deficits, producing a moment of genuine fear within the administration and the country. Because of that failure, Republicans came to learn over the next two decades that there was no longer a political or economic price to pay for creating deficits. These lessons ultimately destroyed the balanced budget wing and transformed the Republican Party.

The Rediscovery of Tax Cuts in the 1990s

In 1983, after the seeming defeat of the tax cut agenda, the Republican Party was back to searching for policies to propose. The suggestions ranged from "advanced technology with traditional values in a free- and market-oriented society . . . to ensure neighborhoods safe from domestic crime or foreign aggression" to "an active, involved senior citizenship" and "life with dignity for the truly disabled or handicapped American."[8]

Several events brought attention back to tax cuts. One was the peculiar manner in which Vice President Walter Mondale went down to defeat in the presidential campaign of 1984. In his speech accepting the Democratic Party nomination, Mondale, trying to be the truth-telling grown-up in the room, had said, "Mr. Reagan will raise taxes, and so will I. He won't tell you. I just did."[9] Mondale was right—Reagan did raise taxes over the next few years—but taking a correct and unpopular stance has never been particularly helpful in a presidential campaign. When Mondale lost in a landslide, many pundits identified this moment as crucial. Whether or not Mondale's truth-telling about taxes was the actual reason for his defeat, it became an increasingly popular explanation for the results.[10]

In 1986 Grover Norquist of Americans for Tax Reform came up with the "Taxpayer Protection Pledge." Norquist was a rich kid who burned with passion for the cause of capitalism. He had realized a truth that progressives still have not, a generation later, been able to counteract: progressivism depends on stable taxes. If you kill the tax base of the state, you kill the state and all of the social programs that it supports. And so he focused single-mindedly on identifying the vulnerabilities of the American tax state—namely, that its costs are highly visible, and its benefits invisible—and on increasing those vulnerabilities by making the costs of taxation even more visible.[11]

The content of the pledge, to be signed by policymakers, was simple: "I pledge to the taxpayers of the District of the State of _____ and to the American people that I will: ONE, Oppose any effort to increase marginal tax rates from the 15 percent and 28 percent rates for individuals and the 34 percent top rate for businesses; and TWO, Oppose any further reduction or elimination of deductions and credits, unless matched dollar for dollar by further reducing tax rates." Norquist's main strategy was threatening politicians with the bad publicity of breaking the pledge. Newspapers such as the *Wall Street Journal* helpfully listed every member who had signed the pledge.[12]

The pledge has taken on such mythic status that it almost seems as if any piece of paper pushed under the nose of a politician will create a political revolution. But the pledge had such power because politicians thought it would be politically costly not to sign it, and once they had signed it, they knew it would be politically costly not to uphold it. Norquist and his supporters could make a plausible claim that breaking the pledge, or not signing it, did have electoral consequences as they pointed to examples where breaking the pledge had become a major issue in Republican primaries.[13] Bob Dole's refusal to sign the pledge in 1988 haunted him for years afterwards. Dole had won the Iowa caucus in the Republican primaries that year and become the frontrunner. In a televised debate, one of the other candidates pulled out a copy of the antitax pledge. "Sign it," he demanded. Dole refused. The weekend before the New Hampshire primary the Bush campaign aired attack ads saying Dole "just won't promise not to raise taxes, and you know what that means." Some polls showed Dole up by 8 percentage points on the eve of the voting, but ultimately Bush won. Polls showed late deciders breaking for Bush, and the attacks on Dole for not signing the pledge were taken to be the reason for the outcome. Ironically, Dole's pollster, the one who had told him not to worry too much about taxes because they weren't turning up in the polls, was Wirthlin.[14]

The Taxpayer Protection Pledge was also a pledge that was actionable. Norquist could have written a pledge making politicians promise to increase economic growth, but everyone would have known that this was an empty promise because it is not possible to predict accurately which specific actions increase economic growth. And politicians would have quickly violated any pledge requiring them to cut spending because the political costs of cutting spending for specific programs would have been greater than the costs of breaking the pledge. Thus, a pledge to cut taxes gave Republicans the main thing they needed: a way to demonstrate that they were acting in ways that voters said they wanted.

This increasing concern with taxation in the party led George H.W. Bush to try to portray himself as a tax cutter during his campaign for the presidency in 1988. Bush's pollsters had told him in 1987 that social issues such as abortion were controversial, but that economic issues such as lower taxes have "a strong appeal to the Republican grassroots and the general electorate."[15] But given Bush's famous disparagement of supply-side as "voodoo economics," conservatives were skeptical of him. He was down in the polls. To shore up his support with that wing of the party he departed from his moderate reputation and campaigned on holding the line on taxes. In speechwriter Peggy Noonan's memorable phrase—toxically memorable, as it turned out—he had said at the nominating convention, "Read my lips. No new taxes."[16]

The statement might have helped him get into office, but the scale of the deficit he faced once he got there was frightening: Reagan had left him with an estimated deficit of $100 billion, but it actually turned out to be over $218 billion. Proposing his own budget the next year, Bush got the deficit down to $63 billion, but the state of the economy was such that it had to be revised to over $168 billion—"$231 billion if the federal government's share of the savings and loan bailout was included, and nearly $300 billion if the temporary surplus generated by the Social Security Trust Fund was excluded from the computation." Bush held out through a government shutdown, but given these numbers, it is not hard to understand why he eventually compromised and accepted tax increases, even over the opposition of members of his own party.[17]

In 1992, Bush lost the presidential election to Governor Bill Clinton of Arkansas. Just as progressives were appalled by the results of the 2016 election, so conservatives in 1992 could not understand how a draft-dodging, pot-smoking philanderer with no Washington experience could have won the presidency over a military hero and successful businessman who had been ambassador to the United Nations and to China, and head of the Republican National Committee and the CIA. Many Republicans settled on the explanation that it must have been because Bush broke his promise not to cut taxes—and that cutting taxes, as Reagan had done, was the route to victory.[18]

A kind of tax cut fever swept Republican legislators at state and local level in the 1990s. It began, by many accounts, because of Christine Todd Whitman of New Jersey. Fresh off a near-upset of popular senator Bill Bradley, Whitman had decided to run for governor of New Jersey in 1993. But she handled the early campaign poorly and at one point was trailing by double digits. As a last-ditch move, she adopted a tax cut as her main plank—a 30 percent across-the-board cut over three years, an exact replica of Reagan's plan. One of its architects had worked for Reagan. This position marked an abrupt turnaround for Whitman, who in June had said it was "cynical" to dangle tax cuts before voters in an election year. By September, that is exactly what she was doing. And she won. The campaign immediately attributed her victory to focusing on the tax issue: "We decided we'd have a

Figure 8.2 State-Level Republican Success, 1937–2011

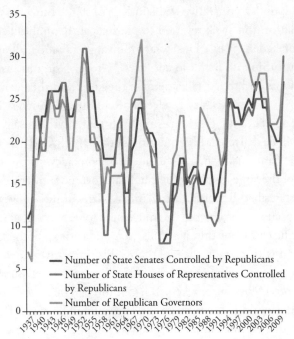

Legend:
— Number of State Senates Controlled by Republicans
— Number of State Houses of Representatives Controlled by Republicans
— Number of Republican Governors

Source: Klarner 2013.

single message and drive it every day. . . . We drove it everywhere and it broke through." Although earlier in the summer polls had shown voters unconvinced by her tax plan, all of that was wiped away by the victory, and it came to be celebrated as proof of the power of the tax cut issue.[19]

More and more Republican governors and legislators flocked to the tax cut banner. In 1994, the Republicans had a major victory when they took over the House of Representatives based on New Gingrich's "Contract with America," which included many provisions that dealt with taxes, including reductions in estate and gift taxes and capital gains taxes and a child tax credit, but no large across-the-board tax cut.[20] The 1990s were also a time when Republicans were increasingly capturing state governorships (figure 8.2). Although this may have been the effect of Southern Democratic dealignment from the Democratic Party on the issue of race, many Republicans concluded that the tax cut issue had strong political legs.

It was around this time that the party began consciously to brand itself as the party of tax cuts, to point to politics as the reason for this branding, and to retrospectively rehabilitate Reagan's tax cut, ignoring his later tax increases. Republican operative William Kristol said, "Bush ran on a Reaganesque platform in 1988, reverted to pre-Reagan Republicanism in '90, and got clobbered in '92 by a Democrat promising a tax cut. Call me simpleminded, but I think it's better to cut taxes." Grover Norquist insisted that the Republicans had to cut taxes because they had said they would in the Contract with America. Newly elected Republican congressman Sam Brownback agreed, saying, "There's no faith that anything said during a campaign will be delivered. It's a question of trust, faith, and that's an enormously important quality in a representative democracy."[21]

Because of the large number of Republican governors entering office, by 1995 thirty states had Republican governors. Many of these governors embarked on tax cutting programs. This movement for tax cuts in the late 1990s was not conjured out of thin air. Polls were indicating another round of dissatisfaction with taxes in the late 1990s, this time driven by objectively higher tax burdens.[22] The prosperity of the late 1990s was putting more Americans into higher tax brackets, Bill Clinton had increased tax rates especially on the wealthy, and because the Alternative Minimum Tax was not yet indexed to inflation, more people were caught in its net every year. Moreover, the general prosperity of the times, including the very high stock market, was creating state budget surpluses. With all these factors in play, governors offering tax cuts were often successful. Tax cuts may or may not have been the main cause of the Republicans' victories, but they were coming at the same time as those victories and therefore causing excitement. One Republican observer concluded: "State tax cuts have been a political and economic triumph for the GOP. Republicans are riding the pro-growth, antitax message to victory. Some six hundred legislative seats switched to the Republican side in last November's elections, and big GOP gains are expected again this November. The state experience raises the puzzling question: Why do Republicans on Capitol Hill approach tax cutting with fear and loathing?"[23]

Other developments in the 1990s magnified the tax cut momentum. The Cato Institute began to publish "report cards" of governors assessing how they had done on reducing spending and keeping taxes down, providing a seemingly objective way for Republicans to keep up the pressure on officeholders, and providing a way for governors to prove their tax cut credentials in hopes of higher office.[24] And academic economists generated a useful concept that is essentially the Laffer curve under a different name, "dynamic scoring." Martin Feldstein of Harvard argued most strongly that economic models need to account for the effect of taxes on economic activity.[25] While reasonable in theory, in practice the effects of tax cuts on economic activity are unclear, and introducing small differences in assumptions can produce large differences in outcomes, so that politicians are given a relatively unconstrained set of options that can justify their preferred policies. Republicans had been trying to get dynamic scoring made official since the days of the Contract with America, but there was too much skepticism about it, including among audiences that Republicans cared about, such as financial markets.[26] Of course, a truly objective attempt to account for all the effects of a tax cut would also include the positive effects of government programs on economic activity,[27] but proponents of dynamic scoring are more interested in the negative effects.

Eventually the local-level tax cut fever made it to the national level. In 1996, not only did the Republican presidential candidate, Bob Dole, run on the platform of an across-the-board tax cut, but he even chose Jack Kemp as his running mate—mollifying the conservatives who had always thought Kemp, not George H. W. Bush, was Reagan's rightful heir.[28] But Dole had been a tax cut skeptic for so long that he could not mount a convincing campaign on the issue.[29] Republicans concluded that simply promising tax cuts was not enough. Candidates had to have the experience of actually delivering tax cuts.[30]

In addition to the political lesson that tax cutting is more popular than balanced budgets, the ERTA also taught Republicans a key economic lesson. Traditionally, American investors worried that government deficits would compete with private firms looking for capital. This was one reason the stock market fell after the passage of the ERTA. In the 1980s, orthodox economists such as Walter Heller insisted that deficits led to inflation or higher interest rates, or both, and Robert Solow wrote that nearly all economists thought deficits crowded out investment.[31]

Interest rates did remain at startlingly high levels in the early 1980s, but crisis was averted because between 1973 and 1983 the amount of international investment in the American economy more than quadrupled—and careful observers thought that even this figure might have been understating the amounts of foreign capital flowing into the United States. Thus, firms looking for capital were able to find it easily. At first, opinions diverged on what to think about the development. The investment banker Felix Rohatyn voiced the fears of many in worrying that international capital was "becoming an addiction, and a sudden withdrawal could produce convulsions." Chairman of the Federal Reserve Paul Volcker cautioned that international borrowing, if "left unchecked, will sooner or later undermine the confidence in our economy essential to a strong currency and to prospects for lower interest rates." Senator William Proxmire worried that "foreign investors . . . get into a position where they can impose tough terms or cut off the credit." But others were more optimistic. As one banker put it, "There's no place else for the foreign capital to go, nor will there be." Another argued that the United States was "one of the few countries in the world creating jobs, so an entrepreneur can make a buck and keep it."[32]

At this point there was no consensus on what foreign financing of the deficit meant, and therefore deficit concerns made a comeback in the presidency of Bill Clinton. Despite Clinton's populist predilections, he followed the counsel of advisers who told him that his agenda would hinge on the health of the bond market, and that pleasing the bond market meant reducing the deficit. Following the bond market became such a fetish within the administration that Clinton aide James Carville said that he wanted to be reincarnated as the bond market, so that he could intimidate everyone. With a Democratic president open to balancing the budget, and with Congress controlled by Republicans who still had a balanced budget wing, the budget came into balance for the first time in decades.[33]

But Republicans concluded from this episode that budget balance was not an issue that brought votes. William Kristol had warned in 1995: "Reducing the deficit more than Clinton won't be an effective Republican platform. It will always be an uncertain claim, in any event, given the macroeconomic exigencies of interest rates. And let's face it—deficit reduction has a patchy record as a political bragging point. Ask our current President [Bill Clinton], who's just devoted the first half of his Administration to that goal, with notably disastrous results."[34] After the Republicans barely held on to their majority in the 1998 midterm elections, several analysts converged on the conclusion that the Republican leadership had not been conservative enough on tax policy: "Republicans should have campaigned on a Reaganite platform in 1998. Four years earlier, they captured the House running on the Contract With America, a ten-point agenda for lower taxes, less regulation, welfare reform, and a strong defense . . . By contrast, in 1998 most

Republicans in the House and Senate from their leaders on down voted for the budget compromise with Clinton, and the Senate refused even to vote on the House's small tax cut of $80 billion over five years. . . . In 1998, the Senate's refusal to consider a tax cut made it hard for House Republicans to argue that the GOP stood for lower taxes."[35] "Republicans have been unable to unite behind their most important weapon, and the only one that scares liberals: Tax Cuts."[36] "Tax cuts are the sugar that helps the medicine— all of those 'nos' Republicans have to say—go down. But since the public doesn't believe Republicans are serious about tax cuts, it tells pollsters tax reduction is a low-priority issue, and Republicans don't bother to get serious about cutting taxes."[37] "The Democratic Party, the party of government, has a natural advantage on the entitlements it created. Republicans should have a corresponding natural advantage on taxes, but their missteps have allowed Democrats to pull even. Without tax cuts to offer voters, it is a wonder Republicans have done as well as they have. . . . Republicans should reclaim the tax issue by offering voters, not tax reform, not tax fairness, but tax cuts. . . . Republicans can either start paying more attention to Americans, or get used to Americans' not paying attention to them."[38] "The party of small government cannot win a stable majority without reclaiming the tax issue."[39]

Or as one Republican commentator succinctly put it: "Who ever saw his poll numbers drop for proposing to cut taxes?"[40]

The George W. Bush Tax Cuts

Into this context—with a conservative right mobilized around the issue of tax cuts thanks to the state-level races and the D.C. policy entrepreneurs, and a budget in balance—walked George W. Bush, the son of the candidate who had gone down to defeat because he reneged on his tax cut promise. As governor of Texas, George W. Bush had failed at pushing through a big tax reform, but was lucky enough to be in office at a time of budget surplus, which he used to cut taxes.[41] As his campaign for the presidency became official, he announced a tax cut plan that would reduce revenues by about 9 percent over the next decade.[42] A conservative magazine noted "tax cuts are back, after years of being written off as yesterday's issue."[43]

In the primaries Bush defeated Senator John McCain, who wanted a smaller tax cut to leave money for reform of Social Security and debt reduction. In the general election Bush tried to attack Democratic nominee Al Gore's character, but when that failed he shifted to making the tax cut a central issue. Gore repeatedly attacked the proposal as irresponsible but—fitting the general pattern for tax cut proposals—although Americans said they would have preferred to use the money for Social Security or Medicare, they approved of Bush's tax cut proposal 61 percent to 28 percent.[44] Bush implemented a tax cut in each of the four years of his first term, including the second and third largest tax cuts in American history; although as analysts have noted, given the intense mobilization of Republican activists and office-holders around taxation, it would have been hard for any Republican president not to focus on cutting taxes at that point.[45]

Bush's tax cuts, combined with increases in military spending, produced large deficits. But something interesting happened at this point: many investors seemed to become convinced that deficits did not crowd out investment after all, and they were no longer fearful of international capital. Indeed, by the early 2000s, the bond market had itself been reincarnated into something James Carville would not have recognized. The late 1990s budget-balance effort itself had convinced investors that deficits were not something to worry about long term; that is, that one should not panic about deficits in bad times, because they would be resolved in good times.[46] Moreover, many thought that given the alternatives, the United States continued to be the best investment bet: stagnant Japan, crisis-ridden Europe, and volatile emerging markets meant "the United States starts to look a lot better and a lot of this starts to make more sense."[47] All of a sudden, the big concern that everyone had had for two generations, the concern over deficits that led Reagan to abandon Jack Kemp and turn his back on his big policy achievement, had vanished. Economic debate about the debt-to-GDP ratio continued, but did not seem to have practical effects on investor concern about the deficit.

And once the markets did not care, voters did not seem to care much either. Republicans discovered in the 1990s and 2000s that although voters say they worry about deficits, they do not vote on that concern. The percentages who prefer a balanced budget to a deficit have hardly changed for several decades, remaining at around 80 percent, but only a very small percentage of respondents consider deficits the most important problem.[48] Republicans concluded that fighting the deficit makes for poor political strategy. This was the moment when Republicans definitively abandoned budget balance in favor of tax cuts.

There was and continues to be worry that the deficit situation may not be sustainable, and occasional deficit reduction efforts continue. Indeed, there is a strange dynamic visible in the events: confidence in the bond market undercuts the willingness to cut deficits that that confidence is based on. All the effort Clinton and Congress had made to get the budget back into balance allowed the Republicans in the 2000s to push it back into deficit without much response from Wall Street. Politicians thus decided that if the bond market is not worried about deficits, then voters will not be worried about deficits, and therefore policymakers do not need to be worried about deficits. In the absence of indications of crisis, the political world has settled on the unstated conclusion that if the United States can run deficits at low cost, it should. When Dick Cheney allegedly said in 2002 that "deficits don't matter," he was voicing what many others had silently concluded.[49]

The demonstration that nothing terrible happened politically because of Reagan's deficits was crucial for the Republican Party. The Bush deficits showed that nothing terrible happened economically either. This is how the ERTA is most important historically: not in itself, but rather, because it taught the Republicans that they could open up an analogue to the extremely appealing politics that the Democrats had developed based on offering popular social programs, and because it therefore inaugurated a sequence that ended with the Republicans' abandonment of budget balance. If the deficit is no longer a concern, then Republicans could have their tax cut Santa Claus after all, developing a power structure based on the offer of tax cuts. As Republicans saw it, Democrats had recklessly been using government spending to keep a coalition together for decades. It wasn't that Republicans decided to be equally reckless with tax cuts. Rather, they thought tax cuts would be the lever that could keep spending down, and would therefore be the responsible policy. The arrival of international capital changed the calculations, making the politics more successful than they could have thought, but only at the cost of completely reorienting the party away from the goal of budget balance.

After Bush: The States Pull Back

Precisely because taxes have been going down continuously since 1997, the objective factors that were raising dissatisfaction with taxes are no longer present, and tax dissatisfaction is now at the lowest levels it has been since the beginning of the surveys. This confluence of circumstances has made tax cuts a less than perfect issue for bringing Republican politicians to the national stage, as encapsulated in the histories of two recent tax cutters, Bobby Jindal, governor of Louisiana, and Sam Brownback, governor of Kansas. Both pushed through big, president-making tax cuts, only to see those cuts swamped in controversy and catastrophe. Louisiana went from a large surplus when Jindal took office to a large deficit, his poll numbers plummeted, and the state found itself in a dire situation—epitomized by the months that accused prisoners who could not afford private defense attorneys had to sit in jail waiting for public defenders.[50]

Kansas's situation is even more notable, because Governor Brownback had called it an experiment in supply-side economics. The key element of his 2010 campaign, Brownback's tax cuts were released with great fanfare, and familiar figures on the right, including Arthur Laffer, weighed in and gave advice. Observers saw the Kansas tax cuts as a test of supply-side theory and compared the initiative to programs to raise taxes in other states, such as California and Maryland.[51] Brownback said, "We believe this is a strategy that builds a strong state in the future on the red state model. . . . It's not as if we haven't tried the blue state model, because we have." Opponents speculated that it was all designed to bring him national attention.[52] But the state quickly ran into trouble, facing a shortfall in school funding, and job growth was slower after the tax cut than in three of four neighboring states. The budget moved into deficit, and Moody's downgraded the state's debt. Brownback won reelection but was faced with even worse budget numbers. He eventually proposed an increase in sales taxes and slowing down his plan to cut the state income tax, and when even that wasn't enough, he increased alcohol and cigarette taxes. The *New York Times* wrote: "The grand myth of modern Republican politics—the trickle-down theory that sweeping tax cuts generate rising revenues—has come crashing down in Kansas. . . . Even some Republican supporters of Mr. Brownback, finding their schoolchildren threatened by declining standards, are calling for the reversal of some of the tax cuts."[53] Brownback became one of the least popular governors in the country. Finally, when public education began to be threatened, in 2017 the Republican-controlled legislature stepped in to raise taxes, overriding the governor's veto.[54] Brownback remained defiant to the end, blaming the weak national economy and the price of oil and wheat for his state's fiscal woes.[55]

Observers, concluding that tax cut politics had run its course in the states, tried to read in the Kansas story the prospects for tax reform at national level: "Something strange has been happening to taxes in Republican-dominated states: They are going up. Conservative lawmakers in Kansas, South Carolina and Tennessee have agreed to significant tax increases in recent weeks to meet demands for more revenue. They are challenging what has become an almost dogmatic belief for their party. . . . And now some Republicans say that what has played out in these states should serve as a cautionary tale in Washington, where their party's leaders are confronting a set of circumstances that looks strikingly similar."[56]

But something quite different would unfold at the national level.

The Tax Cuts and Jobs Act of 2017

Marx didn't say what happens the third time. In 2017, the Republican Party, in control of both branches of Congress and with a Republican in the White House, and having failed to repeal the Affordable Care Act, put together a tax cut plan that cut corporate tax rates severely and raised many other taxes to pay for it.

The business community opposed Reagan's tax cut and was ambivalent about Bush's, but business wanted and supported the tax cut of 2017, whose main plank was intended to benefit business. Moreover, tax dissatisfaction was not particularly high among the public, and unlike the Reagan and Bush tax cuts, the 2017 tax cut was not popular among the general public at the time it was passed. These factors suggest a change in the dynamics of tax cuts.

Nevertheless, it is still worth remembering the historical origins of the tax cut movement, because the 2017 cut retained those traces. Like the Reagan and Bush tax cuts, we see in this most recent cut the need for the Republican Party to do something—anything. As one analyst dissected the issue in the fall of 2017, after they failed to repeal the Affordable Care Act, "Republicans are staggering, knocked off kilter by internecine conflict. . . . Incumbents are under aggressive challenge from conservative activists. Frustrated veteran lawmakers are bailing out. Given the swirling tumult, one political and legislative reality is suddenly becoming crystal clear: Republicans must deliver a tax cut or face an epic backlash that would pose a significant threat to their governing majority and long-term political health."

It seemed that after decades of tax cuts, tax cuts were the only thing the party knew how to do. Without them,

> the party would have virtually no argument for re-election in 2018 and Senate and House incumbents would be wide open to challenge from both the right and the left. Big donors who are already sitting on their wallets would have no motivation to open them up. . . . The Republican Party really has no choice—it must find a way to get a tax cut to the president's desk. . . . Eventual success on a tax plan could ease a lot of the criticism they have come under for their legislative failures and demonstrate they have the capacity to run Washington.[57]

Corporations seem to have jumped on the tax cut bandwagon because it was the only wagon rolling. Despite controlling the presidency and both houses of Congress, Republicans were still unable to cohere on any other policy issue. Knowing that tax cuts of one kind or another must happen, business groups seem to have decided to make sure the cuts were designed in their interest. Although this most recent tax cut was very different in the sources of its support, in one way it represented the culmination of the tax cut movement: now even businesses had signed on to the argument that deficits don't matter.

Because of the deep unpopularity of the 2017 tax cut, an ACRS-style rollback is possible if Democrats manage to win control of Congress or the presidency. But even if it is rolled back, the lesson of the 2017 tax cut is that the Republican Party, once the party of budget balance, the party of fiscal hawks, has completed its transformation and brought its donor base along with it. All those who once stood to obstruct the path of tax cuts at the national level—the Republicans themselves, the media, voters, business groups, economists, Congress and the Democrats, and the stock market—have been overcome, rendered inoperative by the deus ex machina of international finance.

The Balance Sheet

Reagan's defenders point to the healthier economy of the 1980s and 1990s, compared with the 1970s, as proof that Reagan must have done something right. His critics point out that credit for controlling inflation should go to

Paul Volcker rather than Reagan; that inflation was brought down by causing a recession (contrary to the supply-side argument that a recession would
not be necessary); that it probably took the brutal experience with inflation
in the 1970s to summon the determination to withstand a recession; and
that the real effects of tax cuts have been a higher deficit and worsening inequality.[58] In truth, Reagan does not deserve most of the praise or blame
for any of these things because, as we have seen, a large part of his tax cut
was rolled back the next year, and what remained was not far out of line
with what many analysts from across the political spectrum thought was
necessary given the effects of inflation on taxes.

What Reagan's tax cut actually did was enable future tax cuts—by
demonstrating the political appeal of cutting taxes even at the expense of
deficits and by eventually showing that deficits could be financed with foreign borrowing—and those further tax cuts have had an effect. Thanks to
them the share of American tax revenue has held stable as a percentage of
GDP, even though in other countries tax revenue as a percentage of GDP
tends to rise as GDP rises.

Scholars have mapped out a similar dynamic in attacks on the welfare
state. Examining the effects of Thatcherism and Reaganism in the 1980s,
several scholars, most prominently Claus Offe and Göran Therborn, developed the "irreversibility thesis," that "the size of the population benefiting
from the welfare state ensures that as long as democracy accompanies advanced capitalism, the core of the welfare state is safe."[59] Other scholars
such as Ramesh Mishra pointed out that although the core of the welfare
state may be safe, the attacks from the right meant the welfare state could
not keep up with new issues such as the transition to a less labor-intensive
economy.[60] In Paul Pierson's evocative phrase, attempts to cut back the
welfare state have outflanked it instead, as if going around a Maginot line:
"the evidence now seems clear that welfare state programs have been quite
durable . . . Rather than directly assaulting the welfare state, those seeking
to remake the American political economy have mostly outflanked it"[61]
by ensuring that the welfare state has been unable to keep up with new
demands.

Partly because of those trends in the welfare state, a very similar dynamic
is visible in tax policy. It has proven impossible to reduce tax revenue as a
proportion of GDP, despite a concerted effort. But the effort has ensured
that there will not be new revenue to address new problems—automation,

Figure 8.3 Average Federal Tax Rates (Income, Payroll, Corporate, Excise), by Quintile, 1979–2013

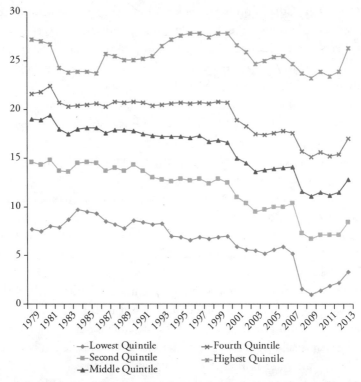

Source: Congressional Budget Office, "Distribution of Household Income and Federal Taxes," https://www.cbo.gov/topics/taxes/distribution-federal-taxes (accessed August 15, 2018).

new family forms with two working parents, the needs of an aging population, rising immigration and consequent exclusion of larger numbers from full integration into society, the need for retraining caused by globalization-induced job losses. What is interesting about taxation is that, unlike the welfare state, there is no one really defending taxation. Tax revenues have held the line because reductions in tax rates have been limited to the bottom four quintiles and the top 1 percent, but these do not generate much loss of tax revenue, as it is the top quintile that pays most of the taxes, and tax rates on the top quintile have not systematically declined (figure 8.3).

As these figures show, the federal tax system has not become less progressive if we examine it by quintiles. In fact, the share of federal income taxes that the wealthy pay, compared to the share of income that they earn, has not changed very much over the last several decades. According to Internal Revenue Service (IRS) data, in 1980, before Reagan's tax cut launched the Republicans on the path of pursuing tax cuts as their main domestic priority, the top 1 percent of federal income taxpayers earned 6.99 percent of total income and paid 14.69 percent of total federal income taxes, for a ratio of 2.1 times the share of taxes paid compared to the share of income earned. In 1986, after Reagan had backed down and raised taxes several times, the top 1 percent earned 10.41 percent of the income and paid 21.88 percent of the tax, the ratio remaining at 2.1 times the share of taxes paid compared to the share of income earned.[62]

The same thing happened after the George W. Bush tax cuts. In 2001, before the cuts, the top 1 percent of federal income taxpayers earned 17.53 percent of the income and paid 33.89 percent of the tax, for a ratio of 1.9. By 2009, they were earning 16.93 percent of the income and paying 36.73 percent of the tax, for a ratio of 2.2. In 2015—after over three decades of a relentless Republican focus on cutting taxes—the top 1 percent earned 20.65 percent of income and paid 39.04 percent of federal income tax, for a ratio of 1.9. The main story here is clearly the rise in the *pre-tax* income share of the wealthy, which is a story of factors such as executive compensation, technological trends, and deregulation of finance. The tax structure itself has not become systematically less progressive if we examine it by quintiles, although it can be argued that it should have become much *more* progressive given the concentration of incomes at the top.

What has happened is that Republican presidents reduce tax rates for everyone, and when Democratic presidents come in they increase tax rates for the rich but not everyone else. Overall tax rates have gone down continually for the bottom four quintiles. This is an odd facet of the movement that has fed its longevity, because after each round of tax cuts, Republicans can point to how much of the tax burden the wealthy are carrying, justifying another round of tax cuts. David Stockman's complaint about the tax cut being a Trojan horse for the rich, while false for the ERTA itself, is in a larger and metaphorical sense true about the tax cut movement: it has benefited the wealthy, in that tax rates on the wealthy have held steady despite a dramatic rise in incomes at the top of the income distribution, and this probably could not have happened without taxes going down for the middle classes and the poor.

This is even clearer if we examine what happens *within* the top quintile.

The total effective tax rate has been relatively stable for the bottom half of the top 1 percent (from 32.3 percent in 1979 to 29.7 percent in 2005) as well as those below them, has dropped somewhat for those slightly richer, and has dropped *dramatically* for the top .01 percent (from 42.9 percent in 1979 to 31.5 percent in 2005). This is the most substantial change the tax cut movement has produced, and it is not likely that this could have happened without simultaneous and popular cuts in taxes on the bottom four quintiles.

The cuts for the top 0.01 percent seem to be a result of significant cuts in the capital gains tax rate, as effective rates for income taxes and other taxes for these taxpayers have remained stable or gone down only slightly. However, as we will see in the next chapter, it is not clear what to make of this, because those capital gains taxes were falling from unusually high levels.

The Evolution of Business Interests

The role of business interests is more difficult to pin down in the more recent tax cut episodes. Many developments since the early 1980s suggest an evolution of the role of business and of the wealthy more generally, including changes in campaign finance laws and the rise of business mobilization at state level. Moreover, if the main reason business interests opposed Reagan's tax cut was fear of the deficit, and if the intervening decades have dampened concern about the deficit, it stands to reason that business interests may not only be more amenable to tax cuts now, but could even be initiators of tax cuts.

A full accounting of this issue cannot be made until more archival research on the recent decades has been conducted, but there are several reasons to think that business interests are not the main part of the story, even for the more recent decades.

First, tax cuts do seem to have electoral benefits for Republicans. Many scholars point out that respondents do not prefer tax cuts to budget balance or spending cuts and therefore conclude that tax cuts are not popular. This ignores a broader lesson: tax cuts have helped to cement the Republican Party's reputation as an economically responsible party, bringing it to parity with the Democrats on this dimension (figure 8.4). Indeed, Mark A. Smith argues that if one subtracts general identification with the parties and controls for the actual performance of the economy, Republicans have opened up an advantage on this question. Smith writes:

Figure 8.4 Public Opinion on Which Party Will Keep the Country Prosperous, 1951–2017

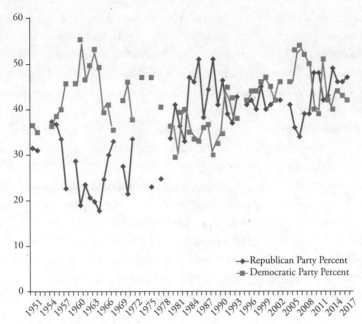

Source: Gallup polls, "Party Images," 1951–2017, https://news.gallup.com/poll/24655/party-im-ages.aspx (accessed August 27, 2018).

The Republican message of lowering taxes, eliminating regulations, and streamlining the welfare state has been clear and consistent. The Democrats, by contrast, changed their economic themes over time and offered arguments—particularly regarding the need for deficit reduction—that were difficult to convey lucidly and compellingly to the mass public. . . . The GOP's economic reputation . . . added votes to the party's tally in six of the last eight presidential elections. By linking the party's key stances clearly, directly, and repeatedly to a healthy economy, Republicans crafted a message that helped them both win elections and then construct coalitions in subsequent struggles over policy.[63]

Although voters say they prefer budget balance or preserving spending to cutting taxes, politicians who try to follow those stated preferences, such as Walter Mondale or John McCain, have not always been successful at using that strategy to get into office.

Smith also shows that since 1980 the American public has become more concerned with economic issues, because of stagnant wages, job insecurity, and rising debt; thus, Republicans have developed a reputation for being more attentive to the economy at precisely the moment when Americans have become more concerned about the economy. Tax cuts may not be the top priority for voters, but they do seem to have brought Republicans votes. Martin Gilens argues that economic and tax policy are the domains "in which interest groups have the least sway over policy outcomes," and that the popularity of tax cuts and the unpopularity of tax increases contributes to making Republicans the party that is more responsive to public preference.[64]

Another reason to doubt the business interest explanation is the divergence in tax policy at state and national level. Many scholars argue that business interests and the wealthy are more powerful at state level, because progressives have by and large concentrated their attention at the national level. But it is precisely at state level that we have seen tax cut politicians pull back more recently, while tax cut politics continues fervently at the national level. What drives the difference in state- and federal-level outcomes is that many states have constitutional requirements for balanced budgets, whereas at national level the country continues to be able to borrow cheaply. Where Republicans have to balance budgets, at state level, they do so. Where they do not have to, they continue to pursue tax cuts.

This story puts the analyses given by some scholars in different perspective. Alexander Hertel-Fernandez and Theda Skocpol have argued that Democrats were pressured by small business groups into supporting the 2001 Bush tax cut and its 2010 extension.[65] But when Democratic presidents take office, taxes on the wealthy rise; this would seem to be the wrong policy if appeasing small business is the goal.

Jacob Hacker and Paul Pierson have pointed to various odd features of the Bush tax cuts that served to hide the true size and the true distribution of the cuts, and have interpreted this as evidence that Republicans were trying to deceive the public.[66] But given that, in Martin Gilens's words, "the public almost uniformly displays antitax preferences tempered only slightly by variations in the distributional character of the proposed tax changes,"[67] and that voters did indicate awareness that the wealthy would receive most of the benefits from the Bush tax cuts, it is not clear that public preferences would have changed significantly if voters had understood that the wealthy were receiving even more of the benefits. Moreover, another possibility that explains the odd features of the Bush tax cuts is that these were necessary because of the organizational imperative to have a big, headline-grabbing tax cut, the kind that makes it clear to everyone that Republicans are the tax-cutting party and that Bush can deliver major policy. Observers sometimes ask why Republicans do not cut taxes that fall more heavily on the middle classes and the poor, such as payroll taxes. But because payroll taxes are tied to Social Security and Medicare, cutting them means cutting Social Security and Medicare, an incendiary proposition. Sales taxes also fall more heavily on the middle classes and the poor, but sales taxes are the province of the states. A president who wants a huge tax cut has to cut federal income or corporate taxes, and that will generally mean cutting taxes on the wealthy; and because cutting taxes on the wealthy is not particularly popular, a process of camouflaging those cuts is likely. Note the curious circumstance here of an unpopular policy being used to boost electoral chances, an oddity we take up in more detail in chapter 11.

The Republican focus on tax cuts has coincided with a remarkable renaissance in the fate of the Republican Party, which has gone from predictions of its extinction in the mid-1970s after Watergate, to holding even with Democrats in the presidency and Congress, and even pulling ahead at state and local level. Progressives often point to gerrymandering as an explanation, but the trend is exactly the same where gerrymandering is not an issue, such as in governorships. The racial realignment of the parties is probably the overarching factor in this story, but, whether or not tax cuts got them into power, Republicans certainly thought they did. Of course, Republicans have both ideological and financial reasons to cut taxes on the wealthy. But they *also* have electoral reasons to do so. Which ultimately drove the more recent tax cut episodes is a question that can only be answered as archives on these eras become available.

Finally, there is an overarching reason to be skeptical of the power of money in American politics: for all of their efforts, American businesses and the wealthy have not yet managed to get taxes on business or the wealthy lower than other countries, as we will examine in the next chapter.

Ronald Reagan promised that his tax cut would not create deficits. But this chapter has argued that Reagan's tax cut had long-term influence precisely because it did create very large deficits. Reagan won re-election despite record-breaking deficits, and the political world learned that deficits could be financed by international capital and therefore would not necessarily lead to higher interest rates. Republicans concluded that neither voters nor markets would punish politicians for creating deficits. It took nearly two decades for those lessons to be absorbed, but once they were, Republicans abandoned for good the balanced budget ideology that had driven them for decades, and that, Jack Kemp had thought, kept them out of power.

Inflation brought tax cuts onto the Republican agenda, but although inflation came under control in the 1980s the tax cut issue remained. As Republican politicians increasingly invoked Ronald Reagan and especially his tax cut, in its afterlife the ERTA became more important than it had been at the time of its first passage. By the 2000s, the issue of tax cuts had become the centerpiece of Republican economic policy because of deficit financing, plus the demonstrated possibility of constructing electoral victories around tax cuts and the absence of other significant issues for Republicans.

Despite this long tradition, tax cuts are not very popular right now. The party continues to propose them because there are no other traditionally Republican issues around which to unite a fractious coalition. Except for one: racism. The party is balanced between its history of tax cuts and the appeal of creating a new political history around explicit racism and xenophobia. It's possible that a new Jack Kemp will come along to wrest the future of the party away in a completely new direction. Or a moderate sort of racism and xenophobia could win the day, concentrating on immigration restrictions, control of the border, and trade protectionism; it could continue to be combined with tax cuts as we saw in 2017, or it could eventually take the party away from free market policies. Or, if we're unlucky, in its quest for votes the Party of Lincoln may get pulled down a much darker path. When last heard from, Grover Norquist was engaged in a battle with extremists in the Republican Party who are convinced that he and his group Americans for Tax Reform are a front for radical Islam.[68]

Part II

AMERICAN CONSERVATISM AND AMERICAN HEGEMONY

CHAPTER 9

Running to Stay in Place

THE STORY OF American conservatism as usually told goes like this. In the 1970s, a series of economic and political crises came together: stagflation—caused by Lyndon Johnson's "guns and butter" policy, a domestic wage-price spiral, poor monetary steering, and international developments, particularly in the price of oil—combined with a wider crisis of confidence arising from the Vietnam War, the riots and protests of the sixties, the trauma of Watergate, and changing racial and sexual norms. Conservatism was one response, promising a return to a time before all of these troubles. Although triggered by the recent developments, resurgent conservatism was rooted in long-lasting traditions and organizational efforts that had continued even during the flourishing of the New Deal. Conservatism drew oxygen from the increasing suburbanization of American society, which had led to greater numbers of homeowners eager to preserve their racial and economic privileges, as well as from the weakening of organized labor as manufacturing declined and less organized service-sector jobs increased. The main actors in the conservative movement were organized business groups, grassroots activists, foreign policy hawks, and religious leaders, brought together within the Republican Party under the overarching theme of anti-Communism. This coalition eventually proved strong enough to rival the Democratic Party's coalition of farmers, workers, white ethnic minorities, and African Americans. In economic policy, conservative principles have since become orthodoxy.[1]

This story does capture many elements of what we have seen in the tax cut episode—such as its precipitation by economic crisis—but cannot explain some of its major aspects. For one, why did some conservative policies become law while others fell by the wayside? For all of the seamlessness of the conservative victory that this narrative implies, conservatives have had to tolerate the onward march of women's rights, civil rights, and gay rights, as well as the arrival of the first African American president. Even in economic policy conservative achievements are mixed: the costliest parts of the welfare state, Social Security and Medicare, have not been touched, welfare cuts have been matched by increases in the Earned Income Tax Credit (EITC), other social programs have continued to grow, the costs of regulation have nearly quadrupled since 1980, and when Democratic presidents come into office they undo much of what Republican presidents have managed to accomplish.[2] Taken as a whole, the scholarly literature has done an excellent job of explaining the origins of the conservative movement, but has been less successful at explaining the translation of that movement into specific changes either at the level of policy or at the level of society more broadly.

Second, if business leaders were part of the conservative coalition, why in our story do we find them opposing the leader of that coalition? Even scholars who do not see business as central believe that it played a supporting role. But in the tax cut story business groups were initially opponents, then allies who were won over through a quid pro quo, and then ex-allies who felt betrayed. And what business leaders did support was a policy that turns out to have been the norm in other capitalist countries. What explains the surprising struggle of American capitalists to persuade government to enact policies that Swedish capitalists had been taking for granted since the 1930s?

To answer these questions this chapter builds on a small but growing scholarship that is starting to explore the role of an important background factor: the different political economy that arose in America compared to other rich countries after the Second World War. America emerged from the war as the undisputed champion of the free world, while Europe lay in rubble. Even European countries that had not been devastated by war were surprised by, and then fearful of, America's increasing economic might. Indeed, from 1943 to 1946—before Europe embarked on its three decades of postwar prosperity—total American GDP was higher than the *combined* GDPs of Austria, Belgium, Denmark, Finland, France, Germany, Italy, the Netherlands, Norway, Sweden, Switzerland, the United Kingdom, Ireland, Greece, Portugal, Spain, Australia, New Zealand, and Canada.[3]

Europeans adopted many different strategies in response, to such an extent that, as the historian Sven Beckert points out, three of the main themes of European history in the twentieth century—late colonialism, the economic integration of the European economy, and intervention and conflict in Eastern Europe—can be seen as attempts to catch up to the United States.[4]

But like "late industrializers" throughout history, Europe's main catch-up strategy was to press the state into the service of the project of economic expansion. Domestic political economy was reoriented around the attainment of economic growth. And how did a twentieth-century economy attain economic growth? At midcentury, many observers took for granted that industrialization was a consequence of capital accumulation. Since labor was abundant, it seemed obvious at the time that what led to industrialization was the money that allowed the great factories to be built, the roads to be laid, the canals to be dug. And the way to raise capital for investment was to restrain consumption.

Although there is today debate on the importance of capital accumulation to growth,[5] at midcentury the need to focus on investment seemed clear to everyone, and European countries struggled to restrain consumption and channel available funds toward investment. The result was that "net investment rates in Europe were nearly twice as high in the 1950s and 1960s as before or since." These investments were channeled toward exports, and the export sector was the driver of growth. Even today, many analysts see this strategy as the cause of Europe's miraculous postwar growth. This focus on investments, and consequent restraint of consumption, was made possible by institutions that allowed for cooperation between labor, business, and the state. In the face of the crisis, labor and business both subordinated their demands in the interest of regenerating the economy, drawing on older traditions of cooperation. Well-organized labor associations that could credibly claim to speak on behalf of labor acquiesced to policies such as wage restraint and regressive taxes, and businesses channeled profits toward investment. The result of these cooperative European arrangements was a model of government that scholars have called corporatism. In exchange for wage restraint and restraint of consumption, European workers would receive increasingly generous welfare protections, which they would largely pay for themselves: taxation on capital would remain low, and regulation of business would be minimal. Although it is American unions at midcentury that are generally considered moderate, examining this broader set of policies allows us to see the essentially moderate nature of labor across the advanced industrial countries in the early postwar period. With their low wages, regressive taxes, and minimal regulation, European countries in many ways seem to have been more supply-side than the United States. Over time, as the welfare state expanded, the strategy seemed vindicated, as European poverty and inequality rates declined.[6]

It is this focus on investment that we are seeing in the other countries' surprisingly business-friendly investment environments, and it is the focus on consumption that American businesses were struggling against in ACRS. What seems surprising from one perspective—How could Sweden actually be more business-friendly than the United States?—is not at all surprising when considering the postwar political economy of the different countries.

Historians have examined in detail how the United States adopted a model of increasing purchasing power while other countries focused on policies that led their populations to increase savings.[7] Economists have shown that this pattern originated in the 1930s: before 1930, European countries consumed more, suggesting that the reason for the divergence was not some innate American propensity to consume but rather the different experiences of the countries during these periods.[8] Sociologists and political scientists have identified these two patterns as two different "growth models" and traced their origins to the different problems that the United States faced during the Great Depression and the Second World War compared to its European counterparts.[9] The upshot is that over the postwar period the European countries posted high levels of investment while the United States posted lower levels, as seen in figure 9.1. Not all European countries managed high levels of savings. The Mediterranean countries and the United Kingdom have been strong consumers, which may have been either cause or consequence of their relatively poorer economic performance over the postwar period. But there is a major difference between the consuming United States and the continental and Scandina-

Figure 9.1 Investment as Share of GDP in the United States and Twenty-Two OECD Countries, 1950–2014

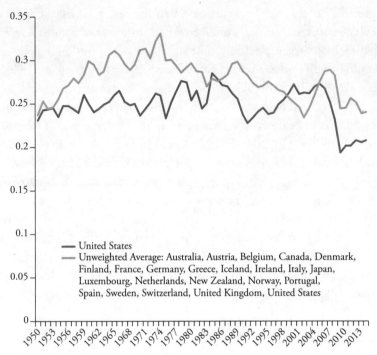

Source: Penn World Tables, Feenstra, Inklaar, and Timmer 2015.

vian countries, which focused on increasing savings. Although this litera-ture identifying different political economy regimes has developed across the social sciences, it has not yet been brought into our understanding of the rise of conservatism. Scholars of conservatism have been groping for a more global explanation, but, with some important exceptions,[10] tend to examine different conservative movements comparatively, for example "the connections between American conservatism and the conservative intel-lectual and political tradition in Europe . . . the contributions that Amer-ican conservatives made to right-wing movements elsewhere [and] how conservative movements around the world were able to gain strength from the economic and cultural changes of the late twentieth century."[11] This approach sees the different countries as individual units that may learn from each other, rather than as part of an overarching global system that constrains what each of them can do.

In this chapter, we examine one of the most surprising aspects of the divergence in American and European political economy at midcentury: because the European states were desperately focused, especially after the wars, on reconstruction and economic growth, they were often able to overcome divisions between capital and labor and achieve cooperation in policies that would benefit both. In particular, welfare benefits became part of a bargain in return for the favorable tax and regulatory treatment of capital.

In the United States, on the other hand, many policies adopted during the decades after the war, a period seen in retrospect as one of relative harmony between capital and labor,[12] were in fact comparatively hostile to both capital and labor. Because the United States could take production more or less for granted, capitalists did not receive favorable treatment in areas such as investment incentives, nor were they brought into coalitions that extended social programs in return. As a result of these divergent orientations, Europe not only had lower poverty than the United States but was also more accommodating toward capital throughout its golden age. This difference in treatment was behind the business complaints about taxation of capital in the Reagan era and helps to explain the appeal of ACRS.

The Tax Treatment of Capital

If European countries fostered investment and exports, starting in the early twentieth century the United States was surprisingly punitive to its corporations. In many domains American politics at this time was driven not by a labor-capital divide, but by a split between the agrarian Midwest and South against the industrial Northeast. The former two were often able to unite, sometimes in coalition with the West, and translate political animus against corporations into tax policies that would be paid for by the Northeast.[13] In consequence, as one observer wrote: "While in the United States Socialism as a political creed has little following, yet in few countries have there been tax laws so pleasing to Socialists as those of the United States."[14] In 1980, at the eve of the tax cut revolution, effective tax rates on capital were higher in the United States than other countries.[15]

Reagan and the Republicans continually invoked the example of Europe in promoting the ERTA. During the 1980 campaign, Reagan's Advisory Group on International Trade and Competitiveness received position papers from various industrial groups. The American Electronics Association, citing policies in Japan, Germany, France, and Canada that included R&D subsidies, accelerated depreciation, low-interest loans, tax credits and deductions and exemptions, lower taxes for research-related sales, and even cash grants for investment, argued that innovation was declining in the United States.[16]

A common complaint was that "in principle, the present U.S. system of taxing foreign source income (through the use of the 'foreign tax credit' and 'deferral') is equitable and sensible. However, when contrasted to the policies used by our major trading partners, they fall considerably short and therefore should be reviewed in that light. France, the Netherlands, and Belgium, for example, do not tax foreign source income at all, and other countries, including the United Kingdom, Germany, and Japan have tax policies which offer preferential treatment on income earned abroad."[17] "American corporations are penalized because the cost of keeping a home country sales person, technical person or manager overseas to promote U.S. business is much more expensive than for their foreign competitors."[18]

The value-added tax and its favorable effects on exports was another key theme of the Reagan campaign:

When goods are shipped from a common market country to the U.S., the exporter receives a rebate of the value added tax ranging from 13 percent in Germany to 22 percent in Italy. In other words, on exported goods, the government foregoes the revenue it would otherwise receive on that production. In effect, the rebate becomes a tax incentive, or subsidy, for exports. On arrival in the U.S., no tax is levied on the arriving goods. So they can be sold at a lower price in the U.S. than in their home country. The U.S. product with which it competes has already made its full contribution to the U.S. government through direct taxes. But the imported product makes no tax contribution at all. Turning the coin over, when a U.S. product is exported to a common market country, no U.S. rebate whatsoever is given the U.S. exporter. Therefore, unlike the European import into the U.S., it enters Europe at the same price it sold for in the U.S. Then the European government adds a value added tax, which makes it sell in Europe for a higher price than in the U.S.A. The VAT is a tax disincentive or penalty on imports.[19]

One writer noted, "In Germany, industry paid a mere $7.8 billion in taxes in 1973 or 6.5% of the total budget for all government operations, against

American industry's $53.1 billion which represented 16% of the taxes collected by local and state and the Federal governments. Corporate real estate in Germany paid $500 million in taxes in 1973 as against $16.4 billion in the U.S."[20]

Charles Pilliod of Goodyear argued that American firms were disadvantaged because they complied with tax laws, whereas compliance was interpreted more flexibly in other countries. He compared the situations of tire companies in France and the United States, complaining first about antitrust policies in the latter:

> Several years ago the U.S. Justice Department filed anti-trust suits against the two leading U.S. tire companies, charging each of them with efforts to monopolize the market. Yet each of these companies had far less than half the position which the French company had in its market. Clearly, such dominance of one's home market provides a much firmer, and presumably more profitable, base from which to operate as an exporter, or as a multinational. It provides the economics of volume, to yield lower costs, and the ability to price in the marketplace with less competitive pressure.

In addition, the French company's earnings and fixed assets were taxed at a lower rate, and it was allowed to pool profits and losses from different countries to lower its taxes.[21]

Lawrence Fox of the National Association of Manufacturers hammered the point that "the savings-consumption-business investment ratios must be altered in the direction of increased *personal* savings, and this requires a recognition that the growth in personal consumption will have to yield some to increase savings on a long-term basis."[22] A major conclusion was that "foreign government policies fostered export-led growth."[23] A briefing book in Ed Meese's papers argues that the U.S. share of world trade had declined because the "U.S. reduced capital investment, increased regulation, decreased productivity," while "other countries [were] developing new technology, increasing capital investment and supporting exporters through government programs."[24] Another observer complained European countries "do not, so it would seem, place their trust in Adam Smith. They do aggressively and in a variety of ways stimulate and encourage export business. To them, it is not plus business, it is bread and butter business."[25]

While progressives have been busily comparing the United States to Europe over the last several decades and finding it wanting, business-oriented conservatives have been doing the exact same thing. Progressives want the United States to imitate Europe's social programs. Conservatives want it to imitate Europe's investment orientation and favorable treatment of capital. As we have seen, Kemp-Roth was not the brainchild of American business. ACRS was, but in fighting so hard for it, American businesses were simply trying to achieve what businesses in other countries could take for granted. American businesses were running to stay in place.

Running to Stay in Place

In fact, "running to stay in place" describes the power of business in America for a surprisingly large number of issues. Consider corporate taxation in general. Table 9.1 shows the statutory tax rate on corporations in the United States (that is, the tax rate before exemptions, deductions, and so on), and the effective average tax rate (the total tax that corporations actually pay after all the exemptions and deductions and loopholes have been accounted for, as a percent of total income) and marginal effective tax rate (the tax on the marginal increment of investment). The statutory tax rate in the United States in 2012 was nearly 40 percent, but the average effective tax rate was under 30 percent. There is reason to think that this discrepancy was at least partly caused by lobbying, and indeed, some research suggests that tax exemptions are the key benefit that most corporations receive for their lobbying.[26] However, the table also shows that in comparative perspective, the actual taxes that corporations pay were still slightly higher in the United States than in Europe. At least until the tax reform of 2017, all the lobbying that American corporations did for tax exemptions got them tax rates that European corporations got *without* lobbying. This is running to stay in place.

This chapter briefly detours from the story of the ERTA to show that this phenomenon is widespread in American political economy and can be seen in a substantial number of issues on which businesses have won victories. Again and again, the power of money buys American corporations policies that European corporations do not have to expend money or time fighting for. This phenomenon does not affect all of the issues on which businesses have won victories, but it does affect a substantial number.

The dominant tradition of studying the influence of money on politics examines the effect of campaign contributions, donations, or lobbying, from either business groups or individual firms, on either the outcome of

Table 9.1 Statutory, Effective Average, and Effective Marginal Corporate Tax Rates, G20 Countries, 2012

Statutory Tax Rates, Highest to Lowest		Effective Average Tax Rates, Highest to Lowest		Effective Marginal Tax Rates, Highest to Lowest	
United States	39.1	Argentina	37.3	Argentina	22.6
Japan	37	Indonesia	36.4	Japan	21.7
Argentina	35	United States	29	United Kingdom	18.7
South Africa	34.6	Japan	27.9	United States	18.6
France	34.4	Italy	26.8	Brazil	17
Brazil	34	India	25.6	Germany	15.5
India	32.5	South Africa	23.5	India	13.6
Italy	31.4	Brazil	22.3	Mexico	11.9
Germany	30.2	Russia	21.3	Indonesia	11.8
Australia	30	South Korea	20.4	France	11.2
Mexico	30	Mexico	20.3	Australia	10.4
Canada	26.1	France	20	China	10
China	25	Turkey	19.5	South Africa	9
Indonesia	25	China	19.1	Canada	8.5
South Korea	24.2	Australia	17	Saudi Arabia	8.4
United Kingdom	24	Canada	16.2	Turkey	5.1
Russia	20	Germany	14.5	Russia	4.4
Saudi Arabia	20	United Kingdom	10.1	South Korea	4.1
Turkey	20			Italy	−23.5

Source: Congressional Budget Office, CBO International Comparisons of Corporate Income Tax Rates, March 2017.

elections or on votes on specific legislation. Despite widespread public belief in the power of money, research findings are mixed; reviews of the research conclude that the evidence for the influence of money is weak. The largest study of lobbying to date concludes that although there are isolated examples of lobbying success—which draw disproportionate media attention—these are not representative. Examining a representative sample of attempts to lobby reveals that the influence of lobbyists is minimal, because on many policy issues the business community is divided. For example, legislation that helps trucking will hurt airlines, and vice versa, and therefore the power of different corporations or sectors cancels out. Moreover, some scholars find that even when businesses manage to overcome such fragmentation, they do not necessarily win in the policymaking arena, because issues that unify business—and the process of business unification itself—attract attention from the media and the public. Recently, Martin Gilens has shifted the focus from business groups to wealthy individuals, arguing that wealthy individuals systematically see their preferences reflected in policy to a greater extent than others; but other scholars have pointed out that this conclusion may be overstated, because on most issues there is not significant difference in preferences between income groups.[27]

On the narrower question of the role of money in the rise of free market policies, however, the orthodoxy is that either business groups or wealthy individuals have been influential. We discussed some of the most prominent of these works earlier, including David Harvey, Jacob Hacker and Paul Pierson, Lawrence Lessig, and Kim Phillips-Fein, but these represent only the tip of the iceberg.[28]

Table 9.2 lists the free market policies that scholars argue have been particularly influenced by business power. The table was generated by searching for scholarship on free market policies that argues for the power of business and then examining the legislation or failed or absent legislation studied in this literature. Although the scholarship on money in politics is vast, the criteria for inclusion in table 9.2 are narrow. A free market policy was included in this list only if a scholarly work has defended an explicit argument that business groups or the wealthy influenced it. Much scholarship on money in politics is excluded because it focuses only on the independent variable—tracing, for example, the rise in corporate lobbying without investigating its consequences.[29] Other free market policies, such as welfare reform legislation under Clinton, are excluded because of absence of scholarly arguments for the influence of business groups or the wealthy on the policy.[30] There may be other policies where money was influential that have not yet been identified by scholars; if so, it will be for future scholars to address whether the phenomenon identified here holds for those policies as well.

These works of scholarship define business power in various ways, either in terms of initiating change, or joining in coalitions for change, or accepting change or resisting it. As expected, there is much debate about the origins of these free market policies and the specific importance of business groups versus other factors. Because the overarching argument here is that the power of business has been overestimated, I extend to scholars who argue that business is powerful the benefit of the doubt in these debates. That is, I assume that the scholars arguing that these pieces of legislation

Table 9.2 Were Free Market Policies "Running to Stay in Place"?

	Was This a "Running to Stay in Place" Policy?
Failure of labor law reform (1977)	No
Defeat of consumer protection agency (1978)	Yes
Defeat of Common Situs Picketing Bill (1978)	No
Cutting capital gains tax rate in half (1978)	Yes
Garn–St. Germain Depository Institutions Act (deregulation of savings and loans) (1982)	No
North American Free Trade Agreement (1993)	Yes
Financial Accounting Standards Board's hostility to restrictions on stock options (1993)	No
Failure of Clinton health care reform (1994)	No
Riegle Neal Interstate Banking and Branching Efficiency Act (deregulation of branch banking) (1994)	Yes
Carried interest provision (allowing some income to be treated as capital gains) (1993, 2005)	Yes
Repeal of Glass-Steagall (1999)	Yes
Commodity Futures Modernization Act (2000)	No
Bankruptcy Abuse Prevention and Consumer Protection Act (2005)	Yes

Source: Author's review of scholarship on free market policies (see text).

were at least partly brought about by the mobilization of business are correct, and then I place the phenomenon in comparative perspective. (If these scholars are wrong—if business mobilization was not responsible for these victories—then the overarching argument about the overestimation of American business power holds without needing to examine the phenomenon in comparative perspective.)

This discussion is necessarily brief, meant to illustrate a trend that has remained unnoticed rather than to provide definitive conclusions. But even a brief overview shows that when we deploy a comparative perspective, business can be seen to have been running to stay in place in many of the cases listed in table 9.2.

The defeat of a bill to establish a consumer protection agency in 1978 has been cited as the first major demonstration of the power of business in the postwar period. The public supported such an agency, but business opposed it in what was described by one congressman as "the most intense lobbying I've ever seen against any bill."[31] The U.S. Chamber of Commerce, the National Association of Manufacturers, the National Federation of Independent Business, and the Business Roundtable joined with over four hundred corporate organizations and trade associations to defeat the bill, and many scholars argue that this mobilization was central to its defeat.[32]

But the defeat looks different when placed in comparative perspective, because consumer protection was more advanced in the United States than in any other country at this time. The Food and Drug Administration (FDA), for example, was more aggressive in keeping dangerous drugs off the market than most European countries were. The most spectacular case was thalidomide, a drug that led to severe birth defects when taken during pregnancy. Thalidomide was permitted on the market in Europe—leading to thousands of cases of stillbirth or birth defects there—but was kept off the American market thanks to the FDA.[33] This case was not an outlier either. One study found that Great Britain had approved four times as many new drugs as the United States in the 1960s; another study found that drug approval took up to two years longer in the United States than in France, Great Britain, and Germany.[34] Pharmaceutical companies complained about the drug lag, but the longer drug approval times in the United States did seem effective at protecting consumers: between 1972 and 1994, 12 percent of drugs on the British market were found to be unsafe, compared to only 3 percent in the United States.[35] When business mobilized against the proposed consumer protection agency, then, it was doing so in the context of a regime of consumer protection that was already more protective of the consumer than was the case in Europe.

The same is true for a surprising number of other regulations that businesses fought in the 1970s and 1980s. Comparative case studies of regulation before the 1980s routinely concluded that environmental and health and safety regulations were stronger in the United States than in European countries at this time. The United States fought pollution more aggressively than Sweden, regulated possible carcinogens more heavily than several European countries, adopted health and safety regulations that were more adversarial to industry, was more punitive to business in the regulation of mines, quickly banned chlorofluorocarbons and led the fight against them while most European countries dragged their feet, and had much more stringent drug approval criteria and more stringent water pollution regulations.[36]

Similar dynamics are evident in other domains. The cut in capital gains taxes of 1978 has been cited as a central example of the power of business, and as we saw, capital gains tax cuts represent the most significant change in the tax code over several decades, dramatically reducing the tax liabilities of the top 0.01 percent. But a comparative perspective suggests that business groups were organizing because capital gains taxes as a percentage of GDP were considerably higher in the United States than in other countries at the time (figure 9.2). The interpretation of this figure is not straightforward, as capital gains tax revenue can increase for reasons other than high rates (for example, because capital gains may be more likely to be realized when rates are lower, because capital gains may play a larger role in some economies than others, or simply because some countries do not tax capital gains separately). Nevertheless, careful studies of the tax burden before 1980 do find effective tax rates on capital to be higher in the less well-developed welfare states (including the United States) than in the more developed welfare states.[37]

The Riegle-Neal Interstate Banking and Branching Act of 1994 repealed restrictions on branch banking, but most other advanced industrial countries had never had such restrictions against branch banking to begin with. Indeed, the absence of this restriction is often cited as the reason why Canadian banks have been able to withstand economic crises much better than American banks in the postwar period.[38]

The story is similar for the most famous deregulation of recent years, the repeal of the Glass-Steagall Act, the Depression-era regulation that separated commercial and investment banking. Scholars have argued that the repeal was initiated and promoted by commercial banks, which had opposed Glass-Steagall since the 1970s.[39] However, the repeal of Glass-Steagall is a classic example of the "running to stay in place" dynamic, because Glass-Steagall is a curiously American phenomenon. Most other advanced industrial countries had never had restrictions separating commercial and investment banking and practiced what is called, by contrast, "universal banking"; the unusual American structure seems again to have been a result of the agrarian-industrial divide.[40] Thus, what American businesses achieved, after some thirty years of effort and campaigning, was simply the status quo ante in Europe. Indeed, allowing American firms to compete with their European counterparts was routinely given as a reason for the repeal of Glass-Steagall by both Democrats and Republicans.[41]

In 2005, bankruptcy reform made it harder for consumers to declare bankruptcy. This was widely interpreted by commentators as a victory for

Figure 9.2 Capital Gains Taxes on Individuals in the United States and Nineteen OECD Countries as a Percentage of GDP, 1965–2016

United States

Unweighted Average: Australia, Austria, Belgium, Canada, Denmark, Finland, France, Germany, Greece, Ireland, Italy, Japan, Luxembourg, Netherlands, New Zealand, Norway, Sweden, Switzerland, United Kingdom, United States

Source: OECD Revenue Statistics (OECD.Stat, "OECD Revenue Statistics—OECD Countries: Comparative Tables," https://stats.oecd.org/Index.aspx?DataSetCode=REV, accessed August 15, 2018).

the credit card industry, which had pushed for such a change for years. But even after the passage of this law, American consumers still have greater bankruptcy protections than consumers in any other country. The reform achieved a result that European corporations took for granted.[42]

The same is true for the North American Free Trade Agreement (NAFTA), which was widely supported by business.[43] As figure 9.3 shows, American tariffs have consistently been higher than European tariffs for several decades.

In these instances—which make up the backbone of the case for business

Figure 9.3 Applied Tariff Rates (Simple Mean), All Products, Percent, in United States and in European Union, 1988–2016

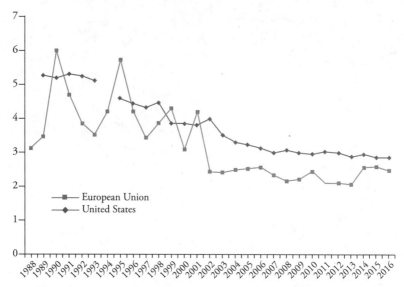

Source: The World Bank, "Tariff Rate, Applied, Simple Mean, All Products," https://data.worldbank .org/indicator/tm.tax.mrch.sm.ar.zs (accessed August 15, 2018).

influence in the rise of recent free market policies—it turns out that American businesses were working hard to achieve an outcome that European businesses did not have to work for at all.

This discussion has focused only on national-level regulations, leaving a full investigation of state-level regulations for future research. But there are indications that American businesses may be "running to stay in place" at the state level as well—for example, in right-to-work laws, which are highly contentious at the state level in the United States but are common in Europe.[44]

This discussion has drawn on the secondary literature on money in politics, and most of that literature was written before the changes introduced in the United States by the Supreme Court's *Citizens United* and *SpeechNow* decisions. Thus, the situation today—which is developing rapidly—may be different from what can be seen in the historical record. Moreover, there is a clear distinction in the historical record before and after 1980. Before the rise of Ronald Reagan, the United States was considerably more adversarial to corporations than it is now. The free market revolution has had an effect, and in general American policies are more business-friendly now, in some domains even more so than in Europe. The regulation of genetically modified organisms (GMOs) is perhaps the most prominent example, but scholars have identified many others.[45]

For both of these reasons, this discussion of the European and American models may explain the recent past better than the present or the future. It is nevertheless important to understand the historical dynamics, because they explain why free market policies were so advanced in the United States: businesses organized a massive mobilization in the 1970s because they were trying to address policies that were more hostile to business than was the case in other countries. That mobilization did have some effects. Even if it is not the main factor in our story here, it often pulled the United States back to the European average, and in a few cases even went beyond that. Money may be more powerful now, or may become more powerful in the future, but we misunderstand the history of the recent past if we do not keep these comparative points in mind.

Another problem with relying on the secondary literature is that this chapter is unable to assess business power on less salient issues on which corporations may be able to exercise power in ways that are not visible to researchers.[46] This is indeed a problem any time researchers are attempting to examine issues that actors are interested in concealing. Nevertheless, scholars who do attempt to examine less visible forms of power conclude that the main thing businesses get from this behind-the-scenes kind of influence is tax exemptions;[47] and as we have discussed above, tax exemptions are a prime example of running to stay in place. As other research emerges giving other examples of less visible power, it will be up to researchers to examine whether the running to stay in place dynamic holds in those other cases.

Our story here may also help explain why scholars find that the affluent are more likely than the poor to see their views represented in European policies.[48] European businesses and the European wealthy have mechanisms of power other than lobbying, but the workings of these mechanisms are less visible in most European countries than lobbying activity in the United States. This lower visibility means that the surprising European combination of lower poverty levels and less inequality with extensive business power has not been sufficiently appreciated or investigated.

Does it matter what happens in other countries? One could argue that power is simply the ability to exercise influence in a situation, and certainly American business showed that power at multiple points in the story. But the comparison with other countries matters first for a simple definitional reason, but more importantly, because it points a way forward for American political economy.

First, if a despot is torturing dissidents, and after a concerted effort of resistance the situation improves to where the despot is only imprisoning the dissidents for life, it's true that from one perspective the resistance has been powerful in achieving a better outcome, but it still does not seem that one can conclude the resistance is powerful compared to the despot. A proper analysis of the situation demands a counterfactual that can serve as a baseline for what should even count as power. In our case, the European countries, generally seen as more economically progressive, should provide a fair counterfactual for what is a realistic level of business power under capitalism.

Moreover, the comparison suggests some very practical policy implications. One may conclude from this discussion not that business and the wealthy are less powerful in the United States, but rather that business and the wealthy are *also* or even *more* powerful in Europe. This would be an accurate interpretation of the argument, and it has several important implications. European businesses exercise this power without having to conduct active lobbying efforts, as they are often embedded in domestic decision-making structures for which there is no analogue in the United States.[49] Because American modes of exercising business power are more visible, observers overestimate the power of business in America. More importantly, this greater power of European corporations, indexed by their ability to take for granted the policies that American corporations struggle for, is combined with levels of poverty and inequality that are lower than in the United States, partly owing to more extensive welfare states in Europe. It seems that privileging the ability of corporations to accumulate has been the price of the European welfare state. This is why the comparison with Europe is fruitful: the European experience suggests a path could be taken that would require less wasted effort on lobbying *and* achieve lower poverty and inequality. But this path runs through policies that are more—not less—favorable to capital.

As table 9.2 shows, there are some clear exceptions to the argument that American businesses are running to stay in place, as well as some policies that are difficult to code one way or the other. The deregulation of savings and loans is difficult to code because these organizations are not equivalent in the different countries. And the relatively greater power of American business against labor explains why the United States is generally considered a state oriented to capitalists. In 1977, for instance, businesses organized against a labor law reform that would have made it harder for businesses to retaliate against employees involved in union activities, and they also helped defeat a bill that would have allowed workers to picket against all employers located at a particular site.[50]

The exceptions in the table show that "running to stay in place" does not explain every victory for American business. The most important exception to the running to stay in place phenomenon is the welfare state. One of the business victories listed in table 9.2 that cannot be explained as simply a matter of American business catching up to Europe is the failure of Bill Clinton's health care reform. The United States has been considerably behind Europe since the Second World War in developing a public welfare state, with the consequence that poverty and inequality have been consistently lower in European countries than in the United States throughout the postwar period. This "exception," moreover, turns out to be the key to explaining the whole phenomenon of running to stay in place, as we will discuss in chapter 11.

But first, if "running to stay in place" helps to explain why American business supported ACRS, we know by now that ACRS was only a small part of the ERTA. We turn next to examining Kemp-Roth in comparative perspective.

CHAPTER 10

Pocketbook Politics and the Rise of Conservatism

KEMP-ROTH HAPPENED BECAUSE Americans were calling for a response to inflation in the 1970s, and entrepreneurial politicians discovered in tax cuts a possible response to inflation. But why were Americans so upset about inflation, and why were tax cuts the particular response that Republicans gave?

Objective assessments of the costs of inflation do not find it to be so troublesome. Scholars have noted that in the 1970s even those at the lowest end of the socioeconomic scale saw their taxes rise due to inflation, because inflation brought some people into the lowest tax bracket who otherwise would not have been paying any taxes at all, and because there were more and smaller brackets in the tax code at the low end than at the high end.[1] But estimates of the actual costs of inflation find the most heavily affected were taxpayers at twice median income—many of whom were two-income families—who saw marginal tax rates almost double in the course of thirteen years, from 22 percent to 43 percent; and for those at the 95th percentile, marginal rates increased from 26 percent to 38 percent between 1961 and 1979. For the general population, inflation resulted in only about a 1.5 to 3 percent lower standard of living—for most families, a few hundred dollars a year.[2] It's hard to see why that would trigger over 80 percent of respondents calling it the most important problem in the nation, more important even than unemployment, why little children would be puzzling about it and drawing pictures about it. After all, although inflation harms creditors, it should benefit debtors.

Any time objective material conditions seem out of line with subjective responses to them, we have to wonder if some sort of manipulation is at work. There are some arguments along this line,[3] and it's quite possible that fear of inflation could have been constructed out of the usual factors that drive American journalism, such as extreme attentiveness to issues that affect the upper middle classes, and a search for novelty and sensation. Murders in gas lines, no matter how unrepresentative, are going to lead the news.

There is also the possibility of something more universal in the response to inflation. Karl Polanyi noted in *The Great Transformation* the effects that price volatility has in history: it seems to be not the level of prices, but their rise or fall that most affects people.[4] One study of over thirty thousand people in nearly forty countries found the poor more likely than the rich to worry about inflation.[5] Those who are harmed by inflation are often hard-working elderly people whose savings are disappearing, a sympathetic population even if those elderly when seen in cross-section are part of the upper middle classes. Keynes thought what made inflation intolerable is that it detached well-being from effort, creating winners and losers by lottery.[6]

Between the social constructionist argument and the universal response argument is a more historically conditioned possibility that sees the response to inflation as rooted in objective material conditions, but sees those conditions as unique to the United States: specifically, all the ways in which the consumer economy of midcentury led to a rising panic about inflation.

The Creation of the Consumer Economy

Figure 9.1 in the previous chapter showed that the countries of the advanced industrial world differ considerably in the extent to which they devote resources to investment. Figure 10.1 shows the obverse, the extent to which countries devote resources to household consumption. The United States is particularly marked as having a high proportion of GDP devoted to consumption since at least 1950.

This focus on consumption is not the outgrowth of some deep element in American character that favors material consumption. In fact, at the beginning of the twentieth century, the United States was the country that

Figure 10.1 Household Consumption as Share of GDP in the United States and Twenty-Two OECD Countries, 1950–2014

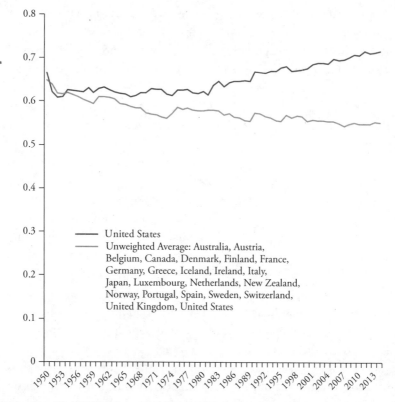

Source: Penn World Tables, Feenstra, Inklaar, and Timmer 2015.

had the highest savings for those on which we have systematic comparative data, as would be expected for the country that had the highest wealth (figure 10.2). But the different experiences of the countries in the first half of the twentieth century led to different formations of political economy, such that by the 1950s, the situation had reversed. Savings rose in the European countries as they became wealthier, in line with standard understandings of the relationship between savings and GDP, but the United States held steady at a constant rate of savings despite the unprecedented prosperity of the postwar period. Some analysts such as Alexander Gerschenkron had already in 1962 noticed that less developed countries generally try to restrain consumption and try to "increase supply of capital to the nascent industries."[7] But a comparative historical examination reveals a startling fact that was

Figure 10.2 Total Gross Savings as Percentage of GDP in Nine Countries, 1870–1987

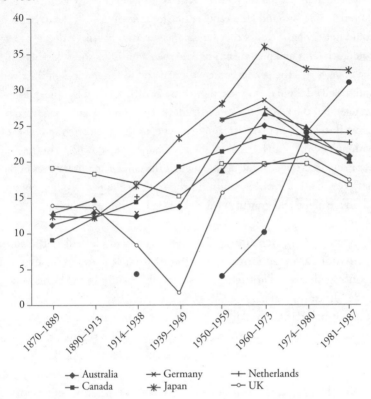

Legend:
- Australia
- Canada
- Germany
- Japan
- Netherlands
- UK

Source: Maddison 1992.

not predicted by Gerschenkron, and in some ways directly contradicts the main thrust of his argument predicting greater state intervention in backward countries: in the early to mid-twentieth century the American state launched an extensive program of state interventions aimed at increasing consumption and *decreasing savings* during this period, preventing the savings rate from rising with GDP as one would expect.

Many American observers believed at this time that the productive capacity of the United States had come to outpace its ability to consume, causing problems that shook the economy: agricultural "overproduction" drove down prices, leaving farmers unable to repay loans, which rattled the banks that had made those loans. What happened next is memorialized in the title of one of the great American novels:

The works of the roots of the vines, of the trees, must be destroyed to keep up the price, and this is the saddest, bitterest thing of all. Carloads of oranges dumped on the ground. The people came for miles to take the fruit, but this could not be. How would they buy oranges at twenty cents a dozen if they could drive out and pick them up? And men with hoses squirt kerosene on the oranges . . . The people come with nets to fish for potatoes in the river, and the guards hold them back; they come in rattling cars to get the dumped oranges, but the kerosene is sprayed. And they stand still and watch the potatoes float by, listen to the screaming pigs being killed in a ditch and covered with quick-lime, watch the mountains of oranges slop down to a putrefying ooze; and in the eyes of the people there is the failure; and in the eyes of the hungry there is a growing wrath. In the souls of the people the grapes of wrath are filling and growing heavy, growing heavy for the vintage.[8]

Why are the pigs screaming? Why are they being killed? Is this all just hallucination, a metaphorical rendering of what it feels like to live inside an economy that is collapsing? This is the only passage in the book in which the title phrase appears.

It is not hallucination. All of this actually happened. It was all a part of the price-management programs that were one of President Franklin Delano Roosevelt's attempted solutions to the Great Depression. Because farmers had been so productive in so many areas, prices for agricultural goods were falling. In fact they fell to such an extent that farmers found themselves unable to sell their crops at prices that would allow them to pay back their loans. This was the case for pork, cotton, wheat, corn, sugar, and tobacco. All over the country, farmers were launching riots and political actions. To appease farmers required keeping the prices of agricultural products up. And the simplest way to keep prices up was to reduce the amount of goods that were for sale by destroying them.[9] This is what produced the crop destruction that so haunted Steinbeck.

The real culprit was tight monetary policy, but that was not yet recognized. And so the United States created a permanent Keynesian economy in which consumption would be the motor of growth. As European countries focused on reconstruction and catching up with the "American danger," America tried to address agricultural "overproduction" by raising the ability of consumers to consume. These policies to promote consumption were supported by all elements of the American political world, from unions to corporations, Democrats and Republicans, economists and journalists.

Where European labor unions were demanding social welfare spending and restraining wages, American unions fought for higher wages to keep up purchasing power—with the approval of economists and policymakers. While European economic reconstruction was led by large export firms, American corporations supported an agenda of domestic consumption.[10]

The promotion of consumption was accomplished most concretely and consequentially with the inauguration of a regime of debt-financed home ownership as the centerpiece of the economic system. Many identified housing as a sector capable of reviving the economy at large, because housing and construction could absorb so much productive capacity and were linked to so many other sectors. A sophisticated infrastructure of credit developed and expanded, from the subsidized home mortgage loans that allowed a generation of returning GIs to move to the suburbs, to the rapid spread of credit cards, to home equity loans, to fights for increased credit access for women and minorities. The single-family home in the suburbs increasingly came to be the center of how Americans organized their lives: the largest purchase most would ever make, for which they saved for years, and the loans for which they paid off over decades. Housing increasingly determined children's life chances too, in an educational system dependent on local property taxes, and the tax code gave large exemptions for home mortgage interest and property tax.[11]

And at the heart of this midcentury focus on consumption and the ideal of the single-family home with its intensive use of appliances was the face of Ronald Reagan. In the 1950s, after his Hollywood career was over but before his political career had begun, Reagan worked for many years as a spokesman for General Electric (GE). Biographers identify this period as crucial in his transition from New Deal Democrat to conservative Republican.[12]

Reagan often identified the hand of Providence at work in his life, and indeed, in retrospect, it is remarkable how his failures made his successes possible. Observers speculate that had Reagan's Hollywood career been successful, had he been able to get the kinds of movies that had him playing a strong president, he would never have wanted to run for president. And had Reagan been elected president in 1976, when he came close to securing the Republican nomination but ultimately lost it, he would likely have been a one-term president felled by inflation, because it took many more years of inflation for the American political world to be ready for Volcker's strong medicine.

In the 1950s the job at GE, which seems somewhat tiresome—spending weeks traveling on the train to speak to the workers of GE plants around the country—ended up being an education in public speaking. He learned "how to conserve his voice and how to fill his martini glass with water until the last reception of the day. He made mental notes about which jokes succeeded and which statistics served to make his points."[13] He became such a good salesman that a joke circulated about the audience member who had heard Reagan's pitch for the GE nuclear submarine and said, "I didn't really need a submarine, but I've got one now."[14] GE also flooded its employees, including Reagan, with material on the virtues of the free market and the dangers of collectivism, thus providing Reagan with the language and vision of midcentury American "free enterprise" that he would spend the rest of his life trying to get the country back to—a subtle way in which business influence operated on the rise of American conservatism.[15]

Part of Reagan's mandate at GE was precisely to communicate the virtues of the American consumer economy, particularly as made possible by GE appliances.

> The Reagan family was enlisted to represent the slogan "live better electrically" in their new, modernist ranch house, which was kitted out as a showcase for GE products. It had a retractable roof over the atrium, a heated swimming pool with underwater lights, intercoms in every room, and an elaborate lighting system that could produce a variety of colored effects. There was an electric barbecue, a refrigerated wine cellar, three TVs, three refrigerators, two freezers, two ovens, and a dishwasher with a built-in garbage disposal. The company had to install a three-thousand-pound switch box to handle the electric current. A series of three-minute commercials featured the Reagans telling three-year-old Patti about their "electrical servants," such as the vacuum and waffle iron that "make Mommy's work easier." Dad told viewers that "when you live better electrically, you lead a richer, fuller, more satisfying life."[16]

Living in his expensive single-family home, Reagan exemplified the ideals of consumption and homeownership. And through the television sets made possible by that focus on consumption his confident gaze arrived in millions of those suburban homes every week, on the third-highest rated show in America,[17] the consumer economy at its peak.

Inflation Rocks the Consumer Economy

The American consumer economy was based on the mortgage-financed suburban single-family home. Every element of that agreement—the price of housing, the availability and price of the credit that gave access to the housing, and the price of the gasoline that allowed workers to travel to those suburbs and brought low-cost goods all over the country—came undone by inflation.

Between 1970 and 1974 the nominal median price for a single family home rose by 50 percent. Housing price increases in the 1970s receive less attention than they deserve, because we are used to adjusting our historical statistics for inflation to make for comparable numbers. But although economists tried to explain even at the time that wages were also going up due to inflation, the sticker shock of the higher prices remained.[18] Moreover, the struggle to control inflation had also led to high interest rates. In conjunction with Regulation Q, which placed ceilings on interest rates, it was often the case that credit simply was not available for those wanting to purchase housing.[19] Inflation benefited those who had already purchased homes at fixed repayment rates, but they were hit in another way—through rising property taxes on the inflated values of their homes.[20] Whether you were in the market for a home, or already owned one, inflation got you one way or another. The nail in the coffin was the rise of gas prices, which raised not just the cost of transportation to and from those homes, but also the cost of all the goods that a network of trucks delivered throughout the far-flung suburbs.[21]

Inflation in the context of an economy oriented to consumption may also have helped to hasten the decline of labor. In the 1970s unions did what unions had always done in postwar America, fight for higher wages for their workers to keep up purchasing power—unlike unions in Europe that knew how to restrain wages when necessary. But whereas labor unions fighting for higher wages had once been welcome partners in the creation of purchasing power to keep the American consumer economy running, in the context of inflation higher wages were blamed for higher prices, alienating the public. Reagan's assault on PATCO was only one of several similar responses to striking unions in the 1970s by policymakers.[22]

In short, American dissatisfaction with inflation was part and parcel of the consumer economy and the politics of lower prices that had been pioneered over the three decades after the Second World War. As a few scholars have begun to argue, it was pocketbook politics in a new form.[23] Thus, when inflation shook the consumer economy, Republicans, perpetually stuck in the minority, got their chance—an opening to attack the entire postwar order.

Pocketbook Politics and Tax Dissatisfaction

This still does not explain why the Republicans turned to taxation as their solution to inflation, however. Two elements of the midcentury compromise over taxation prove crucial for understanding this. First, the American focus on consumption and the very high rates of taxation led John Kennedy and Lyndon Johnson to inaugurate a policy of cutting tax rates, and Jack Kemp and Ronald Reagan could then seize on that policy to justify their own. In other countries there were neither the astonishingly high rates nor the desire to stimulate consumption. Second, the United States relies disproportionately on income, profit, and capital gains tax, and these can be shown to rise with inflation more than other kinds of taxes.

Income tax rates were much higher in the United States than in other countries until the 1980s. The agrarian populists had defended high tax rates as a way to spread the fruits of capitalism as far as possible, to maintain purchasing power. But at midcentury, with deflation no longer a concern, John F. Kennedy's advisers thought it would be lower tax rates that would boost consumption and stimulate the economy, particularly if they were financed through deficits. One of the main figures involved with the Kennedy/Johnson bill gave arguments supporting it that sound remarkably like Kemp's:

> Congress believes that, in the long run, we will collect more taxes with lower rates. The principle should be readily recognizable to Americans. It shows up in our industrial practice of lowering the cost of items whenever appropriate to increase volume and profits. . . . The stimulative effect of tax reduction will boost demand and heighten the incentive for investment and risk-taking. It will also alleviate our unemployment and excess capacity problems, encourage modernization and expansion of plant and equipment, and increase the gross national product and national income. In brief, we expect to collect more revenue by creating a larger pool of taxable income to be taxed at lowered rates. . . . There are important collateral benefits flowing from rate re-

duction. It takes the pressure off Congress to provide relief for different groups of activities, which in the past, for example, led to a wide extension of the capital gains concept. It also lessens the incentives for businessmen and tax practitioners to seek such legislative relief, to tailor their affairs to fit into artificial patterns, or to risk experimenting with borderline transactions or tax gadgets. Rate reduction, in other words, should lessen our intense focus on tax planning and increase our concentration on more productive pursuits.[24]

The Kennedy/Johnson bill was remarkably supply-side. Elizabeth Popp Berman and Nicholas Pagnucco show that the Kenney/Johnson and Reagan bills were similar in many ways, and were defended in similar terms—with the exception that in 1964 it was the Democrats arguing that tax cuts would pay for themselves, and the Republicans worrying about the deficit. But the original impetus for the 1964 bill had been a Keynesian one of increasing demand and providing economic stimulus.

According to the Kemp aide who drew up the first version of Kemp-Roth, the Kennedy/Johnson bill was its direct model.[25] Moreover, Republicans referred to the Kennedy bill several times in the Congressional debate over Kemp-Roth, both to argue that that tax cut had paid for itself, to use Kennedy's own language to support their cut, and to harangue the Democrats for their change of heart over taxation. (Democrats argued that the two cuts were not comparable because tax rates had been so much higher under Kennedy, and because the role of inflation was different.) One of the chief architects of Kemp-Roth, Norman Ture, had worked for Kennedy.[26]

Thus, the high tax regime of midcentury America, combined with the American economy's consumer orientation, led Kennedy to set a precedent that may have been a model for, and was at the least used as rhetorical justification for, Reagan's tax cut.

Another aspect of the midcentury compromise was the focus on income, property, and capital gains taxes. These are exactly the taxes that are most affected by inflation. As early as the mid-1970s—before the era of the tax revolts—scholars had noticed that countries that relied proportionately more on direct taxes (income and property taxes) had more difficulty collecting taxes than countries that relied on indirect taxes (sales and payroll taxes and social security contributions).[27] Over the last few decades, economists have argued that consumption taxes are better for economic growth than income taxes.[28] The reasons why are still subject to debate. It may be

Figure 10.3 Income, Profit, and Capital Gains Tax as Percent Total Tax Revenue in the United States and Twenty-Two OECD Countries, 1965–2016

Source: OECD Revenue Statistics (OECD.Stat, "OECD Revenue Statistics—OECD Countries: Comparative Tables," https://stats.oecd.org/Index.aspx?DataSetCode=REV, accessed August 15, 2018).

that by restraining consumption, consumption taxes help to channel income toward savings, which can then be used for investment.[29] The United States is the only advanced industrial country without a national-level consumption tax, although a handful of other countries have proportionately low sales tax collections (figure 10.3).

Reliance on different kinds of taxes produces different responses to inflation: because income taxes are progressive, a taxpayer pays more taxes as her income increases. Progressive tax systems divide income into brackets and levy different rates on different brackets. Other taxes, such as sales taxes, do not differentiate between taxpayers of different income levels. A pauper who buys a soft drink will pay the same eight or ten cents of tax as Bill Gates. Bill Gates will certainly spend a higher absolute amount on consumption, but consumption does not rise proportionately to income: with each extra dollar earned, people spend less and save more. Bill Gates spends a lower proportion of his income on consumption and therefore pays a lower proportion of his income on consumption tax. Some countries try to offset this by levying lower tax rates on basic items, such as food, and higher taxes on luxury goods, but overall economists still think that tax systems that rely heavily on consumption taxes tend to be slightly regressive.[30]

Particularly notable for our purposes is what happens to these different kinds of systems under inflation. Bracket creep increases the proportion of progressive taxes as a percent of GDP, but for taxes that are not progressive, there is no such bracket creep, and consequently inflation would not increase the proportion of taxes as a percent of GDP in this way. Thus we would expect inflation to have a greater effect on tax revenues for income taxes (which are progressive and charge higher rates the more money a taxpayer makes) than for other kinds of taxes that are not linked to income, or are regressive.

Figure 10.4 shows the evolution of tax structures in the OECD from 1965 to 1982, the years identified by economists as the period of the "Great Inflation." The figure shows unweighted averages of each kind of tax as a percentage of GDP in Australia, Austria, Belgium, Canada, Denmark, Finland, France, Germany, Greece, Ireland, Italy, Japan, Luxembourg, the Netherlands, New Zealand, Norway, Portugal, Spain, Sweden, Switzerland, the United Kingdom, and the United States. Of the three largest taxes, income taxes and social security taxes rose as a percentage of GDP over this period, as expected. And as expected, taxes on goods and services were remarkably stable as a percentage of GDP, despite the economic growth and inflation of this period.

The appendix shows that this dynamic holds even after controlling for other factors that may affect the level of taxes. The results show several different estimations of the effects of inflation on different kinds of taxes, with the outcome variable measured both as a proportion of total tax revenue and as a proportion of GDP. Because we are interested in the short-term effects of inflation on taxes, the estimations use fixed effects. The estimations show the same story regarding income taxes: inflation is associated with rises in income, profit, and capital gains taxes, but is not reliably associated

Figure 10.4: Evolution of Tax Structure under the Great Inflation, OECD, 1965–1982

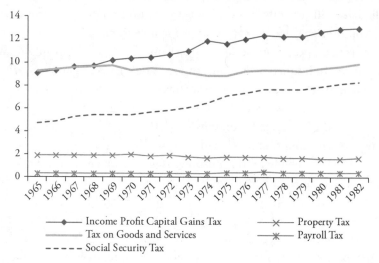

Source: OECD Revenue Statistics (OECD.Stat, "OECD Revenue Statistics—OECD Countries: Comparative Tables," https://stats.oecd.org/Index.aspx?DataSetCode=REV, accessed August 15, 2018).

with taxes on goods and services. Either income taxes worsen inflation, or inflation drives up income taxes because of bracket creep, or both. It is not clear whether it is the absolute amount of income taxes as a percent of GDP that is the key factor or the proportion in the revenue structure, which would suggest the mechanism is about the visibility of taxation for a given amount of spending. Social security taxes, however, do not rise with inflation when we control for other factors; only income, profit, and capital gains taxes do.

In short, inflation interacts differently with income, profit, and capital gains tax than it does with other taxes. This is not surprising, and indeed is exactly what we would expect from the nature of the taxes. But the consequences have not been noted for our understanding of comparative political economy over the last several decades.

One final piece of evidence links this macroeconomic picture—that the United States relies disproportionately on taxes on income, profit, and capital gains, which are exactly the taxes most vulnerable to inflation—to the history on the ground. Figure 10.5, which is based on the work of the political scientist Andrea Campbell, shows that tax dissatisfaction can be predicted from just a few variables: GDP, GDP growth, inflation, and the total

Figure 10.5 Predicting Tax Dissatisfaction among Americans, 1956–2017

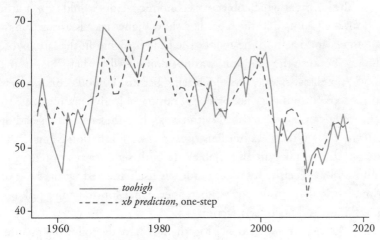

Source: Author's calculations based on Campbell 2009.

tax burden as a percentage of GDP.[31] The solid line in the figure, based on General Social Survey (GSS) and Gallup poll data, shows the percentage of respondents who believed that their taxes were "too high." The dotted line is a predictive equation made up of the variables GDP, the rate of growth of GDP, the inflation rate, and the total tax burden. Using only these four variables, it is possible to predict the proportion of respondents who say their taxes are "too high," with a correlation between the predicted and actual values of 0.84.

The evidentiary base for this picture is not as strong as we would wish, as the question was asked only a handful of times in the period that concerns us (just six times between 1973 and 1982). Nor is it possible to conduct a comparative evaluation of this question, because the international survey data of the World Values Survey and the International Social Survey Programme as well as indices constructed from newspapers such as the European Protest and Coercion Data do not begin until the 1980s, missing the key effects of inflation in the 1970s. This is an area for further research; a cross-national index of public opinion on taxes in the 1970s, built from newspaper sources or other sources, would be a useful contribution to the scholarship, and could help to answer the question of whether the relationships identified here for the United States hold in other countries.

But the evidence we do have suggests that tax dissatisfaction was growing at exactly the points at which objective economic factors would expect it to grow. Both the Gallup and the GSS data show higher tax dissatisfaction in the late 1970s and again in the 1990s. The peak is higher in the late 1970s, presumably because the economy was not doing well at that time; in the late 1990s, tax dissatisfaction was increasing because a good economy was pushing people into higher tax brackets, raising objective tax burdens. In general, Americans are dissatisfied with taxes when the economy is bad or not growing, when their tax burdens rise, and when inflation is high. The inflation and total tax burden variables are both significant in predicting tax opposition. Since the total tax burden is itself affected by the level of inflation, particularly in the 1970s, there is evidence for drawing a link between inflation and tax dissatisfaction.

Putting these sources of evidence together, we have the following picture. First, we know that the Reagan team was picking up evidence in the polls of citizen dissatisfaction with tax burdens. We also know that this dissatisfaction can be explained by objective factors, as it can be predicted by GDP, GDP growth, the total tax burden, and inflation. And we know that, because inflation is associated with rising taxes on income, profit, and capital gains in particular, countries that rely disproportionately on those taxes in their tax structure will see more tax dissatisfaction than countries that rely on other kinds of taxes. Income, profit, and capital gains taxes are the only taxes that rise systematically with inflation. There is a relationship across the advanced industrial world between inflation and the burden of income, profit, and capital gains taxes, and there is a relationship in the United States between objective economic factors and tax dissatisfaction.

The full story is not quite so mechanistic, because after all inflation is not the main reason why income taxes grow, nor are inflation and tax burdens the only factors affecting tax dissatisfaction. Most importantly, tax dissatisfaction was neither unmixed (voters also preferred increased spending and balanced budgets) nor highly salient to voters.

Tax dissatisfaction is best understood as a *resource for politicians* in crafting political victory: something politicians sought out and nurtured, but did not invent from scratch. The crucial role of the entrepreneurial politician also explains why some analysts have found that the shape of the tax mix (that is, which kinds of taxes predominate in the revenue structure) leads to lower growth in spending across the advanced industrial countries, but others have found no relationship between the tax mix and tax protest, at least for the post-1980 period.[32] Reliance on particular kinds of taxes may generate not tax protest, but tax dissatisfaction—a willingness to accept cuts when they are offered, not an active demand for lower taxes. After all, at the height of the peak of tax dissatisfaction, Jimmy Carter was not getting letters complaining about taxes.

Despite these qualifications, there is a clear material thread here that should not be ignored in our understanding of the rise of American economic conservatism in the 1970s: Inflation rose, driven partly by the exogenous oil shock when OPEC decided to restrain production, and partly by longer-term factors that are still being debated, such as wage-price spirals.[33] When inflation rose, it caused taxes on income, profit, and capital gains to rise, and the burden of these taxes may have worsened inflation in ways that were not as prominent in countries that did not rely so disproportionately on income, profit, and capital gains taxes. When tax burdens rose, especially in the context of inflation, tax dissatisfaction rose. This is what Dick Wirthlin was picking up in his opinion polls all over the country. The Republicans pinned their electoral hopes on it.

The tax cut movement was both reaction to, and outgrowth of, the mid-century American consumer economy. While business interests lobbied to bring the United States closer to European norms regarding the promotion of investment, American consumers saw their interests as tied to lower prices. The unusual nature of American tax collection allowed a political party trying to get into power to capitalize on these concerns. The consumer economy helped Jack Kemp and his allies both by providing the precedent of Kennedy's tax cuts, and by producing a tax structure that was generating tax dissatisfaction and therefore potential popularity of tax cuts. Business and consumers had two different responses to the problem of inflation in the consumer economy. These two different responses collided in the tax cut, producing the specter of business fighting Ronald Reagan.

The most successful and durable aspects of American conservatism are precisely those that coincide with the purchasing-power paradigm, while those that do not coincide with it, such as preventing gay rights or civil rights or women's rights, have largely failed. Even if we examine only economic issues, financial deregulation—which helps to subsidize purchasing power in a time of stagnant wages—coincides with the consumption paradigm and has proven difficult to dislodge; environmental deregulation does not coincide with it, and is undone by Democratic presidents and policy-makers, and even by Republican policymakers at the state level. Even the rise of xenophobia is partly a result of policies and policy omissions that ensure that Americans can depend on low prices. There is a straight line from the screaming pigs to Jack Kemp, and beyond.

CHAPTER 11

Democracy's Deficits

THE ELECTORAL POTENTIAL of tax cuts affected every stage of the story, as we can see from Republicans' efforts to scrutinize the political appeal of large across-the-board tax cuts at the very early stages of policy formulation in the mid-1970s, when Jack Kemp and others saw in tax cuts a way to dislodge the Democrats' hold on Congress; before the congressional elections of 1978, when tax cut fever briefly gripped the land; throughout the 1980 primaries, when the promise of tax cuts became a point of contention between Ronald Reagan and George H. W. Bush; and during the general election, when tax cuts became the Reagan team's main answer to the most important problem of the day, inflation, over other issues that could not run the political gauntlet, such as the gold standard. After the election, Democrats, also noting the polls, decided not to resist tax cuts but to offer an alternative tax cut of their own.

We have also seen that there were objective reasons for increased tax dissatisfaction in the mid-1970s, particularly the rise in inflation and the rise of real tax burdens. And we have seen that the peculiar tax structure of the United States, which relies less on consumption taxes than other countries do, may help explain the greater tax dissatisfaction during the "Great Inflation" of the 1970s.

The optimistic version of these findings is that the tax cut was a triumph of democracy. Taxes had gone up to levels where people were dissatisfied with them, and politicians responded appropriately by lowering them.

Arrayed against this more optimistic picture, however, is a range of evidence that casts doubt on the thesis that public opinion drove the tax cut movement. First is the simple fact that public opinion was inconsistent, even contradictory, and changed quickly. As we have seen, the tax cut fervor already seemed to be waning by the time of the 1980 general election, although even this is hard to state unequivocally given the fluctuating and sometimes contradictory nature of the polls. More damaging to the argument that public opinion drove policy, even at the height of tax dissatisfaction polls showed that respondents did not want tax cuts if they would lead to spending cuts or a rise in the deficit. Support for tax cuts was only high if they were presented without a tradeoff.[1]

At no point in the story do Reagan's tax cuts actually win a democratic contest. The Proposition 13 revolts were about local property taxes, not federal income taxes. The 1978 midterm elections were run on the issue of tax cuts, but the results were mixed at best, and a disaster in some reckonings. Reagan's campaign knew and admitted that tax cuts were not the reason for his primary wins. Tax cuts did lead to a small electoral boost in the general election, but the 1980 election was such a landslide that one cannot conclude that tax cuts were a decisive factor. And at the very end of the ERTA process, it's possible that the supposed public support that overwhelmed Congress was orchestrated by business groups.

Moreover, some scholars have argued that elites create the mass opinions to which they then claim to be responding. Andrea Campbell notes that objective tax burdens have not always led people to say that taxes are too high: in the early postwar period, the fit between objective burdens and opinions about taxes was not so tight, and she suggests that elite discourse on taxation makes the fit tighter than it would otherwise be—that is, that tax burdens only become noticeable when elites draw attention to them, as Jack Kemp and others were doing.[2] In their examination of editorials in the *Wall Street Journal,* John Burns and Andrew Taylor show that editorials in favor of across-the-board tax cuts were being written years before the Proposition 13 revolt.[3] Other scholars argue that in general, politicians follow the masses only when the masses want what the politician already prefers.[4] Benjamin Page and Robert Shapiro suggest that business and political elites manipulated public opinion to oppose inflation in the 1970s.[5]

Fitting this model is how Reagan talked about "waste and fraud." Polls have found that, when pressed to reconcile their seemingly contradictory preferences for lower taxes and more spending and balanced budgets, respondents suggest this can be done if waste is cut from government.[6] Americans have startlingly high estimations of how much government money is wasted, and this has been the case for decades, with guesses ranging from 39.8 cents of every tax dollar in 1979, to 51.2 cents in 2014.[7]

Jimmy Carter had campaigned against tax cuts because polls showed that voters did not want tax cuts if tax cuts came at the cost of a balanced budget. At least some analysts thought the 1978 midterm effort failed because voters did worry about deficits and spending cuts.[8] But the Reagan team discovered that those worries could be allayed by reminding voters about waste and fraud in government spending. For example, speechwriter Ken Khachigian took careful notes during a meeting with Wirthlin to discuss polls after Reagan's February 1981 speech, and concluded that to make the case that his program could work and would not hurt the poor, Reagan had to "start including waste & fraud – get some specifics going."[9] Reagan had already been hammering the theme during the campaign: "The subject of waste, fraud and abuse in government programs is one so important . . . when HEW alone reported over $6 billion lost, strayed or stolen, surely there is more reason than ever to see to it that tax dollars are used more effectively. The Office of Management and Budget estimates that the annual waste in federal government programs could reach as high as $25 billion and Jimmy Carter tells us we can't have a tax cut."[10] In office Reagan took various steps to reduce waste such as including "an immediate moratorium on all production and procurement of new audiovisual products and publications."[11] And he appointed a commission to investigate waste in government, as other presidents have also done.[12] In fact studies of waste, fraud, and abuse of government spending find that it is nowhere near the scales that would be needed to reconcile the kind of tax cuts and spending increases that politicians offer.[13] Vanessa Williamson interviewed voters and found that in many cases, what they mean by "waste" is simply policies they don't agree with.[14] But it is just as unrealistic to think that agreement can be found on which policies constitute "waste" as it is to think that cutting inefficiency and abuse can solve the problem. Over the decades the terms waste, fraud, and abuse have become an all-purpose solution to the question of how taxes can be cut without cutting spending.

Thus, some would argue that tax cuts were clearly not an instance of democracy if by that we mean representatives following the wishes of the public. In particular, cutting taxes was not an instance of the median voter driving policy, as the median voter seems to have preferred balanced budgets. There was certainly no groundswell of public opinion in favor of tax cuts at the expense of spending cuts or a deficit, and the Republicans could only create the semblance of popularity of their policy by talking about it in a particular way. Many scholars have argued that the success of free market policies is both result and index of a larger rise in individualism in American culture[15] but in fact the popularity of tax cuts was equivocal, and Americans remained as committed to government programs as they had ever been.

But it turns out that here things get tricky, and we cannot reach a confident conclusion of elites leading the masses either. Page and Shapiro's own work shows that public opposition to taxation dropped as soon as the ERTA indexed tax brackets to inflation, suggesting that there were objective reasons for the antitaxation climate of the 1970s. As for the tighter fit between objective factors and public opinion on taxes in the later period, perhaps this arises from consumers becoming more attuned to objective factors as a result of the rising inflation during the later period: as we have seen, inflation unraveled a great deal of the postwar consumer economy, and some of that may have emerged as tax dissatisfaction. If it was business rather than political elites who were somehow causing the public opposition to inflation—through the kind of attempts to influence attitudes that historians have documented for other periods,[16] or efforts such as the long-term campaign of persuasion that Ronald Reagan got from General Electric—*the strategy backfired,* for the individual income tax cuts that resulted were not favored by business. Moreover, one could argue that it is unrealistic to expect congruence between policy and general public opinion, because politicians operating in healthy democracies don't try to meet the wishes of the people, but rather of their base. And on major issues there can be such congruence between what the public wants and what politicians do that pollsters don't even bother to poll many issues: no politician in America today is going to suggest restricting credit access for women, for example, and no pollster is going to poll it. For all these reasons, arguments about persuasion and manipulation can be overdrawn.

Even the question of whether Reagan was doing something wrong or undemocratic by highlighting the issue of waste, fraud, and abuse is unclear. As several analysts note, when voters say they want lower taxes and higher spending, they are making the same demand as shoppers who want lower prices for greater value.[17] Although demands to cut government waste may be politically unrealistic, they are not irrational. Nor is it irrational to think that government, because of lack of competition, has no incentive to be efficient. For example, even if waste is not as widespread as responents think, it is hard to defend the high costs of medicines and the high salaries that American doctors earn compared to doctors in other countries, and some of those high profits and high salaries are being funded by taxpayers. One could argue that this is precisely an example of waste or abuse that responsible politicians could address. Moreover, one could point out that at least so far, tax cuts have not come at the cost of cuts in popular spending programs, and deficits have proved to be manageable and have not caused economic problems for voters. And one could note that asking Reagan *not* to make the best case for his program seems too high a bar to set in a democratic context: by that standard, Democratic politicians should have been emphasizing the tax costs of every spending program they promoted for decades.

Thus, there are reasons to think that one could call the tax cut democratic. In fact, the main reason to call the tax cut a democratic outcome is the simple and overwhelming observation that Americans did want something done about inflation. No problem has ever elicited a larger number of respondents calling it the most important problem in Gallup's poll than inflation did in the 1970s—not even unemployment in peak periods of unemployment. The genuinely democratic politician, the one who wants to do only what the people want, must respond to inflation. But none of the possible solutions to inflation was popular. Perhaps the responsible course would have been to do nothing, if we didn't know exactly how to cure inflation. But that would have been undemocratic, because doing nothing is clearly not what the people wanted. One could argue that if inflation was the problem, we had to create a recession, which is what Volcker eventually did. But that was an extremely unpopular—even undemocratic—course.

Indeed, although people clearly wanted something done about inflation, all of the things that politicians tried to do were unpopular or ineffective. Nixon's wage and price controls were popular when first implemented, but soon recognized to be ineffectual; Ford's WIN buttons and Carter's solar panels were unpopular, and therefore undemocratic.[18] One could argue that if the belief was that deficits were causing inflation, and what the median voter really wanted was balanced budgets, then the politician should have increased taxes and cut spending. But is there any understanding of democracy in which higher taxes and lower spending would have been considered a democratic outcome in the late 1970s, given that people expressed preferences for precisely the opposite? If Reagan had simply taken his victories on spending cuts and not tried to do anything about tax cuts—which would have been more favorable to balancing the budget—we would surely now be pointing to all the polls that showed respondents did not want spending cuts and calling him undemocratic.

The definition of democracy as a system of politician responsiveness to opinion polls, and critiques of policies for not matching opinion polls, are incoherent. The public wanted a solution to inflation, and the public did not want any of the specific solutions to inflation that were proposed. There is no course of action that could pass the test of public responsiveness, and therefore no democratic option by this definition of democracy.

The only possible conclusion to draw is that democracy cannot mean responding to opinion polls. But then what on earth could it mean?

Responsible Parties and Agonistic Democracy

At midcentury a group of political scientists made a simple and powerful argument: democracy means offering voters a choice. This means not only presenting a policy program at election time, but actually attempting to implement that program once in office. In America, with its fragmentation of power, implementing policies requires agreement among a broad coalition of policymakers, and the political parties are the best vehicle to achieve that widespread agreement. As the famous American Political Science Association report on responsible party systems wrote, "unless the parties identify themselves with programs, the public is unable to make an intelligent choice between them. . . . When the parties lack the capacity to define their actions in terms of policies, they turn irresponsible because the electoral choice between the parties becomes devoid of meaning. . . . The voter's political choice when confined to candidates without a common bond in terms of program amounts to no more than taking a chance with an individual candidate." They concluded: "An effective party system requires, first, that the parties are able to bring forth programs to which they commit themselves and, second, that the parties possess sufficient internal cohesion to carry out these programs. In such a system, the party program becomes the work program of the party, so recognized by the party leaders in and out of the government, by the party body as a whole, and by the public." Such a party allows voters to hold it accountable.[19]

More recently a set of democratic theorists has, from a different direction, developed similar ideas around the concept of "agonistic" democracy. Bonnie Honig, for example, argues that many conceptions of politics attempt to get rid of disagreement and conflict. Models of politics that assume politicians should simply be responding to public preference do something similar. Honig instead articulates an alternative understanding of conflict as central to political freedom.[20] Nancy Rosenblum develops this empirically by defending political parties as the main actors that structure and channel conflict, setting the stage for democracy.[21]

This understanding is more realistic with respect to the interests of state actors. For example, consider a piece of evidence that Hacker and Pierson see as proof that the Bush tax cuts were not democratic as shown by surveys taken from 1999 through early 2001: "Voters consistently saw tax cuts as a lower priority than plausible alternative uses of the forecasted surpluses. . . . Versus Social Security, tax cuts lost by a 74 to 21 percent margin. Versus Medicare, the margin is 65 to 25 percent. Even when Social Security is taken out of consideration, 69 percent of respondents preferred using extra monies on 'education, the environment, health care, crime-fighting, and military defense,' rather than a tax cut, which garnered just 22 percent support."[22]

The problem for a Republican staring at these numbers is that most of these other issues that voters prefer when forced into a tradeoff do not offer a clear contrast with Democrats. Democrats own the protection of government programs, as well as spending on education, the environment, and health care. Crime fighting and military spending have traditionally been Republican issues, but neither would have been a slam dunk at the time, because crime rates were falling and military spending would have been hard to justify given the collapse of the communist threat and the still peripheral role of the terrorist threat.

One response to this structure of public opinion—perhaps the response that an academic or technocrat would prefer—would be for the Republican to become a Democrat. If people see tax cuts as a lower priority than other issues, then perhaps there is no real call for the argument for a smaller state.

But this ignores the basic criterion that democracy means offering a real choice. If we accept that a functioning democracy requires offering a choice, even on issues that majorities prefer, it is a simple step to argue that the normal functioning of democracy requires politicians who not only offer a choice, but actually try to highlight the elements that make the choice they offer more attractive to voters. Reagan arguing that government money is wasted, and therefore that tax cuts would not require a tradeoff, is nothing unusual in this model. Indeed, it would have been unusual—even undemocratic—for him not to try to make a strong case for the choice that he was offering.

In this context it makes a great deal of sense for political activists to choose tax cuts, because tax cuts solve a very specific problem for Republicans. Political scientists have noticed that Americans are ideologically conservative but pragmatically liberal—they love the idea of small government in abstract terms, but in practice they like almost everything that government actually does. This predilection has been stable since the Second World War, as visible in the latest polls as it was under Franklin Roosevelt. So much else has changed since Roosevelt's time—women have transformed the labor market and the labor market has transformed home life, the nation has redefined itself in terms of race and gender, technology has torn up and replaced our everyday several times over—and yet, astonishingly, this remains true: Americans love the idea of small government. And they love almost everything that a big government does.[23]

Traditionally, this asymmetrical structure of opinion left Republicans very little room to maneuver. They could not campaign on cutting back government because the discussion quickly moved to specifics: Which parts of government are you going to cut back? Social Security and Medicare, the largest parts of government spending? The military? Spending on education, libraries, public parks? Spending on research and development? There are those who oppose spending in each of these areas, but broad swathes of the American electorate cannot be mobilized to vote for a candidate who makes cutting any one of these the main goal. As a result, conservative politicians have very few actual policies to run on. They can and do win elections based on factors other than policy, of course, such as charisma, but it's not possible to base a systematic political movement on charisma. At midcentury two Republicans won the presidency based on foreign policy concerns, and out of necessity the Republicans became much better party builders.[24] But this structure of opinion is what ultimately kept Republicans out of power in Congress for four decades.

There are a few major exceptions to the general rule that Americans don't like conservative policies. One is "welfare," to which polls show systematic and sustained opposition. Conservative politicians have made much hay out of this, but as a political strategy it is limited: if we understand "welfare" as welfare programs more broadly, then the term encompasses Social Security and Medicare, programs that are enormously popular. But respondents expressing opposition to "welfare" are thinking of welfare programs that benefit the poor. Attacking such programs was a successful strategy for Republicans in the 1990s, culminating with the Newt Gingrich–led reform of Aid to Families with Dependent Children (AFDC).[25] After that success, however, this effort petered out, first because it turns out that while "welfare" is unpopular, "assistance to the poor" is popular, placing constraints on how far this political strategy can go.[26] It is a strategy based not on substance but on framing, and it did go quite far; at the same time as AFDC was being reformed, however, other forms of aid to the poor, such as the Earned Income Tax Credit, were expanding.[27] Second, and more important, cutting aid to the poor cannot sustain a long-term political strategy because very little of the budget actually goes to aid to the poor. In fact, so little is spent on aid to the poor that even for the Reagan revolutionaries themselves, cutting this area was an afterthought.[28] Any genuine effort to shrink the size of government cannot rely on cutting aid to the poor (or foreign aid, another perennially unpopular but minuscule part of the budget). Moreover, even if the goal isn't actually to shrink the size of government but just to stay in power, attacking welfare has diminishing returns because it inevitably leads to a fight over race, and in that fight the opposition is heavily organized.

Thus, for a Republican politician looking for an issue but not wanting to get into a fight over race, there is a better option: tax cuts. Tax cuts solve the problem by linking the *symbolic* appeal of smaller government to a specific *concrete policy* that, Republicans could argue, would benefit voters. As Charlie Black of the National Republican Committee said a few years later:

> It was a radical idea . . . but politically, it had great value. The Republican Party since Hoover had been viewed as the party of the rich and "Big Business." After Watergate, the corruption image was added into it. Of the first 10 things people thought about Republicans, eight or nine were negative. It didn't take a genius to see the way to shake our terrible image was to take Jack Kemp's bill, and his rhetoric, and spread it to the party's candidates. For the first time in years, Republican candidates were out there running for something, not just against something.[29]

Tax cuts were a policy that could tap the American public's symbolic conservatism, while providing actual concrete material benefits. It wasn't exactly that public opinion drove policy, but that Republicans found in the existing tax preferences raw material that they could work with, a potential for tax opposition that they could ride all the way into Congress and the White House. Public opinion was not the unmoved mover, but a resource used by entrepreneurial politicians to craft political victories. In doing so, they were not following people's true or enlightened preferences—the preferences people might have expressed if they had understood the trade-offs between tax cuts and deficit spending, and the preferences they did express when they were explicitly asked about this trade-off. If the Republicans had been following people's actual preferences, as a median voter model would argue, they would never have given up their focus on balanced budgets. But they had been following that expressed preference all along, and the voters weren't voting for them. The shape of the polls led Republicans to craft an appeal that, they had reason to think, would resonate if they could convince the public that tax cuts would not necessarily lead to spending cuts or deficit increases—something the public was only too willing to believe. There are elements of manipulation in the way Republicans approached the polls: a truly responsible politician would always state the trade-off of tax cuts and balanced budgets given the popularity of the programs supported by government spending. But it is hard to imagine any democratic system that would actually produce that level of responsibility.

In this understanding, all of the elements that are sometimes seen as the initiators of policy—business interests, public opinion, the ideas of economists—are best seen as *resources* in the crafting of political victory.

Although it does a better job of capturing the dynamics of actual democracies, in normative terms this mandate model has several problems. First, preferences can change, whereas a responsible party must adhere to its mandate after it gets into power. Thus a party that is dutifully carrying out its mandate can find itself operating against majority opinion; the mandate model would give this situation high marks.

Second, the mandate model can *create* or *inflame* divisions rather than simply reflecting and redressing them. Given the ambivalence in the polls it seems clear that there would have been no polarization around the tax issue had Republicans not created it, but there is one now. The authors of the APSA report did not think that developing responsible and unified parties would produce a danger of ideological division, because "there is no real

ideological division in the American electorate, and hence programs of action presented by responsible parties for the voter's support could hardly be
expected to reflect or strive toward such division."[30] But as in those social-
psychological experiments in which esentially similar groups are induced
to develop hostility based on nothing, the normal and healthy functioning
of democracy has produced what are today real ideological divisions within
the electorate. Scholars argue from time to time that democracy can exac-
erbate conflict, but this has generally been argued for young democracies
where certain institutions such as the rule of law and a free press are not yet
in place.[31] The tax cut movement shows that mature democracies are not
immune from these dynamics either.

Third, the mandate model can lead parties to emphasize things that are
easy to accomplish, or easy to demonstrate accountability on in the short
term, rather than tackling more important but more difficult problems.[32]
For example, a party could not hope to prevent climate change before the
next election and might well decide to stay away from the whole issue. This
problem explains why the Republican Party slipped from Kemp's wagon,
with one party loading it up with growth and the other unloading with redistribution—complementary tasks—to Wanniski's spending and tax-
cutting Santa Clauses, who together produced a Christmas of deficits. The
Republican Party could not focus on growth because it is not possible to
credibly claim to have delivered economic growth: it often takes a long time
for the effect to show up, and it can be hidden by many other factors oc-
curring at the same time. But it was possible for the party to promise to
deliver tax cuts and then deliver them. The problem is the inability of representatives to *demonstrate* to voters that they are ruling in voters' interests
on the question of economic growth. The demonstrability of the policy in
fact comes to matter more than the actual consequences of the policy, which
are in most cases lost in a blizzard of econometrics. The Republicans thought
of the tax cut platform as an analogue to what they saw as the Democrats'
success in delivering on the promise of redistribution. It may not be easy to
pass legislation to increase the welfare state, but there is a long history of
legislators doing exactly that, and legislators have experience in conducting
both successful and unsuccessful efforts. Once the legislation is passed and
the benefits are flowing, the credit comes easily to the policymakers involved. Tax cuts allowed the Republicans to implement a similar model:
they engineered a contest of accountability on the basis of something they
could be held accountable on. The electoral need to do so ultimately led

Republicans to notice and mobilize the tax dissatisfaction that the unique American political economy had led to in the 1970s.

The Republicans' development of this contest of accountability around tax cuts, based on its perceived electoral potential, provides the best explanation for the rise of the politics of tax cuts—and for its persistence even after the high levels of support for tax cuts withered. It also answers why Democrats have neither opposed the tax cut policy strongly nor gotten on board with it. They don't oppose it because of the shape of the polls, and they don't jump on it because they don't need to, as they have plenty of other policies that potentially resonate with the public.

The need for democracy to offer a choice—the definition of a healthy, functioning democracy—means identifying and mobilizing conflict. Indeed, one could argue that precisely what a democracy should do is identify dissatisfaction even when it's passive, make it a point of concern, and address it. Instead of trying to restrict parties from finding and mobilizing conflict, the goal should be to address the problems that create those potential divisions in the first place.

The European Bargain

One of the problems of the consumer model is that it created conflicts that were papered over during the era of prosperity but that emerged—between labor and capital and between capital and the state—as soon as prosperity ended. On this score, the midcentury European model that has been functioning as the comparison for our case also furnishes some important lessons, because it helps to identify the institutions and policies that can dampen conflict. European democracies, with proportional representation and multiparty systems, have been able to generate and maintain consensus around welfare states that have for decades achieved growth and more equitable distribution than the United States. There are many reasons why these precise institutions and policies are not applicable to the contemporary American situation, but examining precisely how this alternative model worked can help us come up with lessons for our own time.

Although many observers believe that large government programs harm economic growth, in fact economists have spent decades searching for evidence of the trade-off between equity and efficiency without finding it. Europeans are not as wealthy as Americans if one examines brute averages, but those average figures hide the greater concentration of income at the top of the American distribution; moreover, what differences there are seem to be almost entirely because Europeans work for less, forgoing greater wealth for greater leisure time. When scholars take confounding factors into account, there is no strong evidence for the proposition that high taxes and high state spending have damaged economic prosperity in the advanced industrial countries.[33] This may be partly because European policymakers were careful to protect business against the damage (real or imagined) of the European welfare state. This is true of both the Scandinavian and Continental varieties.

Scholars have identified three main reasons why an extensive state did not interfere with economic growth. First, there are aspects of the welfare state that can benefit economic growth. Health care and education are the most obvious examples: well-educated citizens are more capable of making innovations that lead to productivity gains, and healthy workers lose fewer workdays to illness.[34] More recently, researchers have shown that other kinds of programs, such as food stamps and unemployment insurance, have positive economic effects.[35] The welfare state contributes to productivity and economic growth by avoiding the underutilization of the human capital of the poor. A welfare state can also benefit the economy by providing Keynesian stimulus during slumps. The welfare state, Walter Korpi argues, is not a leaky bucket, taking away from productivity, but an irrigation system, ensuring that the economy continues to grow by nurturing the ground from which productivity blooms.[36]

Second, welfare programs were often designed in ways that cushioned negative effects on the economy. The best-developed welfare states have always taken seriously the possibility that welfare programs can harm work incentives and labor supply, and they have attempted to avoid this by putting in place what contemporary observers would call a "disciplinary" welfare regime of various tests, mandates, and requirements for training, job search, and the like.[37] Consider, for example, the case of Sweden, by many measures the most generous and extensive welfare state. But even in Sweden—*especially* in Sweden—the welfare state has always been characterized by efforts not to allow people to stay out of work but rather to get them back into work as soon as possible.[38] The key element of the approach is Sweden's active labor market policy, which allows employers to hire and fire at will but encourages unemployed workers to get back into the labor force and trains them to be able to do so. Sweden pioneered these economic and wage policies in 1951 as part of the Rehn-Meidner model, developed by two

Swedish economists.[39] Moreover, a significant proportion of benefits in Sweden are conditional on employment and dependent on earnings.[40] For example, although in comparative perspective Swedish welfare benefits are certainly more universal than those of other states—applying to the entire population equally—the Swedish pension system has an important regressive element: the universal basic pension is supplemented by a secondary pension that is scaled to earnings, on the model of the continental welfare states.[41] This system induces workers to *increase* their hours of work as they approach retirement.[42] Similarly, only those who earn over a certain threshold are entitled to the sickness benefit, and paid parental leave is by definition available only to those who work—a built-in incentive to continue working.[43] Two scholars conclude: "Because benefit levels are closely related to earnings, the structure of social insurance benefits gives strong incentives for all individuals (men and women) to participate in the labor market."[44] By one accounting, in 1991 universal programs made up only about a quarter of spending on the Swedish welfare state.[45] We cannot completely rule out the existence of work disincentives caused by welfare programs,[46] but their effect is cushioned by the conditional and income-linked nature of many welfare programs. Quite in contrast to Esping-Andersen's praise of the Swedish welfare state for its decommodification, the *goal* of the Swedish welfare state was generally *recommodification*—getting workers back into the workforce as quickly as possible.[47] Other states such as Denmark and Finland are also characterized by the concern of activating workers into the labor market,[48] and the continental welfare states also function on the principle of regressivity, such that those who earn more get more, leading to incentives to earn more;[49] in general the successful European welfare states are characterized by a middle-class orientation, avoiding means tests that would serve as incentives to stay out of work.[50]

Third, European welfare states are embedded in and articulate with broader policies that benefit the economy, often by directly benefiting businesses. The literature has provided six different answers to the question of exactly what the European bargain provides capitalists in return for their acquiescence to extensive regimes of welfare. European capitalists get, to varying degrees in different countries:

(1) Free trade. A set of scholars has long argued that the European welfare state defuses resistance to trade openness and was part of a corporatist bargain of free trade in return for welfare protections.[51] The welfare state cushions citizens from the volatility of international markets and therefore re-

assures them about participation in international trade. The United States, with its large internal market, traditionally had the luxury of higher tariff barriers.

(2) Wage restraint and restraint of labor union militancy. A large literature in comparative political economy identifies the secret of many of the European welfare states to be a cooperative and acquiescent labor force which keeps wage costs low and avoids militant actions, in explicit or implicit return for extensive welfare policies. The precise historical mechanisms through which these bargains were struck, and the specific mechanisms through which they affect the economy, are still the subject of a lively and absorbing debate.[52]

(3) Interdependent production systems that function to generate specific kinds of manufacturing. The "varieties of capitalism" perspective, informed by the earlier "regulation school," has illuminated how coordination between producer groups in many European economies, including coordinated wage bargaining and systems of vocational training, allows the production of high-quality goods that are highly successful on export markets.[53] Welfare states are integral parts of the functioning of such coordinated models, in that they lower uncertainty, reduce turnover, and thus help to generate a labor force with specific skills.

(4) Growth models that are organized around investment and exports, rather than domestic consumption. The varieties of capitalism perspective is feeding into a new literature that emphasizes not only the sources of production, but also the different roles of consumption in different political economies and the roles of monetary and fiscal policy.[54] As we have seen, the United States at midcentury developed a political economy devoted to increasing domestic consumption, while many European countries concentrated on restraining private consumption in order to channel savings toward investment. Growing welfare states helped to bring citizen acceptance of this model.

(5) Tax regimes favorable to capital. Scholarship in the "new fiscal sociology," drawing on an earlier tradition of comparative political economy, has noted that the European state is partially financed by national sales taxes that the American polity has rejected on several occasions for their regressivity, and that payroll taxes play a large role in financing the most extensive welfare states.[55] As a consequence, in the 1970s—when the complaints about capital taxation were building to a crescendo in the United States— the free market United States taxed capital more heavily than countries such

as France and Germany did.[56] Recent research is finding corporatist bargains to be at the origins of the adoption of these modes of financing in Europe.[57]

(6) Regulatory and legal regimes favorable to capital. In comparative legal scholarship several scholars have identified regulatory and legal regimes that work to benefit corporations in Europe. For example, European countries often have much more permissive regulations regarding the right of employers to hire and fire. The model of "flexicurity" has already been mentioned and has received a great deal of attention from scholars; it is a prime example of the pragmatic approach to economic policy in which the European welfare state is embedded and of how the welfare state has been harnessed to support economic growth. Flexicurity ensures the flexibility of the economy by giving employers complete discretion over hiring and firing, allowing them the ability to respond rapidly to market changes. At the same time, workers' security is preserved through training and other programs that strive to get workers who have been fired into new jobs quickly.[58] Until the rise of Reagan's neoliberalism, the United States also regulated corporations more extensively: antitrust regulation, food and drug regulation, and environmental regulation were often more progressive in the United States than in midcentury Europe.[59] These trends are ultimately responsible for the "running to stay in place" phenomenon identified in chapter 9.

These policies allowed the development of the welfare state in Europe both because welfare bought off resistance to policies that favored capital and because policies that favored capital cushioned the economic consequences of the welfare state.[60] Such bargains did not exist in the United States, and the consequence has been both a less developed welfare state and many policies more punitive to capital. Mechanisms have also arisen over time that reinforce the welfare state embedded in capital-friendly regulations in Europe and undermine it in the United States. For example, much of the energies of the American left are drawn into defending a system of regulations that are adversarial to corporations, such as making it easy to sue corporations.[61] Suing corporations is much harder in Europe: punitive damages are not allowed in most European legal systems, class actions have traditionally not been permitted, and litigation is discouraged by the absence of contingency fees for lawyers and rules requiring that a losing plaintiff pay the defendant's legal costs.[62]

American progressives have fought restrictions on the ability to sue corporations because corporate malfeasance can be devastating to victims when there is a weak or nonexistent safety net. But this is not the case in Europe. Consider Robert Kagan's examination of how asbestos-related diseases were handled in the Netherlands and in the United States in the 1970s and 1980s. Although the incidence of the disease was five to ten times as high among Dutch workers, "as of 1991 almost 200,000 asbestos-based tort cases had been filed in the United States. Fewer than *ten* had been filed in the Netherlands," primarily because "disabled Dutch workers are entitled to all needed medical care and lifelong benefits equal to 70 or 80 percent of their lost earnings, without having to prove that an employer or product manufacturer did anything wrong." The American tort system did have the intended effect, driving several asbestos manufacturers into bankruptcy and thus sending a signal to others to take the issue seriously. But two-thirds of the insurance money went to lawyers and experts rather than to victims and their families, and jury awards varied widely.[63] In America, an adversarial approach to capital serves as an inefficient and patchwork welfare state.

The reasons why these corporatist bargains were possible in Europe but not in the United States remain subjects of scholarly controversy. Some have argued that institutions of cooperation were already present in medieval Europe and industrial Europe, where parliamentary representation both allowed and forced parties to work in concert.[64] Another argument is that these bargains arose from the European need to regenerate economic growth during the twentieth-century interwar and postwar periods, whereas the need in the United States was to control price volatility caused by robust economic growth; progressive taxes were intended to break up concentrations of capital in defense of purchasing power, and the geographical fragmentation of power allowed unusual regulations on capital, such as Glass-Steagall.[65]

Whatever the causes, the outcome is that the American polity does not do a good job of reducing poverty, *and* it makes capitalists work very hard for policies that capitalists in other countries take for granted. American capitalists have with their efforts managed to avoid a European-size welfare state that would punish capital. But European welfare states do not punish capital. These states are resilient precisely because they have traditionally been careful not to place the burden of supporting the welfare state on business. And because it is those who benefit from the welfare state who have borne the burden of paying for it, there is less potential for mobilization of dissatisfaction and conflict around these issues.

Perhaps the lessons this comparison reveals cannot be put in place until a time of crisis. But perhaps the crisis is upon us. The great lesson of 2016 was that policies that leave behind significant segments of the population will generate a backlash that cannot be controlled, even by those who promote those policies or who benefit in the short term from the backlash. Examining how to generate prosperity while including all segments of the population within that prosperity has become not a hypothetical or utopian ideal, but a practical necessity.

Conclusion: Lessons and Limitations

"I CAME IN as a balance-the-budget, root canal austere Republican," said Jack Kemp. "Then I looked around and realized . . . people will vote for hope over austerity."[1] The tax cut movement began because Republicans discovered in tax cuts a politically plausible answer to inflation and to their "minority problem"—tax cut clientelism in response to the Democrats' welfare state clientelism. It took time for the electoral potential of tax cuts to be discovered and developed, because of a long-standing belief that politicians would be punished for creating deficits. Perhaps only the post-Watergate life-or-death struggle of the Republican Party could have led to the gamble on big tax cuts, and only because the political world was unsettled by inflation did Republicans get their chance. The tax cut movement persisted because Republicans realized that deficit financing was no longer punished by either the voters or the stock market. Tax cuts solve for Republicans the problem that Americans say they prefer small government but support almost everything the government actually does. For several decades the Republicans have had no alternative policy that has been anywhere near as successful.

The Economic Recovery Tax Act was directly shaped by the American economy's consumption bias, as businesses fought for investment tax credits that would bring the United States in line with European countries in its tax treatment of business, and by the American tax system's disproportionate reliance on income, profit, and captial gains taxation, which interacted with inflation in ways that made the tax issue a potential vote winner for Republicans. Inflation raised the tax burden, and that generated tax dissatisfaction. Politicians noticed this dissatisfaction and mobilized it, claiming that by cutting taxes they could solve the problem of inflation. Meanwhile, the American government's ability to borrow cheaply allowed the "Two Santa Claus" regime to persist. The country's arc from the postwar moment when it emerged as the indisputable economic superpower to the moment when it discovered that it no longer had budget constraints is the background for the tax cut movement.

The most popular explanations for free market policies prove wanting in the case of tax cuts. Polls showed ambivalence about tax cuts, and therefore many scholars assume that business interests must have been behind the policy. But business interests were opposed to the main part of the cut. Some scholars suggest free market policies are about ideology. But the Republican ideology at the time was balanced budgets. In fact the party completely abandoned its ideology in order to accommodate tax cuts. The focus for another set of scholars has been on the power of a set of intellectual ideas. But those ideas were peripheral to the rise of tax cuts in America. Nor does racism prove to be a good explanation for the tax cuts: tax cuts did appeal to racists slightly more than to nonracists, but overall they appealed to many people, including African Americans. In many ways, tax cuts were the alternative to racism within the Republican Party.

These other factors may explain more about other free market policies. Business groups were more interested in deregulation; economists and ideas may have been more influential in free trade and monetarism; race was surely a factor in the repeal of Aid to Families with Dependent Children, and a general factor in the rise of Republicans to electoral parity. Nevertheless, the tax cut story highlights a basic thread of electoral potential in the Republicans' move to free market policies that can also be seen in other areas,[2] and overall the focus on free market policies has given the party an electorally useful reputation as the party that knows how to handle economic problems. The tax cut story also highlights the troubles that inflation caused for the American consumer economy and the underlying fragility of the adversarial political economy developed over the postwar period.

The tax cut movement did not result in lower revenue or lower progressivity, it did not manage to control the growth of the state, it did not raise savings or investment rates over the long term, and it was a sideshow in the attempt to control inflation. What the tax cut movement did is increase the deficit and bring capital gains taxes to levels that are closer to rates in other countries. Moreover, although it proved impossible to undo the tax state, the tax cut movement has assured that progressives have been unable to implement policies to address new issues, such as the rise of automation and globalization, the rise of new family forms, and demographic shifts. Ironically, the movement to wind back the state exemplifies the fears of libertarians that government can become a thing apart from the people, because it was, in fact, the interests of state actors, not any socially located group or broader social currents, that drove tax cuts.

There is no evidence that general tax cuts necessarily lead to economic growth. The effects of taxation on economic growth depend on many factors, including what the tax revenue is spent on. But it is the case that the most successful welfare states, the ones that have managed to reduce poverty and inequality, historically kept taxes on capital and the wealthy low compared to the United States.

There are reasons for thinking that some kind of tax cut would have happened in the 1970s even without Jack Kemp and Ronald Reagan, because the diagnosis of bracket creep was widely accepted at the time. But it would probably not have been such a large cut, it therefore would not have created such a large deficit, and it therefore would not have taught Republicans the lesson that deficits are neither politically nor economically punished.

A tax cut of some kind may have been economically inevitable, but the shape and size it took were political matters. Unwinding this situation, and rebuilding the tax state, are therefore also political matters. The analysis of this book suggests that the main lever for change is not campaign finance reform, building intellectual counternarratives, nor fighting racism, but developing alternative issues that could have equivalent electoral potential for the Republican Party. It seems that only major electoral losses could produce a Republican Party that, as Jack Kemp did in the winter of 1974, is actively searching for new policies. Meanwhile, the struggle for the party is between tax cuts and xenophobia, currently joined in an uneasy coalition because taxes are not particularly unpopular right now.

This book has several limitations, which together constitute an agenda for research. First, I have made a comparative claim, but I have not conducted a detailed comparative analysis. The claim is that the 1981 tax cut was a response to political demands to be seen doing something bold about inflation; that tax cuts offered a way to meet these demands because income taxes (including profit and capital gains taxes) rise in step with inflation while other taxes do not, leading to greater tax dissatisfaction when there is inflation in regimes that rely disproportionately on income taxes; and that the American economy relies on income taxes to a greater extent than the economies of other countries. The first part of the claim is clear from the archival evidence, which shows the Republicans aware of the potential popularity of tax cuts and responsive to the demands to do something about inflation. The third part of the claim, that the American economy relies on income taxes to a greater extent than other national economies, is also clear from comparative data. The middle part of the claim is the weak link: that the impact of inflation on income taxes was the reason for the Reagan administration's mobilization of tax dissatisfaction. I have attempted to marshal evidence for this claim by showing quantitatively the link between income taxes and inflation across the advanced industrial countries, and between inflation and tax dissatisfaction in the United States, but a full treatment would require showing that there is *not* a link between inflation and tax dissatisfaction in other countries, or that politicians are not as responsive to tax dissatisfaction in other countries. Given the absence of cross-national data on these questions for the 1970s, such research would require archival efforts of the kind conducted here only for the United States.

Second, in many ways it is the rediscovery of tax cuts in the 1990s and their persistence on the Republican Party agenda until the present day that is the real story: without those developments, the 1981 tax cut would have remained just a historical curiosity. I updated the story briefly in chapter 8, but a full understanding of more recent events awaits the opening of other archives.

Third, I hope to have convinced readers that corporations and wealthy individuals were not the forces behind the Reagan tax cut, but social forces do not stand still, and it certainly seems that the 2017 tax cut was quite different. The Tax Cuts and Jobs Act of 2017 is the inheritor not of Kemp-Roth but of ACRS. Whether it will follow the fate of ACRS remains to be seen; it could be that Republicans have finally overreached in the tax cut effort. And yet, one broader lesson of the book remains intact: tax cuts continue because the Republican Party has no other issue that is as successful at bringing a broad coalition together. Indeed, in one way the 2017 tax cut is a culmination of the trends discussed here, because now even business groups, which resisted tax cuts under Reagan because of deficit fears and were ambivalent about them under George W. Bush, have finally signed on to them—signaling the triumph of the perspective that deficits do not matter, the apotheosis of American economic hegemony.

In the ERTA episode the entire political world, including business groups, feared deficits and for that reason many opposed tax cuts. Over the next two decades deficit fears subsided, but if businesses and the wealthy were influential over this more recent time period, they were largely influential only in getting capital gains tax to levels commensurate with other countries—they were "running to stay in place." The most recent tax cut, however, may suggest the rise of a new era, in which businesses, the wealthy, and political elites are not just struggling to keep up with European countries, but could even surpass them, getting taxes on corporations and the wealthy even lower than in Europe. It remains to be seen whether such changes would be durable.

A fourth limitation of this book is that it leaves many questions unanswered about the argument that after World War II European countries established welfare states in exchange for policies that favored business. Noticing this bargain allows us to see several facets of politics and economics quite differently—for example, the role of money in the rise of free market politics in America—and suggests the possibilities for a path forward. But much remains to be understood about how the welfare state interacts with other policies. I gave one example of how welfare state commitments reduce the need for adversarial legal policies, but this is an extremely limited start on an important and large research agenda.

Finally, we also need more research into the question of how this country's unique situation as the world's consumer constrained its politics starting after the Second World War, and how its ability to finance its deficits unconstrained its politics starting in the 1980s. An important question for research is whether American politicians' budget shenanigans are starting to affect how the United States is viewed around the world, and how and to what extent that will affect the government's ability to continue to borrow cheaply.

Despite these limitations, three clear lessons arise from the history of the ERTA as detailed in this book. The first is that we should not overestimate the power of money in politics. Even allowing for the possibility that recent trends may have changed, this examination of the major free market policies for which scholars have blamed business power has found either that business power was not at the heart of these policies—as in the Kemp-Roth part of the 1981 tax cut—or that American businesses had to struggle to achieve policies that were the norm in the rest of the developed world—as in the ACRS part of the 1981 tax cut.

This observation is not license to ignore the power of money in politics, as it is precisely the infrastructure of dedicated journalists and activists and scholars keeping watch over the issue that renders money less powerful than it would otherwise be. Without this careful surveillance and the hard work of citizens drawing attention to the power of corporations and wealthy individuals, we would certainly see more systematic victories by businesses and the wealthy. But because this network remains in place, money is less powerful in contemporary American politics than it might be.

Specifically, business power is not enough to explain policies that lead to higher poverty and inequality in the United States. The power of business and the wealthy can be said to be even greater in Europe, because European policies privileging capital do not require the lobbying efforts in which businesses in the United States must stay engaged. But the presence of powerful business interests has not prevented the reduction of poverty and inequality in Europe. The European welfare state may be so robust precisely because policymakers have traditionally been careful not to damage capital accumulation.

The business-power narrative is comforting for progressives, because it suggests that there is no need to examine the failings of progressive policies, and that the only problem is that there is a monster in the way—"the thing that feeds the other ills, and the thing that we must kill first," as a recent book on business power puts it.[3] Kill the monster of business power and everyone lives happily ever after. But progressives had not been able to come up with solutions to stagflation, and the progressive policies of the postwar era proved fragile when inflation struck.

An even less comfortable conclusion is that the tax cut does not show the absence of democracy so much as problems within democracy. The tax cut arose because a political party mobilized an issue on which voters had expressed dissatisfaction, and committed itself to that course because it seemed to offer a route to electoral victory by allowing the party to claim a solution to inflation. While it is not possible to say that the tax cut actually reflected what voters wanted, that's because voters wanted contradictory things: a solution to inflation, but none of the specific possible solutions to inflation. If the tax cut is problematic, it's because there are fundamental problems in the instantiation of democracy itself. In addition to contradictory preferences, a problem can arise if parties decide that their route to victory is to embrace only issues on which accountability can be explicitly demonstrated and to ignore others on which it cannot. In America it led from welfare clientelism to tax cut clientelism, which can coexist because of deficit financing.

Putting together the arguments here about the limits of business power and the problems within democracy, this book is particularly opposed to several recent works that have argued precisely that money is the problem and that changes to democratic rules are the answer. For example, Benjamin Page and Martin Gilens argue, drawing on Gilens's research on public opinion, that the wealthy are disproportionately powerful in America and that we need rule changes to make the system more democratic.[4]

The recent history of advocating rule changes to improve democracy is a cautionary tale, and the main lesson is, be careful what you wish for. Political scientists in the 1950s argued for a "responsible" party system and urged the parties to adopt specific platforms that would provide clear contrasts for voters. In practice, the development of parties that offer clear contrasts has led to hyperpartisanship, political polarization, and gridlock. In the 1960s, in response to activists' demand for more transparent government, the power of centralized committees in Congress was weakened; the result was a Congress more responsive to particularistic interests of specific constituencies, at the expense of careful deliberation.[5] In the 1970s, supporters of direct democracy called for the greater use of referenda and initiatives in government. These were duly implemented in states such as California, and citizens responded by voting for both lower taxes and higher spending, leading to budget dysfunction and widespread calls to reform the reforms.[6] More recently, to counter the problem of parties being driven by their most extreme elements, California introduced a "top two" primary system in which all primary voters receive the same general ballot and can vote for any candidates they like, regardless of party, with the top two vote-getters moving into a runoff. The goal was to allow more moderate voices to win. The result? At least so far, somewhat more ideologically extreme candidates.[7]

Today, if we actually adopted policies that succeeded in making lower-income voters more powerful, one result could be to ride roughshod over minority rights and provide a strong anchor for demagoguery, because it turns out that many of the policies low-income voters favor—and ignoring which makes the country undemocratic—come at the expense of minorities. For example, Gilens's data show that lower-income groups are more likely to want racial profiling of Muslim and Arab Americans.[8] Because the country has not adopted a policy of racial profiling, this case contributes to Gilens's conclusion that money is powerful: if lower-income citizens want racial profiling and do not get it, then according to Gilens, it must be because of money in politics. Gilens's method does not allow him to investigate the mechanisms producing the correlation between affluent Americans' preferences and policies, but he nevertheless concludes: "The complete lack of government responsiveness to the preferences of the poor is disturbing and seems consistent only with the most cynical views of American politics."[9] But hesitations about racial profiling do not necessarily suggest the victory of affluent groups; they may instead reflect independent concerns about minority rights. Similarly, other issues where policy does not generally reflect the preferences of the poor in Gilens's data include gay rights and mandatory AIDS testing, bans on legal immigration, stem cell research, reproductive rights, restrictions on free speech, mandatory school prayer, and allowing government surveillance, areas where lower-income voters have illiberal preferences. Without more direct evidence for affluent individuals or groups exercising influence of emails and telephone calls, it is difficult to agree with Gilens that only the "most cynical" interpretations of politics can explain these outcomes. Page and Gilens dismiss the problem of minority rights in two pages.[10]

Rather than trying to change the rules of representative democracy to better reflect our current preferences, this book suggests another path: develop institutions and policies that dampen the conflicts that the healthy functioning of democracy promotes. The European welfare states in their heyday can provide some lessons in how to do so. In many countries cross-class bargains incorporated the entire population in rising prosperity. For all of its faults and limits, and despite considerable variety across Europe, the European welfare states remain the closest humanity has ever come to eradicating poverty.

This is not an injunction to blindly copy the lessons of 1950s Europe in the twenty-first-century United States, if that were even possible. For one thing, the European welfare state has itself evolved, and under the pressure of the European Union some of the cozy relationships between capital and state have been reformed. It is also implausible to expect an exact replay of the European experience, because that experience depended on a strong demand for exported products, which was made possible in the postwar period by American consumption. The European bargain of strategies to help exporting industries in return for the development of increasingly robust welfare states was a brilliant achievement for its time. The goal now is not to repeat it, but to learn broad lessons from it.

The main lesson is that progressive policies are achieved in concert with, and not in opposition to, business interests. Welfare state policies in Europe in the early postwar period were passed with the interests of a growing economy in mind. Not all government interventions harm the economy, but some do, and identifying those welfare policies that hit the dual goal of encouraging economic growth and reducing risks, as well as examining how other policies interact with welfare state policies, is an important and underdeveloped research agenda.

It may seem dubious to look to Europe for comparisons at a moment when Europe itself is experiencing populist crisis. But the European crisis has not been brought about by the European welfare state, and the welfare state is not a target of European populists. Rather, the European crisis is a consequence of austerity policies in the context of the euro, as well as other exogenous factors, such as the refugee crisis of 2016. The fact that Americans adopted a Keynesian program of stimulus in the face of the crisis whereas Europeans adopted a program of austerity is itself the first clue to something interesting going on that has not received the attention it deserves—a tradition of European free market policies and rejection of Keynesianism as part and parcel of the welfare states that have reduced European poverty to levels that American progressives can only dream of. And this European bargain—maintaining welfare programs in an economy oriented to the needs of business—may be one reason why the catastrophic shocks of the euro, austerity, and the refugee crisis have not yet undone Europe.

So far, the changes that have been made to the European welfare state have been relatively minor, and have been implemented with the intention of—and largely had the effect of—shoring up rather than breaking up the welfare state. As Kathleen Thelen shows, the most successful of the changes have simply extended the European tradition of progressive policies embedded in market-friendly regimes, such as flexicurity; where the European states have been less successful is in responding to new concerns, such as incorporating a rising stream of immigrants, but the core of the European welfare state remains popular and has proven economically sustainable over decades, despite decades of predictions of its imminent collapse.[11] Moreover, many of those concerned about recent trends in European welfare states seem unaware of exactly how market-friendly the classic European welfare state has always been. For example, scholars worry that recent trends have turned many welfare states in Europe into "something that should complement the market, facilitate integration into markets, and encourage competitiveness . . . the commodifying, activating, enabling welfare state."[12] But the European state was always exactly that. The European welfare state—even the Scandinavian welfare state, and even the Swedish welfare state—was always focused on complementing the market, facilitating free trade and wage restraint in order to reconstruct capitalism where it had been destroyed by war.

Some scholars, taking lessons from European states' heavier reliance on a national sales tax, have suggested that the American state should adopt one.[13] An American value-added tax is an important policy to consider, but it is hard to imagine a new tax that falls on the middle classes being implemented in the current environment. Moreover, given the startling extremes of inequality in the United States today, a central justification for national sales taxes—that there simply isn't enough money at the top of the pyramid to pay for extensive welfare states through high income tax rates[14]—may no longer be correct. Levels of wealth at the upper end of the income distribution are unprecedented today, and may both allow levels of revenue generation that were not possible through progressive taxes before, and generate a degree of consensus around such taxation.

If we want to follow the European model of taxing consumption to avoid punishing investment, but combine it with the American focus on tax progressivity, the policy that is most likely to generate revenue and to achieve widespread political consensus would be a progressive consumption tax, such as taxation of luxury consumption. Like consumption taxes more generally, this would avoid taxing investment, and given the high concentration of income at the top, could yield substantial revenue. An equivalent would be to raise capital gains taxes but carve out large exemptions for savings and investments.

The other lesson from Europe is to embed progressive policies in a broader political economy designed to benefit the economy. The European states were successful precisely because they were able to restrain wages among workers, did not extensively regulate corporations, and adopted a tax system that weighed more heavily on labor than on capital. The point is not to imitate these precise policies, but to think about what policies would increase growth while also ensuring that any growth is broadly shared.

For example, a trade-off of higher taxes and greater welfare spending in return for tort reform and lower litigation costs for business is a lesson that America could take from Europe that would satisfy both progressives and business-minded conservatives. Another would be a serious investment into vocational education or infrastructure. Another would be true tax reform. The system of high nominal rates and extensive loopholes generates neither revenues nor legitimacy for the tax code (although it does bring politicians campaign dollars). Closing exemptions and deductions in the tax code, including the home mortgage interest tax deduction, which favors the upper middle class, and the charitable tax deduction, which takes away resources from needed uses and puts them into appealing causes, would generate revenue without damaging economic productivity.

The most pressing need is for a fundamental rethinking of the welfare state, which the focus on business power distracts progressives from conducting. In addition to all of the ways in which the New Deal order proved politically and economically fragile, it never worked for many people. A fundamental problem is that a regime founded on mortgage financing has no good answer for poverty: if credit is not extended to those who may not be credit-worthy, then the poor are excluded from any chance at the American dream; if legislation is passed to force banks to give them credit, it will be given at very high interest rates to compensate for the risks of lending to this population; if interest rates are capped then banks will refuse to offer credit; and if banks are forced to give credit at low interest rates, the banks will bear the costs of the risks, and will pass them on to the broader economy through the costs of bailouts or bank failures. One solution would be to cap interest rates and subsidize banks for offering them to low-income populations, but this is the kind of technical kludge that Steven Teles points to, an inefficient attempt to pretend that what is actually heavy government intervention is the free market at work.[15] It may be time to think about subsidizing saving and renting, rather than borrowing and buying. Moreover, updating the welfare state for an age of automation and globalization may require progressively detaching welfare from work, and responding to new demographic trends means rethinking the public provision of care. Perhaps there is some scope for this kind of rethinking at the state and municipal level, where budget constraints can force actors to work together to produce pragmatic economic development reforms.

If Democrats need to rethink progressivism, instead of focusing on tax cuts—which may have been a reasonable strategy at one point but has diminishing economic and political returns today—Republicans could examine all of the nontax reasons why businesses run into trouble and then work to develop a new Kemp-like struggle to reorient their party around these issues. Indeed, this may be the only solution for Republicans who want to prevent their party from falling back on racism and xenophobia.

It would be naive to think that such a bargain is in the offing—that the American government could suddenly prove itself capable of presiding over a cross-class bargain of this complexity, at this moment of polarization, when such a bargain has eluded it for decades, that someone or some group of actors within the Republican Party could accept the need for the welfare state as part of an accord to ensure economic growth, driven by a wish to resist the party's takeover by racist demagoguery.

But one thing studying history teaches you is that studying history doesn't teach you much. Historically unprecedented things happen all the time. And just as the Reagan tax cut seems entirely predictable in retrospect—of course inflation raised taxes more in regimes dominated by income taxes; of course this made people grumble; of course a party desperately casting about for political issues to mobilize voters noticed this dissatisfaction—so, years from now, we may look back and argue that of course this moment was perfectly ripe for political innovation: automation was deindustrializing the heartland, voter loyalties were up for grabs, Republicans could see that branding themselves the racist party was a demographic dead end and they needed an alternative, and technological developments were making it easier and easier for groups to organize and develop sophisticated collective solutions.

That the United States will overcome its fragmented politics and spontaneously generate a political economy that attends to the needs of the businesses that keep the country prosperous while also bringing poverty levels down certainly seems unlikely today. But like the story of the tax cut itself, unlikely is where the best stories begin.

ACKNOWLEDGMENTS

I AM grateful to the librarians and archivists at the Reagan Library, who made the process of submitting Freedom of Information Act (FOIA) requests almost fun. I also thank the librarians at the Library of Congress, the National Archives, and the other libraries and archives I visited, and I'm grateful to the National Science Foundation (NSF grant 0847725) and Northwestern University (various internal grants) for funding the research trips. The Russell Sage Foundation financed a year-long research leave and provided an ideal context of peace and stimulation in which to write the first draft of this book. The Sociology Department, the Dean's Office, the Institute for Policy Research, and the Buffett Institute for Global Studies at Northwestern University funded a manuscript workshop that proved transformative. None of these funding sources bears any responsibility for the contents of this work.

I thank Theda Skocpol for the title of chapter 7 and Martin Gilens for sharing his data. Parts of this work were published in the *Journal of Policy History* and have been presented at conferences and workshops at various venues. I am grateful to all the comments over the years that have helped me work out the argument. I am particularly grateful to comments from several people who read the entire manuscript: Bruce Bartlett, Niamba Baskerville, Josh Basseches, Tony Chen, Gary Herrigel, Alex Hertel-Fernandez, Emilio Lehoucq, Niko Letsos, Jon Levy, Isaac Martin, Mary McGrath, Ajay Mehrotra, Molly Michelmore, Onur Ozgode, Kumar Ramanathan, Daniel Rodriguez, Charlotte Rosen, Chloe Thurston, and Devin Wiggs. The three anonymous reviewers of the manuscript gave unusually thoughtful and helpful readings that helped me try to speak to multiple disciplinary audiences.

I am grateful to Jason Beckfield, Alex Hertel-Fernandez, Isaac Martin, and Lincoln Quillian for taking a look at the statistical calculations. Since I didn't always take their advice, I can't blame them for any errors or shortcomings.

Without Nancy Reagan's decision to donate the Campaign 1980 papers, the book would not exist. And it would have lost something important without the permission of the students of Mrs. Noble's third-grade class, now in their forties, to use their drawings.

Stefan Henning saw the birth of this book on that first trip to the Reagan Presidential Library when I spent all that time filling out FOIA requests, on our honeymoon. He was there as we spent a year stomping around the outer boroughs on breaks from book drafting. He has by now learned enough about Reagan to give a lecture on him in a pinch, if he had to, and is perhaps the only anthropologist of China with subtle opinions about the varieties of capitalism perspective.

I still remember my father arguing about supply-side economics back in the eighties—he was surely arguing against it, although I was too uninterested back then to pay much attention. I've more than made up for that initial lack of interest. The only sad part about finishing this book is that he won't get to see it. It surprised me that the death from natural causes of an eighty-five-year-old man could feel like such a tragedy, but to us it did. The silver lining, such as it is, is that it brought my mother and my sister and me closer together. My mother remains a model of strength as she struggles to put together her new life. This book is dedicated to my sister Leena Prasad and her family, with love and hope.

TABLES A.1 and A.2 show the effects of inflation on the five main kinds of taxes. In addition to income taxes and sales taxes, countries get most of their revenue from property taxes, payroll taxes, and social security contributions. Table A.1 shows the effect of inflation on the share of these taxes as a part of the overall tax structure, while table A.2 shows the effect of inflation on each tax as a percentage of GDP. Because we are interested in the short-term effects of inflation, estimations are shown using fixed effects. Full calculations are available in the supplemental material available at ICPSR and on my website.[1]

Within each table, each regression shows the result of inflation on the different kinds of taxes. The dependent variables, listed in the column headings, are the different taxes: income, profit, and capital gains taxes as a proportion of total taxes (ipcgtot in table A.1) or as a percentage of GDP (ipcggdp in table A.2); social security taxes as a proportion of total taxes (sstot) or as a percentage of GDP (ssgdp); property taxes as a proportion of total taxes (proptot) or as a percentage of GDP (propgdp); payroll taxes as a proportion of total taxes (pytot) or as a percentage of GDP (pygdp); and taxes on goods and services as a proportion of total taxes (tgstot) or as a percentage of GDP (tgsgdp).

The independent variable is inflation as measured by the percentage change in the consumer price index from the prior year (cpi2).[2]

Several control variables have also been included that may be thought to affect the burden of taxes. The scholarship on taxation has learned that major increases in taxation are nonlinear and generally occur in moments of crisis, especially major war. Thus, scholars generally focus on historical periods that saw large increases. This has left incremental change in taxation less well studied. To identify control variables, I therefore drew on the well-developed scholarship on the welfare state, assuming that many of the mechanisms that cause the welfare state to grow may be similar to those that cause the tax state to grow.

These mechanisms include variables that measure union density (ud) and the degree of wage coordination (wcoord), two variables that scholars in the varieties of capitalism literature have argued are important to the development of the welfare state; economic variables that scholars in the "logic of industrialism" camp argue lead to the growth of the welfare state, including per capita GDP (rgdpecap) and the unemployment rate (hunemr2); trade openness (tradeopen); and partisanship, measured as the proportion of the cabinet that is from left parties (leftcab) and the proportion from Christian right parties of the kind that have been found to be favorable to welfare state expansion (cncrcab). In addition, a measure of the public welfare state is included, as this is likely to be one of the main reasons for higher taxation (sstran). All data are from OECD Revenue Statistics and the Comparative Welfare States Dataset.

Unit root tests showed that many variables were nonstationary, and in the supplemental material the calculations were repeated using first differences of these variables.

Overall, the tables show a uniform story. The first column of each table shows the effect of inflation on income, profit, and capital gains taxes as a percentage of GDP. The second column adds the controls. Column 3 shows the effect of inflation on social security taxes, column 4 adds controls, and this pattern is repeated for property and payroll taxes and taxes on goods and services. Column 11 shows the effect of the controls by themselves on income taxes.

Inflation is associated with a rise in income, profit, and capital gains taxes as a percentage of GDP, but not increases in any other tax. Indeed, in some models inflation is associated with a decline in social security tax as a percentage of GDP, but most models show no robust association of inflation with change in any other kind of tax. The negative association of property taxes and inflation is surprising, but this finding does not survive all the robustness tests. As to inflation and income tax, the variance explained is not large, but the association is strong: inflation is not the main reason for changes in income tax, but it does affect income tax differently from other taxes.

It is possible that increases in income, profit, and capital gains taxes are causing inflation rather than the other way around. For example, an increase in income taxes represents an increase in wages; to cover increases in nominal wages, firms may have to push up prices. It is also possible that increases in prices are leading to increases in wages, and thus to increases in income taxes. Both mechanisms are likely at work, and the phenomenon of wage increases causing rising prices and rising prices causing wage increases was much discussed at the time.

If this reverse causation were the only factor at work, however, we would see payroll and social security contributions increasing too, because firms would also push up prices to cover the costs of higher social security contributions and higher payroll taxes. But when we control for other factors, social security contributions and other payroll taxes do not show an association with inflation. The difference may stem from both social security contributions and payroll taxes being capped at certain levels, which makes them impervious to inflation at the upper end of the income distribution— in other words, the progressivity of income taxes makes them operate differently under conditions of inflation than payroll and social security taxes.

Table A.1 Effect of Inflation on Tax Structure, as Measured by Role Played by Each Tax in Total Tax Revenue

	(1)	(2)	(3)	(4)	(5)	(6)	(7)	(8)	(9)	(10)	(11)
	ipcgtot	ipcgtot	sstot	sstot	proptot	proptot	pytot	pytot	tgstot	tgstot	ipcgtot
cpi2	0.144***	0.0993***	-0.0387*	-0.00779	-0.0512***	-0.0652***	0.00186	0.00306	-0.0717***	-0.0516*	
	(0.0240)	(0.0250)	(0.0168)	(0.0173)	(0.0154)	(0.0170)	(0.00593)	(0.00640)	(0.0212)	(0.0232)	
ud		0.0479+		0.0353+		0.0397***		0.0126		0.0156	0.0488+
		(0.0273)		(0.0192)		(0.0116)		(0.00677)		(0.0247)	(0.0275)
ucoord		-0.00964		-0.0651		0.161**		0.00847		0.0293	-0.00965
		(0.0838)		(0.0581)		(0.0602)		(0.0215)		(0.0777)	(0.0846)
rgdpecap		0.000109*		-0.0000353		0.0000335*		0.0000171		0.0000351	0.0000792
		(0.0000485)		(0.0000359)		(0.0000165)		(0.0000113)		(0.0000418)	(0.0000483)
hunemr2		-0.208***		0.0223		-0.00508		0.0107		0.134+	-0.262***
		(0.0627)		(0.0437)		(0.0349)		(0.0159)		(0.0575)	(0.0617)
tradeopen		0.0101		-0.000496		0.00266		-0.00151		-0.000641	0.0206+
		(0.0111)		(0.00770)		(0.00635)		(0.00281)		(0.0102)	(0.0108)
leftcab		0.00497*		-0.00239		0.000453		0.000878		-0.00156	0.00499*
		(0.00241)		(0.00167)		(0.00160)		(0.000616)		(0.00223)	(0.00243)
cncrcab		-0.0261+		0.0220*		0.00166		0.00128		0.00594	-0.0286*
		(0.0142)		(0.00985)		(0.00911)		(0.00362)		(0.0131)	(0.0143)
strran		-0.118		0.348***		-0.0843*		-0.00944		0.0176	-0.137+
		(0.0752)		(0.0528)		(0.0391)		(0.0188)		(0.0685)	(0.0756)
_cons	39.21***	36.74***	26.34***	20.27***	6.333***	4.464***	1.175***	1.192***	27.90***	25.46***	37.81***
	(0.0504)	(0.187)	(0.0354)	(0.117)	(0.0407)	(0.265)	(0.0125)	(0.0534)	(0.0444)	(0.189)	(0.187)
N	916	916	916	916	916	916	916	916	916	916	916
adj. R^2	0.015	0.070	-0.019	0.077	-0.012	0.014	-0.025	-0.030	-0.012	-0.012	0.055

Source: OECD Revenue Statistics (OECD.Stat), "OECD Countries: Comparative Tables," https://stats.oecd.org/Index.aspx?DataSetCode=REV, accessed August 15, 2018) and Comparative Welfare States Data Set (Brady, Huber, and Stephens 2014).

Notes: Standard errors are in parentheses.

$^+ p < 0.1$; $^* p < 0.05$; $^{**} p < 0.01$; $^{***} p < 0.001$

Table A.2 Effect of Inflation on Tax Structure, as Measured by Tax as Proportion of GDP

	(1) ipcggdp	(2) ipcggdp	(3) ssgdp	(4) ssgdp	(5) propgdp	(6) propgdp	(7) pygdp	(8) pygdp	(9) tgsgdp	(10) tgsgdp	(11) ipcggdp
cpi2	0.0730***	0.0576***	-0.00264	0.00792	-0.0176**	-0.0169**	0.000530	0.000827	-0.0000514	0.00860	
	(0.0119)	(0.0127)	(0.00638)	(0.00638)	(0.00544)	(0.00603)	(0.00228)	(0.00246)	(0.00786)	(0.00846)	
ud		0.0118		0.00589		0.0118**		-0.0000910		0.00350	0.0127
		(0.0137)		(0.00721)		(0.00416)		(0.00257)		(0.00880)	(0.0138)
wcoord		-0.00663		-0.0197		0.0464*		0.00215		0.0108	-0.00645
		(0.0425)		(0.0214)		(0.0213)		(0.00825)		(0.0284)	(0.0430)
rgdpecap		0.00000932		-0.0000645***		0.0000194**		0.000000501		0.0000350	-0.00000601
		(0.0000237)		(0.0000142)		(0.00000589)		(0.00000422)		(0.0000143)	(0.0000234)
hunemr2		-0.128***		-0.0235		0.00539		0.00185		0.0173	-0.159***
		(0.0316)		(0.0163)		(0.0124)		(0.00607)		(0.0208)	(0.0312)
tradeopen		0.000420		-0.00213		0.000453		-0.000562		-0.00249	0.00651
		(0.00560)		(0.00285)		(0.00227)		(0.00108)		(0.00370)	(0.00549)
leficab		0.00219+		-0.0000839		0.000517		0.000337		0.000213	0.00220+
		(0.00122)		(0.000616)		(0.000568)		(0.000237)		(0.000813)	(0.00124)
cncrcab		-0.0107		0.0128***		0.00105		0.000420		0.00570	-0.0122+
		(0.00719)		(0.00364)		(0.00324)		(0.00139)		(0.00478)	(0.00727)
sstran		0.0375		0.126***		-0.0147		-0.00197		0.0679**	0.0283
		(0.0378)		(0.0198)		(0.0140)		(0.00719)		(0.0246)	(0.0381)
_cons	14.23***	13.64***	10.91***	10.36***	2.053***	1.061***	0.446***	0.474***	10.28***	9.024***	14.13***
	(0.0249)	(0.0991)	(0.0135)	(0.0382)	(0.0145)	(0.0930)	(0.00479)	(0.0212)	(0.0165)	(0.0737)	(0.101)
N	916	916	916	916	916	916	916	916	916	916	916
adj. R^2	0.017	0.037	-0.024	0.112	-0.013	0.018	-0.025	-0.031	-0.025	-0.013	0.015

Source: OECD Revenue Statistics (OECD.Stat, "OECD Revenue Statistics—OECD Countries: Comparative Tables," https://stats.oecd.org/Index.aspx?DataSetCode=REV, accessed August 15, 2018) and Comparative Welfare States Data Set (Brady, Huber, and Stephens 2014).

Note: Standard errors are in parentheses.

+ $p < 0.1$; * $p < 0.05$; ** $p < 0.01$; *** $p < 0.001$

ARCHIVAL SOURCES

Ronald Reagan Presidential Library

- 1980 Transition Papers
- Martin Anderson Files
- Martin Anderson Papers [pre-presidential]
- James A. Baker III Files
- Cabinet Council on Economic Affairs Meeting Files
- Council of Economic Advisers—Staff Economists Files
- James W. Cicconi Files
- T. Kenneth Cribb Files
- Richard G. Darman Files
- Michael K. Deaver Files
- Economic Policy Council Records
- Elizabeth Dole Files
- Executive Secretariat, NSC [National Security Council]: VIP Visits
- Craig Fuller Files
- David Gergen Files
- Wendell Gunn Files
- Francis Hodsoll Files
- Jerry Jordan Files
- Kenneth Khachigian Files
- Edwin Meese III Files
- William Niskanen Files
- Franklyn [Lyn] Nofziger Files
- M. B. Oglesby Files
- Office of Policy Development: Records
- Office of the Presidential Diary: President's Daily Diary
- Office of White House Correspondence: Records

- Pre-Presidential Papers
- Presidential Briefing Papers
- Presidential Handwriting File
- Ronald Reagan 1980 Presidential Campaign Papers, 1964–1980 ["Campaign 1980"]
- Ronald Reagan Radio Broadcast Typescript
- Margaret Tutwiler Files
- Murray Weidenbaum Files
- White House Office of Public Affairs: Records
- White House Office of Records Management Alphabetical Files
- White House Office of Records Management Subject Files
- White House Office of Speechwriting
- White House Staff Exit Interviews

Library of Congress

- Jack Kemp Papers
- Donald T. Regan Papers
- Alice M. Rivlin Papers
- United States Congress Senate Committee on the Budget Oral History Project

Gerald R. Ford Presidential Library

- John O. Marsh Files
- A. James Reichley Interview Transcripts
- L. William Seidman Files
- White House Central Files
- White House Congressional Mail Files

Jimmy Carter Presidential Library

- Susan Clough Papers
- Council of Economic Advisers Papers
- Press Office Papers
- Inflation [Special Adviser to the President] Papers
- Anne Wexler Papers
- White House Central File Papers

National Archives at College Park

- Record Group 56, General Records of the Department of Treasury
- Record Group 58, Records of the Internal Revenue Service

Hoover Institution

- Annelise Anderson Papers
- Milton Friedman Papers
- Deaver and Hannaford, Inc., Records
- Peter Hannaford Papers
- Edwin Meese Papers
- Jude Wanniski Papers

Hagley Museum and Library

- National Association of Manufacturers Records
- Chamber of Commerce of the United States Records

NOTES

Introduction

1. For example, a larger proportion of the U.S. population lives in material deprivation than in Sweden, Denmark, Luxembourg, Germany, France, and most other wealthy OECD countries; the United States is much wealthier than Italy, but the two countries have similar proportions of the population living in material deprivation (Boarini and d'Ercole 2006, 30). Of the thirteen Anglophone, Continental, and Nordic European countries, the United States has the highest rates of absolute poverty among all persons, among all children, and among young children (Gornick and Nell 2017, 18, table 1). Timothy Smeeding (2006) shows the United States at or near the top in poverty rankings by several different measures; see also Kenworthy (2011).
2. OECD.Stat, "Revenue Statistics—OECD Countries: Comparative Tables," Organization for Economic Cooperation and Development (OECD), https://stats.oecd.org/Index.aspx?DataSetCode=REV (accessed August 15, 2018).
3. Piketty 2014, 508–12, 515–39, 572.
4. Scorsone and Bateson 2011.
5. Blow 2015; Prasad 2017.
6. Robertson 2016.
7. Blumenson and Nilsen 1998, 73–74. For some of the libertarian response see, for example, Suprynowicz 1999, 77–78; *St. Louis Post-Dispatch* 1995; Boaz 1999; Lochhead 1999.
8. And still is, by some measures. The tax cuts of George W. Bush, even combined, were much smaller. Other big tax cuts were implemented in 1945 and 2010, both under Democratic presidents (see Tempalski 2013).
9. Modigliani and Modigliani 1987; Erskine 1964, 154–68, 162–63.
10. McCartin 2011; Jacobs and Myers 2014; Hays and Hays 1989; Noble 1986; Niskanen 1988. On the rise of free market policies more broadly see Jones 2012; Mirowski and Plehwe 2015; Prasad 2006. On state-level environmental policy Rabe (2004).

11. Buckley (2011) 2012; Patashnik 2014.
12. Stockman 1986; Sykes et al. 2015; Dudley and Warren 2018, 21.
13. Tempalski 2013.
14. Davey 2015; Stillman 2013; Blumenson and Nilsen 1998, 73–74; Scorsone and Bateson 2011; Harris 2016.
15. Perlstein 2001; Mason 2012.
16. Perlstein 2001, 422; Huret 2014; Martin 2013.
17. Sundquist 1968, 42.
18. Huret 2014, 205.
19. Matusow 1998.
20. Moran 2011.
21. Piketty 2014, 507.
22. Mendoza, Razin, and Tesar 1994.
23. OECD.Stat, "Revenue Statistics—OECD Countries: Comparative Tables," Organization for Economic Cooperation and Development (OECD), https://stats.oecd.org /Index.aspx?DataSetCode=REV (accessed August 15, 2018).
24. Durevall and Henrekson, 2011.
25. Baumol and Bowen 1965.
26. Tilly 1975; Skocpol, Evans, and Rueschemeyer 1985; Tilly 1992.
27. Notes on Cabinet Meeting, February 13, 1981, taken by Kenneth Khachigian, Kenneth Khachigian Files, 1981, Box 1, Folder Cabinet Meetings [Notes] (February 1981), Ronald Reagan Presidential Library Ronald Reagan Library (hereafter "RRPL").
28. Gorski 1976.
29. Prasad 2006.
30. Ronald Reagan 1980 Presidential Campaign Papers, 1964–1980 (hereafter referred to as "Campaign 1980"). In addition to this and other collections at the Ronald Reagan Presidential Library, Simi Valley, California, I have also drawn on several recently released collections from the Hoover Institution, the Library of Congress, and other archives.
31. Eichengreen 2008, 33–34.
32. Kato 2003; Morgan and Prasad 2009.
33. Aldrich and Niemi 1996.
34. American Political Science Association 1950.
35. Ashworth 2012, 183.
36. Mickey Edwards to the president, July 13, 1981, M. B. Oglesby Files, "Misc—Members of Congress," CA 8618, RRPL.
37. Jude Wanniski, quoted in Landon 2000.
38. See, for example, Chivvis 2010, 108–11.
39. Prasad 2006, 2012.

Chapter 1: The Tax Cut Santa Claus

1. Kondracke and Barnes 2015, 21; Clymer 2009.
2. Clymer 2009.

3. Young 2009; Martin 2009. Even allowing for the inflation of praise common in obituaries, these are not the kind of comments often given to Republicans.

4. DeParle 1993.

5. Noah 2015.

6. Greg Daugherty, "The Education of Jack Kemp," *Success,* September 1981, Jack Kemp Papers, Box 382, Folder 2: "Scrapbooks," Vol. 18, August 31, 1979–December 28, 1981, 1 of 4, Manuscript Division, Library of Congress, Washington (hereafter "LC"); Paul A. Gigot, "Republicans Are People Too," Jack Kemp Papers, Box 84, Folder 11: "Mueller, Press about Kemp," 1979, Manuscript Division, LC.

7. Daniel P. Moynihan to Jack Kemp, October 13, 1978, Jack Kemp Papers, Box 381, Folder 11: "Scrapbooks," Vol. 16, February 10, 1978–January 3, 1979, 3 of 3, LC.

8. Frank 2016.

9. Brands 2015, 199.

10. Clymer 2009.

11. Large 1970.

12. Carlson 2009.

13. On the effects of Watergate, McLeod, Brown, and Becker 1977, 184; Republican pollster Robert Teeter, quoted in Apple 1975; sun party and moon party, Lubell 1952.

14. Gallup 1974.

15. Gallup 1974.

16. Mays 1974; *Guardian* 1974.

17. Donovan 1974.

18. Nolan 1975; Peter J. Wallison, "Memorandum for the Vice President," April 28, 1975, Philip Buchen Files, Box 59, Folder: "Republican National Committee (2)," Gerald R. Ford Presidential Library, Ann Arbor, Mich. (hereafter "GFPL"), https://www.fordlibrarymuseum.gov/library/document/0019/28469421.pdf (accessed May 9, 2018).

19. Smith 1975.

20. Kondracke and Barnes 2015, 30.

21. As of 2011, the medal remained at the Ford Library. Thomas A. Klinck to Jack Kemp, January 22, 1976, and Russell A. Rourke to Jack Kemp, February 4, 1976, both in John Marsh Files, Congressional Correspondence File: "Hruska, Roman L.," Box 102, Folder: "Kemp, Jack (1)," GFPL.

22. Hibbs 1982, 215–16.

23. Saad 2008. Hibbs (1982, 215) notes that the Gallup data confound the question of "rising prices" and "high cost of living," but for our concerns both concepts seem relevant. Heffington, Park, and Williams's dataset (2017) shows lower numbers and slightly different peak years, but still shows inflation in the 1970s with higher numbers than any other issue in any other year (using the Singer coding scheme, which breaks out inflation as a separate issue).

24. Jacobs 2016, 191.

25. Jacobs 2016, 5, 90–110, 162.

26. Stein 2010; Gannon 1976; Collins 1998, 167–74.

27. Rowe 1978.

28. Silk 1978.
29. Golden 1980.
30. Blinder 1979, 189; Jianakoplos 1976, 8.
31. Quoted in Cowie 2010, 223. Years later, economists would criticize the events chronicled here (see, for example, Krugman 1994). As one of the figures involved with the origins of supply-side policies noted (Anderson 1988, 112), scholars never attempt to provide comprehensive policy proposals about the economy: "Yet when someone decides to run for president, one of the first questions a reporter will put to him or her is, 'Can you please tell us what your economic policy is going to be?' And the distinguished economists who have never had the audacity to write about this themselves will be the first ones to look up from their newspapers to see how this wretch of a politician will respond to the question on the evening network television news."
32. Waterhouse 2013; Stein 2010, 113; Mattson 2010; Jacobs 2016.
33. Mason 2012.
34. Jack Kemp to the editor, April 8, 1976, Jack Kemp Papers, Box 103, Folder 3: "Correspondence General 1975–80," Manuscript Division, LC.
35. Bruce Bartlett, "Revolution of 1978," Jack Kemp Papers, Box 89, Folder 6: "Mueller, Kemp, Jack, Economics 'Model Notebook,'" 1975–1980, 4 of 4, Manuscript Division, LC.
36. Kondracke and Barnes 2015, 31.
37. Kondracke and Barnes 2015, 33.
38. Benko 2017.
39. Martin 2005.
40. Koestler et al. 1949; Oppenheimer 2016; Moss 2017; Gaston 2013.
41. Hershey 2014.
42. Noble 2006; Bloom 1986; Oppenheimer 2016.
43. Bartlett 2009, 100–101; Laffer 1999; Kondracke and Barnes 2015.
44. Collins 1998, 184; Krugman 1994 86–87 (see footnote 3 for an interesting example of how Laffer and his defenders tried to burnish his reputation).
45. Nobel Prize 1999.
46. Burgin 2012, 180.
47. Mundell 2003, 238.
48. Robert Mundell, quoted in Wanniski 1974. Mundell may have been influenced by renewed attention in economics on how taxes influence incentives (Mirrlees 1971), but given the absence of scholarly attention to Mundell this is only speculation.
49. Robert Mundell, quoted in Wanniski 1974.
50. Robert Mundell, quoted in Wanniski 1974.
51. Wanniski 1974.
52. Robert Mundell, quoted in Wanniski 1974.
53. "Model Notebook K-R: Q&As," Jack Kemp Papers, Box 89, Folder 4, Manuscript Division, LC; Tobin 1989; Anderson 1988, 149.
54. Applebaum 2017.
55. Kondracke and Barnes 2015, 37.

56. See Bruce Bartlett's three-part history of the Laffer curve for historical examples (Bartlett 2012a, 2012b, 2012c).

57. Kennedy 1962.

58. Keynes was desperately trying to argue *against* the view that it was necessary to increase supply (Keynes 1933/2009, 3–5).

59. See, for example, Kneller, Bleaney, and Gemmell 1999; Korpi 1985. Effects on income shifting, Goolsbee 1999.

60. For a thorough catalog of how economists saw the supply-siders, see Krugman 1994.

61. Dunn 1978.

62. Kondracke and Barnes 2015, 38; see also Irwin Ross, "Jack Kemp Wants to Cut Your Taxes—A Lot," *Fortune,* April 10, 1978, Jack Kemp Papers, Box 89, Folder 5, Manuscript Division, LC; Sandy Grady, "Could the Champagne Turn Sour for Tax-Cut Superstar Jack Kemp?" August 8, 1981, Jack Kemp Papers, Box 382, Folder 3: "Scrapbooks," Vol. 18, August 31, 1979–December 28, 1981, 2 of 4, Manuscript Division, LC; Collins 1998, 185.

63. Jude Wanniski to Karl O'Lessker, November 2, 1984, Jack Kemp Papers, Box 41, Folder 3: "Correspondence Wall-Wann 1984–1988," Manuscript Division, LC.

64. (Unsigned), "The 1981 Tax Cuts—Their Origin and Evaluation, Part I—1976–1980," Donald T. Regan Papers, Box 176, Folder 1: "Tax Legislation Economic Recovery Tax Act of 1981, Miscellaneous Materials," n.d., 2 of 2, Manuscript Division, LC; Bartlett 2012a; Roberts 1984, 27–31.

65. Jack Kemp to William E. Simon, March 26, 1975, Jack Kemp Papers, Box 88, Folder 4: "Mueller, Jobs Creation Act," 1976, 3 of 4, Manuscript Division, LC.

66. (Unsigned), "The 1981 Tax Cuts—Their Origin and Evaluation, Part I—1976–1980," Donald T. Regan Papers, Box 176, Folder 1: "Tax Legislation Economic Recovery Tax Act of 1981, Miscellaneous Materials," n.d., 2 of 2, Manuscript Division, LC; Bartlett 2012a; Roberts 1984, 27–31.

67. Jack Kemp to Ronald Reagan, October 10, 1975, Jack Kemp Papers, Box 88, Folder 4: "Mueller, Jobs Creation Act," 1976, 3 of 4, Manuscript Division, LC.

68. Kemp 1975.

69. Jack Kemp, remarks at the Republican National Committee luncheon meeting, February 28, 1976, Sheraton National Hotel, Arlington, Va. (Kesaris 1986); "small entrepreneurial spirit," 21; taxation of savings and investment, 22–24. A bit of the "vee have vays of making you stop talking" can be seen in this speech: on pages 16–17, Kemp notes that he has been given a time limit; on page 22, he says, "That's where I will close"; on page 25, he again promises "just to close"; and on page 27, he is still giving "one last note."

70. Burns and Taylor 2000, 430; *Wall Street Journal* 1975a, 1975b.

71. *Wall Street Journal* 1977. Bartlett 1981, 130; Kondracke and Barnes 2015, 45.

72. Roberts 1984, 32–33.

73. Anderson 1988; Golden 1975. Anderson (1988, 144–45) also claims that Arthur Burns had unsuccessfully proposed a three-year 5 percent rate reduction to Nixon. Bartlett (1981, 135) notes that Roberts had in 1971 produced a Laffer-like curve tracing the

response of the productivity of a system to the number of rules governing management (Roberts 1971, 54); this curve was not concerned with taxation, but it does show
that the idea that too much government regulation impedes productivity was in the
air.

74. Jack Kemp, quoted in Margolis 1978. For other verbatim examples months apart, see
Steigerwald 1979; Sobran 1980. The idea articulated by this wording isn't necessarily
true; as other free marketers would argue—when not engaged in rhetorical battle—
subsidies can make recipient firms less efficient, which would imply that taxes can
force them into needing to be more efficient.

75. For example, "The more you tax something, the less of it you get. The less you tax
something or the more you subsidize it, the more of it you get." "Questions and
Answers," March 1981, T. Kenneth Cribb Files: Office of Cabinet Affairs, Box 1,
Folder OA3809: "Background on the President's Tax Program," 2 of 2 (binder), RRPL.

76. Wanniski 1976.

77. Mason 2012, 128. Even the Santa Clause metaphor was not new: in 1951 Kenneth
Wherry wrote to Nixon, "It is true everybody loves Santa Claus, yet I think there is
another issue on which the Democrats are vulnerable, and that is the wasteful expenditure of money for these welfare ideas and the toll in taxes it has taken from the
individual" (quoted in Mason 2012, 136).

78. Kemp 1976.

79. Jack Kemp, "A Republican Renaissance," remarks prepared for participants at the
Tidewater Conference, Easton, Md., sponsored by the National Republican Con-
gressional Committee, the National Republican Senatorial Committee, and the
Republican Governors Association, April 28, 1978, Digital Collections, Carnegie
Mellon University, http://digitalcollections.library.cmu.edu/awweb/awarchive?type
=file&item=690102 (accessed January 21, 2018).

80. Raymond Clapper, quoted in Mason 2012, 49.

81. Arthur Vandenberg, quoted in Mason 2012, 50. NHA pamphlet, Plotke 2006, 224.

82. Quoted in Mason 2012, 158.

83. Roberts 1984, 21. For an analysis of the argument and its proponents on the eve of the
Reagan Revolution, see Bartlett 1981, 159–65.

84. Pfiffner 1979; Cannon 2003, 368–79.

85. Including perhaps the neoconservative Irving Kristol (Dawn Gifford, interview with
A. James Reichley, November 17, 1980, A. James Reichley Interview Transcripts,
1977–1981, "Politician Interviews: Politician Interviews—General," Box 3, Folder:
"1980 Campaign and Transition, Gifford, Dawn," GFPL); Murray Friedman (Friedman 2005, 177–84); and maybe even the economist Herb Stein (Jack Kemp, interview
with A. James Reichley, October 4, 1977, A. James Reichley Interview Transcripts,
1977–1981, "Domestic Policy Interviews: Domestic Policy Interviews—General," Box
2, Folder: "Congress Jack Kemp," GFPL).

86. Jack Kemp to Gerald Ford, December 15, 1976, Campaign 1980, Box 493: "Rep. Jack
Kemp (R-N.Y.)," RRPL.

87. Jack Kemp to Republican members of Congress, February 22, 1977, Campaign 1980,
Box 85: "Black—Personal Correspondence 1977," RRPL.

Chapter 2: Convincing the Republicans

1. Brownlee 1996a, 1996b; McCaffery and Cohen 2006; Michelmore 2012; Stein 1969; Steuerle 2004; Zelizer 2000; Pollack 2003, 45–54; Linder 1996; Perlstein 2001; Mason 2012; Cannon 2003; Huret 2014; Martin 2013; Prasad 2012; Sanders 1998, 217–32.

2. Quoted in Roberts 1984, 3.

3. Gerald Ford, quoted in Moran 2011, 50.

4. *Human Events* 1975.

5. *Boston Globe* 1976; *Baltimore Sun* 1977. Richard Nixon did skate close to the tax cut issue in the wake of his campaign against McGovern, when advisers suggested adopting the "apparently popular position against tax increases." But Nixon's stance on taxes remained opposition to tax increases rather than a determined course of tax reduction (Michelmore 2012, 121).

6. James T. Lynn to Max Friedersdorf, April 13, 1976, John Marsh Files, Congressional Correspondence File: "Hruska, Roman L.," Box 102, Folder: "Kemp, Jack (2)," GFPL. For and interesting example of the Nixon administration's opposition to tax cuts, see Shanahan 1972.

7. Klinkner 1994, 786.

8. Charlie Black to Jack Kemp, May 23, 1977, Campaign 1980, Box 85: "Black—Personal Correspondence 1977," RRPL.

9. Quoted in Burns and Taylor 2000, 432.

10. Kondracke and Barnes 2015, 43–49; Roberts 1984, 7–20; Farney 1978. There were already dozens of measures for tax cuts in Congress before Proposition 13.

11. *Boston Globe* 1977. See Galvin 2009, 247, for the argument that party-building has been a durable response from the Republicans for their minority problem.

12. Klinkner 1994, 787.

13. For an example of inflation inspiring an episode of the tax revolt, see Martin 2008, 50.

14. Hume 1978; Dorsey 1978; Neikirk 1978; Berman and Pagnucco 2010, 258–59.

15. Tolchin 1978.

16. W. H. von Dreele, quoted in Domitrovic, 2009, 175.

17. Wanniski 1978b.

18. "Briefings: Republican Tax Cut Blitz Briefing Book," Campaign 1980, Box 52, September 20–22, 1978, 1 and 2 of 2, RRPL.

19. "Roth-Kemp = Tax Cut = Jobs = Economic Growth," *First Monday,* June 1978, Campaign 1980, Box 459: "Research Files—Kemp [Jack] (Hopkins/Bandow)," RRPL.

20. "Remarks of Congressman Jack Kemp (R-N.Y.) at the 44th Annual Convention of the International Longshoremen's Association, AFL-CIO, Miami, 16 July 1979," Campaign 1980, Box 473: "Research Policy—Issues Material—Kemp, Jack," 2 of 2 (Hopkins/Bandow), RRPL; Ed Kelly, "How Kemp Wooed ILA," *Buffalo Evening News,* August 8, 1979, Campaign 1980, Box 437: "Research Policy—Issues Material— Kemp, Jack," 1 of 2 (Hopkins/Bandow), RRPL.

21. Anonymous [perhaps Randall Teague?], "The Economic Program," May 5, 1975, Jack

Kemp Papers, Box 88, Folder 5: "Mueller, Jobs Creation Act," 1976, 4 of 4, Manuscript Division, LC.

22. Cannon 1991, 147.
23. Coste 2015; Perlstein 2014, 27–49.
24. Anderson 1988, 166.
25. Cannon 2003, 368–79; Cannon 1991, 69; Reagan 1990, 231–32; Gourse 2015, 234 –79.
26. "Ronald Reagan Speaks Out on Carter Tax Plan," *CFTR Newsletter,* December 1, 1977, Campaign 1980, Box 38: "Hannaford/CA HQ—*Citizens for the Republic* [newsletter]," August 1977–December 1977, 2 of 3, RRPL; "Ronald Reagan Speaks Out: Republicans Ride the Tax Cut Ride," *CFTR Newsletter,* July 17, 1978, Campaign 1980, Box 39: "Hannaford/CA HQ—*Citizens for the Republic,*" Vol. 2, June 1978–October 1978, 2 of 3 (General), RRPL.
27. Williams and Wilson 1979.
28. Lyons 1978.
29. Hunt 1978.
30. Gergen 1978.
31. Harris 1978.
32. Reinhold 1978.
33. Beckman 1978.
34. On interpreting the meaning of midterm elections, see Tufte 1975; Bafumi, Erikson, and Wlezien 2010.
35. Reinhold 1978.
36. Shogan 1979.
37. Cannon 2003, 194–99.
38. Bergholz 1979.
39. Clymer 2011.
40. Jacobs and Burns 2004; Wirthlin 1981; Murray 2006; Beal and Hinckley 1984; Murray and Howard 2002.
41. Levy 1984, 90; Jacobs and Burns 2004, 548–51.
42. "A National Survey of the American Electorate," May–June 1978, 83, Campaign 1980, Box 183, RRPL.
43. Steering Committee meeting, January 13, 1979, 16, 22, Campaign 1980, Box 105: "Meese Files—Campaign Ops—*Citizens for the Republic,*" May 1979 (background, status, and meeting minutes), RRPL.
44. Anderson 1988, 117; Brands 2015, 260; Kondracke and Barnes 2015, 66–67.
45. Lindsey 1980.
46. Peterson 1980.
47. Ronald Reagan to Fred Lennon, n.d., Campaign 1980, Box 1: "RR—Dictation," n.d., RRPL; Germond and Witcover 1979; Evans and Novak 1980b.
48. Thimmesch 1979.
49. *Washington Post* 1980b.
50. Endicott 1980a; Witcover and Germond 1980.
51. Stall 1980b.

52. Taylor 1980.
53. *Washington Post* 1980b.
54. *New York Times* 1980a.
55. *Christian Science Monitor* 1980; on Bush's stance on deregulation, Jacobs 2016, 21–22.
56. Clymer 1980; Stall 1980a.
57. Bergholz 1980b.
58. "A Statewide Survey of Republican Primary Voters in New Hampshire," January 1980, 5–7, Campaign 1980, Box 193, RRPL; "Two Brushfire Surveys of New Hampshire Republican Voters," February 1980, 10, Campaign 1980, Box 196, RRPL; Richard Wirthlin to John Sears, February 16, 1980, 3, Campaign 1980, Box 109: "Meese, Ed—Campaign Operations—Polling Data," 1 of 2, RRPL.
59. Ronald Reagan to Keith Ferguson, n.d., Campaign 1980, Box 1: "RR—Dictation," January 1, 1980–June 1980, 1 of 3, RRPL.
60. Mollison 1980.
61. Shirley 2009, 147–48.
62. Broder and Cannon 1980; Nyhan 1980b; Brands 2015, 222–23. See Ronald Reagan, "I Am Paying for This Microphone (1980)," https://www.youtube.com/watch?v=Rd_KaF3-Bcw (accessed May 9, 2018).
63. Nyhan 1980a.
64. Wirthlin and Hall 2004, 44.
65. Smith 1980.
66. Shirley 2009, 154.
67. "A Statewide Survey of Republican Primary Voters in New Hampshire," January 1980, 5–7, Campaign 1980, Box 193, RRPL.
68. Warsh 1980.
69. Shirley 2009, 259–64.
70. "A Panel Survey of Vermont Republicans," February 1980, Campaign 1980, Box 197, RRPL.
71. "A Statewide Survey of Republican Primary Voters in Illinois Wave II," February 9–10, 1980, 17, Campaign 1980, Box 195, RRPL.
72. Shirley 2009, 238–39.
73. On Kemp's name recognition, see "A Statewide Survey of Republican Primary Voters in Florida," November–December 1979, 25–26, Campaign 1980, Box 191, RRPL. On Kemp as a possible vice presidential pick, see "Kemp's Talk to Convention May Be Biggest of Career" and "Reagan Nearly Chose Kemp, Aide Reveals," Jack Kemp Papers, Box 382, Folder 8: "Scrapbooks," Vol. 20, July 15, 1980–February 13, 1981, Manuscript Division, LC. On Kemp as the "good soldier," see Jack Kemp to Ronald Reagan, n.d., "Presidential Handwriting File," Series II: Presidential Records, December 17, 1980–December 13, 1981, Box 1, Folder 15, November 19, 1981–December 1, 1981, RRPL.
74. Evans and Novak 1979; Bunch 2009, 38–39.
75. *New York Times* 1982.

Chapter 3: Convincing the Voters

1. *Washington Post* 1980a.
2. Shirley 2009, 493–94.
3. Hunt 1980. Wanniski tried to defend himself by saying that he had been trying to make Reagan look more intellectual. Jude Wanniski to Peter Hannaford, April 10, 1980, Campaign 1980, Box 37: "Hannaford/CA HQ General—Advertising (1980 Campaign) I," 1 of 3, RRPL.
4. Jude Wanniski to Jack Kemp, June 10, 1980, Campaign 1980 Box 124: "Meese, Ed—Memos—RR & Positions for May & June 1980," RRPL.
5. "Strategy," Campaign 1980, Box 101: "Meese, Ed—Campaign Planning—Campaign 80 Marketing Plan," August 8, 1980, RRPL.
6. Atkinson 1980; Anderson 1988, 126, 133.
7. *Wall Street Journal* 1980.
8. "A Statewide Survey of Republican Voters in Pennsylvania," April 1980, 11, Campaign 1980, Box 199, RRPL.
9. *Wall Street Journal* 1980.
10. Silk 1980; Wanniski 1975, 1978a; Bartley 1979.
11. Eichengreen and Flandreau 1997.
12. *New York Times* 1981a.
13. "Meeting on Public Policy Issues," September 8, 1979, Campaign 1980, Box 103: "Meese, Ed—Campaign Planning—Meetings," RRPL.
14. Silk 1981.
15. "Meeting Re: Economic Affairs," January 21, 1980, Campaign 1980, Box 103: "Meese—Campaign Planning—Meetings," January 1980, RRPL.
16. Martin Anderson, "An Economic Program for the 1980s," rough draft, March 20, 1980, Campaign 1980, Box 468: "Research Policy—Speech Material—Economy (General) (Hopkins/Bandow)," RRPL.
17. Martin Anderson, "An Economic Program for the 1980s," rough draft, March 20, Campaign 1980, Box 468: "Research Policy—Speech Material—Economy (General) (Hopkins/Bandow)," RRPL.
18. Richard B. Wirthlin to Reagan, Casey, and Meese, May 26, 1980, "Strategy for the Doldrums," Box 104: "Meese, Ed—Campaign Planning—Tactics," 3 of 4, RRPL.
19. William J. Casey to Governor Reagan et al., April 7, 1980, 2–3, Campaign 1980, Box 128, Meese Subject Files, "Domestic—Briefing Papers/Memos," 1 of 2, RRPL; Robert J. Geis, "The Economic Benefits of the Gold Reserve Act of 1981," T. Kenneth Cribb Files: Office of Cabinet Affairs, Box 1, 013809, 4821, Folder "The Gold Reserve Act of 1981 OA4821 Cribb, T. Kenneth: Files Cabinet Affairs Series I," RRPL; Folder OA3809: "Background on the President's Tax Program," RRPL; T. Kenneth Cribb Files: Office of Cabinet Affairs Series I, Folder OA4821: "The Gold Reserve Act of 1981," RRPL; "14 Key Economic Questions on Reagan Economic Plan," attachment to memo from Ed Meese and Jim Baker to Governor Reagan, October 2, 1980, Campaign 1980, Box 140: "Messe, Ed—Debate—Baltimore 9/21/80 (Reagan-Anderson)—Post-Debate," RRPL.

20. "Report on a Focus Group Discussion of the 1980 Presidential Election," 12–13, Campaign 1980, Box 250: "Political Ops—General—Polling & Strategy (Wirthlin, Beal)," 1 of 5 (Timmons), RRPL; Meeting, July 9, 1980, Campaign 1980, Box 105: "Meese, Ed—Campaign Planning Meetings," July 1980, RRPL; Richard B. Wirthlin to Governor Ronald Reagan et al., Campaign 1980, Box 152: "Meese, Ed—Staff/Advisors—Wirthlin, Dick," 2 of 2, RRPL; "Campaign 80," October 8, 1980, Campaign 1980, Box 221: "Media Campaign—(Campaign '80, 10/8/80 Meeting) (Peter Dailey)," RRPL; "Some Initial Strategic and Tactical Considerations for the 1980 Presidential Campaign," March 28, 1980, Campaign 1980, Box 104: "Meese, Ed—Campaign Planning—Tactics," 3 of 4, RRPL.

21. Bob Garrick to Ed Meese, memorandum re: "Mail Report for the Week of October 18–24," October 25, 1980, Campaign 1980, Box 108: "Meese Files—Campaign Operations—Miscellaneous (Reports, Memos, Correspondence)," 2 of 3, RRPL.

22. "Business Politics: Controversial Reagan Economic Positions," Campaign 1980, Box 246: "Debate File—Debate Strategies," 2 of 3 (Baker), RRPL.

23. July 9, 1980, meeting, Campaign 1980, Box 105: "Meese, Ed—Campaign Planning Meetings," July 1980, RRPL.

24. Michael J. Boskin to Ed Meese, March 26, 1980, Campaign 1980, Box 116: "Ed Meese—Correspondence File—EM Correspondence," March 1980, 2 of 2, RRPL.

25. Ronald Reagan to Clair Burgerner, Campaign 1980 Box 1: "Reagan, Ronald—Dictation—1980," RRPL.

26. Neikirk 1980.

27. Anderson 1988, 131.

28. Martin Anderson to Governor Reagan, August 22, 1980, 6, Campaign 1980, Box 129, Meese Subject Files: "Federal Spending [Anderson to RR re: economic conditions]," RRPL.

29. Anderson 1988, 126–39; White and Wildavsky 1989, 77.

30. Bartlett 2011, 628.

31. Donald Regan, "Testimony of the Honorable Donald T. Regan, Secretary of the Treasury, before the Senate Appropriations Committee," January 27, 1981, Wendell Gunn Files, Folder OA6851: "Economic Program" (2), RRPL.

32. "Testimony of the Honorable Donald T. Regan," January 27, 1981, Wendell Gunn Files, Folder OA6851: "Economic Program" (2), RRPL; Murray Weidenbaum to Jake Garn, February 25, 1981, Weidenbaum Files, Folder OA11004: "MLW General Correspondence," February 19–22, 1981 (2), RRPL; Murray Weidenbaum to James R. Jones, March 13, 1981, Weidenbaum Files, Folder OA11004: "MLW General Correspondence," March 12–31, 1981 (5), RRPL; Martin Anderson to Governor Reagan, August 22, 1980, 6, Campaign 1980, Box 129, Meese Subject Files: "Federal Spending [Anderson to RR re: economic conditions]," RRPL. Michael Boskin's (1978) work on savings played a particularly important role and is discussed in greater detail in chapter 5.

33. Rattner 1980.

34. Pine 1980.

35. *Washington Post* 1980c; White and Wildavsky 1989, 77.

36. Richard B. Wirthlin to Governor Reagan et al., August 13, 1980, Campaign 1980, Box 152: "Meese, Ed—Staff/Advisors—Wirthlin, Dick," 1 of 2, RRPL.

37. Richard Nixon to Jack Kemp, March 5, 1981, Jack Kemp Papers, Box 382, Folder 2: "Scrapbooks," Vol. 18, August 31, 1979–December 28, 1981, 1 of 4, Manuscript Division, LC.

38. Wilentz 2008, 141.

39. Madden 1980.

40. "Consumer Attitudes toward Government Taxation and Spending," September 3, 1980, Campaign 1980, Box 252: "Political Ops—Issues—Taxes" (Timmons), RRPL.

41. Jude Wanniski, "The Campaign Homestretch," Peter Hannaford Papers, Box 6, Folder 6–9, Hoover Institution, Stanford University, Stanford, Calif.

42. "Some Initial Strategic and Tactical Considerations for the 1980 Presidential Campaign," March 28, 1980, 11, Campaign 1980, Box 104: "Meese, Ed—Campaign Planning—Tactics," 3 of 4, RRPL.

43. Kevin Hopkins and Doug Bandow to Dick Wirthlin, May 21, 1980, Campaign 1980, Box 107: "Meese—Campaign Ops—[Issues, Memos re:]," RRPL.

44. Richard B. Wirthlin to Reagan/Bush Campaign, October 21, 1980, Campaign 1980, Box 140: "Meese, Ed—Debate—Cleveland OH," October 28, 1980 (Reagan-Carter), 2 of 3, RRPL.

45. Ed Meese to Richard Wirthlin, August 13, 1980, Campaign 1980, Box 127, "Meese Subject Files, "Carter Strategy," RRPL.

46. Jude Wanniski to Peter Hannaford, April 10, 1980, Campaign 1980, Box 37: "Hannaford/CA HQ General—Advertising (1980 Campaign) I," 1 of 3, RRPL.

47. Richard B. Wirthlin to Governor Ronald Reagan, Bill Casey, and deputy campaign directors, memorandum re: "Status of the Campaign and Some Strategic Considerations with 25 Days to Go," October 11, 1980, Campaign 1980, Box 152: "Meese, Ed—Staff/Advisors—Wirthlin, Dick," 2 of 2, RRPL.

48. Jeff Peterson to Gene E. Godley, memorandum re: "The Tax Cut Issue," June 27, 1980, Archives II (National Archives), Record Group 56, General Records of the Department of the Treasury, Office of the Assistant Secretary for Legislative Affairs, Subject Files of Robert E. Moss, 1980, Box 4, Folder: "81 Tax Cuts," 3 of 3, National Archives and Records Administration (NARA), College Park, Md.

49. Busch 2005.

Chapter 4: Beasts and Dogs

1. Marie Allen, "Interview with Dr. Martin Anderson, February 26, 1982," White House Staff Exit Interviews: Transcripts: "Martin Anderson," RRPL.

2. Green 2009; Jacobs 2016.

3. For an example of the "starve the beast" explanation, see Krugman 2010.

4. Moynihan 1983.

5. Dionne 1988.

6. Allan H. Ryskind, quoted in Dionne 1988.

7. Reagan 1981.

8. Robert H. Michel to Republican colleagues, May 29, 1981, M. B. Oglesby Files, Folder: "Strategy—Republican," CA 8618, RRPL.

9. See Bartlett 2007.

10. Richard G. Darman, "Meeting of Legislative Strategy Group," May 12, 1981, Craig Fuller Files, Box 10972: "Economic/Budget Policy," May 81, RRPL.

11. See Charles E. Walker to Richard V. Allen, White House Office of Records Management (WHORM) Subject Files: "Meetings—Conferences," Box 1, Folder MC013298, February 18, 1981: "There are billions upon billions of dollars around the world that will flow into U.S. bonds and stocks just as soon as foreign investors become convinced that the program will work." But for a discussion of the general absence of attention to the role of foreign markets in financing the deficit at this time see Krippner 2011, 95.

12. U.S. Department of the Treasury, "Background on the President's Tax Program," Edwin Meese III Files, Binder 1, Folder OA2990: "Background on the President's Tax Program," RRPL.

13. David A. Stockman, "Reagan Economic Program II–General Materials," White House Office of Public Affairs: Records, Folder OA9020, 2 of 5, RRPL. See also Morgan 2008, 104.

14. Murray Weidenbaum, "Interest Rates and Monetary Policy," May 7, 1981, Craig Fuller Files, Box 10972: "Economic/Budget Policy," May 1981, RRPL (emphasis in original).

15. Martin Anderson, "Memorandum for Governor Reagan," August 22, 1980, Campaign 1980, Box 129, Meese Subject Files: "Federal Spending [Anderson to RR re: economic conditions]," RRPL.

16. Anderson 1988.

17. Brownlee and Steuerle 2003.

18. Reagan 1990, 232.

19. White and Wildavsky 1989, 79–81.

20. *Neshoba Democrat* 2007; Sitton 1964; *Baltimore Sun* 1964; Bates 2011, 25.

21. López 2014.

22. Turner 2009; Bates 2011, 23, 27–28.

23. Ward 2011; Manly 1962; Moyers 2004, 197; Boyd 1970.

24. Barry Goldwater, quoted in Ward 2011, 170.

25. Lyndon Johnson, quoted in Moyers 2004, 197.

26. Boyd 1970, 105.

27. Kevin Phillips, quoted in Boyd 1970, 111; Phillips 1969.

28. Carmines and Stimson 1989, 38–39; Frymer and Skrentny 1998, 138–39; López 2014.

29. López 2014, 25; Scammon and Wattenberg 1970.

30. Sanders 1992, 627–30, 638.

31. Edsall and Edsall 1991; Ward 2011; Manly 1962, 7; Moyers 2004, 197; Boyd 1970, 105; Carmines and Stimson 1989, 38–39; Frymer and Skrentny 1998, 131–61, 138–39; Bass and DeVries 1995, 30; Kotlowski 1998; Orfield 1975, 95; Graham 1996, 94; López 2014, 24. Randolph Hohle (2015) has recently argued for a racial angle to free market pol-

icies by showing elements of free market ideology in three Southern states from long before the Reagan era, on the assumption that a Southern origin implies origins in racism. But such policies are found outside the South as well. For example, Kathryn S. Olmsted (2015) finds them in California in the 1930s and Elizabeth Tandy Shermer (2013) in Phoenix starting in the 1940s.

32. Wirthlin with Hall 2004, 68.
33. Wirthlin with Hall 2004, 68.
34. See chapter 1, page 20.
35. Bates 2011, 18–27.
36. Wirthlin with Hall 2004, 65–66.
37. *Neshoba Democrat* 2007.
38. These data are made available by the Inter-University Consortium for Political and Social Research and were originally collected by the Institute for Social Research at the University of Michigan, director Warren E. Miller, director for 1980 Maria Elena Sanchez. The data are currently available at http://www.electionstudies.org/ (accessed September 28, 2018), and the calculations in this chapter are available at my website (https://www.sociology.northwestern.edu/people/faculty/core/monica-prasad.html) and through the ICPSR.
39. Feldman and Huddy 2005.
40. Quotations from American National Election Studies 1980.
41. Throughout this analysis, I did not impute for missing data, as the results are similar whether or not cases with missing values are dropped.
42. Lacy 1998.
43. Feldman and Huddy 2005.
44. *Neshoba Democrat* 2007.
45. Green 2012.
46. Baron 1979.
47. Hurst 1981.
48. Greenberger 1980.
49. Bergholz 1980a.
50. Nolan 1980; *Baltimore Sun* 1980.
51. Los Angeles Times 1980; Bernstein and Eaton 1981; Brown 1981a, 1981b; Bernstein 1980.
52. Broder 1981.
53. Endicott 1980b.
54. Shogan 1980.
55. Kraft 1981.
56. McCartin 2011.
57. Pontusson 2013.

Chapter 5: "Thank God, and Bring Down Prices"

1. Jacobs 2016, 207–17; *New York Times* 1979.
2. Pupils of Miss Rutland's fourth-grade class to Ronald Reagan, January 1981, WHORM

Subject Files: "Business—Economics," Box 87, Folder BE004-02 (BEGIN–005999), RRPL.

3. Pupils of Mrs. Faulkner's fifth-grade class to Ronald Reagan, January 1981, WHORM Subject Files: "Business—Economics," Box 87, Folder BE004-02 (BEGIN–005999), RRPL.

4. Pupils of Mrs. Noble's third-grade class to Ronald Reagan, ca. February 1981, WHORM Subject Files: "Business—Economics," Box 87, Folder BE004-02 (006000–008499), RRPL.

5. This interesting confusion presages the argument of this book that the tax cut was born in the politics of inflation.

6. Laffer 1980; Poulos 1981; Smith 1988, 50–51.

7. *Chicago Tribune* 1981.

8. Welch 2000, 44.

9. Notes on meeting with Dick Wirthlin, 2-27[or 29?]-81, taken by Kenneth Khachigian, Kenneth Khachigian Files, 1981, Box 1, Folder Communications Meetings [Notes] (January 1981–April 1981), RRPL. Not clear if "they buy it" is Khachigian's phrase of Wirthlin's. Welch 2008, 15.

10. Collins 2006, 62–63, 179–83; 1998, 189.

11. For example, the attempts by Daniel Stedman Jones (2012) to tie economists to the Reagan tax cuts are brief and unconvincing. In one such attempt, he writes, "James Buchanan and Milton Friedman *provided prominent and vocal ballast* to the supporters of the tax revolts" (172, emphasis added), but showing that economists supported tax cuts is not the same thing as showing that their ideas caused it. In fact, the time line shows that economists joined the effort after it was already under way. Similarly, Jones quotes an article by Friedman arguing that Republicans should focus on tax cuts rather than deficit reduction (172), but the article is dated 1978—several years after Republicans had begun pushing for tax cuts. Friedman did push for a negative income tax, as Jones notes, but of course the key word there is "negative": the negative income tax is not a tax cut, but a form of welfare spending (allegedly one that distorts incentives less than current forms of welfare spending).

12. U.S. Senate, Budget Committee 1978. Note however that the Senate was controlled by Democrats, and the economists surveyed may not have constituted a representative sample.

13. Richard R. Nelson to Murray Weidenbaum, March 16, 1981, Weidenbaum Files, Folder OA11004: "MLW General Correspondence," March 12–31, 1981 (3), RRPL.

14. George Stigler and Alan Greenspan, quoted in Zucker 1978.

15. Evans and Novak 1979.

16. Bill Brock to William Armstrong, January 26, 1979, Jack Kemp Papers, Box 103, Folder 10: "Brunette," 1977–1979, Manuscript Division, LC.

17. Jack Kemp to the editor, *Wall Street Journal,* April 4, 1980, Jack Kemp Papers, Box 89, Folder 5: "Mueller, Kemp, Jack, Economics 'Model Notebook,'" 1975–1980, 3 of 4, Manuscript Division, LC.

18. See, for example, James Tobin to Al Ullman, August 3, 1978, Council of Economic Advisers Papers, Box 84, Charles L. Schultze Subject Files, Folder: "Tax Reduction

Exercise 1980 [Reagan-Kemp-Roth]," (3), Jimmy Carter Presidential Library, Atlanta, Ga. (hereafter "JCPL").

19. "Questions and Answers," March 1981, T. Kenneth Cribb Files: Office of Cabinet Affairs, Box 1, Folder OA3809: "Background on the President's Tax Program," 2 of 2 (binder), RRPL.

20. Lucas 1982, 5.

21. Frey et al. 1984, 994; Klein and Stern 2007. By 1992, a more comprehensive survey found that 54.7 percent of economists disagreed with the statement, "The major source of macroeconomic disturbances is supply-side shocks," with only 40.3 percent agreeing; 43.8 percent disagreed with the statement, "Lower marginal income tax rates reduce leisure and increase work effort," and 55.4 percent agreed with it; and 49.8 percent disagreed with the statement, "Reducing the tax rate on income from capital gains would encourage investment and promote economic growth," with 49.3 percent agreeing (Alston, Kearl, and Vaughan 1992, 205; I have included "agree with provisos" in the agreement figures here). Interestingly, by 2003 economists were more likely to agree that lower marginal rates increase work effort (66.8 percent) and that lower capital gains tax rates increase investment and economic growth (61.4 percent) (Fuller and Geide-Stevenson 2003, 376–77). Far from economists driving the supply-side revolution, it may be that the supply-side revolution has subsequently shaped the field of economics. More recent work finds more consensus in the discipline on support for free trade and school vouchers as well as more opposition to subsidies and the postal monopoly, but there is less agreement on other issues; it is also worth noting that over 45 percent of economists express support for universal health insurance (Whaples 2006).

22. Joyce 2011, 56–57.

23. Evans and Novak 1981b.

24. Williams 1998, 221–22.

25. Joyce 2011, 58.

26. Suggested response to the charge that "The President's package will not reduce inflation, or increase saving," Donald T. Regan Papers, Box 176, Folder 1: "Tax Legislation, Economic Recovery Tax Act of 1981, Miscellaneous Materials," n.d., 1 of 2, Manuscript Division, LC.

27. Council of Economic Advisers, March 17, 1981, "The Current Status of the President's Program for Economic Recovery," Donald T. Regan Papers, Box 138, Folder 4: "Economic Recovery Program," March 17–April 3, 1981, Manuscript Division, LC.

28. "President's Tax Proposals Economic Rationale," Office of the Secretary of the Treasury, Donald T. Regan Papers, Box 138, Folder 3: "Economic Recovery Program," February 18–March 3, 1981, Manuscript Division, LC.

29. "Questions and Answers," February 17, 1981, U.S. Department of the Treasury, Donald T. Regan Papers, Box 138, Folder 3: "Economic Recovery Program," February 18–March 3, 1981, Manuscript Division, LC.

30. See, for example, Kemp 1976.

31. For a lively denial, Anderson 1988, 140–63.

32. Hayward 2009, 70–71.

33. Skelton 1981a.

34. Reagan 1990, 232, 244.

35. White House, "President Reagan's Program for Economic Recovery," April 1981, Craig Fuller Files, Folder OA10972: "Economic/Budget Policy," April 1981 (3), RRPL.

36. David A. Stockman, "Reagan Economic Program II—General Materials," White House Office of Public Affairs: Records, Folder OA9020, 2 of 5, RRPL.

37. "Savings and Investment in the Program for Economic Recovery," White House Office of Public Affairs: Records, Folder OA9015: "Reagan Tax Cut Plan," 4 of 8, RRPL.

38. Boskin 1978.

39. U.S. Department of the Treasury, "Background on the President's Tax Program," Edwin Meese III Files, Folder OA2990: "Background on the President's Tax Program," Binder 1, RRPL.

40. Congressional Budget Office, "Congress and the Budget," April 10, 1981, Alice M. Rivlin Papers, Box 26, Folder: "Congress and the Budget," April 16, 1981, Manuscript Division, LC.

41. Walter Heller, "Memorandum for the President," January 3, 1980, Council of Economic Advisers Papers, Charles L. Schultze Correspondence Files, Box 191, Folder: "[General Correspondence: H] [10]," JCPL.

42. *New York Times* 1981b.

43. Pechman 1981, 431; Thurow 1981, 16–17; Gordon 1981, 2; Jorgenson 1981a, 1788; 1981b, 347.

44. Rutledge 1981, 437–43; Bradford 1981, 11–14; Rabushka 1981, 49; Feldstein 1981b, 141; Meiselman 1981, 82.

45. Quoted in Reay 2012, 71.

46. Jacob 1985, 14.

47. Galbraith 1988, 224.

48. Weidenbaum 1988, 242.

49. Ronald Reagan, quoted in Orr 1984.

50. Reagan 1985, 1247.

51. Cannon 1991, 98.

52. Berry 1984.

53. Blinder 1987, 1, 3.

54. Samuelson 1966, 1515.

55. Crittenden 1976; see also Golden 1980.

56. Fairbrother 2014. Hirschman and Berman (2014) argue that for economists to be influential, they must have professional authority and institutional presence, and their mechanisms of influence are styles of reasoning as well as policy devices. But economists did have professional authority and institutional presence in this case, without much influence, and their styles of reasoning and policy devices either did not lead to specific courses of action or were used in ways that undermined the expertise of economists (as with Anderson's use of the SBC numbers).

57. Heller 1978, 20.

58. Quoted in Morgan 1981.

59. Paul Craig Roberts to Donald Regan, 13 May 1981, Donald T. Regan Papers, Box 175, Folder 6, Tax Legislation, Economic Recovery Tax Act of 1981, Miscellaneous Materials, May–Dec. 1981, Manuscript Division, Library of Congress.

60. John Sears interview with A. James Reichley, January 12, 1981, A. James Reichley Interview Transcripts, 1977–81, "Politician Interviews, Politician Interviews—General," Box 3, Folder "1980 Campaign and Transition, Sears, John," Gerald R. Ford Library.

61. *Baltimore Sun* 1981.

62. Notes on Cabinet Meeting, 3-19-81, taken by Kenneth Khachigian, Kenneth Khachigian Files, 1981, Box 1, Folder Cabinet Meetings [Notes] (March 1981), RRPL.

63. See, for example, U.S. House of Representatives, Ways and Means Committee 1981, part I.

64. White and Wildavsky 1989, 111.

Chapter 6: Tax Cut versus Tax Cut

1. Mickey Edwards to the president, July 13, 1981, M. B. Oglesby Files, "Misc-Members of Congress," CA 8618, RRPL.

2. O'Neill and Novak 1987, 203, 330–31; Reagan 2007, 80.

3. O'Neill and Novak 1987, 344; Farrell 2001, 543–62; Cohen 1981.

4. Tate 1981a, 376.

5. Arieff 1981.

6. Farrell 2001, 543–62; White and Wildavsky 1989, 115–17; Cohen 1981; Tate 1981c.

7. Collins 2006, 60; "Biographical," Jack Kemp Papers, Box 43, Folder 9: "Biographical Material," 1973–1977, Manuscript Division, LC.

8. Ronald Reagan to Jack Kemp, July 26, 1979, Jack Kemp Papers, Box 381, Folder 14: "Scrapbooks," Vol. 17, January 5, 1979–January 11, 1980, 3 of 4, Manuscript Division, LC.

9. "The Daily Diary of President Ronald Reagan," March 30, 1981, The President's Daily Diary, March 25–April 10, 1981, Office of the Presidential Diary, RRPL.

10. "Attack on Ronald Reagan," https://www.youtube.com/watch?v=e-cKPe7E-wI (accessed January 26, 2018); Brands 2015, 284–88; Reeves 2005, 35–42; Giordano 1981; "The Daily Diary of President Ronald Reagan," March 30, 1981, The President's Daily Diary, March 25–April 10, 1981, Office of the Presidential Diary, RRPL; Marie Allen, "Interview with Ken Duberstein," December 15 and 29, 1983, White House Staff Exit Interviews, Transcripts: "Kenneth Duberstein," (1), RRPL.

11. Brands 2015, 284–88; Reeves 2005, 35-42; *Boston Globe* 1981; Notes on Cabinet Meeting, 4-24-81, taken by Kenneth Khachigian, Kenneth Khachigian Files, 1981, Box 1, Folder Cabinet Meetings [Notes] (April 1981), RRPL.

12. Reeves 2005, 43.

13. Marie Allen, "Interview with Ken Duberstein," December 15 and 29, 1983, White House Staff Exit Interviews, Transcripts: "Kenneth Duberstein" (1), RRPL.

14. "Memos, Articles/Public Support," M. B. Oglesby Files, Folder OA8618, RRPL.

15. Reagan quoted in *New York Times* 1981c.

16. Nelson 1981.

17. Marie Allen, "Interview with Ken Duberstein," December 15 and 29, 1983, White House Staff Exit Interviews, Transcripts: "Kenneth Duberstein" (1), RRPL.

18. Marie Allen, "Interview with Ken Duberstein," December 15 and 29, 1983, White House Staff Exit Interviews, Transcripts: "Kenneth Duberstein" (1), RRPL.

19. Fessler 1981a, 1981b; Tate 1981b.

20. Edsall 1981.

21. Dale 1977.

22. *Chicago Tribune* 1978b.

23. See, for example, "Tax Policy," January 31, 1980, Campaign 1980, Box 372, RPD Files: "Field Ops—Issues—Tax Policy," RRPL.

24. Arenson 1981.

25. *Chicago Tribune* 1978a. White and Wildavsky 1989, 170–75.

26. Charles Stenholm, quoted in Safire 1981.

27. Barnes 1981.

28. Farrell 2001, 560; Fessler 1981c.

29. Edsall 1981.

30. Congressional contact reports, "Telephone Calls—Cabinet," 1 of 2, M. B. Oglesby Files, CA 8618, RRPL.

31. Congressional contact reports, "Telephone Calls—Cabinet," 2 of 2, M. B. Oglesby Files, CA 8618, RRPL.

32. Ken Duberstein to Max Friedersdorf, "The Gypsy Moth Tentative Wish List," M. B. Oglesby Files, "Misc—Members of Congress," CA 8618, RRPL.

33. Marie Allen, "Interview with Ken Duberstein," December 15 and 29, 1983, White House Staff Exit Interviews, Transcripts: "Kenneth Duberstein" (1), RRPL.

34. Wehr 1981.

35. "Telephone Calls—President," 1 of 2, M. B. Oglesby Files, CA 8618, RRPL; "Telephone Calls—President," 2 of 2, M. B. Oglesby Files, CA 8618, RRPL; Marie Allen, "Interview with Ken Duberstein," December 15 and 29, 1983, White House Staff Exit Interviews, Transcripts: "Kenneth Duberstein" (1), RRPL.

36. Max L. Friedersdorf, "Meeting with Selected Democratic Members of the House of Representatives, July 27, 1981," July 24, 1981, Presidential Briefing Papers, Box 5, July 27, 1981, Folder 043488 (1), RRPL.

37. Max L. Friedersdorf, "Suggested Talking Points for Meeting with Selected Democratic Members of the House of Representatives," July 24, 1981, Presidential Briefing Papers, Box 5, July 27, 1981, Folder 043488 (1), RRPL.

38. Ronald Reagan to Glenn [presumably either Glenn English of Oklahoma or Glenn Anderson of California], July 26, 1981, "Misc—Members of Congress," M. B. Oglesby Files, CA 8618, RRPL; Max L. Friedersdorf, "Meeting with Congressman John T. Myers, July 27, 1981," July 26, 1981, Presidential Briefing Papers, Box 5, July 27, 1981, Folder 043488 (1), RRPL.

39. Barnes 1981.

40. Weatherford and McDonnell 2005, 8.
41. Wehr 1981.
42. Weaver 1988, 203.
43. "Talking Points," Francis Hodsoll Files S.M., Series I: Subject File, Box 5: "Tax Bill," RRPL.
44. Congressional contact reports, "Telephone Calls—Cabinet," 2 of 2, M. B. Oglesby Files, CA 8618, RRPL.
45. Wehr 1981.
46. Marie Allen, "Interview with Ken Duberstein," December 15 and 29, 1983, White House Staff Exit Interviews, Transcripts: "Kenneth Duberstein" (1), RRPL; Wehr 1981.
47. "An Economic, Political Victory," Jack Kemp Papers, Box 84, Folder 13: "Mueller, Press about Kemp," 1981, Manuscript Division, LC.
48. Fessler 1981c.
49. Tip O'Neill, quoted in Neikirk 1981.
50. Skelton 1981b.
51. Cannon 1981.
52. *National Journal* 1981.
53. Sandy Grady, "Could the Champagne Turn Sour for Tax-Cut Superstar Jack Kemp?" August 8, 1981, Jack Kemp Papers, Box 382, Folder 3: "Scrapbooks," Vol. 18, August 31, 1979–December 28, 1981, 2 of 4, Manuscript Division, LC.
54. "Kemp's Lonely Road Makes Victory Sweet," Jack Kemp Papers, Box 84, Folder 13: "Mueller, 'Press about Kemp,'" 1981, Manuscript Division, LC.

Chapter 7: How Ronald Reagan Betrayed Business

1. Ehrman 2005, 57. Domitrovic 2009, 230–31.
2. Bartlett 2011, 628.
3. Stockman 1986, 269.
4. For example, that the stock market fell because the business tax cuts had led to a situation in which the cost of new equipment was so low that the value of old equipment was falling by comparison, leading to rationally justified lower share prices. Feldstein 1981a.
5. Jude Wanniski, "Sent to the New York Times Op-Ed Page," Jack Kemp Papers, March 8, 1983, Box 134, Folder 6: "Taxes and Taxation, General," 1979–1984, Manuscript Division, LC.
6. *Wall Street Journal* 1982.
7. Jenkins, Aylward, Napolitano, Masterton, Laguarte, and Green to the President, February 25, 1982, WHORM Subject Files, Folder BE004: "National Economy" (062644), 5 of 5, RRPL.
8. Ernest F. Hollings to the President, March 10, 1982, WHORM Subject Files, Folder BE004: "National Economy" (062644), 5 of 5, RRPL.
9. Elizabeth H. Dole, "Tax Cut," Elizabeth Dole Files, Folder OA5459, RRPL.
10. Edwin L. Harper to Regan, Baker, Meese, and Stockman, March 25, 1982, Edwin Meese III Files, Folder OA9449: "Economic Policy Advisory Board," RRPL.

11. Edwin L. Harper to Regan, Baker, Meese, and Stockman, March 25, 1982, Edwin Meese III Files, Folder OA9449: "Economic Policy Advisory Board," RRPL.

12. Edwin L. Harper to Regan, Baker, Meese, and Stockman, March 25, 1982, Edwin Meese III Files, Folder OA9449: "Economic Policy Advisory Board," RRPL.

13. Harvey 2005, 43.

14. Hacker and Pierson 2010; Lessig 2011.

15. Phillips-Fein 2009, xii.

16. Joint Committee on Taxation 1981, 380. For a breakdown of the costs of the tax bill as of that date, see Steuerle 1992, 186–87. Indexing taxes to inflation did not in the end prove as costly as feared, because inflation came under control within a few years.

17. Waterhouse 2014, 206–7.

18. McCoy 1981.

19. Samuelson 1981a, 557; 1981b, 344.

20. Collins 1998, 53.

21. Waterhouse 2014, 207–12; Murray and Birnbaum 1988, 17–18.

22. McCoy 1981.

23. Samuelson 1981a, 558.

24. Larry Lindsey to the Council, February 8, 1982, "One of the most controversial parts …," Box 73: "Council of Economic Advisors: Staff Economists (Susan Nelson)," Folder 14789: "Tax Package Memo—April 1982," RRPL. The document, written in the face of criticism of ACRS, concludes weakly that, "although ACRS is not the most optimal means of treating depreciable property, it is defensible." On the difficulties of business unification, Pollack 2003, 62; Martin 1991, 118–19.

25. White and Wildavsky 1989, 28, 163–64.

26. Pine 1981.

27. Farnsworth 1980.

28. Dewar 1979.

29. U.S. House of Representatives. Ways and Means Committee 1978, 46.

30. Waterhouse 2014, 207–12.

31. Blumenthal 1980.

32. Lemann 1981.

33. Evans and Novak 1981a; Waterhouse 2014, 211.

34. "Cautions from Conservatives," David Gergen Files, Box 10533: "Tax Bill '81," 1 of 2, 2/5, RRPL.

35. John Davidson to Edwin Meese [enclosure: John Davidson to the editor of the *Wall Street Journal*], February 29, 1980, Campaign 1980, Box 108: "Meese, Ed—Meese Phone Conversations—Campaign Operations," RRPL.

36. Enclosed in Peter O'Donnell, Jr., to Anne Armstrong, August 18, 1980, Campaign 1980, Box 129, Meese Subject Files: "Economic Policy," RRPL.

37. Jude Wanniski [?], "FYI: With Reagan in California," n.d., Campaign 1980, Box 104: "Meese, Ed—Campaign Planning—RFP Planning, Budget & Personnel," January 1980–February 1980, RRPL.

38. *Washington Post* 1980d.

39. Drew 1978, 33.

40. Walker 1977a.
41. Walker 1977b.
42. Walker 1978a.
43. Walker 1978b.
44. Walker 1979.
45. National Association of Manufacturers (NAM), *Business Activity Report,* December 2, 1976–February 16, 1977, and January 21, 1979–May 8, 1979, Hagley Museum and Library, NAM Records.
46. NAM, *Business Activity Report,* May 13, 1980–October 11, 1980, Hagley Museum and Library, NAM Records.
47. U.S. Chamber of Commerce, board of directors meetings, June 24, 1977–February 18, 1982, Series I, Box 3: "Board of Directors Meetings/Minutes, June 24, 1977–May 2, 1983, 399th Meeting–423rd Meeting," Hagley Library, Chamber of Commerce of the United States Records.
48. Jack Carlson, "Fighting Inflation for a Healthy Economy," November 16, 1978, Series I, Box 6: "Board Report, 404th Meeting, Nov. 16, 1978," Hagley Library, Chamber of Commerce of the United States Records; see, for example, pp. 12–13.
49. "Report to the Board of Directors," January 30, 1979, Series I, Box 6: "Board Report, 404th Meeting, Feb. 14, 1979," Hagley Library, Chamber of Commerce of the United States Records.
50. "Report to the Board of Directors," February 6, 1980, Series I, Box 6: "Board Report, 409th February 21, 1980–81," Hagley Library, Chamber of Commerce of the United States Records.
51. Quoted in Waterhouse 2014, 214.
52. McQuaid 1994, 165.
53. James W. Fuller to William J. Casey, June 12, 1980, Campaign 1980, Box 105: "Ed Meese Files—Campaign Ops—Business Advisory Panel Meeting," June 1980, RRPL.
54. Business Advisory Panel meeting, June 17, 1980, Campaign 1980, Box 105: "Ed Meese—Campaign Planning Meetings," June 1980, RRPL.
55. Evans and Novak 1980a.
56. Business Advisory Panel meeting, 17 June 1980, Campaign 1980, Box 105, Ed Meese–Campaign Planning Meetings, June 1980, RRPL.
57. Charls Walker, quoted in Blumenthal 1980.
58. Hacker and Pierson 2010, 134.
59. Blyth 2002, 175–76.
60. Citizens for Tax Justice, "Tax Policy Guide, Number One, 'How the States Can Respond to the 1981 Changes in Federal Depreciation Rules,'" Box 73: "Council of Economic Advisors: Staff Economists (Susan Nelson)," Folder 14789: "Tax Cut: Effect on State & Locals," RRPL.
61. Yemma 1980.
62. Mouat 1980.
63. "How We Deal with a 1981 Tax Cut," June 24, 1980, Archives II (National Archives), Record Group 56, General Records of the Department of the Treasury, Office of the

Assistant Secretary for Legislative Affairs, Subject Files of Robert E. Moss, 1980, Box 4, Folder: "'81 Tax Cuts," 2 of 3, NARA; Bacon 1980.

64. Louis Harris, "Federal Tax Cut Opposed," July 10, 1980, Archives II (National Archives), Record Group 56, General Records of the Department of the Treasury, Office of the Assistant Secretary for Legislative Affairs, Subject Files of Robert E. Moss, 1980, Box 4, Folder: "'81 Tax Cuts," 1 of 3, NARA.

65. Diamond 1981.

66. Jacobs 1981; Bronstein and Waldenberg 1983; Pollack 2003, 61–64.

67. Booth 1972, 9.

68. Martin 1971.

69. Kumpa 1962.

70. Crowther 1962.

71. Fowler 1962.

72. Quoted in Cowan 1966.

73. *Guardian* 1971.

74. Steinmo 1986, 30–41 (emphasis added).

75. Price Waterhouse 1980, 48–49, 87; HM Revenue and Customs 2016.

76. Price Waterhouse 1975, 84–86.

77. Price Waterhouse 1978, 77–79, 168.

78. Ronald Reagan, Ronald Reagan radio broadcast, taped July 31, 1978, "Economics II," typescript 2/3, RRPL.

79. Ronald Reagan, Ronald Reagan radio broadcast, taped March 6, 1979, "Higher Standard of Living," typescript 3/4, RRPL.

80. Martin 1991, 114–20.

81. Neikirk 1980.

82. Hershey 1981.

83. Waterhouse 2014, 214; Jenkins and Eckert 2000, 319; Martin 1991, 120–23.

84. Jenkins and Eckert 2000, 319. Jenkins and Eckert assert that business organizations originated both ACRS and Kemp-Roth, but give no evidence for the claim that Kemp-Roth's across-the-board tax reductions originated in business groups (see, for example, their discussion of the origins of these policies on page 316).

85. See Reeves 2005, 80–81.

86. Waterhouse 2014, 216–19; Pollack 2003, 64. As Waterhouse notes, corporations can often pass along higher corporate taxes to consumers, so it is incorrect to assume that the entire corporate tax increase would have been borne by corporations (or that all corporate tax cuts would benefit corporations). But those higher prices could reduce sales, explaining why the business community was generally opposed to corporate tax increases.

87. Martin 1991, 135–58.

88. Eric I. Hemel to Murray L. Weidenbaum, handwritten comments on "Senate Finance List of Options for Raising Revenue," Box 73: "Council of Economic Advisors: Staff Economists: (Susan Nelson)," Folder 14788: "Senate Finance Tax Options," June 1982, RRPL.

89. Susan Nelson to Greg Ballentine and Larry Dildine, Box 73: "Council of Economic Advisors: Staff Economists (Susan Nelson)," Folder 14789: "Tax Package Memo," April 1982, RRPL.
90. Waterhouse 2014, 215–20.
91. Waterhouse 2014, 227–30.
92. Briner 1983; Steuerle 1992, 58–61; Pollack 2003, 64.
93. Greider 1982. John Sears also claims that this was what the team truly wanted, but it is not clear exactly why he believed this. John Sears, interview with A. James Reichley, January 12, 1981, A. James Reichley Interview Transcripts, 1977–1981, "Politician Interviews: Politician Interviews—General," Box 3, Folder: "1980 Campaign and Transition, Sears, John," GFPL.
94. Domitrovic 2009, 235; White and Wildavsky 1989, 159.
95. John [Mueller] to Jack Kemp, November 16 1981, "Ideas on the Trickle-Down Problem," Jack Kemp Papers, Box 82, Folder 13: "Mueller Correspondence 1981," October–December, Manuscript Division, LC.
96. Jack Kemp, "Statement by Congressman Jack Kemp on Ways and Means Chairman Dan Rostenkowski's Tax Proposal," April 10, 1981, Jack Kemp Papers, Box 134, Folder 6: "Taxes and Taxation General," 1979–1984, Manuscript Division, LC.
97. Jack Kemp, "Why Corporate Taxes Should Be Slashed," *Human Events* 25 (20, May 17, 1975), Jack Kemp Papers, Box 134, Folder 5: "Taxes and Taxation, 1975–1977, General," Manuscript Division, LC.
98. Keller 1981, 1137.
99. Martin 1991, 132.
100. Smith 2000.
101. Indeed, Page and Gilens note that in an examination of polled issues over several decades, "For those proposed policy changes on which at least one business-oriented group took a position, another business-oriented group was found on the opposite side less than 5 percent of the time" (2017, 579).

Chapter 8: After Reagan

1. McGrory 1982; Friedman 1981.
2. Waterhouse 2014, 229–30. The 1986 Tax Reform Act (TRA) was effective in some ways, but its attempt to close "loopholes" was neither particularly successful nor durable: it did not touch the most significant tax expenditures, and over the course of time thousands of tax expenditures have crept back into the tax code (Buckley 2011/2012).
3. Bartels 2005; Hacker and Pierson 2005, 2012; Crum 2010; Gilens 2012, 230–31.
4. Morgan 2001; Morgan and Babington 2001; Morgan and Day 2001.
5. Morgan 2001.
6. Morgan and Day 2001.
7. Dataset for Martin Gilens (2012), items 1676 and 1777.
8. Smith 2012, 89.

9. Smith 1984.

10. Hershey 1992, 951–52.

11. Easton 2002, 78–80; Mettler 2011.

12. *Wall Street Journal* 1990.

13. *Wall Street Journal* 1996.

14. Shalit 1995; Matthews 1988; Matthews and West 1988; Shribman 1988; Kelly 1988; Matthews and Kelly 1988; Hunt 1988.

15. Quoted in Jacobs 2016, 291.

16. Woodward 1992.

17. Pollack 2003, 68–69.

18. McFaden (2008) conducts a more careful analysis and suggests breaking the pledge was not the reason for Bush's loss. On a draft dodger beating a war hero, see, for example, Denton 1992.

19. Gray 1993a, 1993b, 1993c, 1993d; McLarin 1993; King 1993; Moore 1995.

20. Pollack 2003, 80–81.

21. Toner 1995.

22. See chapter 10; Johnston 1999; *Wall Street Journal* 2000.

23. Moore 1995, 50–52.

24. https://www.cato.org/fiscal-policy-report-card-americas-governors (accessed August 6, 2018).

25. Tyson 1995.

26. Chandler and Pianin, 1995. For a critique of dynamic scoring, see *New York Times* 1994.

27. See, for example, Hoynes, Schanzenbach, and Almond 2016.

28. Easton 2002, 144.

29. *National Review* 1996; Ponnuru 1996; Moore 1996, 40.

30. *National Review* 1998a; *National Review* 1998c.

31. Solow 1985. Solow also noted that "there is one dissident school of thought for whom 'deficits don't matter,' but it is very small and uninfluential."

32. Tolchin 1985; see also Krippner 2011.

33. Woodward 1994; James Carville, quoted in Woodward 1994, 139.

34. Toner 1995. The "disastrous results" are presumably the 1994 Republican takeover of Congress.

35. Norquist 1999.

36. Bethell 1999.

37. Ponnuru 1998.

38. *National Review* 1998c.

39. *National Review* 1998b.

40. Frum 1998.

41. O'Sullivan 1998.

42. *National Review* 1999.

43. *National Review* 2000.

44. Seib 2000; Calmes 2000; Balz and Connolly 2000; Elder 2000.

45. Hacker and Pierson 2012.

46. Leonhardt 2004; Fuerbringer 2002; Beattie and McGregor 2004.

47. Scott Minerd, quoted in Sommer 2011.

48. "Federal Budget Deficit," Gallup polls, 1994–2018, http://news.gallup.com/poll/1476 26/federal-budget-deficit.aspx (accessed August 14, 2018); "In the Balance: The Public, the Budget, and the Deficit," Cornell University, Roper Center for Public Opinion Research, https://ropercenter.cornell.edu/in-the-balance-the-public-the-budget -and-the-deficit/' (accessed August 14, 2018); "Most Important Problem," Gallup polls, 1956–2018, http://news.gallup.com/poll/1675/most-important-problem.aspx (accessed August 14, 2018).

49. *Chicago Tribune* 2004. See Labonte 2012 for reasons to remain concerned about the deficit.

50. Robertson 2016.

51. Cooper 2012; Eligon 2012.

52. Eligon 2014a.

53. Graff and Eligon 2014; Barro 2014b; Krugman 2014; Bosman 2014; Eligon 2014b, 2014c, 2014d, 2014e, 2015a, 2015b; Barro 2014a; *New York Times* 2016.

54. Bosman, Smith, and Davey 2017.

55. Eligon and Bosman 2017.

56. Peters 2017.

57. Hulse 2017.

58. For attempts to defend Reagan's record, see Lindsey 1990; Nau 2015; for a criticism of such attempts, see Krugman 1994. For recent contributions, generally arguing against an effect of tax cuts on economic growth, see Piketty, Saez, and Stantcheva 2014; Alvaredo et al. 2013.

59. Therborn and Roebroek 1986; Offe 1984, 152–53.

60. Mishra 1990, 32–42.

61. Pierson 2015, 293.

62. Figures in this and the next paragraphs are from McCubbin and Scheuren 1988–1989; IRS 2017; Dungan 2017; SOI Tax Stats—Individual Income Tax Rates and Tax Shares, https://www.irs.gov/statistics/soi-tax-stats-individual-income-tax-rates-and -tax-shares (accessed August 14, 2018), Selected Descending Cumulative Percentiles of Returns Based on Income Size Using the Definition of AGI for Each Year, Table 5, 1986–2009, Selected Descending Cumulative Percentiles of Returns Based on Income Size Using the Definition of AGI for Each Year, Table 1, 2001–2015; Congressional Budget Office, Historical Effective Tax Rates, 1979 to 2005, December 2008, https://www.cbo.gov/sites/default/files/110th-congress-2007-2008/reports/12 -23-effectivetaxratesletter.pdf (accessed August 14, 2018).

63. Smith 2007, 190–91, 202.

64. Gilens 2012, 149, 183.

65. Hertel-Fernandez and Skocpol 2015.

66. Hacker and Pierson 2005.

67. Gilens 2012, 183.
68. Ball 2017.

Chapter 9: Running to Stay in Place

1. For just some of the more notable works on American conservatism, see Cowie 2010; Edsall and Edsall 1991; Fones-Wolf 1994; Hamilton 2008; Himmelstein 1990; Kabaservice 2012; Lassiter 2005; McGirr 2001; Moreton 2009; Phillips-Fein 2009; Stein 2010.
2. See, for example, Sykes et al. 2015; Dudley and Warren 2018. On the mixed outcome of conservatism, Zelizer 2010.
3. Maddison 2010.
4. Beckert 2017.
5. For recent contributions to the debate, see, for example, Aghion et al. 2016; Bond, Leblebicioğlu, and Schiantarelli 2010; Opschoor 2015.
6. Eichengreen 1996, 38; Prasad 2012. On the need for capital accumulation see, for example, Gerschenkron 1962, 354; Pollard 1958. On the rise of corporatism Maier 1975.
7. Cohen 2003; Jacobs 2005; Garon 2012.
8. Maddison 1992.
9. Baccaro and Pontusson 2016; Prasad 2012.
10. Judith Stein in *Pivotal Decade* (2010) conducts a truly global examination of the crisis of the 1970s. But she misses the reasons why the United States focused on consumption (and therefore settles on an excessively voluntary argument that explains manufacturing decline in America as driven by decisions of 1970s politicians who forgot workers) and understates the role of inflation (and therefore misunderstands the context of those decisions).
11. Phillips-Fein 2011.
12. See, for example, Mizruchi 2013.
13. Prasad 2012; Sanders 1998, 217–32.
14. Quoted in Mehrotra 2013, 260.
15. See, for example, Mendoza, Razin, Tesar 1994.
16. Noel J. Fenton to Edmund T. Pratt Jr., August 19, 1980, Campaign 1980, Box 43, Series I: Hannaford/California Headquarters: General Campaign Files, Folder: "Hannaford CA/HQ—International Trade & Competitiveness—Draft Materials," 1 of 5 (General), RRPL.
17. Edmund T. Pratt Jr., to James W. Fuller, September 24, 1980, Campaign 1980, Box 43, Series I: Hannaford/California Headquarters: General Campaign Files, Folder: "Hannaford CA/HQ—International Trade & Competitiveness—Draft Materials," 1 of 5 (General), RRPL.
18. Charles Pilliod to Edmund T. Pratt Jr., September 2, 1980, Campaign 1980, Box 43, Series I: Hannaford/California Headquarters: General Campaign Files, Folder: "Hannaford CA/HQ—International Trade & Competitiveness—Draft Materials," 2 of 5 (General), RRPL.

19. Charles Pilliod to Edmund T. Pratt Jr., September 2, 1980, Campaign 1980, Box 43, Series I: Hannaford/California Headquarters: General Campaign Files, Folder: "Hannaford CA/HQ—International Trade & Competitiveness—Draft Materials," 2 of 5 (General), RRPL.

20. Oscar Boline, "German Model Is the Key," n.d., Jack Kemp Papers, Box 82, Folder 11: "Mueller—Correspondence," 1978–1980, Manuscript Division, LC.

21. Charles Pilliod to Edmund T. Pratt Jr., September 2, 1980, Campaign 1980, Box 43, Series I: Hannaford/California Headquarters: General Campaign Files, Folder: "Hannaford CA/HQ—International Trade & Competitiveness—Draft Materials," 2 of 5 (General), RRPL.

22. Lawrence A. Fox to Edmund T. Pratt Jr., September 12, 1980, Campaign 1980, Box 43, Series I: Hannaford/California Headquarters: General Campaign Files, Folder: "Hannaford CA/HQ—International Trade & Competitiveness—Draft Materials," 4 of 5 (General), RRPL.

23. Lawrence A. Fox and William F. Avery, "The U.S. Trade Deficit: A Hard Look at Bad News," Campaign 1980, Box 43, Series I: Hannaford/California Headquarters: General Campaign Files, Folder: "Hannaford CA/HQ—International Trade & Competitiveness—Draft Materials," 4 of 5 (General), RRPL.

24. International Briefing Book, prepared by David Gergen and Frank Hodsoll, October 13, 1980, Campaign 1980, Box 156, Series III: Ed Meese Files: Briefing Books, Folder: "Ed Meese Files—Briefing Books—International Briefing Book" (Ed Meese personal copy), October 13, 1980, 2 of 2, RRPL.

25. Jon Michael Hofgren to Dave Durenberger and Bill Frenzel, August 13, 1981, Box TA003, ID# 036952, Folder 036000-039299, RRPL.

26. Richter, Samphantharak, and Timmons 2009; Clawson, Neustadtl, and Weller 1998. Money in politics can change the distribution of costs and benefits even if it does not change the overall level. For example, in one sample only 10 percent of corporations lobbied at all (Richter, Samphantharak, and Timmons, 2009). These corporations bought themselves lower taxes, but if overall tax rates are similar in the United States and Europe, then corporations that do not lobby must be paying higher tax rates than in Europe. This is clearly an important problem, as it works to the benefit of larger and better-connected corporations. But that some businesses are paying higher tax rates is a different problem from what we generally worry about when we are concerned with money in politics. Moreover, this problem only applies to some of the domains examined in this chapter, specifically corporate taxes. Distributional issues remain an avenue for future research, but do not change the main argument being made here.

27. Ansolabehere, De Figueiredo, and Snyder 2003; Walker and Rea 2014; Baumgartner et al. 2009; Hojnacki et al. 2015; on media, see Ansolabehere, Snowberg, and Snyder 2005; Baumgartner and Leech 1998.; Smith 2000. For the argument that the wealthy are influential, see Gilens 2012; Gilens and Page 2014. For critiques, see Enns 2015; Branham, Soroka, and Wlezien 2017.

28. Harvey 2005, 43; Hacker and Pierson 2010; Lessig 2011; Phillips-Fein 2009, xii. For

just a few other examples, see Duménil and Lévy 2004; Ferguson and Rogers 1986; Page and Gilens 2017; Fones-Wolf 1994; Clawson, Neustadtl, and Weller 1998; Jenkins and Eckert 2000, 319; Akard 1992; Volscho 2017. Benjamin Waterhouse (2014, 2–3) is an interesting case, as he argues for the power of business interests, but the strength of his archival research in fact lies in showing the limits of that power.

29. See, for example, Drutman 2015.

30. Weaver 2000, 216.

31. New York congressman Benjamin Rosenthal, quoted in Cohen 2010, 239.

32. Cohen 2010, 239–40; Waterhouse 2014, 155–71; Vogel 2003, 160–63.

33. Carpenter 2014; Prasad 2012, 3–7.

34. Wardell 1973; Wardell and Lasagna 1975.

35. Wiktorowicz 2003, 625.

36. Lundqvist 1980; Brickman, Jasanoff, and Ilgen 1985; Jasanoff 1991; Kelman 1981; Badaracco 1985; Wilson 1985; Braithwaite 1985; Benedick 1998; Vogel 1986; Verweij 2000.

37. For example, Mendoza, Razin, and Tesar 1994, 308–09. On the 1978 capital gains tax cut as an example of the power of business, see Hacker and Pierson 2010, 133–34.

38. Carr, Mathewson, and Quigley 1995; Calomiris 2000; Haubrich 1990; White 1984, 131–32; Grossman 1994; Bordo, Rockoff, and Redish 1994; Bordo, Redish, and Rockoff 2011.

39. Suárez and Kolodny 2011, 96.

40. Benston 1994, 121–22; Barth, Brumbaugh, and Wilcox 2000, 201; Calomiris 2000; Prasad 2012, 216–20.

41. Komansky, Purcell, and Weill 1997; U.S. Senate 1999, 28356–357; Gramm 2009; Barack Obama, quoted in Gramm 2009.

42. Day 2005; Warren 2005; Tabb 2005, 775–76.

43. Fairbrother 2014, 1342–46.

44. Dimick 2012; Lenhoff 1956; Summers 1964; Mitchnick 1993; Addison and Siebert 1998.

45. Vogel 2012.

46. Culpepper 2011.

47. Clawson, Neustadtl, and Weller 1998, 71. Many scholars argue that what business gets for its donations is access to politicians: but if that access is not actually resulting in some action or some benefit, either particularistic or general, short term or long term, it's not clear why access matters. And if it does result in some action or some benefit, we can focus on the action or the benefit, rather than the access.

48. Elsässer, Hense, and Schäfer 2016.

49. Binderkrantz and Rasmussen 2015.

50. Akard 1992.

Chapter 10: Pocketbook Politics and the Rise of Conservatism

1. Michelmore 2012, 205.

2. Steuerle 1992, 23–26; Pressman 1987.

3. Page and Shapiro 1992, 149.

4. Polanyi 2001, 201.

5. Easterly and Fischer 2001.

6. Keynes 1920, 235–36.

7. Gerschenkron 1962, 354.

8. Steinbeck 2002, 348–49.

9. Olmstead and Rhode 2006, Table Da995-1019; Kennedy 1999, 241–48; Schlesinger 2003.

10. Stapleford 2007; Currarino 2006; on "American danger," Beckert 2017.

11. Garon 2012, 329–51; Cohen 2003; Jacobs 2005.

12. Evans 2006.

13. Cannon 2003, 108.

14. Evans 2006, 62.

15. Evans 2006, 69–80.

16. Weisberg 2016, 35.

17. Weisberg 2016, 34–35.

18. Shafer 1974.

19. Krippner 2011, 62–63.

20. Martin 2008.

21. Hamilton 2008.

22. Kraft 1981.

23. Hamilton 2008, 2–4, 237; Jacobs 2016, 269.

24. Caplin 1964, 858-60; see Berman and Pagnucco 2010 for similarities between the Kennedy/Johnson tax cut and the Reagan tax cut.

25. Bruce Bartlett, quoted in Kondracke and Barnes 2015, 45.

26. Berman and Pagnucco 2010.

27. For example, Harold Wilensky, whose work is summarized in his magnum opus, *Rich Democracies* (Wilensky 2002).

28. See, for example, Widmalm 2001; Kneller, Bleaney, and Gemmell 1999.

29. Lindert 2004.

30. For a detailed attempt to compare the progressivity of tax systems, see Landais, Piketty, and Saez 2011.

31. Campbell 2009.

32. Brady and Lee 2014; Martin and Gabay 2013.

33. Hung and Thompson 2016.

Chapter 11: Democracy's Deficits

1. Ladd et al. 1979, 131; Modigliani and Modigliani 1987, 460–62, 466.

2. Campbell 2009.

3. Burns and Taylor 2000, 430.

4. Canes-Wrone 2010.

5. Page and Shapiro 1992, 149 (on elites manipulating public opinion), 163 (on opposition to taxation dropping after ERTA).

6. Ladd et al. 1979, 134.
7. Riffkin 2014.
8. Harris 1978.
9. Notes on meeting with Dick Wirthlin, 2-27[or 29?]-81, taken by Kenneth Khachigian, Kenneth Khachigian Files, 1981, Box 1, Folder Communications Meetings [Notes] (January 1981–April 1981), RRPL.
10. "A Strategy for Growth: The American Economy in the 1980s," draft, Martin Anderson Papers 1976, 1979–1980, Handwritten Reagan Speeches and Edits, Box 1, Folder 9/4/80 Econ Speech Edits [2 of 2], RRPL. See also *New York Times* 1980b.
11. "The President's Campaign Against Waste and Fraud," July 1981, Box T. Kenneth Cribb Files: Office of Cabinet Affairs Box 1 OA3809, 4821, Folder "Cabinet Meeting, 08/04/1981 OA3809 Cribb, T. Kenneth: Files," RRPL.
12. Kelman 1985.
13. For a thoughtful review of the issue, see Kelman 1985.
14. Williamson 2017, 142–64.
15. For example, Collins 2006; Rodgers 2011.
16. Fones-Wolf 1994.
17. Beck et al. 1987, 228–29; Gilens 2012, 232.
18. Waterhouse 2013; Stein 2010; Mattson 2010; Jacobs 2016.
19. American Political Science Association 1950, 22, 27–28, 17–18.
20. Honig 1993.
21. Rosenblum 2010.
22. Hacker and Pierson 2005, 38.
23. See, for example, Grossman and Hopkins (2016), who argue that because of the American preference for small government, Republicans stress ideology rather than policy. In fact, however, the focus on tax cuts gives Republicans a way to offer a very concrete policy.
24. Galvin 2009.
25. Weaver 2000.
26. Smith 1987.
27. Sykes et al. 2015.
28. David Stockman (1986) describes the administration's failed attempts to cut the middle-class entitlements that would have had to go if deficits were to be avoided.
29. Quoted in Roberts 1985.
30. American Political Science Association 1950, 20–21.
31. Chua 2004; Zakaria 2007.
32. Ashworth 2012, 183.
33. Lindert 2004; Mares 2007; Agell, Lindh, and Ohlsson 1997; Atkinson 1995. Studies that do find a negative effect of the welfare state on economic growth include Landau 1985; Hansson and Henrekson 1994; Weede 1986. For studies that find a positive effect of the welfare state on economic growth, see Castles and Dowrick 1990; Korpi 1985. We might expect economists to uniformly find a negative effect of the welfare state on growth, given that discipline's closer affiliation with neoclassical thought, but this

is not the case. Economists who have empirically studied the issue are as divided as other scholars, with some (such as Persson and Tabellini 1994) finding a negative effect and others (such as McCallum and Blais 1987) finding a positive effect. Many scholars have noted that the findings change drastically with very slight adjustments in initial assumptions, the countries or time periods included in the sample, and the measures used (see Saunders 1986). Others note that it is difficult to exclude the possibility of reverse causation—as there are many reasons why poor economic growth might lead to a larger welfare state—or to fully control for factors that lead both to a larger economy and a larger welfare state (Atkinson 1995). Walter Korpi (1985) argues that the case for the welfare state impairing growth is unconvincing even for Sweden, which for much of the postwar period has been the most extensive welfare state in the OECD.

34. Kneller, Bleaney, and Gemmell 1999.
35. Hoynes, Schanzenbach, and Almond 2016; Olds 2016; Hombert et al. 2014.
36. Korpi 1985.
37. Björklund and Freeman 1997, 49. On "disciplinary" welfare regimes, see, for example, Wacquant 2012, 72; Schram et al. 2009, 398–99; King 1995.
38. Erixon 2010, 681.
39. Erixon 2010. Although it is not clear whether these policies actually had the intended effect of getting people back to work (Crépon and Van Den Berg 2016).
40. Rosen 1997, 90; Clayton and Pontusson 1998.
41. Anderson 2004, 293; Lundberg and Åmark 2001, 165; Clayton and Pontusson 1998, 76–77.
42. Aronsson and Walker 1997, 246–47.
43. Clayton and Pontusson 1998, 76–77; Andrén 2001, 8.
44. Aronsson and Walker 1997, 251–52; Clayton and Pontusson 1998, 76–77.
45. Björklund and Freeman 1997, 47–48.
46. Aronsson and Walker 1997, 245-6.
47. Lundberg and Åmark 2001, 161.
48. Leppälä 2016; Emmenegger 2010.
49. Korpi and Palme 1998.
50. Baldwin 1990, 62–94.
51. Cameron 1978; Katzenstein 1985; Ruggie 1982.
52. Maier 1975; Lange and Garrett 1985; Prowe 1985; Castles 1987; Pontusson 1991; Eichengreen 2008; Paster 2013; Kuo 2015; Nijhuis 2015. For a Marxist critique of corporatist bargains, see Panitch 1977.
53. Hall and Soskice 2001; Hall 2017; Schneider and Paunescu 2012.
54. Baccaro and Pontusson 2016; Iversen, Soskice, and Hope 2016; Hall 2017. The "growth models" literature tends to focus on Europe and on the post-1970s period, but see Prasad (2012) for a discussion of postwar American precedents.
55. Lindert 2004; Prasad 2012, 99–124; Baldwin 1990, 62–94.
56. Mendoza, Razin, and Tesar 1994, 308.

57. Helgason 2017; Martin 2015; Beramendi and Rueda 2007; Cusack and Beramendi 2006.
58. Dimick 2012; Emmenegger 2010.
59. For an overview, see Löfstedt and Vogel 2001.
60. Lindert 2004.
61. See, for example, Baker 2005.
62. Kagan 2001, 127–28.
63. Kagan 2001, 126–27.
64. Iversen and Soskice 2009.
65. Prasad 2012.

Conclusion: Lessons and Limitations

1. Quoted in Jacobs 2016, 261.
2. Turner 2009; Prasad 2006, 62–82.
3. Lessig 2011, 2.
4. Page and Gilens 2017; Gilens 2012.
5. Rudder 1983; Strahan 1990; Aldrich and Niemi 1996.
6. Cain and Noll 2010.
7. Kousser, Phillips, and Shor 2016; Ahler, Citrin, and Lenz 2016.
8. Gilens 2012, 185.
9. Gilens 2012, 81.
10. Page and Gilens 2017, 14–15. Gilens's work also has a "running to stay in place" problem: for example, lower-income Americans want more protectionism (108) and less foreign aid (115–16) than affluent Americans do, but the United States already has more protectionism and grants less foreign aid than European countries. If the wealthy are getting their way in trade policy and foreign aid, they are only managing to reach the status quo for other advanced industrial countries.
11. Thelen 2014.
12. Beckfield 2013, 97.
13. For example, Campbell 2011.
14. See the discussion in Linder 1996, 961–62, 1024–25.
15. Teles 2013.

Appendix

1. Available at: https://www.sociology.northwestern.edu/people/faculty/core/monica-prasad.html and at ICPSR.
2. Note that *cpi* and *cpi2* are misdescribed in the Comparative Welfare States data set codebook: *cpi2* is actually the percentage change in the consumer price index from the prior year, while *cpi* is the consumer price index with 2005 as the base year (Brady, Huber, and Stephens 2014, 30–31).

REFERENCES

Addison, John T., and W. Stanley Siebert. 1998. "Union Security in Britain." *Journal of Labor Research* 19(3): 495–517.

Agell, Jonas, Thomas Lindh, and Henry Ohlsson. 1997. "Growth and the Public Sector: A Critical Review Essay." *European Journal of Political Economy* 13(1): 33–52.

Aghion, Philippe, Diego Comin, Peter Howitt, and Isabel Tecu. 2016. "When Does Domestic Savings Matter for Economic Growth?" *IMF Economic Review* 64(3): 381–407.

Ahler, Douglas J., Jack Citrin, and Gabriel S. Lenz. 2016. "Do Open Primaries Improve Representation? An Experimental Test of California's 2012 Top-Two Primary." *Legislative Studies Quarterly* 41(2): 237–68.

Akard, Patrick. 1992. "Corporate Mobilization and Political Power." *American Sociological Review* 57: 597–615.

Aldrich, John H., and Richard G. Niemi. 1996. "The Sixth American Party System: Electoral Change, 1952–1992." In *Broken Contract? Changing Relationships between Americans and Their Government,* edited by Stephen G. Craig. Boulder, Colo.: Westview Press.

Alston, Richard M., James R. Kearl, and Michael B. Vaughan. 1992. "Is There a Consensus among Economists in the 1990s?" *American Economic Review* 82(2): 203–9.

Alvaredo, Facundo, Anthony B. Atkinson, Thomas Piketty, and Emmanuel Saez. 2013. "The Top 1 Percent in International and Historical Perspective." *Journal of Economic Perspectives* 27(3): 3–20.

American National Election Studies. 1980. 1980 INTEGRATED. Principal Investigators, Warren E. Miller and the National Election Studies. ICPSR archive number 7763. Ann Arbor: University of Michigan, Inter-university Consortium for Political and Social Research.

American Political Science Association. Committee on Political Parties. 1950. "Toward a More Responsible Two-Party System." *American Political Science Review* 44(3): S15–36.

Anderson, Karen. 2004. "Pension Politics in Three Small States: Denmark, Sweden, and the Netherlands." *Canadian Journal of Sociology* 29(2): 289–312.

Anderson, Martin. 1988. *Revolution.* New York: Harcourt.

Andrén, Daniela. 2001. "Work, Sickness, Earnings, and Early Exits from the Labor Market: An Empirical Analysis Using Swedish Longitudinal Data." PhD diss., Göteborg University, Department of Economics.

Ansolabehere, Stephen, John M. De Figueiredo, and James M. Snyder. 2003. "Why Is There So Little Money in U.S. Politics?" *Journal of Economic Perspectives* 17(1): 105–30.

Ansolabehere, Stephen, Erik C. Snowberg, and James M. Snyder. 2005. "Unrepresentative Information: The Case of Newspaper Reporting on Campaign Finance." *Public Opinion Quarterly* 69(2): 213–31.

Apple, R. W., Jr. 1975. "GOP Plans a Comeback with TV and Voter Drive." *New York Times,* January 26, 1.

Applebaum, Binyamin. 2017. "A Sketchy Story." *New York Times,* October 14, B1.

Arenson, Karen W. 1981. "Indexing Taxes to Inflation." *New York Times,* July 21, D1.

Arieff, Irwin B. 1981. "Budget Fight Shows O'Neill's Fragile Grasp." *Congressional Quarterly Weekly Report,* May 9, 786.

Aronsson, Thomas, and James R. Walker. 1997. "The Effects of Sweden's Welfare State on Labor Supply Incentives." In *The Welfare State in Transition: Reforming the Swedish Model,* edited by Richard B. Freeman, Robert Topel, and Birgitta Swedenborg. Chicago: University of Chicago Press.

Ashworth, Scott. 2012. "Electoral Accountability: Recent Theoretical and Empirical Work." *Annual Review of Political Science* 15: 183–201.

Atkinson, Anthony B. 1995. "The Welfare State and Economic Performance." *National Tax Journal* 48(2): 171–98.

Atkinson, Caroline 1980. "Reagan Plan Figures Called Way Off Base." *New York Times,* September 5, E1.

Baccaro, Lucio, and Jonas Pontusson. 2016. "Rethinking Comparative Political Economy: The Growth Model Perspective." *Politics and Society* 44(2): 175–207.

Bacon, Kenneth H. 1980. "A Big Role for Uncle Sam." *Wall Street Journal,* September 3, 26.

Badaracco, Joseph L., Jr. 1985. *Loading the Dice: A Five-Country Study of Vinyl Chloride Regulation.* Boston: Harvard Business School Press.

Bafumi, Joseph, Robert S. Erikson, and Christopher Wlezien. 2010. "Balancing, Generic Polls, and Midterm Congressional Elections." *Journal of Politics* 72: 705–19.

Baker, Tom. 2005. *The Medical Malpractice Myth.* Chicago: University of Chicago Press.

Baldwin, Peter. 1990. *The Politics of Social Solidarity: Class Bases of the European Welfare State, 1875–1975.* Cambridge: Cambridge University Press.

Ball, Molly. 2017. "Grover Norquist, the Happiest Man in Washington." *Atlantic,* April 18. https://www.theatlantic.com/politics/archive/2017/04/grover-norquist-the -happiest-man-in-washington/523206/ (accessed January 26, 2018).

Balz, Dan, and Ceci Connolly. 2000. "Nominees Scour West for Votes." *Washington Post,* November 1, A1.

Baltimore Sun. 1964. "3 Bodies Found in Mississippi." *Baltimore Sun,* August 5, 1.

———. 1977. "Candidate Recruitment Stressed: New Chairman Pushing GOP Revival by 1980." *Baltimore Sun,* April 13, A8.

———. 1980. "Reagan Backs Off from Anti-union Stands in Effort to Lure Democrats." *Baltimore Sun,* July 16, A7.

———. 1981. "Reagan Cited 'Mockery' of Tax System." *Baltimore Sun,* March 31, A7.

Barnes, Fred, ed. 1981. "Republican 'Gypsy Moths' Gain Clout as Showdown on Tax Cut Nears." *Baltimore Sun,* July 29, A6.

Baron, Alan. 1979. "Ronald Reagan Trumpets His Traditional Verities in a New Key." *Los Angeles Times,* November 18, F1.

Barro, Josh. 2014a. "Kansas' Budget Gap May Be Worse Than Feared." *New York Times,* November 13, A3.

———. 2014b. "Yes, if You Cut Taxes, You Get Less Tax Revenue." *New York Times,* June 29, BU6.

Bartels, Larry M. 2005. "Homer Gets a Tax Cut: Inequality and Public Policy in the American Mind." *Perspectives on Politics* 3(1): 15–31.

Barth, James R., R. Dan Brumbaugh Jr., and James A. Wilcox. 2000. "Policy Watch: The Repeal of Glass-Steagall and the Advent of Broad Banking." *Journal of Economic Perspectives* 14: 191–204.

Bartlett, Bruce. 1981. *Reaganomics: Supply-Side Economics in Action.* Westport, Conn.: Arlington House.

———. 2007. "'Starve the Beast': Origins and Development of a Budgetary Metaphor." *Independent Review* 12(1): 5–26.

———. 2009. *The New American Economy: The Failure of Reaganomics and a New Way Forward.* New York: Palgrave Macmillan.

———. 2011. "The 1981 Tax Cut after 30 Years: What Happened to Revenues?" *Tax Notes,* August 8, 627–29.

———. 2012a. "The Laffer Curve, Part 1." *Tax Notes* 136(3, July 16).

———. 2012b. "The Laffer Curve, Part 2." *Tax Notes* 136(10, September 3).

———. 2012c. "The Laffer Curve, Part 3." *Tax Notes* 137(1, October 1).

Bartley, Robert L. 1979. "Jack Kemp's Intellectual Blitz." *Wall Street Journal,* November 29, 24.

Bass, Jack, and Walter DeVries. (1976) 1995. *The Transformation of Southern Politics.* New York: Basic Books. Reprint, Athens: University of Georgia Press.

Bates, Toby Glenn. 2011. *The Reagan Rhetoric: History and Memory in 1980s America.* DeKalb, Ill.: Northern Illinois University Press.

Baumgartner, Frank R., Jeffrey M. Berry, Marie Hojnacki, Beth L. Leech, and David C. Kimball. 2009. *Lobbying and Policy Change: Who Wins, Who Loses, and Why.* Chicago: University of Chicago Press.

Baumgartner, Frank R., and Beth L. Leech. 1998. *Basic Interests: The Importance of Groups in Politics and in Political Science.* Princeton, N.J.: Princeton University Press.

Baumol, William J., and William G. Bowen. 1965. "On the Performing Arts: The Anatomy of Their Economic Problems." *American Economic Review* 55(1/2): 495–502.

Beal, Richard S., and Ronald H. Hinckley. 1984. "Presidential Decision Making and Opinion Polls." *The Annals of the American Academy of Political and Social Science* 472(1): 72–84.

Beattie, Alan, and Deborah McGregor. 2004. "Sssh—Don't Mention Federal Deficit to Voters." *Financial Times,* January 14, 9.

Beck, Paul Allen, Hal G. Rainey, Keith Nicholls, and Carol Traut. 1987. "Citizen Views of Taxes and Services: A Tale of Three Cities." *Social Science Quarterly* 68(2): 223–43.

Beckert, Sven. 2017. "American Danger: United States Empire, Eurafrica, and the Territorialization of Industrial Capitalism, 1870–1950." *American Historical Review* 122(4): 1137–70.

Beckfield, Jason. 2013. "The End of Equality in Europe?" *Current History* 112(752): 94–99.

Beckman, Aldo. 1978. "U.S. Tax Angers Public? Carter Doesn't Think So." *Chicago Tribune,* September 28, 5.

Benedick, Richard. 1998. *Ozone Diplomacy: New Directions in Safeguarding the Planet.* Cambridge, Mass.: Harvard University Press.

Benko, Ralph. 2017. "Jack Kemp, Tax Reform, and the Way the World Works." *Forbes,* November 13, 2017. https://www.forbes.com/sites/ralphbenko/2017/11/13/jack-kemp-tax -reform-and-the-way-the-world-works/ (accessed January 21, 2018).

Benston, George J. 1994. "Universal Banking." *Journal of Economic Perspectives* 8: 121–43.

Beramendi, Pablo, and David Rueda. 2007. "Social Democracy Constrained: Indirect Taxation in Industrialized Democracies." *British Journal of Political Science* 37(4): 619–41.

Bergholz, Richard. 1979. "Reagan Leans Toward Running." *Los Angeles Times,* January 14, A3.

———. 1980a. "Reagan Says Carter Hurts Working Class." *Los Angeles Times,* June 7, A28.

———. 1980b. "Reagan Says Iowa Gave Him a New Image." *Los Angeles Times,* January 22, A1.

Berman, Elizabeth Popp, and Nicholas Pagnucco. 2010. "Economic Ideas and the Political Process: Debating Tax Cuts in the U.S. House of Representatives, 1962–1981." *Politics and Society* 38(3): 347–72.

Bernstein, Harry. 1980. "Unions Critical of Both Reagan and President: Labor's Election--Year Dilemma Pointed Up by Steelworker Speeches." *Los Angeles Times,* August 5, B3.

Bernstein, Harry, and William J. Eaton. 1981. "260,000 Protest Reagan Policies: AFL-CIO and 200 Other Groups Launch Counterattack in Capital." *Los Angeles Times,* September 20, A1.

Berry, John M. 1984. "Shaking His Fist at Economists Won't Bring Reagan the Miracle He Needs." *Washington Post,* February 12, B1.

Bethell, Tom. 1999. "Dynamic Scoring." *American Spectator* 32(1): 20–21.

Binderkrantz, Anne Skorkjaer, and Anne Rasmussen. 2015. "Comparing the Domestic and the EU Lobbying Context: Perceived Agenda-Setting Influence in the Multi-Level System of the European Union." *Journal of European Public Policy* 22(4): 552–69.

Björklund, Anders, and Richard B. Freeman. 1997. "Generating Equality and Eliminating Poverty, the Swedish Way." In *The Welfare State in Transition: Reforming the Swedish Model,* edited by Richard B. Freeman, Robert Topel, and Birgitta Swedenborg. Chicago: University of Chicago Press.

Blinder, Alan S. 1979. *Economic Policy and the Great Stagflation.* New York: Academic Press.

———. 1987. *Hard Heads, Soft Hearts: Tough-Minded Economics for a Just Society.* Cambridge, Mass.: Perseus Books.

Bloom, Alexander. 1986. *Prodigal Sons: The New York Intellectuals and Their World.* New York: Oxford University Press.

Blow, Charles. 2015. "'Black Lives Matter' and the GOP." *New York Times,* August 10, A19.

Blumenson, Eric, and Eva S. Nilsen. 1998. "Policing for Profit: The Drug War's Hidden Economic Agenda." *University of Chicago Law Review* 65(1): 35–114.

Blumenthal, Sidney. 1980. "Defining 'Reaganomics.'" *Boston Globe,* November 2, H10.

Blyth, Mark. 2002. *Great Transformations: Economic Ideas and Institutional Change in the Twentieth Century.* Cambridge: Cambridge University Press.

Boarini, Romina, and Marco Mira d'Ercole. 2006. "Measures of Material Deprivation in OECD Countries." OECD Social, Employment, and Migration Working Paper 37. Paris: OECD Publishing.

Boaz, David. 1999. "It's Time to Rethink the Failed War on Drugs." *Las Vegas Review-Journal,* November 12, 11B.

Bond, Steve, Asli Leblebicioğlu, and Fabio Schiantarelli. 2010. "Capital Accumulation and Growth: A New Look at the Empirical Evidence." *Journal of Applied Econometrics* 25(7): 1073–99.

Booth, Arch N. 1972. "A Closer Look at Those Tax Loopholes." *Human Events* 32(22, May 27): 9.

Bordo, Michael D., Angela Redish, and Hugh Rockoff. 2011. "Why Didn't Canada Have a Banking Crisis in 2008 (or in 1930, or 1907, or …)?" Working Paper 17312. Cambridge, Mass.: National Bureau of Economic Research.

Bordo, Michael D., Hugh Rockoff, and Angela Redish. 1994. "The U.S. Banking System from a Northern Exposure: Stability versus Efficiency." *Journal of Economic History* 54(2): 325–41.

Boskin, Michael. 1978. "Taxation, Saving, and the Rate of Interest." *Journal of Political Economy* 86(2, pt. 2): 3–27.

Bosman, Julie. 2014. "Democrat Is Governor Pick of GOP Group in Kansas." *New York Times,* July 16, A16.

Bosman, Julie, Mitch Smith, and Monica Davey. 2017. "Republican Governor Has Tax Cuts Undone by Other Republicans." *New York Times,* June 8, A22.

Boston Globe. 1976. "White, Rich, Male Image Criticized: Dole Urges GOP to Broaden Appeal." *Boston Globe,* December 1, 32.

———. 1977. "Q & A with William Brock: New Signals for GOP from Chairman." *Boston Globe,* July 10, 2.

———. 1981. "Reagan Endured His Ordeal with a Stream of One-Liners." *Boston Globe,* April 1, 16.

Boyd, James. 1970. "Nixon's Southern Strategy; 'It's All in the Charts.'" *New York Times,* May 17, 105.

Bradford, David. 1981. Testimony before U.S. House of Representatives, Budget Committee, *Tax and Program Policy.* Washington: U.S. Government Printing Office (March 12).

Brady, David, Evelyne Huber, and John D. Stephens. 2014. "Comparative Welfare States

Data Set." Chapel Hill and Berlin: University of North Carolina and WZB Berlin Social Science Center.

Brady, David, and Hang Young Lee. 2014. "The Rise and Fall of Government Spending in Affluent Democracies, 1971–2008." *Journal of European Social Policy* 24(1): 56–79.

Braithwaite, John. 1985. *To Punish or Persuade: Enforcement of Coal Mine Safety.* Albany: State University of New York Press.

Brands, H. W. 2015. *Reagan: The Life.* New York: Anchor Books.

Branham, Alexander J., Stuart N. Soroka, and Christopher Wlezien. 2017. "When Do the Rich Win?" *Political Science Quarterly* 132(1): 43–62.

Brickman, Ronald, Sheila Jasanoff, and Thomas Ilgen. 1985. *Controlling Chemicals: The Politics of Regulation in Europe and the United States.* Ithaca, N.Y.: Cornell University Press.

Briner, Merlin G. 1983. "Tax Equity and Fiscal Responsibility Act of 1982." *Akron Tax Journal* 1(2): 29–43.

Broder, David S. 1981. "Labor at the Crossroads." *Boston Globe*, September 6, 47.

Broder, David S., and Lou Cannon. 1980. "A Well-Mannered Republican Race Takes Turn for the Bitter." *Washington Post,* February 24, A1.

Bronstein, Richard J., and Alan S. Waldenberg. 1983. "The Short Life and Lingering Death of Safe Harbor Leasing." *American Bar Association Journal* 69 (December): 1844–47.

Brown, Warren. 1981a. "AFL-CIO Rally: To Belabor Reagan's Points: Reagan Aides Downplay Impact of Labor Protest." *Washington Post*, August 2, H1.

———. 1981b. "Teamsters Meeting Opens with Praise from Reagan, a Blast from Williams." *Washington Post*, June 2, A6.

Brownlee, W. Elliot. 1996a. *Federal Taxation in America: A Short History.* Cambridge: Cambridge University Press/Washington, D.C.: Woodrow Wilson Press.

———, ed. 1996b. *Funding the Modern American State, 1941–1995: The Rise and Fall of the Era of Easy Finance.* Cambridge: Cambridge University Press.

Brownlee, W. Elliot, and C. Eugene Steuerle. 2003. "Taxation." In *The Reagan Presidency,* edited by W. Elliot Brownlee and Hugh Davis Graham. Lawrence: University Press of Kansas.

Buckley, John L. (July 18, 2011) 2012. "Tax Expenditure Reform: Some Common Misconceptions." *Tax Notes* 18(February 27): 1122–39.

Bunch, Will. 2009. *Tear Down This Myth: How the Reagan Legacy Has Distorted Our Politics and Haunts Our Future.* New York: Simon and Schuster.

Burgin, Angus. 2012. *The Great Persuasion: Reinventing Free Markets since the Depression.* Cambridge, Mass.: Harvard University Press.

Burns, John W., and Andrew J. Taylor. 2000. "The Mythical Causes of the Republican Supply-Side Economics Revolution." *Party Politics* 6(4): 419–40.

Busch, Andrew E. 2005. *Reagan's Victory: The Presidential Election of 1980 and the Rise of the Right.* Lawrence: University Press of Kansas.

Cain, Bruce E., and Roger Noll. 2010. "Institutional Causes of California's Budget Problem." *California Journal of Politics and Policy* 2(3): 1–37.

Calmes, Jackie. 2000. "Bush Promotes Big Tax Cuts in a Move to Attract Middle-Class Swing Voters." *Wall Street Journal*, September 25, A16.

Calomiris, Charles W. 2000. *U.S. Bank Deregulation in Historical Perspective.* Cambridge: Cambridge University Press.

Cameron, David. 1978. "The Expansion of the Public Economy." *American Political Science Review* 72(4): 1243–61.

Campbell, Andrea Louise. 2009. "What Americans Think of Taxes." In *The New Fiscal Sociology: Taxation in Comparative and Historical Perspective,* edited by Isaac Martin, Ajay Mehrotra, and Monica Prasad. New York: Cambridge University Press.

———. 2011. "The 10 Percent Solution." *Democracy* 19: 54–63.

Canes-Wrone, Brandice. 2010. *Who Leads Whom? Presidents, Policy, and the Public.* Chicago: University of Chicago Press.

Cannon, Lou. 1981. "The Master Politician Has His Day." *Washington Post,* August 2, A1.

———. 1991. *President Reagan: The Role of a Lifetime.* New York: Public Affairs.

———. 2003. *Governor Reagan: His Rise to Power.* New York: Public Affairs.

Caplin, Mortimer M. 1964. "Comment: Reflections on the Revenue Act of 1964." *University of Pennsylvania Law Review* 112: 857–63.

Carlson, Michael. 2009. "Jack Kemp." *Guardian,* May 3, 33.

Carmines, Edward G., and James A. Stimson. 1989. *Issue Evolution: Race and the Transformation of American Politics.* Princeton, N.J.: Princeton University Press.

Carpenter, Daniel. 2014. *Reputation and Power: Organizational Image and Pharmaceutical Regulation at the FDA.* Princeton, N.J.: Princeton University Press.

Carr, Jack, Frank Mathewson, and Neil Quigley. 1995. "Stability in the Absence of Deposit Insurance: The Canadian Banking System, 1890–1966." *Journal of Money, Credit, and Banking* 27(4): 1137–58.

Castles, Francis G. 1987. "Neocorporatism and the 'Happiness Index,' or What the Trade Unions Get for Their Cooperation." *European Journal of Political Research* 15: 381–93.

Castles, Francis G., and Steve Dowrick. 1990. "The Impact of Government Spending Levels on Medium-Term Economic Growth in the OECD, 1960–85." *Journal of Theoretical Politics* 2(2): 173–204.

Chandler, Clay, and Eric Pianin. 1995. "GOP Won't Change Way Tax Cut Impact Measured, Current Methods Had Been Called Inaccurate." *Washington Post,* January 7, D1.

Chicago Tribune. 1978a. "Senate Panel Kills GOP Tax-Cut Plan." *Chicago Tribune,* September 21, 14.

———. 1978b. "Who's Got Our Money? The Tax-Bracket Creep." *Chicago Tribune,* July 17, 3.

———. 1981. "Reagan's Economic Message: Text of Reagan's Economic Speech." *Chicago Tribune,* February 19, 10.

———. 2004. "O'Neill Says Cheney Told Him, 'Deficits Don't Matter.'" *Chicago Tribune,* January 12, 2004, 9.

Chivvis, Christopher S. 2010. *The Monetary Conservative: Jacques Rueff and Twentieth-Century Free Market Thought.* DeKalb: Northern Illinois University Press.

Christian Science Monitor. 1980. "Bush: 'I Just Know How to Go about It Better.'" *Christian Science Monitor,* January 24.

Chua, Amy. 2004. *World on Fire: How Exporting Free Market Democracy Breeds Ethnic Hatred and Global Instability.* New York: Anchor.

Clawson, Dan, Alan Neustadtl, and Mark Weller. 1998. *Dollars and Votes: How Business Campaign Contributions Subvert Democracy.* Philadelphia: Temple University Press.

Clayton, Richard, and Jonas Pontusson. 1998. "Welfare-State Retrenchment Revisited: Entitlement Cuts, Public Sector Restructuring, and Inegalitarian Trends in Advanced Capitalist Societies." *World Politics* 51(1): 67–98.

Clymer, Adam. 1980. "Reagan Age an Issue for New Hampshire." *New York Times,* February 17, 15.

———. 2009. "Jack Kemp, 73, Star on Field and in Politics." *New York Times,* May 2, A1.

———. 2011. "Richard Wirthlin, 80, Pollster and Reagan Adviser, Dies." *New York Times,* March 18, A27.

Cohen, Lizabeth. 2003. *A Consumers' Republic: The Politics of Mass Consumption in Postwar America.* New York: Alfred A. Knopf.

———. 2010. "Colston E. Warne Lecture: Is It Time for Another Round of Consumer Protection?" *Journal of Consumer Affairs* 44(1): 234–46.

Cohen, Richard E. 1981. "Democratic Dilemma—No Credit if They Work with Reagan, Blame if They Don't." *National Journal,* March 21, 482–86.

Collins, Robert. 1998. *More: The Politics of Economic Growth in Postwar America.* Oxford: Oxford University Press.

———. 2006. *Transforming America: Politics and Culture during the Reagan Years.* New York: Columbia University Press.

Cooper, Michael. 2012. "States Face Tough Choices Even as Downturn Ends." *New York Times,* July 11, A15.

Coste, Françoise. 2015. *Reagan.* Paris: Perrin.

Cowan, Edward. 1966. "Belgium Fattens Investment Aid." *New York Times,* July 19, 67.

Cowie, Jefferson R. 2010. *Stayin' Alive: The 1970s and the Last Days of the Working Class.* New York: New Press.

Crépon, Bruno, and Gerard J. Van Den Berg. 2016. "Active Labor Market Policies." *Annual Review of Economics* 8: 521–46.

Crittenden, Ann. 1976. "Economists' Atlantic City Parley Revives Issue of Capital Shortage." *New York Times,* September 18, 41.

Crowther, Rodney. 1962. "Investment Credit Plan Denounced." *Baltimore Sun,* April 3, 9.

Crum, Martha. 2010. "Polling, Media Discourse, and the Construction of Ignorance: Public Opinion Formation on the Bush Tax Cuts." PhD diss., City University of New York.

Culpepper, Pepper. 2011. *Quiet Politics and Business Power: Corporate Control in Europe and Japan.* Cambridge: Cambridge University Press.

Currarino, Rosanne. 2006. "The Politics of 'More': The Labor Question and the Idea of Economic Liberty in Industrial America." *The Journal of American History* 93(1): 17–36.

Cusack, Thomas R., and Pablo Beramendi. 2006. "Taxing Work: Some Political and Economic Aspects of Labor Income Taxation." *European Journal of Political Research* 45(1): 43–73.

Dale, Edwin L., Jr. 1977. "Long-Term Income Tax Reduction Urged as a National Commitment." *New York Times,* January 18, 19.

Davey, Monica. 2015. "Lawsuit Accuses Missouri City of Fining Homeowners to Raise Revenue." *New York Times,* November 4, A15.

Day, Kathleen. 2005. "Bankruptcy Bill Passes; Bush Expected to Sign." *Washington Post,* April 15, E01.

Denton, Mark. 1992. "The Saddest Veterans Day of All?" *Detroit Free Press*, November 19, 12A.

DeParle, Jason. 1993. "How Jack Kemp Lost the War on Poverty." *New York Times,* February 28.

Dewar, Helen. 1979. "Recession Only Inflation Cure, Economist Says: NAM Asserts Inflation Only Cure for Recession." *Washington Post,* March 7, D7.

Diamond, S. J. 1981. "Small Business: Small-Businessmen Speak Out, Know What They Want." *Los Angeles Times,* June 8, E1.

Dimick, Matthew. 2012. "Labor Law, New Governance, and the Ghent System." *North Carolina Law Review* 90(2): 319–78.

Dionne, E. J., Jr. 1988. "Reagan Debt Legacy: His Trap for Democrats?" *New York Times,* December 2, B7.

Domitrovic, Brian. 2009. *Econoclasts: The Rebels Who Sparked the Supply-Side Revolution and Restored American Prosperity.* Wilmington, Del.: Intercollegiate Studies Institute.

Donovan, Robert J. 1974. "Republicans Not the Only Party in a Shambles." *Los Angeles Times,* November 10, J5.

Dorsey, Jasper. 1978. "Capital Gains Proposal Making Steiger a Hero." *Atlanta Constitution*, July 9, J3.

Drew, Elizabeth. 1978. "Charlie." *New Yorker,* January 9, 32–58.

Drutman, Lee. 2015. *The Business of America Is Lobbying: How Corporations Became Politicized and Politics Became More Corporate.* Oxford: Oxford University Press.

Dudley, Susan, and Melinda Warren. 2018. "Regulators' Budget: More for Homeland Security, Less for Environmental Regulation." St. Louis, Mo., and Washington, D.C.: Washington University Weidenbaum Center on the Economy, Government, and Public Policy and George Washington University Regulatory Studies Center (May).

Duménil, Gérard, and Dominique Lévy. 2004. *Capital Resurgent: Roots of the Neoliberal Revolution.* Cambridge, Mass.: Harvard University Press.

Dungan, Adrian. 2017. "Individual Income Tax Shares, 2014." *IRS Statistics of Income (SOI) Bulletin* 36(4, Spring): 12–24.

Dunn, Robert M., Jr. 1978. "The Laffer Curve: A Dangerous Mirage." *Washington Post,* July 9, B7.

Durevall, Dick, and Magnus Henrekson. 2011. "The Futile Quest for a Grand Explanation of Long-Run Government Expenditure." *Journal of Public Economics* 95(7–8): 708–22.

Easterly, William, and Stanley Fischer. 2001. "Inflation and the Poor." *Journal of Money, Credit and Banking* 33(2): 160–78.

Easton, Nina J. 2002. *Gang of Five: Leaders at the Center of the Conservative Ascendancy.* New York: Touchstone Books.

Edsall, Thomas B. 1981. "Reagan Goes to the Hill on Tax Bill." *Washington Post,* July 25, A1.

Edsall, Thomas Byrne, and Mary D. Edsall. 1991. *Chain Reaction: The Impact of Race, Rights, and Taxes on American Politics.* New York: W. W. Norton and Co.

Ehrman, John. 2005. *The Eighties: America in the Age of Reagan.* New Haven, Conn.: Yale University Press.

Eichengreen, Barry. 1996. "Institutions and Economic Growth: Europe after World War II." In *Economic Growth in Europe since 1945,* edited by Nicholas Crafts and Gianni Toniolo. Cambridge: Cambridge University Press.

———. 2008. *The European Economy since 1945: Coordinated Capitalism and Beyond.* Princeton, N.J.: Princeton University Press.

Eichengreen, Barry J., and Marc Flandreau, eds. 1997. *The Gold Standard in Theory and History.* 2nd ed. London: Routledge.

Elder, Janet. 2000. "The Polls: Poll Shows Americans Divided Over Election." *New York Times,* December 18, A22.

Eligon, John. 2012. "In Kansas, Conservatives Vilify Fellow Republicans." *New York Times,* August 6, A11.

———. 2014a. "Brownback Leads Kansas in Sharp Right Turn." *New York Times,* February 14, A1.

———. 2014b. "Conservative Experiment Faces Revolt in Reliably Red Kansas." *New York Times,* September 15, A1.

———. 2014c. "Incumbents Withstand Strong Challenge to Republican Control." *New York Times,* November 5, 4.

———. 2014d. "Kansas' Advice to Republicans, Stay to the Right." *New York Times,* November 6, P7.

———. 2014e. "Tax Cuts Not Set in Stone as Kansas Faces Shortfall." *New York Times,* December 15, A12.

———. 2015a. "Education Is Newest Target of Kansas Budget Cuts." *New York Times,* February 12, A15.

———. 2015b. "Pressed by Budget Squeeze, Kansas Governor Pulls Back on Tax Cuts." *New York Times,* January 17, A11.

Eligon, John, and Julie Bosman. 2017. "Kansas Governor's Tenure May Serve as a Warning for Conservatives." *New York Times,* July 28, A12.

Elsässer, Lea, Svenja Hense, and Armin Schäfer. 2016. *Systematisch verzerrte Entscheidungen? Die Responsivität der deutschen Politik von 1998 bis 2015: Endbericht.* Bonn: Bundesministerium für Arbeit und Soziales.

Emmenegger, Patrick. 2010. "The Long Road to Flexicurity: The Development of Job Security Regulations in Denmark and Sweden." *Scandinavian Political Studies* 33(3): 271–94.

Endicott, William. 1980a. "Setback for Leader in GOP Race." *Los Angeles Times,* January 1, 1.

———. 1980b. "The Times Poll: Reagan Gains Strength with Blue-Collar Voters." *Los Angeles Times*, October 15, 1.

Enns, Peter K. 2015. "Relative Policy Support and Coincidental Representation." *Perspectives on Politics* 13(4): 1053–64.

Erixon, Lennart. 2010. "The Rehn-Meidner Model in Sweden: Its Rise, Challenges, and Survival." *Journal of Economic Issues* 44(3): 677–715.

Erskine, Hazel Gaudet. 1964. "The Polls: Some Gauges of Conservatism." *Public Opinion Quarterly* 28(1): 154–68.

Evans, Rowland, and Robert Novak. 1979. "Reagan Talks Out of School." *Washington Post,* October 12, A15.

———. 1980a. "Reagan: Once Invincible, Now Invisible." *Washington Post,* January 14, A23.

———. 1980b. "Tax Cut Idea Worked Accidentally." *The Atlanta Constitution,* July 7, 4A.

———. 1981a. "Big Business Is Furious, Too." *Washington Post,* June 8, A15.

———. 1981b. "Captain General of the Tax Counterrevolution." *Washington Post,* February 11, A19.

Evans, Thomas W. 2006. *The Education of Ronald Reagan: The General Electric Years and the Untold Story of His Conversion to Conservatism.* New York: Columbia University Press.

Fairbrother, Malcolm. 2014. "Economists, Capitalists, and the Making of Globalization: North American Free Trade in Comparative-Historical Perspective." *American Journal of Sociology* 119: 1324–79.

Farney, Dennis. 1978. "Middle Class 'Apprehension.'" *Wall Street Journal,* April 27, 22.

Farnsworth, Clyde H. 1980. "N.A.M. President Urges Delay in Tax-Cut Plans." *New York Times,* November 12, D24.

Farrell, John Aloysius. 2001. *Tip O'Neill and the Democratic Century.* Boston: Little, Brown, and Co.

Feenstra, Robert C., Robert Inklaar, and Marcl P. Timmer. 2015. "The Next Generation of the Penn World Table." *American Economic Review* 105(10): 3150–82.

Feldman, Stanley, and Leonie Huddy. 2005. "Racial Resentment and White Opposition to Race-Conscious Programs: Principles or Prejudice?" *American Journal of Political Science* 49(1): 168–83.

Feldstein, Martin. 1981a. "The Tax Cut: Why the Market Dropped." *Wall Street Journal,* November 11, 26.

———. 1981b. Testimony before U.S. Senate, Finance Committee, *Tax Reduction Proposals,* part 1. Washington: U.S. Government Printing Office, May 13, 14, 18.

Ferguson, Thomas, and Joel Rogers. 1986. *Right Turn: The Decline of the Democrats and the Future of American Politics.* New York: Hill and Wang.

Fessler, Pamela. 1981a. "House Floor Battle Looming on Tax Cut Bill." *Congressional Quarterly Weekly Report,* July 25, 1323–26.

———. 1981b. "Positions Harden as Panels Kick off Tax Cut Markups." *Congressional Quarterly Weekly Report,* June 13, 1027–28.

———. 1981c. "Reagan Tax Plan Ready for Economic Test." *Congressional Quarterly Weekly Report,* August 8, 1431–36.

Fones-Wolf, Elizabeth A. 1994. *Selling Free Enterprise: The Business Assault on Labor and Liberalism, 1945–60.* Urbana: University of Illinois Press.

Fowler, Elizabeth M. 1962. "Accounting Abroad: It Can All Be Greek." *New York Times,* September 23, 155.

Frank, Jeffrey. 2016. "The Ghost of Jack Kemp." *New Yorker,* May 10. https://www.newyorker .com/news/daily-comment/the-ghost-of-jack-kemp (accessed February 19, 2018).

Frey, Bruno S., Werner W. Pommerehne, Friedrich Schneider, and Guy Gilbert. 1984. "Consensus and Dissension among Economists: An Empirical Inquiry." *American Economic Review* 74(5): 986–94.

Friedman, Murray. 2005. *The Neoconservative Revolution: Jewish Intellectuals and the Shaping of Public Policy.* Cambridge: Cambridge: University Press.

Friedman, Robert. 1981. "Tempo: Preppy Rep Rocks Congress with His 'Republican Punk.'" *Chicago Tribune,* July 7, A1.

Frum, David. 1998. "The Dow of Social Security." *Weekly Standard,* September 14, 10.

Frymer, Paul, and John David Skrentny. 1998. "Coalition-Building and the Politics of Electoral Capture during the Nixon Administration." *Studies in American Political Development* 12: 131–61.

Fuerbringer, Jonathan. 2002. "Deficits Are Back. But Maybe They Aren't as Dangerous." *New York Times,* August 25, B6.

Fuller, Dan, and Doris Geide-Stevenson. 2003. "Consensus among Economists: Revisited." *Journal of Economic Education* 34(4): 369–87.

Galbraith, James K. 1988. "The Grammar of Political Economy." In *The Consequences of Economic Rhetoric,* edited by Arjo Klamer, Deirdre N. McCloskey, and Robert M. Solow. Cambridge: Cambridge University Press.

Gallup, George. 1974. "GOP Affiliation Drops to an All-Time Low." *Boston Globe,* July 18, 17.

Galvin, Daniel J. 2009. *Presidential Party Building: Dwight D. Eisenhower to George W. Bush.* Princeton, N.J.: Princeton University Press.

Gannon, James P. 1976. "Unemployment as a Political Issue." *Wall Street Journal,* February 12, 16.

Garon, Sheldon. 2012. *Beyond Our Means: Why America Spends While the World Saves.* Princeton, N.J.: Princeton University Press.

Gaston, K. Healan. 2013. "The Cold War Romance of Religious Authenticity: Will Herberg, William F. Buckley Jr., and the Rise of the New Right." *Journal of American History* 99(4): 1133–58.

Gergen, David. 1978. "Wanted: A GOP Program: A Minority Party with a Majority Philosophy." *Washington Post,* November 19, C8.

Germond, Jack W., and Jules Witcover. 1979. "Reagan Is Following a Debatable Strategy." *Chicago Tribune,* November 23, B4.

Gerschenkron, Alexander. 1962. *Economic Backwardness in Historical Perspective.* Cambridge, Mass.: Belknap Press of Harvard University Press.

Gilens, Martin. 2012. *Affluence and Influence: Economic Inequality and Political Power in America.* Princeton, N.J.: Princeton University Press.

Gilens, Martin, and Benjamin I. Page. 2014. "Testing Theories of American Politics: Elites, Interest Groups, and Average Citizens." *Perspectives on Politics* 12(3): 564–81.

Giordano, Joseph M. 1981. "Doctor's Story of Reagan Emergency." *Los Angeles Times,* April 4, 1, 22.

Golden, Soma. 1975. "Reporter's Notebook: Economists Ready with a Plan for U.S. Income Distribution." *New York Times,* January 2, 65.

———. 1980. "Superstar of the New Economists." *New York Times,* March 23, SM8.

Goolsbee, Austan. 1999. "Evidence on the High-Income Laffer Curve from Six Decades of Tax Reform." *Brookings Papers on Economic Activity* 2: 1–64.

Gordon, Robert. 1981. Testimony before U.S. House of Representatives, Budget Committee, *Tax and Program Policy.* Washington: U.S. Government Printing Office, March 12.

Gornick, Janet C., and Emily Nell. 2017. "Children, Poverty, and Public Policy: A Cross-National Perspective." Luxembourg Income Study (LIS) Working Paper 701. Luxembourg: Cross-National Data Center.

Gorski, James M. 1976. "Access to Information? Exemptions from Disclosure under the Freedom of Information Act and the Privacy Act of 1974." *Willamette Law Journal* 13(1): 135–71.

Gourse, Alexander. 2015. "Restraining the Reagan Revolution: The Lawyers' War on Poverty and the Durable Liberal State, 1964–1989." PhD diss., Northwestern University, Department of History.

Graff, Trevor, and John Eligon. 2014. "Kansas School Funding Is Faulted, State's Supreme Court Orders Legislature to Fix Disparities." *New York Times,* March 8, A9.

Graham, Hugh Davis. 1996. "Richard Nixon and Civil Rights: Explaining an Enigma." *Presidential Studies Quarterly* 26(1): 93–106.

Gramm, Phil. 2009. "Deregulation and the Financial Panic." *Wall Street Journal,* February 20, A17.

Gray, Jerry. 1993a. "Florio-Whitman Debate Zeroes in on Ethics." *New York Times,* October 23, B1.

———. 1993b. "Going on Offensive, Whitman Plans Cuts in New Jersey Taxes." *New York Times,* September 22, A1.

———. 1993c. "In New Jersey Campaign, Cries of 'Class Warfare.'" *New York Times,* August 4, 1.

———. 1993d. "New Jersey Anger over Taxes Propels Challenger." *New York Times,* November 3, A1.

Green, Joshua. 2009. "The Elusive Green Economy." *Atlantic,* August 15.

Green, Penelope. 2012. "Family, Southern Style." *New York Times,* August 1, D1.

Greenberger, Robert S. 1980. "Reagan Revises Tune in Bid to Harmonize with Unions; Carter Calls It a 'Flip-Flop.'" *Wall Street Journal,* October 13, 5.

Greider, William. 1982. *The Education of David Stockman and Other Americans.* New York: Dutton.

Grossman, Matt, and David A. Hopkins. 2016. *Asymmetric Politics: Ideological Republicans and Group Interest Democrats.* New York: Oxford University Press.

Grossman, Richard S. 1994. "The Shoe That Didn't Drop: Explaining Banking Stability during the Great Depression." *Journal of Economic History* 54(3): 654–82.

Guardian. 1971. "Brake on Investment Incentives." *Guardian,* October 13, 3.

————. 1974. "An Elephantine Decline." *Guardian,* November 7, 12.

Hacker, Jacob S., and Paul Pierson. 2005. "Abandoning the Middle: The Bush Tax Cuts and the Limits of Democratic Control." *Perspectives on Politics* 3(1): 33–53.

————. 2010. *Winner-Take-All Politics: How Washington Made the Rich Richer—and Turned Its Back on the Middle Class.* New York: Simon & Schuster.

————. 2012. "Presidents and the Political Economy: The Coalitional Foundations of Presidential Power." *Presidential Studies Quarterly* 42(1): 101–31.

Hall, Peter A. 2017. "Varieties of Capitalism in Light of the Euro Crisis." *Journal of European Public Policy* 2017: 1–24.

Hall, Peter A., and David W. Soskice, eds. 2001. *Varieties of Capitalism: The Institutional Foundations of Comparative Advantage.* Oxford: Oxford University Press.

Hamilton, Shane. 2008. *Trucking Country: The Road to America's Wal-Mart Economy.* Princeton, N.J.: Princeton University Press.

Hansson, Pär, and Magnus Henrekson. 1994. "A New Framework for Testing the Effect of Government Spending on Growth and Productivity." *Public Choice* 81(3/4): 381–401.

Harris, Alexes. 2016. *A Pound of Flesh: Monetary Sanctions as Punishment for the Poor.* New York: Russell Sage Foundation.

Harris, Louis. 1978. "Harris Survey: The Voters' Message." *Chicago Tribune,* November 16, B3.

Harvey, David. 2005. *A Brief History of Neoliberalism.* Oxford: Oxford University Press.

Haubrich, Joseph G. 1990. "Nonmonetary Effects of Financial Crises: Lessons from the Great Depression in Canada." *Journal of Monetary Economics* 25: 223–52.

Hays, Samuel P., and Barbara D. Hays. 1989. *Beauty, Health, and Permanence: Environmental Politics in the United States, 1955–1985.* Cambridge: Cambridge University Press.

Hayward, Steven. 2009. *The Age of Reagan: The Conservative Counterrevolution, 1980–1989.* New York: Crown Forum.

Heffington, Colton, Brandon Beomseob Park, and Laron K. Williams. 2017. "The 'Most Important Problem' Dataset (MIPD): A New Dataset on American Issue Importance." *Conflict Management and Peace Science.* Published online March 31. DOI: 10.1177/0738894217691463.

Helgason, Agnar Freyr. 2017. "Unleashing the 'Money Machine': The Domestic Political Foundations of VAT Adoption." *Socio-Economic Review* 15(4): 797–813.

Heller, Walter W. 1978. "The Kemp-Roth-Laffer Free Lunch." *Wall Street Journal,* July 12, 20.

Hershey, Marjorie Randon. 1992. "The Constructed Explanation: Interpreting Election Results in the 1984 Presidential Race." *Journal of Politics* 54(4): 943–76.

Hershey, Robert D., Jr. 1981. "Mr. Reagan Gives Business a Jolt." *New York Times,* June 7, F1.

————. 2014. "Murray L. Weidenbaum, Reagan Economist, Dies at 87." *New York Times,* March 21, A22.

Hertel-Fernandez, Alexander, and Theda Skocpol. 2015. "Asymmetric Interest Group Mobilization and Party Coalitions in U.S. Tax Politics." *Studies in American Political Development* 29(2): 235–49.

Hibbs, Douglas A., Jr. 1982. "Public Concern about Inflation and Unemployment in the

United States: Trends, Correlates, and Political Implications." In *Inflation: Causes and Effects,* edited by Robert A. Hall. Chicago: University of Chicago Press.

Himmelstein, Jerome L. 1990. *To the Right: The Transformation of American Conservatism.* Berkeley: University of California Press.

Hirschman, Daniel, and Elizabeth Popp Berman. 2014. "Do Economists Make Policies? On the Political Effects of Economics." *Socio-Economic Review* 12(4): 779–811.

HM Revenue and Customs. 2016. *Capital Allowances Manual.* GOV.UK, April 16. http://www.hmrc.gov.uk/manuals/camanual/Index.htm (accessed June 5, 2018).

Hohle, Randolph. 2015. *Race and the Origins of American Neoliberalism.* New York: Routledge.

Hojnacki, Marie, Kathleen M. Marchetti, Frank R. Baumgartner, Jeffrey M. Berry, David C. Kimball, and Beth L. Leech. 2015. "Assessing Business Advantage in Washington Lobbying." *Interest Groups and Advocacy* 4(3): 205–24.

Hombert, Johan, Antoinette Schoar, David Sraer, and David Thesmar. 2014. "Can Unemployment Insurance Spur Entrepreneurial Activity?" Working Paper 20717. Cambridge, Mass.: National Bureau of Economic Research.

Honig, Bonnie. 1993. *Political Theory and the Displacement of Politics.* Ithaca, N.Y.: Cornell University Press.

Hoynes, Hilary, Diane Whitmore Schanzenbach, and Douglas Almond. 2016. "Long-Run Impacts of Childhood Access to the Safety Net." *American Economic Review* 106(4): 903–34.

Hulse, Carl. 2017. "Republicans Need a Victory, and Fear What Happens if They Don't Get One." *New York Times,* October 11, A17.

Human Events. 1975. "Tax Cut Bill Points up Ford Weakness." *Human Events* 35(14, April 5).

Hume, Craig R. 1978. "Proposition 13 'Bomb' Explodes in Washington." *Atlanta Constitution,* June 11, 15C.

Hung, Ho-fung, and Daniel Thompson. 2016. "Money Supply, Class Power, and Inflation: Monetarism Reassessed." *American Sociological Review* 81(3): 447–66.

Hunt, Albert R. 1978. "GOP Gains Miss Targets: Republicans Set Anti-Government Tone of Elections, but Democrats Joined Them in Reaping the Rewards; Elections Give GOP Four More Statehouses but Little in Congress." *Wall Street Journal,* November 9, 2.

———. 1980. "Right Angles: Which Conservatism, Traditional or Populist, Will Reagan Stress?" *Wall Street Journal,* March 27, 1.

———. 1988. "Reagan's Coattails and Anti-Tax Feeling Are Cited in Bush's New Hampshire Win." *Wall Street Journal,* February 17, 58.

Huret, Romain D. 2014. *American Tax Resisters.* Cambridge, Mass.: Harvard University Press.

Hurst, Sam. 1981. "The New Democratic Coalition: Old One Is in Shambles, but Party Can Regroup for Future." *Los Angeles Times,* January 22, C11.

Internal Revenue Service (IRS). 2017. "SOI Tax Stats: Individual Income Tax Rates and Tax Shares." Updated October 25, 2017. https://www.irs.gov/statistics/soi-tax-stats-individual-income-tax-rates-and-tax-shares (accessed August 15, 2018).

Iversen, Torben, and David Soskice. 2009. "Distribution and Redistribution: The Shadow of the Nineteenth Century." *World Politics* 61: 438–86.

Iversen, Torben, David Soskice, and David Hope. 2016. "The Eurozone and Political Economic Institutions." *Annual Review of Political Science* 19(1): 163–85.

Jacob, Charles E. 1985. "Reaganomics: The Revolution in American Political Economy." *Law and Contemporary Problems* 48(4): 7–30.

Jacobs, David, and Lindsey Myers. 2014. "Union Strength, Neoliberalism, and Inequality: Contingent Political Analyses of U.S. Income Differences Since 1950." *American Sociological Review* 79(4): 752–74.

Jacobs, Lawrence R., and Melanie Burns. 2004. "The Second Face of the Public Presidency: Presidential Polling and the Shift from Policy to Personality Polling." *Presidential Studies Quarterly* 34(3): 536–56.

Jacobs, Meg. 2005. *Pocketbook Politics: Economic Citizenship in Twentieth-Century America.* Princeton, N.J.: Princeton University Press.

———. 2016. *Panic at the Pump: The Energy Crisis and the Transformation of American Politics in the 1970s.* New York: Hill and Wang.

Jacobs, Sanford L. 1981. "How Changes in the Tax Law Will Affect Small Companies." *Wall Street Journal,* October 19, 31.

Jasanoff, Sheila. 1991. "Acceptable Evidence in a Pluralistic Society." In *Acceptable Evidence: Science and Values in Risk Management,* edited by Deborah J. Mayo and Rachelle D. Hollander. New York: Oxford University Press.

Jenkins, J. Craig, and Craig M. Eckert. 2000. "The Right Turn in Economic Policy: Business Elites and the New Conservative Economics." *Sociological Forum* 15(2): 307–38.

Jianakoplos, Nancy. 1976. "The FOMC in 1975: Announcing Monetary Targets." *Federal Reserve Bank of St. Louis Review* (March): 8–22.

Johnston, David Cay. 1999. "Funny, They Don't Look Like Fat Cats." *New York Times,* January 10, 1.

Joint Committee on Taxation. 1981. *General Explanation of the Economic Recovery Tax Act of 1981.* Washington: U.S. Government Printing Office.

Jones, Daniel Stedman. 2012. *Masters of the Universe: Hayek, Friedman, and the Birth of Neoliberal Politics.* Princeton, N.J.: Princeton University Press.

Jorgenson, Dale. 1981a. Testimony before U.S. House of Representatives, Ways and Means Committee, *Tax Aspects of the President's Economic Program,* part 3. Washington: U.S. Government Printing Office, April 1–3, 7.

———. 1981b. Testimony before U.S. Senate, Finance Committee, *Tax Reduction Proposals,* part 2. Washington: U.S. Government Printing Office, May 19 and 20.

Joyce, Philip G. 2011. *The Congressional Budget Office: Honest Numbers, Power, and Policymaking.* Washington, D.C.: Georgetown University Press.

Kabaservice, Geoffrey. 2012. *Rule and Ruin: The Downfall of Moderation and the Destruction of the Republican Party, from Eisenhower to the Tea Party.* Oxford: Oxford University Press.

Kagan, Robert. 2001. *Adversarial Legalism: The American Way of Law.* Cambridge, Mass.: Harvard University Press.

Kato, Junko. 2003. *Regressive Taxation and the Welfare State: Path Dependence and Policy Diffusion.* New York: Cambridge University Press.

Katzenstein, Peter J. 1985. *Small States in World Markets: Industrial Policy in Europe.* Ithaca, N.Y.: Cornell University Press.

Keller, Bill. 1981. "Democrats and Republicans Try to Outbid Each Other in Cutting Taxes for Business." *Congressional Quarterly Weekly Report,* June 27, 1132–37.

Kelly, Michael. 1988. "In N.H., 12 Desperate Men Try Anything." *The Sun,* February 16, 1A.

Kelman, Steven. 1981. *Regulating America, Regulating Sweden: A Comparative Study of Occupational Safety and Health.* Cambridge, Mass.: MIT Press.

———. 1985. "The Grace Commission: How Much Waste in Government?" *Public Interest* 78(Winter): 62–82.

Kemp, Jack. 1975. "The Tax Bias Against Savings Shrinks Everyone's Pie." *Evening Star,* September 21, 21.

———. 1976. "Congress' First Priority: Lower Federal Tax Rates." *Human Events,* November 27.

Kennedy, David M. 1999. *Freedom from Fear: The American People in Depression and War, 1929–1945.* New York: Oxford University Press.

Kennedy, John F. 1962. "549: Address and Question and Answer Period at the Economic Club of New York," December 14, 1962. American Presidency Project, edited by Gerhard Peters and John T. Woolley. http://www.presidency.ucsb.edu/ws/?pid=9057 (accessed August 15, 2018).

Kenworthy, Lane. 2011. *Progress for the Poor.* Oxford: Oxford University Press.

Kesaris, Paul L., ed. 1986. *Papers of the Republican Party.* Frederick, Md.: University Publications of America.

Keynes, John Maynard. 1920. *The Economic Consequences of the Peace.* New York: Harcourt, Brace, and Howe.

———. (1933) 2009. *General Theory of Employment, Interest, and Money.* London: Macmillan. Reprint, New York: Harcourt, Brace, and World.

King, Desmond. 1995. *Actively Seeking Work? The Politics of Unemployment and Welfare Policy in the United States and Great Britain.* Chicago: University of Chicago Press.

King, Wayne. 1993. "Whitman and Florio Attack as New Jersey Battle Begins." *New York Times,* June 10, A1.

Klarner, Carl. 2013. "State Partisan Balance Data, 1937–2011." Harvard Dataverse, V1. https://hdl.handle.net/1902.1/20403 (accessed August 15, 2018).

Klein, Daniel B., and Charlotta Stern. 2007. "Is There a Free-Market Economist in the House? The Policy Views of American Economic Association Members." *American Journal of Economics and Sociology* 66(2): 309–34.

Klinkner, Philip A. 1994. "Beyond Pseudo-Science: Political Parties and Policymaking." *Polity* 26(4): 769–91.

Kneller, Richard, Michael F. Bleaney, and Norman Gemmell. 1999. "Fiscal Policy and Growth: Evidence from OECD Countries." *Journal of Public Economics* 74(2): 171–90.

Koestler, Arthur, Ignazio Silone, Richard Wright, André Gide, Louis Fischer, and Stephen Spender. 1949. *The God That Failed.* New York: Harper & Brothers.

Komansky, David H., Philip J. Purcell, and Sanford I. Weill. 1997. "1930s Rules Ensnare 1990s Finance." *Wall Street Journal,* October 30, A22.

Kondracke, Morton, and Fred Barnes. 2015. *Jack Kemp: The Bleeding-Heart Conservative Who Changed America.* New York: Sentinel.

Korpi, Walter. 1985. "Economic Growth and the Welfare State: Leaky Bucket or Irrigation System?" *European Sociological Review* 1(2): 97–118.

Korpi, Walter, and Joakim Palme. 1998. "The Paradox of Redistribution and Strategies of Equality: Welfare State Institutions, Inequality, and Poverty in the Western Countries." *American Sociological Review* (1998): 661–87.

Kotlowski, Dean J. 1998. "Nixon's Southern Strategy Revisited." *Journal of Policy History* 10(2): 207–38.

Kousser, Thad, Justin Phillips, and Boris Shor. 2016. "Reform and Representation: A New Method Applied to Recent Electoral Changes." *Political Science Research and Methods* (November): 1–19.

Kraft, Joseph. 1981. "Labor's Troubles…" *Washington Post*, September 6, C7.

Krippner, Greta. 2011. *Capitalizing on Crisis: The Political Origins of the Rise of Finance.* Cambridge, Mass: Harvard University Press.

Krugman, Paul R. 1994. *Peddling Prosperity: Economic Sense and Nonsense in the Age of Diminished Expectations.* New York: W. W. Norton & Co.

———. 2010. "The Bankruptcy Boys." *New York Times,* February 22, A19.

———. 2014. "Charlatans, Cranks, and Kansas." *New York Times,* June 30, A19.

Kumpa, Peter J. 1962. "The Common Market: U.S. Investments Rising Rapidly in West Europe." *Baltimore Sun,* March 26, 5.

Kuo, Alexander G. 2015. "Explaining Historical Employer Coordination: Evidence from Germany." *Comparative Politics* 48(1): 87–106.

Labonte, Marc. 2012. "The Sustainability of the Federal Budget Deficit: Market Confidence and Economic Effects." Congressional Research Service, 7-5700, R40770, December 14.

Lacy, Dean. 1998. "Electoral Support for Tax Cuts: A Case Study of the 1980 American Presidential Election." *American Politics Quarterly* 26(3): 288–307.

Ladd, Everett Carll, Jr., Marilyn Potter, Linda Basilick, Sally Dantels, and Dana Suszkiw. 1979. "The Polls: Taxing and Spending." *Public Opinion Quarterly* 43(1): 126–35.

Laffer, Arthur B. 1980. "Fed Monetary Policy to Backfire." *Los Angeles Times,* January 22, F3.

———. 1999. "Economist of the Century." *Wall Street Journal,* October 15, A16.

Landais, Camille, Thomas Piketty, and Emmanuel Saez. 2011. *Pour une révolution fiscale.* Paris: Le Seuil.

Landau, Daniel L. 1985. "Government Expenditure and Economic Growth in the Developed Countries: 1952–76." *Public Choice* 47(3): 459–77.

Landon, Thomas, Jr. 2000. "The Laffer-Curve Crew Reunites for Steve Forbes at Treasury!" *New York Observer,* September 11, http://observer.com/2000/09/the-laffercurve-crew -reunites-for-steve-forbes-at-treasury/ (accessed January 17, 2018).

Lange, Peter, and Geoffrey Garrett. 1985. "The Politics of Growth: Strategic Interaction and Performance in Advanced Industrial Democracies, 1974–1980." *Journal of Politics* 47: 792–827.

Large, Arlen. 1970. "Stars on the Stump." *Wall Street Journal,* May 4, 1.

Lassiter, Matthew D. 2005. *The Silent Majority: Suburban Politics in the Sunbelt South.* Princeton, N.J.: Princeton University Press.

Lemann, Nicholas. 1981. "Trying to Turn a Collective Sentiment into a Government." *Washington Post,* February 24, A4.

Lenhoff, Arthur. 1956. "The Problem of Compulsory Unionism in Europe." *American Journal of Comparative Law* 5(1): 18–43.

Leonhardt, David. 2004. "That Big Fat Budget Deficit, Yawn." *New York Times,* February 8, BU1.

Leppälä, Heli. 2016. "Welfare or Workfare?: The Principle of Activation in the Finnish Postwar Disability Policy, Early 1940s to Late 1980s." *Journal of Social History* 49(4): 959–81.

Lessig, Lawrence. 2011. *Republic, Lost: How Money Corrupts Congress—and a Plan to Stop It.* New York: Twelve.

Levy, Mark R. 1984. "Polling and the Presidential Election." *The Annals of the American Academy of Political and Social Science* 472(March): 85–96.

Linder, Marc. 1996. "Eisenhower-Era Marxist-Confiscatory Taxation." *Tulane Law Review* 70(4): 905–1040.

Lindert, Peter. 2004. *Growing Public,* vol. 1, *The Story: Social Spending and Economic Growth since the Eighteenth Century.* New York: Cambridge University Press.

Lindsey, Lawrence. 1990. *The Growth Experiment: How the New Tax Policy Is Transforming the U.S. Economy.* New York: Basic Books.

Lindsey, Robert. 1980. "As Reagan Goes, so Goes John P. Sears 3d." *New York Times,* January 27, E4.

Lochhead, Carolyn. 1999. "Do Guilt and Innocence Still Count in America?" *San Francisco Chronicle,* May 16.

Löfstedt, Ragnar E., and David Vogel. 2001. "The Changing Character of Regulation: A Comparison of Europe and the United States." *Risk Analysis* 21(3): 399–416.

López, Ian Haney. 2014. *Dog Whistle Politics: How Coded Racial Appeals Have Reinvented Racism and Wrecked the Middle Class.* Oxford: Oxford University Press.

Los Angeles Times. 1980. "Conferees Advise Reagan on Economy: Tax Cuts Won't Help, Labor Warns." *Los Angeles Times,* December 11, G2.

Lubell, Samuel. 1952. *The Future of American Politics.* New York: Harper.

Lucas, Robert E., Jr. 1982. "The Death of Keynes." In *Viewpoints on Supply-Side Economics,* edited by Thomas J. Hailstones. Reston, Va.: Reston Publishing Company.

Lundberg, Urban, and Klas Åmark. 2001. "Social Rights and Social Security: The Swedish Welfare State, 1900–2000." *Scandinavian Journal of History* 26(3): 157–76.

Lundqvist, Lennart J. 1980. *The Hare and the Tortoise: Clean Air Policies in the United States and Sweden.* Ann Arbor: University of Michigan Press.

Lyons, Richard L. 1978. "Democrats Retain the House, but GOP Begins a Comeback." *Washington Post,* November 9, A15.

Madden, Richard L. 1980. "Anderson, in Manhattan, Says Rivals Flip-Flopped." *New York Times,* October 10, A1.

Maddison, Angus. 1992. "A Long-Run Perspective on Saving." *Scandinavian Journal of Economics* 94(2): 181–96.

———. 2010. "Statistics on World Population, 2010." https://www.rug.nl/ggdc/historical development/maddison/ (accessed August 15, 2018).

Maier, Charles. 1975. *Recasting Bourgeois Europe: Stabilization in France, Germany, and Italy in the Decade After World War I.* Princeton, N.J.: Princeton University Press.

Manly, Chesly. 1962. "Goldwater, Rocky Clash over Strategy." *Chicago Daily Tribune,* December 28, 7.

Mares, Isabela. 2007. "The Economic Consequences of the Welfare State." *International Social Security Review* 60(2/3): 65–81.

Margolis, Jon. 1978. "Jack Kemp Thinks He Has a Capital Idea." *Chicago Tribune,* June 25, A2.

Martin, Cathie J. 1991. *Shifting the Burden: The Struggle over Growth and Corporate Taxation.* Chicago: University of Chicago Press.

———. 2015. "Labour Market Coordination and the Evolution of Tax Regimes." *Socio-Economic Review* 13(1): 33–54.

Martin, Douglas. 2005. "Jude Wanniski, 69, Journalist Who Coined the Term 'Supply-Side Economics,' Dies." *New York Times,* August 31, A17.

Martin, Isaac William. 2008. *The Permanent Tax Revolt.* Stanford, Calif.: Stanford University Press.

———. 2013. *Rich People's Movements: Grassroots Campaigns to Untax the One Percent.* Oxford: Oxford University Press.

Martin, Isaac William, and Nadav Gabay. 2013. "Fiscal Protest in Thirteen Welfare States." *Socio-Economic Review* 11(1): 107–30.

Martin, Michel. 2009. "Football Taught Jack Kemp Early Lessons in Equality." May 4. *Tell Me More,* National Public Radio. https://www.npr.org/templates/story/story.php ?storyId=103773159 (accessed August 15, 2018).

Martin, Richard. 1971. "Too Little, Too Late: Capital Expenditures Seen Rising at Last—But Not by Very Much." *Wall Street Journal,* December 28, 1.

Mason, Robert. 2012. *The Republican Party and American Politics from Hoover to Reagan.* Cambridge: Cambridge University Press.

Matthews, Mark. 1988. "Dole Runs Ahead on Eve of Voting." *The Sun,* February 16, 1A.

Matthews, Mark, and Michael Kelly. 1988. "New Aggressiveness Pays Off for Bush." *The Sun,* February 17, 1A.

Matthews, Mark, and Paul West. 1988. "Republicans Squabble in N.H. Debate." *The Sun,* February 15, 1A.

Mattson, Kevin. 2010. *"What the Heck Are You Up to, Mr. President?": Jimmy Carter, America's "Malaise," and the Speech That Should Have Changed the Country.* New York: Bloomsbury Publishing.

Matusow, Allen J. 1998. *Nixon's Economy: Booms, Busts, Dollars, and Votes.* Lawrence: University Press of Kansas.

Mays, Benjamin E. 1974. "It's Democrats' Responsibility Now." *Chicago Defender,* November 30, 8.

McCaffery, Edward J., and Linda R. Cohen. 2006. "Shakedown at Gucci Gulch: The New Logic of Collective Action." *North Carolina Law Review* 84 (2006): 1159–252.

McCallum, John, and André Blais. 1987. "Government, Special Interest Groups, and Economic Growth." *Public Choice* 54(1): 3–18.

McCartin, Joseph A. 2011. *Collision Course: Ronald Reagan, the Air Traffic Controllers, and the Strike that Changed America.* Oxford: Oxford University Press.

McCoy, Michael R. 1981. "ACRS New Method for Regulating Taxes." *Los Angeles Times,* December 5, SF15.

McCubbin, Janet, and Fritz Scheuren. 1988–1989. "Individual Income Tax Shares and Average Tax Rates, Tax Years 1951–1986." *IRS Statistics of Income (SOI) Bulletin* 8(3, Winter): 39–74. https://www.irs.gov/pub/irs-soi/51-86inintxshatr.pdf (accessed August 15, 2018).

McFaden W. Clay. 2008. "Reneging on the 'Read My Lips' Tax Pledge." PhD diss., University of Houston.

McGirr, Lisa. 2001. *Suburban Warriors: The Origins of the New American Right.* Princeton, N.J.: Princeton University Press.

McGrory, Mary. 1982. "Victory Cigar Is Sweet for Speaker Tip O'Neill." *Atlanta Constitution,* November 5, 19A.

McLarin, Kimberly. 1993. "Whitman Finds Her Voice in New Jersey Race." *New York Times,* September 8, 1.

McLeod, Jack M., Jane D. Brown, and Lee B. Becker. 1977. "Watergate and the 1974 Congressional Elections." *Public Opinion Quarterly*, 41(2): 181–95.

McQuaid, Kim. 1994. *Uneasy Partners: Big Business in American Politics, 1945–1990.* Baltimore: Johns Hopkins University Press.

Mehrotra, Ajay. 2013. *Making the Modern American Fiscal State.* New York: Cambridge University Press.

Meiselman, David. 1981. U.S. Senate, Finance Committee, *Tax Reduction Proposals,* part 1. Washington: U.S. Government Printing Office, May 13, 14, and 18.

Mendoza, Enrique G., Assaf Razin, and Linda L. Tesar. 1994. "Effective Tax Rates in Macroeconomics: Cross-Country Estimates of Tax Rates on Factor Incomes and Consumption." *Journal of Monetary Economics* 34(3): 297–323.

Mettler, Suzanne. 2011. *The Submerged State: How Invisible Government Programs Undermine American Democracy.* Chicago: University of Chicago Press.

Michelmore, Molly C. 2012. *Tax and Spend: The Welfare State, Tax Politics, and the Limits of American Liberalism.* Philadelphia: University of Pennsylvania Press.

Mirowski, Philip, and Dieter Plehwe, eds. 2015. *The Road from Mont Pèlerin: The Making of the Neoliberal Thought Collective.* Cambridge, Mass.: Harvard University Press.

Mirrlees, James A. 1971. "An Exploration in the Theory of Optimum Income Taxation." *Review of Economic Studies* 38(2): 175–208.

Mishra, Ramesh. 1990. *The Welfare State in Capitalist Society.* London: Routledge.

Mitchnick, Morton G. 1993. "Recent Developments in Compulsory Unionism." *International Labour Review* 132(4): 453–68.

Mizruchi, Mark S. 2013. *The Fracturing of the American Corporate Elite.* Cambridge, Mass.: Harvard University Press.

Modigliani, Andre, and Franco Modigliani. 1987. "The Growth of the Federal Deficit and the Role of Public Attitudes." *Public Opinion Quarterly* 51(4): 459–80.

Mollison, Andrew. 1980. "Reagan Antes up $3,500 to Debate Bush." *Atlanta Constitution,* February 22, 7A.

Moore, Stephen. 1995. "Welfare States." *National Review* 47(21, November 6): 50–52.

———. 1996. "Middle Muddle." *National Review,* 48(23, December 9): 40.

Moran, Andrew D. 2011. "More Than a Caretaker: The Economic Policy of Gerald R. Ford." *Presidential Studies Quarterly* 41(1): 39–63.

Moreton, Bethany. 2009. *To Serve God and Wal-Mart: The Making of Christian Free Enterprise.* Cambridge, Mass.: Harvard University Press.

Morgan, Dan. 1981. "Getting Our Ideology in the Wall Street Journal." *Washington Post,* February 15, C1, C5.

———. 2001. "Business Backs Bush Tax Cut; Under Pressure, Groups Agree to Defer Push for Wider Relief." *Washington Post,* March 4, A1.

Morgan, Dan, and Charles Babington. 2001. "Lobbyists in Final Tax Bill Scramble." *Washington Post,* May 25, A7.

Morgan, Dan, and Kathleen Day. 2001. "Early Wins Embolden Lobbyists for Business." *Washington Post,* March 11, A1.

Morgan, Iwan. 2008. "Reaganomics and Its Legacy." In *Ronald Reagan and the 1980s,* edited by Cheryl Hudson and Gareth Davies. New York: Palgrave Macmillan.

Morgan, Kimberly J., and Monica Prasad. 2009. "The Origins of Tax Systems: A French-American Comparison." *American Journal of Sociology* 114(5): 1350–94.

Moss, Richard. 2017. *Creating the New Right Ethnic in 1970s America: The Intersection of Anger and Nostalgia.* Madison, N.J.: Fairleigh Dickinson University Press.

Mouat, Lucia. 1980. "Wisconsin Senate Race Suddenly Tight." *Christian Science Monitor,* October 16, 6.

Moyers, Bill. 2004. *Moyers on America: A Journalist and His Times.* New York: Anchor Books.

Moynihan, Daniel Patrick. 1983. "Reagan's Bankrupt Budget." *New Republic* 189(27, December 31): 18–21.

Mundell, Robert. 2003. "A Reconsideration of the Twentieth Century." In *Prize Lectures in Economic Sciences 1996–2000,* edited by Torsten Persson. Singapore: World Scientific Publishing Co.

Murray, Alan, and Jeffrey Birnbaum. 1988. *Showdown at Gucci Gulch: Lawmakers, Lobbyists, and the Unlikely Triumph of Tax Reform.* New York: Vintage Books.

Murray, Shoon Kathleen. 2006. "Private Polls and Presidential Policymaking: Reagan as a Facilitator of Change." *Public Opinion Quarterly* 70(4): 477–98.

Murray, Shoon Kathleen, and Peter Howard. 2002. "Variation in White House Polling Operations: Carter to Clinton." *Public Opinion Quarterly* 66(4): 527–58.

National Journal. 1981. "Seizing the Helm." *National Journal,* August 8, 404.

National Review. 1996. "Seeing the Right Light." *National Review* 48(16, September 2): 16–17.

———. 1998a. "November and After." *National Review* 50(October 26): 14–19.

———. 1998b. "Number Crunch." *National Review* 50(24, December 21): 16.

———. 1998c. "Without Issue." *National Review* 50(23, December 7): 14–16.

———. 1999. "The Week." *National Review,* 51(25, December 31): 6.

———. 2000. "The Tax Man Goeth." *National Review* 52(15, August 14): 16.

Nau, Henry. 2015. "The 'Great Expansion': The Economic Legacy of Ronald Reagan." In *Reagan's Legacy in a World Transformed,* edited by Jeffrey L. Chidester and Paul Kengor. Cambridge, Mass.: Harvard University Press.

Neikirk, Bill. 1978. "Capital Gains Bill Puts Carter in Corner." *Chicago Tribune,* July 16, A7.

———. 1980. "Reagan Tax Plan Skeptics Are Told to Have Faith." *Chicago Tribune,* September 10, A1.

———. 1981. "Reagan Tax-Cut Plan Wins." *Chicago Tribune,* July 30, 1.

Nelson, Jack. 1981. "Lift the Burden of Inflation—Reagan: Repeatedly Cheered by Congressmen, He Presses for His Economic Program." *Los Angeles Times,* April 29, B1.

Neshoba Democrat. 2007. "Transcript of Ronald Reagan's 1980 Neshoba County Fair Speech." *Neshoba Democrat,* November 15. http://neshobademocrat.com/Content/NEWS/News/Article/Transcript-of-Ronald-Reagan-s-1980-Neshoba-County-Fair-speech/2/297/15599 (accessed August 10, 2018).

New York Times. 1979. "Notes from the Gas Line." *New York Times,* June 22, B6.

———. 1980a. "Excerpts from Forum in Iowa of 6 GOP Presidential Candidates." *New York Times,* January 7, B4.

———. 1980b. "Transcript of the Presidential Debate between Carter and Reagan in Cleveland." October 29, A26.

———. 1981a. "Handcuffs of Gold." *New York Times,* August 23, E20.

———. 1981b. "Measuring a Mandate: Budget Themes and Variations." *New York Times,* May 3, E1.

———. 1981c. "Transcript of Reagan Speech to Houses of Congress." *New York Times,* April 29, A22.

———. 1982. "Briefing." *New York Times,* February 12, A20.

———. 1984. "Do the Large Deficits Matter?" *New York Times,* February 2, B7.

———. 1994. "Keeping Score on the Budget." *New York Times,* December 5, A18.

———. 2016. "Kansas Schools, Victims of Bad Tax Policy." *New York Times,* June 2, A22.

Nijhuis, Dennie Oude. 2015. "Incomes Policies, Welfare State Development and the Notion of the Social Wage." *Socio-Economic Review* 13(4): 771–90.

Niskanen, William A. 1988. *Reaganomics: An Insider's Account of the Policies and the People.* Oxford: Oxford University Press.

Noah, Timothy. 2015. "Holding the Line." *New York Times,* November 8, BR14.

Nobel Prize. 1999. "The Sveriges Riksbank Prize in Economic Sciences in Memory of Alfred Nobel: Robert Mundell." Nobelprize.org, press release, October 13. http://www.nobelprize.org/nobel_prizes/economic-sciences/laureates/1999/press.html (accessed May 21, 2018).

Noble, Charles. 1986. *Liberalism at Work: The Rise and Fall of OSHA.* Philadelphia: Temple University Press.

Noble, Holcomb. 2006. "Milton Friedman, the Champion of Free Markets, Is Dead at 94." *New York Times,* November 17, A1.

Nolan, Martin. 1975. "The Nation: Political Credibility on the Tube." *Boston Globe,* June 10, 26.

———. 1980. "GOP Takes to the Air to Sell Its Candidates." *Boston Globe*, August 27, 11.

Norquist, Grover G. 1999. "Stalemate." *American Spectator* 32(1): 60–62.

Nyhan, David. 1980a. "A Golden Night for Reagan." *Boston Globe,* June 1, A1.

———. 1980b. "'Just Politics' or a 'Lockout'?" *Boston Globe*, February 25, 1.

Offe, Claus. 1984. *Contradictions of the Welfare State.* Cambridge, Mass.: Massachusetts Institute of Technology Press.

Olds, Gareth. 2016. "Food Stamp Entrepreneurs." Working Paper 16-143. Boston: Harvard Business School.

Olmstead, Alan L., and Paul W. Rhode. 2006. "Beef, Veal, Pork, and Lamb—Slaughtering, Production, and Price: 1899–1999." In *Historical Statistics of the United States, Earliest Times to the Present: Millennial Edition,* edited by Susan B. Carter, Scott Sigmund Gartner, Michael R. Haines, Alan L. Olmstead, Richard Sutch, and Gavin Wright. New York: Cambridge University Press.

Olmsted, Kathryn, S. 2015. *Right Out of California: The 1930s and the Big Business Roots of Modern Conservatism.* New York: The New Press.

O'Neill, Thomas P., Jr., with William Novak. 1987. *Man of the House: The Life and Political Memoirs of Speaker Tip O'Neill.* New York: Random House.

Oppenheimer, Daniel. 2016. *Exit Right: The People Who Left the Left and Reshaped the American Century.* New York: Simon & Schuster.

Opschoor, S. J. A. 2015. "The Effects of Saving on Economic Growth." PhD diss., Erasmus University, Rotterdam.

Orfield, Gary. 1975. "Congress, the President, and Anti-Busing Legislation, 1966–1974." *Journal of Law and Education* 4(1): 81–140.

Orr, Richard. 1984. "Economist: Recovery Going Well." *Chicago Tribune,* April 18, 12.

O'Sullivan, John. 1998. "Wilsonianism." *National Review,* 50(16, September 1): 17–20.

Page, Benjamin I., and Martin Gilens. 2017. *Democracy in America? What Has Gone Wrong and What We Can Do about It.* Chicago: University of Chicago Press.

Page, Benjamin I., and Robert Y. Shapiro. 1992. *The Rational Public: Fifty Years of Trends in Americans' Policy Preferences.* Chicago: University of Chicago Press.

Panitch, Leo. 1977. "The Development of Corporatism in Liberal Democracies." *Comparative Political Studies* 10(1): 61–90.

Paster, Thomas. 2013. "Business and Welfare State Development: Why Did Employers Accept Social Reforms?" *World Politics* 65(3): 416–51.

Patashnik, Eric M. 2014. *Reforms at Risk: What Happens after Major Policy Changes Are Enacted.* Princeton, N.J.: Princeton University Press.

Pechman, Joseph. 1981. Testimony before U.S. House of Representatives, Ways and Means Committee, *Tax Aspects of the President's Economic Program,* part 1. Washington: U.S. Government Printing Office, February 24, 25, March 3–5.

Perlstein, Rick. 2001. *Before the Storm: Barry Goldwater and the Unmaking of the American Consensus.* New York: Nation Books.

———. 2014. *The Invisible Bridge: The Fall of Nixon and the Rise of Reagan*. New York: Simon & Schuster.

Persson, Torsten, and Guido Tabellini. 1994. "Is Inequality Harmful for Growth?" *American Economic Review* 76(1): 191–203.

Peters, Jeremy W. 2017. "Cut Taxes? In States, GOP Goes Other Way." *New York Times,* July 3, A10.

Peterson, Bill. 1980. "Reagan Returns to WHO … What Hit Him?" *Washington Post,* January 19, A1.

Pierson, Paul. 2015. "Reflections on the Evolution of a Research Program." *PS: Political Science & Politics* 48(2): 292–94.

Pfiffner, James P. 1979. *The President, the Budget, and Congress: Impoundment and the 1974 Budget Act.* Boulder, Colo.: Westview Press.

Phillips, Kevin. 1969. *The Emerging Republican Majority.* New York: Arlington House.

Phillips-Fein, Kim. 2009. *Invisible Hands: The Making of the Conservative Movement from the New Deal to Reagan.* New York: W. W. Norton.

———. 2011. "Conservatism: A State of the Field." *The Journal of American History* 98(3): 723–43.

Piketty, Thomas. 2014. *Capital in the Twenty-First Century.* Cambridge, Mass.: Harvard University Press.

Piketty, Thomas, Emmanuel Saez, and Stefanie Stantcheva. 2014. "Optimal Taxation of Top Labor Incomes: A Tale of Three Elasticities." *American Economic Journal: Economic Policy* 6(1): 230–71.

Pine, Art. 1980. "Campaign Economics: Numbing Jibes and Jibing Numbers." *Washington Post,* September 14, F1.

———. 1981. "DuPont's Irving S. Shapiro." *Washington Post,* February 8, G1.

Plotke, David. 2006. *Building a Democratic Political Order: Reshaping American Liberalism in the 1930s and 1940s.* Cambridge: Cambridge University Press.

Polanyi, Karl. (1944) 2001. *The Great Transformation.* Boston: Beacon Press.

Pollack, Sheldon D. 2003. *Refinancing America: The Republican Antitax Agenda.* Albany: State University of New York Press.

Pollard, Sidney. 1958. "Investment, Consumption and the Industrial Revolution." *The Economic History Review* 11(2): 215–24.

Ponnuru, Ramesh. 1996. "The Right Agenda." *National Review,* 48(19, October 14): 46–52.

———. 1998. "CAMPAIGN AUTOPSY; Running on Empty." *National Review* 50(22, November 23): 37.

Pontusson, Jonas. 1991. "Labor, Corporatism, and Industrial Policy: The Swedish Case in Comparative Perspective." *Comparative Politics* 23(2): 163–79.

———. 2013. "Unionization, Inequality and Redistribution." *British Journal of Industrial Relations* 51(4): 797–825.

Poulos, Nick. 1981. "Volcker Does Reagan Favor with 'Little' Recession: Fed Chairman Used Transition to Renew Squeeze." *Atlanta Constitution,* January 19, 10C.

Prasad, Monica. 2006. *The Politics of Free Markets: The Rise of Neoliberal Economic Policies in Britain, France, Germany, and the United States.* Chicago: University of Chicago Press.

———. 2012. *The Land of Too Much: American Abundance and the Paradox of Poverty.* Cambridge, Mass.: Harvard University Press.

———. 2017. "Deadly Deficits." *Contexts* 16(1): 22–23.

Pressman, Steven. 1987. "The Myths and Realities of Tax Bracket Creep." *Eastern Economic Journal* 13(1): 31–39.

Price Waterhouse. 1975. *Doing Business in France.* London: Price Waterhouse Center for Transnational Taxation.

———. 1978. *Doing Business in Germany.* London: Price Waterhouse Center for Transnational Taxation.

———. 1980. *Doing Business in the United Kingdom.* London: Price Waterhouse Center for Transnational Taxation.

Prowe, Diethelm. 1985. "Economic Democracy in Post-World War II Germany: Corporatist Crisis Response, 1945–1948." *Journal of Modern History* 57(3): 451–82.

Rabe, Barry. 2004. *Statehouse and Greenhouse: The Emerging Politics of American Climate Change Policy.* Washington, D.C.. Brookings Institution Press.

Rabushka, Alvin. 1981. Testimony before U.S. Senate, Judiciary Committee, *Balancing the Budget.* Washington: U.S. Government Printing Office, May 29.

Rattner, Steven. 1980. "Candidates' Statistics Don't Add Up." *New York Times,* September 14, E2.

Reagan, Ronald. 1981. "Address to the Nation on the Economy." February 5, 1981. American Presidency Project, edited by Gerhard Peters and John T. Woolley. http://www.presidency.ucsb.edu/ws/?pid=43132 (accessed January 24, 2018).

———. 1985. "Remarks at a Fundraising Dinner for Senator Robert W. Kasten, Jr., in Milwaukee, Wisconsin," October 15, 1985. In *Public Papers of the Presidents of the United States: Ronald Reagan.* Washington: U.S. Government Printing Office.

———. 1990. *An American Life.* New York: Simon & Schuster.

———. 2007. *The Reagan Diaries.* New York: HarperCollins.

Reay, Michael. 2012. "The Flexible Unity of Economics." *American Journal of Sociology* 118(1): 45–87.

Reeves, Richard. 2005. *President Reagan: The Triumph of Imagination.* New York: Simon & Schuster.

Reinhold, Robert. 1978. "Poll Indicates Congress Candidates Were More Extreme Than Voters." *New York Times,* November 9, A21.

Richter, Brian Kelleher, Krislert Samphantharak, and Jeffrey F. Timmons. 2009. "Lobbying and Taxes." *American Journal of Political Science* 53(4): 893–909.

Riffkin, Rebecca. 2014. "Americans Say Federal Gov't Wastes 51 Cents on the Dollar." *Gallup News,* September 17. http://news.gallup.com/poll/176102/americans-say-federal-gov-wastes-cents-dollar.aspx (accessed May 2, 2018).

Roberts, Paul Craig. 1971. *Alienation and the Soviet Economy.* Albuquerque: University of New Mexico Press.

———. 1984. *The Supply-Side Revolution.* Cambridge, Mass.: Harvard University Press.

Roberts, Steven B. 1985. "Jack Kemp's Year of Decision." *New York Times,* February 3, SM40.

Robertson, Campbell. 2016. "In Louisiana, the Poor Lack Legal Defense." *New York Times,* March 20, A1.

Rodgers, Daniel T. 2011. *Age of Fracture.* Cambridge, Mass.: Harvard University Press.

Rosen, Sherwin. 1997. "Public Employment, Taxes, and the Welfare State in Sweden." In *The Welfare State in Transition: Reforming the Swedish Model,* edited by Richard B. Freeman, Robert H. Topel, and Birgitta Swedenborg. Chicago: University of Chicago Press.

Rosenblum, Nancy L. 2010. *On the Side of the Angels: An Appreciation of Parties and Partisanship.* Princeton, N.J.: Princeton University Press.

Rowe, James L. 1978. "Inflation Succeeds Unemployment as No. 1 Worry." *Washington Post,* January 2, D8.

Rudder, Catherine E. 1983. "Tax Policy: Structure and Choice." In *Making Economic Policy in Congress,* edited by Allen Schick. Washington, D.C.: American Enterprise Institute for Public Policy Research.

Ruggie, John Gerard. 1982. "International Regimes, Transactions, and Change: Embedded Liberalism in the Postwar Economic Order." *International Organization* 36(2): 379–415.

Rutledge, John. 1981. Testimony before U.S. House of Representatives, Ways and Means Committee, *Tax Aspects of the President's Economic Program,* part 1. Washington: U.S. Government Printing Office, February 24 and 25, March 3–5.

Saad, Lydia. 2008. "Economy Entrenched as Nation's Most Important Problem." *Gallup News,* December 10. http://news.gallup.com/poll/113041/economy-entrenched-nations-most-important-problem.aspx (accessed February 12, 2018).

Safire, William. 1981. "The Reagan Administration's Tax Cut Brought out the Insects in Congress." *Baltimore Sun,* August 16, D4.

Samuelson, Paul Anthony. 1966. *The Collected Scientific Papers of Paul A. Samuelson,* edited by Joseph Stiglitz, vol. 2. Cambridge, Mass.: MIT Press.

Samuelson, Robert J. 1981a. "Business Tax Cuts." *National Journal,* February 28, 556–61.

———. 1981b. "Reagan's Tax Package." *National Journal,* February 28, 340–45.

Sanders, Elizabeth. 1998. *Roots of Reform: Farmers, Workers, and the American State, 1877–1917.* Chicago: University of Chicago Press.

Sanders, Randy. 1992. "'The Sad Duty of Politics': Jimmy Carter and the Issue of Race in His 1970 Gubernatorial Campaign." *Georgia Historical Quarterly* 76(3): 612–38.

Saunders, Peter. 1986. "What Can We Learn from International Comparisons of Public Sector Size and Economic Performance?" *European Sociological Review* 2(1): 52–60.

Scammon, Richard, and Ben Wattenberg. 1970. *The Real Majority: An Extraordinary Examination of the American Electorate.* New York: Coward-McCann.

Schlesinger, Arthur M., Jr. (1958) 2003. *The Coming of the New Deal.* New York: Houghton Mifflin.

Schneider, Martin R., and Mihai Paunescu. 2012. "Changing Varieties of Capitalism and Revealed Comparative Advantages from 1990 to 2005: A Test of the Hall and Soskice Claims." *Socio-Economic Review* 10(4): 731–53.

Schram, Sanford F., Joe Soss, Richard C. Fording, and Linda Houser. 2009. "Deciding to Discipline: Race, Choice, and Punishment at the Frontlines of Welfare Reform." *American Sociological Review* 74(3): 398–422.

Scorsone, Eric, and Nicolette Bateson. 2011. "Long-Term Crisis and Systemic Failure: Taking the Fiscal Stress of America's Older Cities Seriously." East Lansing: Michigan State University Extension. https://www.cityofflint.com/wp-content/uploads/Reports/MSUE_FlintStudy2011.pdf (accessed September 28, 2018).

Seib, Gerald F. 2000. "Bush Seeks to Regain the Initiative with Emphasis on Tax-Cut Plan." *Wall Street Journal,* February 3, A4.

Shafer, Ronald G. 1974. "A Fading Dream." *Wall Street Journal,* September 3, 1.

Shalit, Ruth. 1995. "Uncle Bob." *New York Times,* March 5, SM33.

Shanahan, Eileen. 1972. "An Administration Slide Show Attacks the Idea of Tax Reform." *New York Times,* April 24, 1.

Shermer, Elizabeth Tandy. 2013. *Sunbelt Capitalism: Phoenix and the Transformation of American Politics.* Philadelphia: University of Pennsylvania Press.

Shirley, Craig. 2009. *Rendezvous with Destiny: Ronald Reagan and the Campaign That Changed America.* Wilmington, Del.: Intercollegiate Studies Institute.

Shogan, Robert. 1979. "GOP Leaders Seek Stance on Fiscal Policy: Shift Emphasis from Tax Cuts to Limits on Federal Spending." *Los Angeles Times,* April 10, B16.

———. 1980. "'GOP Majority' Hopes Revived: Reagan Has Opportunity to Solidify His Broad Support." *Los Angeles Times,* November 6, 1.

Shribman, David. 1988. "Bungled Campaign." *Wall Street Journal,* March 14, 1.

Silk, Leonard. 1978. "Carter Economic Strategy." *New York Times,* January 3, 45.

———. 1980. "Economic Scene: Reagan's Gold Advisers." *New York Times,* March 14, D2.

———. 1981. "Economic Scene: Clash over Gold Standard." *New York Times,* April 29, D2.

Sitton, Claude. 1964. "Tragedy in Mississippi." *New York Times,* August 9, E6.

Skelton, George. 1981a. "Reagan Assails Wall Street's Economic Advice." *Los Angeles Times,* May 29, 1.

———. 1981b. "The Times Poll: Americans Prefer Smaller Tax Cut to Reagan's Plan." *Los Angeles Times,* March 26, A12.

Skocpol, Theda, Peter B. Evans, and Dietrich Rueschemeyer. 1985. *Bringing the State Back In.* New York: Cambridge University Press.

Smeeding, Timothy M. 2006. "Poor People in Rich Nations: The United States in Comparative Perspective." *Journal of Economic Perspectives* 20(1): 69–90.

Smith, Hedrick. 1980. "Excluded from GOP Debate, Four Attack Bush." *New York Times,* February 24, 1.

———. 1984. "Reagan-Mondale Clashes May Foreshadow the First Debate." *New York Times,* October 7, 30.

———. 1988. *The Power Game: How Washington Works.* New York: Ballantine Books.

Smith, Mark. 2000. *American Business and Political Power.* Chicago: University of Chicago Press.

Smith, Mark A. 2007. *The Right Talk: How Conservatives Transformed the Great Society into the Economic Society.* Princeton, N.J.: Princeton University Press.

Smith, Seymour S. 1975. "Kemp Feels Sports Trained Him for Politics." *Baltimore Sun,* February 16, B12.

Smith, Tom W. 1987. "That Which We Call Welfare by Any Other Name Would Smell

Sweeter: An Analysis of the Impact of Question Wording on Response Patterns." *Public Opinion Quarterly* 51(1): 75–83.

Smith, Zachary C. 2012. "From the Well of the House: Remaking the House Republican Party, 1978–1994." PhD diss., Boston University.

Sobran, Joseph. 1980. "Bringing Back the Golden Goose." *Washington Post,* July 22, A13.

Solow, Robert M. 1985. "Why People Make Fun of Economists." *New York Times,* December 29, F2.

Sommer, Jeff. 2011. "Why Are Investors Still Lining up for Bonds?" *New York Times,* May 29, BU4.

Stall, Bill. 1980a. "Despite Good Look at All GOP Hopefuls, Many N.H. Voters Are Still Undecided." *Los Angeles Times,* February 20, B22.

———. 1980b. "Flushed with Iowa Victory, Bush Learns Price of Success as Well as Its Benefits." *Los Angeles Times,* January 28, B14.

Stapleford, Thomas A. 2007. "Market Visions: Expenditure Surveys, Market Research, and Economic Planning in the New Deal." *The Journal of American History* 94(2): 418–44.

Steigerwald, Bill. 1979. "Kemp Blitzes U.S. Government Policy." *Los Angeles Times,* October 14, O8.

Stein, Herbert. 1969. *The Fiscal Revolution in America.* Chicago: University of Chicago Press.

Stein, Judith. 2010. *Pivotal Decade: How the United States Traded Factories for Finance in the Seventies.* New Haven, Conn.: Yale University Press.

Steinbeck, John. (1939) 2002. *The Grapes of Wrath.* New York: Penguin.

Steinmo, Sven. 1986. "So What's Wrong with Tax Expenditures? A Reevaluation Based on Swedish Experience." *Public Budgeting and Finance* 6(2): 27–44.

Steuerle, C. Eugene. 1992. *The Tax Decade, 1981–90.* Washington, D.C.: Urban Institute.

———. 2004. *Contemporary U.S. Tax Policy.* Washington, D.C.: Urban Institute.

Stillman, Sarah. 2013. "Taken." *New Yorker,* August 12 and 19, 48–61.

St. Louis Post-Dispatch. 1995. "Abolish Forfeiture Law, Sen. Flotron Urges." *St. Louis Post-Dispatch,* December 10, 11C.

Stockman, David. 1986. *The Triumph of Politics: Why the Reagan Revolution Failed.* New York: Harper & Row.

Strahan, Randall. 1990. *New Ways and Means: Reform and Change in a Congressional Committee.* Chapel Hill: University of North Carolina Press.

Suárez, Sandra, and Robin Kolodny. 2011. "Paving the Road to 'Too Big to Fail': Business Interests and the Politics of Financial Deregulation in the United States." *Politics and Society* 39(1): 74–102.

Summers, Clyde W. 1964. "Freedom of Association and Compulsory Unionism in Sweden and the United States." *University of Pennsylvania Law Review* 112: 647–96.

Sundquist, James L. 1968. *Politics and Policy: The Eisenhower, Kennedy, and Johnson Years.* Washington, D.C.: Brookings Institution.

Suprynowicz, Vin. 1999. *Send in the Waco Killers: Essays on the Freedom Movement, 1993–1998.* Las Vegas, Nev.: Mountain Media.

Sykes, Jennifer, Katrin Križ, Kathryn Edin, and Sarah Halpern-Meekin. 2015. "Dignity and

Dreams: What the Earned Income Tax Credit (EITC) Means to Low-Income Families." *American Sociological Review* 80(2): 243–67.

Tabb, Charles J. 2005. "Lessons from the Globalization of Consumer Bankruptcy." *Law and Social Inquiry* 30(4): 763–82.

Tate, Dale. 1981a. "Congress Shapes Strategy for Reagan Economic Plan." *Congressional Quarterly Weekly Report,* February 28, 376–78.

———. 1981b. "Tax Cut Agreement Proves Elusive." *Congressional Quarterly Weekly Report,* May 30, 937.

———. 1981c. "Tax Cut Compromise Barred as Committee Markups Near." *Congressional Quarterly Weekly Report,* April 18, 670–71.

Taylor, Benjamin. 1980. "Bush Not about to Concede." *Boston Globe,* February 27, 14.

Teles, Steven. 2013. "Kludgeocracy in America." *National Affairs* 17: 97–114.

Tempalski, Jerry. 2013. "Revenue Effects of Major Tax Bills: Updated Tables for All 2012 Bills." Working Paper 81. Washington: U.S. Department of the Treasury, Office of Tax Analysis (February).

Thelen, Kathleen. 2014. *Varieties of Liberalization and the New Politics of Social Solidarity.* New York: Cambridge University Press.

Therborn, Göran, and Joop Roebroek. 1986. "The Irreversible Welfare State: Its Recent Maturation, Its Encounter with the Economic Crisis, and Its Future Prospects." *International Journal of Health Services* 16(3): 319–38.

Thimmesch, Nick. 1979. "Bush: 'Confidence Itself.'" *Washington Post,* May 3, A19.

Thurow, Lester. 1981. Testimony before U.S. Senate, Finance Committee, *Tax Reduction Proposals,* part 2. Washington: U.S. Government Printing Office, May 19 and 20.

Tilly, Charles. 1975. *The Formation of National States in Western Europe.* Princeton, N.J.: Princeton University Press.

———. 1992. *Coercion, Capital, and European States, AD 990–1992.* Cambridge, Mass.: Blackwell.

Tobin, James. 1989. "Reaganomics in Retrospect." In *Policies for Prosperity: Essays in a Keynesian Mode.* Cambridge, Mass.: MIT Press.

Tolchin, Martin. 1978. "Jack Kemp's Bootleg Run to the Right." *Esquire,* October 24, 59–69.

———. 1985. "Foreign Capital Growth in U.S. Causes Concern." *New York Times,* April 1, 1.

Toner, Robin. 1995. "Tax Cut Edges out Deficit as GOP's Guiding Tenet." *New York Times,* April 3, A1.

Tufte, Edward R. 1975. "Determinants of the Outcomes of Midterm Congressional Elections." *American Political Science Review* 69(3): 812–26.

Turner, James Morton. 2009. "'The Specter of Environmentalism': Wilderness, Environmental Politics, and the Evolution of the New Right." *Journal of American History* 96(1): 123–48.

Tyson, Laura D'Andrea. 1995. "Dynamic Scoring, Not Ready for Prime Time." *Wall Street Journal,* January 12, A14.

U.S. House of Representatives. Ways and Means Committee. 1978. *Tax Reductions: Economists' Comments on H.R. 8333 and S. 1860.* Washington: Government Printing Office.

————. 1981. *Tax Aspects of the President's Economic Program*. Washington: U.S. Government Printing Office.

U.S. Senate. 1999. *Congressional Record*. Washington: U.S. Government Printing Office.

————. 2000. *Congressional Record*. Washington: U.S. Government Printing Office.

U.S. Senate. Budget Committee (SBC). 1978. *Leading Economists' Views of Kemp-Roth*. Washington: U.S. Congress, SBC.

Verweij, Marco. 2000. "Why Is the River Rhine Cleaner than the Great Lakes (Despite Looser Regulation)?" *Law and Society Review* 34(4): 1007–54.

Vogel, David. 1986. *National Styles of Regulation: Environmental Policy in Great Britain and the United States*. Ithaca, N.Y.: Cornell University Press.

————. 2003. *Fluctuating Fortunes: The Political Power of Business in America*. Washington, D.C: Beard Books.

————. 2012. *The Politics of Precaution: Regulating Health, Safety, and Environmental Risks in Europe and the United States*. Princeton, N.J.: Princeton University Press.

Volscho, Thomas. 2017. "The Revenge of the Capitalist Class: Crisis, the Legitimacy of Capitalism, and the Restoration of Finance from the 1970s to Present." *Critical Sociology* 43(2): 249–66.

Wacquant, Loïc. 2012. "Three Steps to a Historical Anthropology of Actually Existing Neoliberalism." *Social Anthropology* 20(1): 66–79.

Walker, Charls. 1977a. *Charls E. Walker's Washington Economic Report* 5(9, October 4).

————. 1977b. *Charls E. Walker's Washington Economic Report* 5(11, December 29).

————. 1978a. *Charls E. Walker's Washington Economic Report* 6(3, April 7).

————. 1978b. *Charls E. Walker's Washington Economic Report* 6(9, November 27).

————. 1979. *Charls E. Walker's Washington Economic Report* 7(1, February 6).

Walker, Edward T., and Christopher M. Rea. 2014. "The Political Mobilization of Firms and Industries." *Annual Review of Sociology* 40: 281–304.

Wall Street Journal. 1975a. "The Budget Bad News." *Wall Street Journal*, February 4, 20.

————. 1975b. "The House Tax Cut." *Wall Street Journal*, March 5, 14.

————. 1977. "JFK Strikes Again." *Wall Street Journal*, February 23, 24.

————. 1980. "The Reagan Gaffes." *Wall Street Journal*, April 18, 20.

————. 1982. "Voodoo Politics." *Wall Street Journal*, January 14, 29.

————. 1990. "Honor Thy Pledge." *Wall Street Journal*, October 2, A26.

————. 1996. "A Necessary Pledge." *Wall Street Journal*, October 8, A22.

————. 2000. "The Bush Tax Cut." *Wall Street Journal*, December 19.

Wanniski, Jude. 1974. "It's Time to Cut Taxes." *Wall Street Journal*, December 11, 18.

————. 1975. "The Mundell-Laffer Hypothesis—A New View of the World Economy." *Public Interest* (Spring): 31–52.

————. 1976. "Taxes and a Two-Santa Theory." *National Observer*, March 6.

————. 1978a. "Barbaric Metal or Golden Anchor?" *Wall Street Journal*, March 15, 22.

————. 1978b. *The Way the World Works*. New York: Basic Books.

Ward, Jason Morgan. 2011. *Defending White Democracy: The Making of a Segregationist Movement and the Remaking of Racial Politics*. Chapel Hill: University of North Carolina Press.

Wardell, William M. 1973. "Introduction of New Therapeutic Drugs in the United States and Great Britain: An International Comparison." *Clinical Pharmacology and Therapeutics* 14: 773–90.

Wardell, William M., and Louis Lasagna. 1975. *Regulation and Drug Development.* Washington, D.C.: American Enterprise Institute for Public Policy Research.

Warren, Elizabeth. 2005. Testimony before the U.S. Senate Judiciary Committee hearing on Bankruptcy Legislation, 109th Cong., 1st sess., February 10.

Warsh, David. 1980. "New Reagan Aide: Shift to the Right." *Boston Globe,* February 28, 10.

Washington Post. 1980a. "The Battle for Reagan's Mind." *Washington Post,* April 27, F1.

———. 1980b. "George Bush: Hot Property in Presidential Politics." *Washington Post,* January 27, A1.

———. 1980c. "Mr. Reagan's Inflationary Arithmetic." *Washington Post,* September 25, A18.

———. 1980d. "The Ten-Million-Dollar Delegate." *Washington Post,* February 20, A18.

Waterhouse, Benjamin C. 2013. "Mobilizing for the Market: Organized Business, Wage-Price Controls, and the Politics of Inflation, 1971–1974." *Journal of American History* 100(2): 454–78.

———. 2014. *Lobbying America: The Politics of Business from Nixon to NAFTA.* Princeton, N.J.: Princeton University Press.

Weatherford, M. Stephen, and Lorraine M. McDonnell. 2005. "Ronald Reagan as Legislative Advocate: Passing the Reagan Revolution's Budgets in 1981 and 1982." *Congress and the Presidency* 32(1): 1–29.

Weaver, R. Kent. 1988. *Automatic Government: The Politics of Indexation.* Washington, D.C.: Brookings Institution.

———. 2000. *Ending Welfare as We Know It.* Washington, D.C.: Brookings Institution.

Weede, Eriche. 1986. "Sectoral Reallocation, Distributional Coalitions, and the Welfare State as Determinants of Economic Growth Rates in Industrialized Democracies." *European Journal of Political Research* 14: 501–19.

Wehr, Elizabeth. 1981. "White House Lobbying Apparatus ... Produces Impressive Tax Vote Victory." *Congressional Quarterly Weekly Report,* August 1, 1372–73.

Weidenbaum, Murray. 1988. "The Role of the Council of Economic Advisers." *Journal of Economic Education* 19(3): 237–43.

Weisberg, Jacob. 2016. *Ronald Reagan.* New York: Times Books.

Welch, Reed L. 2000. "Is Anybody Watching? The Audience for Televised Presidential Addresses." *Congress and the Presidency* 27(1): 41–58.

———. 2008. "Making an Impression: The Public's Evaluation of Reagan's Televised Address." In *White House Studies Compendium,* vol. 6, edited by Anthony J. Eksterowicz and Glenn P. Hastedt. New York: Nova Science Publishers.

Whaples, Robert. 2006. "Do Economists Agree on Anything? Yes!" *Economists' Voice* 3(9): 1–6.

White, Eugene Nelson. 1984. "A Reinterpretation of the Banking Crisis of 1930." *Journal of Economic History* 44(1): 119–38.

White, Joseph, and Aaron Wildavsky. 1989. *The Deficit and the Public Interest.* Berkeley: University of California Press.

Widmalm, Frida. 2001. "Tax Structure and Growth: Are Some Taxes Better than Others?" *Public Choice* 107: 3–4.

Wiktorowicz, Mary E. 2003. "Emergent Patterns in the Regulation of Pharmaceuticals: Institutions and Interests in the United States, Canada, Britain, and France." *Journal of Health Politics, Policy, and Law* 28(4): 615–58.

Wilensky, Harold. 2002. *Rich Democracies: Political Economy, Public Policy, and Performance.* Berkeley: University of California Press.

Wilentz, Sean. 2008. *The Age of Reagan: A History, 1974–2008.* New York: HarperCollins.

Williams, Philip, and Graham Wilson. 1979. "The American Mid-Term Elections." *Political Studies* 27(4): 603–9.

Williams, Walter. 1998. *Honest Numbers and Democracy: Social Policy Analysis in the White House, Congress, and the Federal Agencies.* Washington, D.C.: Georgetown University Press.

Williamson, Vanessa S. 2017. *Read My Lips: Why Americans Are Proud to Pay Taxes.* Princeton, N.J.: Princeton University Press.

Wilson, Graham K. 1985. *The Politics of Safety and Health.* Oxford: Clarendon Press.

Wirthlin, Dick, with Wynton C. Hall. 2004. *The Greatest Communicator.* Hoboken, N.J.: John Wiley and Sons.

Wirthlin, Richard B. 1981. "The Republican Strategy and Its Electoral Consequences." In *Party Coalitions in the 1980s*, edited by Seymour Martin Lipset. San Francisco: Institute for Contemporary Studies.

Witcover, Jules, and Jack Germond. 1980. "Bush Gaining on Reagan." *Atlanta Constitution,* January 13, 3C.

Woodward, Bob. 1992. "Origin of the Tax Pledge." *Washington Post,* October 4, A1.

———. 1994. *The Agenda: Inside the Clinton White House.* New York: Simon & Schuster.

Yemma, John. 1980. "U.S. Steelmakers: $30 Billion Fixup." *Christian Science Monitor,* July 2, 1.

Young, Sam. 2009. "Former Representative Jack Kemp Dies, Leaves Tax Policy Legacy." *Tax Notes,* May 11, 665.

Zakaria, Fareed. 2007. *The Future of Freedom: Illiberal Democracy at Home and Abroad.* Rev. ed. New York: W. W. Norton & Co.

Zelizer, Julian E. 2000. *Taxing America: Wilbur D. Mills, Congress, and the State, 1945–1975.* Cambridge: Cambridge University Press.

———. 2010. "Rethinking the History of American Conservatism." *Reviews in American History* 38(2): 367–92.

Zucker, Seymour. 1978. "The Fallacy of Slashing Taxes without Cutting Spending." *Business Week,* August 7, 62.

INDEX

Boldface numbers refer to figures and tables.